# THE MATHESON MONOGRAPHS

The principal objective of the Matheson Trust is to promote the study of comparative religion from the point of view of the underlying harmony of the great religious and philosophical traditions of the world. This objective is being pursued through such means as audio-visual media, the support and sponsorship of lecture series and conferences, the creation of a website, collaboration with film production companies and publishing companies as well as the Trust's own series of publications.

The Matheson Monographs will cover a wide range of themes within the field of comparative religion: scriptural exegesis in different religious traditions; the modalities of spiritual and contemplative life; in-depth mystical studies of particular religious traditions; broad comparative analyses taking in a series of religious forms; studies of traditional arts, crafts and cosmological sciences; and contemporary scholarly expositions of religious philosophy and metaphysics. The monographs will also comprise translations of both classical and contemporary texts as well as transcriptions of lectures by, and interviews with, spiritual and scholarly authorities from different religious and philosophical traditions.

# THE GOSPEL OF THOMAS

# THE GOSPEL OF THOMAS

In the Light of Early Jewish, Christian
and Islamic Esoteric Trajectories

*with a contextualized commentary and
a new translation of the* Thomas *Gospel*

## Samuel Zinner

THE MATHESON TRUST
For the Study of Comparative Religion

© The Matheson Trust, 2011

The Matheson Trust
PO Box 336
56 Gloucester Road
London SW7 4UB, UK

ISBN: 978 1 908092 04 5 paper

*All rights reserved. No part of this publication may be reproduced, stored in a retrieval system, or transmitted in any form or by any means, electronic, mechanical, photocopying, recording, or otherwise, without the prior written permission of the Publisher.*

British Library Cataloguing-in-Publication Data.
A catalogue record for this book is
available from the British Library

# CONTENTS

Introduction . . . . . . . . . . . . . . . . . . . . . . . . . . . . . . . . . . *ix*

PART I: A RECONSTRUCTION OF ANCIENT JEWISH, CHRISTIAN
AND ISLAMIC ESOTERIC TRAJECTORIES . . . . . . . . . . . . . . . . .1

1. The Matrix of Orality and Textuality . . . . . . . . . . . . . . . . . .3
2. Overcoming the Historicist Paradigm. . . . . . . . . . . . . . . .19
3. Ancient Jewish Esoteric Traditions . . . . . . . . . . . . . . . . . .25
4. The Reality and Nature of the Esoteric Teachings
   of Jesus. . . . . . . . . . . . . . . . . . . . . . . . . . . . . . . . . . . . . . . . 44
5. Recovering the Esoteric James . . . . . . . . . . . . . . . . . . . . . .65
6. Jewish Esoteric Traditions in 2nd-Century
   "Gnosticism". . . . . . . . . . . . . . . . . . . . . . . . . . . . . . . . . . . . .88
7. From Jewish Christianity to Islam . . . . . . . . . . . . . . . . . .97

PART II: A RECONSTRUCTION OF EARLY JEWISH CHRISTIANITY
AND GENTILE CHURCH HISTORY AND THOUGHT. . . . . . . .121

1. Reconstructing the Jerusalem Church's Ebionite
   Faith through an Indirect Reading of the
   Pauline Corpus . . . . . . . . . . . . . . . . . . . . . . . . . . . . . . . . .123
2. Reconstructing the Jerusalem Church's Ebionite
   Faith through the Jerusalem Pillars Peter
   and John. . . . . . . . . . . . . . . . . . . . . . . . . . . . . . . . . . . . . . .153
3. A Reconstruction of the Ebionite Faith in the Diaspora:
   Late 1st to Early 2nd Centuries, and Beyond . . . . . . . . .162
4. From Jerusalem to Syria: The Esoteric Heritages
   of James and Thomas. . . . . . . . . . . . . . . . . . . . . . . . . . . .184
5. Models of Early Christologies: Part I: The Gospel
   of the Hebrews: Jerome and Cyril . . . . . . . . . . . . . . . . . .198

6. Models of Early Christologies: Part II: Transfiguration
   and Crucifixion . . . . . . . . . . . . . . . . . . . . . . . . . . . . . . . .213
7. Models of Early Christologies: Part III: The Angelic
   Christ and the Resurrection. . . . . . . . . . . . . . . . . . . . . . .222
8. Models of Early Christologies: Part IV: Ebionite
   Christic and Marian Pneumatology. . . . . . . . . . . . . . . . .230

PART III: THE GOSPEL OF THOMAS . . . . . . . . . . . . . . . . . . . .243

1. Jewish-Christian Features of the Gospel of Thomas . . . . .245
2. The Gospel of Thomas: A Contextualized
   Commentary . . . . . . . . . . . . . . . . . . . . . . . . . . . . . . . . . .261
3. The Gospel of Thomas: A New Translation. . . . . . . . . . . .291

Bibliography . . . . . . . . . . . . . . . . . . . . . . . . . . . . . . . . . . . . . .309
Index. . . . . . . . . . . . . . . . . . . . . . . . . . . . . . . . . . . . . . . . . . . .325

# INTRODUCTION

The present work represents a portion of the results of over twenty years of research by the author on the *Gospel of Thomas*. This monograph concentrates on an historical reconstruction of the early Jewish, Christian, and Islamic esoteric trajectories that may help shed light on *Thomas'* conceptual background. We include Islamic sources in our study despite their later origin on account of their preservation of both Jewish and Jewish-Christian (i.e., Ebionite) traditions which often have not been preserved elsewhere. Additionally, much in Islam exists on a line of continuity with the previous revelations of Judaism and Christianity so that texts from all three Abrahamic religions often shed mutual light on the beliefs and practices of the others.

As we note in our text, we have consistently employed the terms "Jewish Christian" and "Ebionite" as synonyms. This by no means is intended to imply that there were not a variety of ancient Judaic-Christian sects. Yet all of the various Jewish-Christian congregations shared certain distinctive traits in common which united them in a general and functionally useful sense. The usual attempt to create a disjunction between the earliest Jewish Christians of Jerusalem under James the Just (the *Tsaddiq*) and the Ebionites (from the Hebrew term meaning the Poor Ones) is the apologetically and ideologically driven need to deny that Jesus and his earliest direct followers were fully faithful Torah observant Jews who simultaneously possessed a deeply esoteric 'gnostic' orientation. Our historical reconstruction indicates that the Ebionites were precisely what they portrayed themselves as, namely, descendents of the Jerusalem church led by James the *Tsaddiq*, and that even the self-designation of the Ebionites is to be traced back to the earliest days of the Jerusalem Jamesian (or Jacobean) community.

The *Thomas* gospel as a whole is not understandable apart from the history and thought of the general heritage of Ebionite Jewish Christianity. A separate and much lengthier volume is in preparation in which we present a textual-philological analysis of *Thomas*. However, more than philology or linguistic arguments alone, it is a comparative *textual* approach that would best help to narrow the search for the geographic and temporal provenance of this deeply profound and provocative ancient text. In our textual-philological volume in preparation we present previously overlooked parallels between *Thomas* and Jewish sources ranging from the Dead Sea Scrolls, the *Book of Enoch*, and Rabbinic literature. A surprising number of the *Thomas* logia are also clearly paralleled in Mandaean (the Qur'anic Sabaeans) literature to a previously overlooked degree, which we document in a separate volume from this historical-esoteric exegetical work. Such Jewish and Mandaean parallels have not been generally noticed previously principally because of bias among various scholars who are predisposed to prematurely label *Thomas*' more esoteric logia as Hellenistic or as Hermetic in an Alexandrian sense. As a result, even a certain number of Hebrew Biblical parallels to *Thomas* have gone unnoticed, for few have thought to look in such *Jewish* places for *Thomas*' background.

The final chapter of the present study's Part III presents what we call a contextualized commentary on the *Thomas* gospel. Rather than including all the historical and exegetical materials useful for the interpretation of each of the individual logia in the contextualized commentary chapter, we have instead distributed the diverse evidence throughout the various chapters in Parts I and II. We reserve the contextual commentary chapter solely for an analysis of the separate logia by means of intra-textual comparison; that is, in this particular chapter we interpret each logion by comparing it with other logia of the same gospel. We have done this because our research indicated to us that in order to understand *Thomas* properly, various reorientations or revisions were called for re-

*Introduction*

garding some of the generally prevailing interpretative paradigms relating to ancient esoteric trajectories. Such reorientation is necessitated in part by the regrettable anti-Jewish bias of some Christian scholars who find it difficult to accept that the earliest form of Christianity may have been thoroughly Judaic rather than Gentile-oriented in a Pauline sense. Additionally, valuable Jewish and Jewish-Christian traditions on esoteric matters preserved in early Islamic sources have been ignored by Christian scholars as irrelevant to their historical or theological endeavors. Some Islamic scholars have similarly been reluctant to study Jewish esoteric sources which might shed light on various of the more arcane aspects of the Islamic revelation, as if somehow Islam were not a confirmation and continuation of the earlier revelations. Alternatively, some non-Muslim scholars find it difficult to see how Islamic sources could help shed light on ancient Jewish and Christian theology and metaphysics, as if Islam had not emerged from the same Abrahamic monothesistic matrix from which Judaism and the Church arose. Given this conflicted situation, it should go without saying that our citation of a particular scholar's work does not necessarily imply agreement with all their published views. According to a well-known Ebionite metaphorical logion of Jesus on the necessity of correct interpretation of spiritual teachings, one should be a good money changer, able to distinguish between authentic and counterfeit coins.

Our translation of the *Thomas* gospel incorporated at the close of this volume contains only brief footnotes and is designed for the general, non-specialized reader. Our goal here is to remain faithful to the Coptic and Greek texts as preserved in the various manuscripts. In the separate textual-philological study we will present an emendational reconstructed translation with an often different logia sequence and a pericope-based, rather than a logion-based, numbering scheme. Both of the two volumes will be complementary works, but each will represent independent studies, since both this volume's historical reconstruction of ancient esoteric trajectories and the additional volume's textual-philological results designed for a more specialized audience with a knowledge of Hebrew, Aramaic, Mandaic, Syriac, Greek, and Coptic, represent different domains of our findings on the *Gospel of Thomas*.

As we argue in this volume, the central esoteric concern of *Thomas* is self-knowledge, but not a knowledge of the earthly self or of the lower ego, but a knowledge of the divine Self which is mediated through the discovery first of one's primordial androgynous Edenic self and then of one's celestial self or image of light that pre-exists in the supernal kingdom, which anticipates in several respects the later-attested Kabbalistic feminine hypostatic *Malkhut* and *Shekhinah*. Self-knowledge is the only knowledge which is truly necessary, for to adapt the Islamic profession of faith to our present theme, there is no self but the Self; or alternatively, to abbreviate the words of the Jewish Shema, the Lord is *One*.

SAMUEL ZINNER
October 2010
Casablanca, Morocco

## ADDENDA

Page 27, in the first full paragraph, line 3, after "the Divine as such," the following footnote inadvertently dropped out: "The characterization of *ma'aseh bereshit and ma'aseh merkabah* as lesser and greater mysteries stems from Philo; our selection in this chapter of Philonic passages has been guided in part by M. Friedländer, *Der vorchristliche jüdische Gnosticismus* (Göttingen: Vandenhoeck und Ruprecht, 1898), a work which in many respects is still quite relevant and rewarding for the question of the Jewish origins of various components of Gnosticism."

Page 149, line 14, after "Roman citizenship," the following footnote inadvertently dropped out: "This and related matters are treated in a polemical tone in Hyam Maccoby, *The Myth-Maker: Paul and the Invention of Christianity* (NY: Harper Collins, 1987)."

PART I

# A Reconstruction of Ancient Jewish, Christian, and Islamic Esoteric Trajectories

# 1. The Matrix of Orality and Textuality

THE VIEWS of modern scholars are often determined by a culture myopically dominated by written texts; this contrasts with ancient cultures in which both textuality and orality freely interpenetrated. Modern scholarly obsession with written texts may lead to reductionistic paradigms which predispose interpreters to view compositional and redactional activities as exclusively "written" phenomena. When we free ourselves from such artificial schemata, and recognize the possibility of reciprocal oral and textual dynamics, we can begin to envision the possibility, for example, that some of the Matthean, Markan, or Lukan redactional phrases, such as Matthew's term "scribes and Pharisees," may in fact represent phrases already current in public preaching of the nascent churches from very early days. Such phrases could have traveled from community to community by word of mouth via theological discussions and homilies. *Matthew* could have employed his particular redactional phrases orally for decades before writing them down. Thus, when we see a Matthean redactional phrase in the *Gospel of Thomas* (or vice versa as the case may be), this would by no means necessitate a *literary* dependence either way.

In order to determine chronological textual priority, each instance of a presence of common redactional phrases in two documents would have to be examined. Yet one would have to remain open to the possibility that in some cases the very concepts of textual or chronological priority may not even be valid categories, given the nature of the fluidity and interpenetration of both ancient orality and textuality. There is therefore, *pace* Koester, no reason why, for example, *2 Clement*'s logia (sayings of Jesus) *must* be based directly or indirectly on a written *Matthew* gospel.[1] After all, the people who authored the canonical and non-canonical gospels were undoubtedly prominent people in the churches wielding wide influence via not only their scribal activity, but via their oral preaching as well.

The above model may enable us to understand why *Thomas* 13, *pace* Bauckham,[2] does not necessarily indicate knowledge of chapter 16 of the written canonical *Matthew*. Here we cite both relevant texts to help illustrate our point:

> *Thomas* 13. Jesus said to his disciples: "Make a comparison and tell me what I am like." Simon Peter said to him: "You are like a righteous angel." Matthew said to him: "You are like a wise sage." Thomas said to him: "Master, my mouth will not allow me at all to say what you are like." Jesus said: "I am not your master; because you drank you were intoxicated from the bubbling spring I have measured out." And he took him aside and spoke to him three things (words). But when Thomas approached his companions, they asked him: "What did Jesus say to you?" Thomas said to them: "If I were to tell you even one of the things he told me, you would gather stones and cast them at me, and fire would come from the stones and burn you."

> *Matthew* 16:13) Now when Jesus came into the district of Caesarea Philippi, he asked his disciples, "Who do people say that the Son of Man is?" 14) And they said, "Some say John the Baptizer, others say Elijah, and others Jeremiah, or one of the prophets." 15) He said to them, "But who do you say that I am?" 16) Simon Peter replied, "You are the Christ, the son of the living God." 17) And Jesus answered him, "Blessed are

---

1. Helmut Koester, *Ancient Christian Gospels. Their History and Development* (Harrisburg, Pennsylvania: Trinity Press International, 1990), 18.

2. Richard Bauckham, *Jesus and the Eyewitnesses. The Gospels as Eyewitness Testimony* (Grand Rapids, Michigan/ Cambridge, U.K., 2006), 236-37.

you, Simon Bar-Jona! For flesh and blood has not revealed this to you, but my father who is in heaven."

Neither *Matthew* 16 nor *Thomas* 13 was created out of thin air, for given early Christian conditions these two texts would likely have been based on so-called floating traditions circulating in both oral and textual modes. The situation in *Thomas* 13, insofar as it contrasts the figures of Matthew and Peter, is paralleled by Paul's open opposition to James and Peter in *Galatians* 2. Indeed, Paul condemns James and Peter outright, whereas *Thomas* 13 merely represents Thomas as having been more insightful upon one occasion than Peter and Matthew. The *Thomas* gospel is in tension with the church of Peter, but this does not necessarily pertain to the Petrine church as described in the canonical *Gospel of Matthew*, for the traditions enshrined in the *Matthew* gospel may have appeared later and independently of *Thomas*. *Matthew* furthermore represents Syrian ecclesiastical traditions of the Antiochene Petrine branch, whereas *Thomas* represents the traditions of the Eddesan branch. Accordingly, *Thomas* 13 may not be commenting upon the canonical written text of *Matthew* 16, but rather upon *oral* traditions concerning Peter which had been current in Antioch and which were later recorded in writing in the canonical *Matthew*. This would account for the simultaneously marked similarity and dis-similarity between *Matthew* 16 and *Thomas* 13.

*Pace* Bauckham, Peter's description of Jesus as a "righteous angel" in *Thomas* 13 does not accord with *Mark*'s Christology, and so may not be used to infer a Thomasine allusion to canonical *Mark*. Rather, it perfectly accords with what we know of Ebionite Jewish-Christian angelic Christology, which we discuss below in this monograph. Perhaps it has been overlooked in previous studies on logion 13 that we have a precise parallel to the term "righteous angel" in "the angel of righteousness"[3] mentioned in the Jewish-Christian text *Shep-*

---

3. The Biblical Aramaic word for the class of angels known as 'watcher',

*herd of Hermas* (Mandate VI,2). Thus Bauckham's suggestion that *Thomas* 13's "a righteous angel" may have been derived from *Mark* 1:2's description of John the Baptist as the "messenger" (*angelos*), but "mistakenly" applied by *Thomas* to the person of Jesus, seems to be a grasping at straws.[4]

Another example of presuppositions determined by a culture of predominant textuality would be the unwarranted contention that the *Apocryphon of James* must be late because it shows the author was acquainted with Paul's thought, based on parallels in the *Apocryphon of James* with certain phrases found in Paul. This would unnecessarily assume that the author of the *Apocryphon* could have had access to Paul's thought only in an exclusively *written* format. Such an approach fails to take into account that the historical James and Paul knew each other personally, or that even the canonical *Letter of James* exhibits a knowledge of some of Paul's theological terminology. In any case, the *Epistle of the Apostles* compared with the *Apocryphon of James* indicates to us that when an ancient author wished to allude to a previously written gospel, it is usually quite clear that he or she has done so. The *Apocryphon of James* exhibits no clear evidence of knowledge of the written canonical gospels or of the Pauline literary corpus. As Kirchner observes, the evidence suggests that the *Apocryphon of James* is a Syro-Palestinian document which may be "as early as the second half of the 1st century,"[5] therefore between 50-100 CE. By contrast, it is universally recognized that the *Epistle of the Apostles* is an early 2nd-century CE

---

עיר, is quite proximate orally to the Biblical word for 'teacher', ירא, which leads one to wonder if Peter's 'righteous angel' (cf. Hermas' 'angel of righteousness') might be connected somehow with the term 'teacher of righteousness' known from the Book of Joel.

4. See Richard Bauckham, *Jesus and the Eyewitnesses. The Gospels as Eyewitness Testimony*, 237.

5. Wilhelm Schneemelcher (ed.), *New Testament Apocrypha*. Vol. 1: *Gospels and Related Writings*. Revised Edition (Louisville/London: Jerome Clarke & Co., Westminster John Knox Press, 2003), 287.

document which alludes to and extensively quotes from previously written gospels, canonical and otherwise.

The early Christian preachers, including the so-called pseudepigraphic authors (many of whom may have sincerely believed that they were speaking authentically under inspiration in the voice and name of the ancient prophets and apostles), constituted both supportive as well as competitive networks of preachers and scribes who influenced entire communities and regions which were engaged in all degrees and varieties of theological and metaphysical exchanges and debates. Scholars who insist that the *Apocryphon of James* must be late because of the presence of "Johannine" parallels again simply assume a *written* source for these Johannine parallels. The same problematic assumption may apply to Quispel's claim that *Thomas* shows knowledge of the *Gospel of John*.[6] Why does Quispel assume that *Thomas'* knowledge of Johannine theology was necessarily mediated to him in a *written* format, especially when the parallels are rather vague, equally as vague as the parallels shared between *John*, the letters of Ignatius, and the *Odes of Solomon*?

Furthermore, some of the earliest pagan converts to Christianity could have been grossly ignorant of Judaism and Palestinian topography, and the latter ignorance could just as well apply to any Jew not resident in Palestine. Thus such features in a text like the *Protevangelium Jacobi* do not necessitate, by themselves, a "late" provenance, and do not always exclude the presence of genuine Jewish traditions.[7] Halperin

---

6. G. Quispel, "The Gospel of Thomas and Christian Wisdom by Stevan L. Davies. Review," *Vigiliae Christianae*, vol. 38, no. 1 (March, 1984), 92-93.

7. Such considerations are not taken into account in Charles L. Quarles, *Midrash Criticism. Introduction and Appraisal* (Lanham/NY/Oxford: University Press of America, 1998), 126-27. Perhaps here Quarles writes out of some sort of anti-Catholic animus directed against Marian traditions when he stresses that the *Protevangelium Jacobi* is "pagan" without "a Judaistic background." By contrast, Jonathan Cohen, without denying historical inaccuracies in the *Protevangelium Jacobi*, nevertheless insists that "one may not simply conclude that all the sources of the PEJ are non-Jewish," and notes several instances of its correct knowledge of Jewish customs and tra-

observes how the ordinary members of an ancient Greek-speaking Jewish community could have been "entirely or almost entirely ignorant of Hebrew."[8] Ignorance of contemporary conditions of other cultures and regions has always existed. Ancient writers would have been avid collectors of traditions, both written and oral, but not everyone could read or write in the ancient world, and this includes the average member of the various primitive churches. The early Christian authors would have been a specialized, prominent group wielding not only local authority, but also wide influence through the direct disemination of their ideas and distinctive phrases through both writing and preaching, and the transmitted written and oral phraseologies would have mutually influenced each other from the very beginning of the process.

The considerations of orality and textuality reach as well into the domain of questions of original compositional languages. As an illustration, scholars still debate the question of the "original" language of the *Odes of Solomon*, whether it was Syriac or Greek. But this question is overly dualistic in its construction and as a consequence might be misleading. Convincing and sound arguments can be put forward alternatingly to support either theory of Greek or Syriac priority. In light of this, the most natural solution would be that the *Odes* were composed simultaneously in Syriac and Greek by a single bilingual Syrian Christian who freely employed wordplays in both versions. Like so many bilingual speakers, he probably also intentionally produced what to scholars would appear as "inaccurate" translational equivalents in both versions. In this scenario the Greek version will have priority, yet it will also be informed by the author's other language, Syriac, that is, his Syriac thought patterns will have influenced

---

ditions found in *Midrash Samuel 2, Abodah Zarah* 26a, *Exodus Rabbah* xxix.9, *Pesikta Rabbati* 26, and many more like references. See Jonathan Cohen, *The Origins and Evolution of the Moses Nativity Story* (Leiden/NY/Köln: E. J. Brill, 1993), 171-72.

8. David J. Halperin, "Origen, Ezekiel's Merkabah, and the Ascension of Moses," *Church History*, vol. 50, no. 3 (Sep., 1981), 269.

his Greek usage. Conversely, with regard to the Syriac version, it will have just as much priority as the Greek, and the Syriac version will be equally as informed (and in some cases possibly misinformed) and influenced by the author's Greek thought patterns.

With regard to the gospels, both canonical and non-canonical, Jesus' words and ideas will have been constantly reformulated to meet the needs of various communities and cultures. Luke changes Matthew's Jewish terminologies, for example, to better communicate Jesus' teachings to a Gentile audience. At a later period, Jesus' teaching on the "new birth" (see *John* 3) was assimilated to the doctrine of transmigration when Syrian Christianity (of partial Nestorian-Ebionite complexion) first spread to China.[9] Thus in all four canonical gospels, as well as in *Thomas*, one would expect a mixture of early and late, as well as Jewish and Hellenistic, formulations and reformulations, which would reflect interpenetrating influences emanating from both textual and oral sources. To argue, therefore, too generally concerning "priority" or "dependence" of *Thomas* (or of any other gospel, canonical or otherwise) would constitute a posture that fails to recognize the situation of mutual interpenetration of regions, mentalities, orality, and textuality which prevailed from the beginning of the nascent churches. Even so-called "secondary" textual and theological elements could have arisen quite early, even from the very beginning of church history, for it would have been necessary from the first day of its preaching to interpret Jesus' message and its significance for a variety of cultural and linguistic audiences. Preaching slogans and catechesis would have existed from the very beginning. All five gospels under consideration here could in principle represent a mixture of both early and late, as well as Jewish and

---

9. See Martin Palmer in association with Eva Wong, Tjalling Halbertsma, Zhao Xiao Min, Li Rong Rong, and James Palmer, *The Jesus Sutras. Rediscovering the Lost Scrolls of Taoist Christianity* (NY: Ballantine Wellspring, 2001).

Hellenistic components. In *Thomas*, at the Syriac level, we see the influence of a pre-Diatessaronic gospel harmony similar to Justin's. This harmony probably developed before the publication of *John*'s gospel, since Justin knew a gospel harmony, but apparently he did not know John's gospel, although he did know traditions paralleled in *John*; the same paradigm applies to Ignatius of Antioch in relation to *Thomas*.[10]

Therefore, no matter when we date the first versions of the canonical gospels, we must still make room for mutual influences, oral and written, behind and between these texts. Moreover, the present version of *Luke* may be later than our present version of *John*,[11] and although *Mark* is generally older than *Matthew* and *Luke*, nevertheless in its present form *Mark* contains various features which arguably might be temporally posterior to *Matthew* and *Luke*. We must keep in mind the rule established by classicists that the first 100 years or so of a text's existence is the period when it will undergo the most redactional changes.[12] Thus the versions of the canonical gospels used in the pre-Diatessaronic harmony could be expected to diverge in several respects from our present canonical gospels. And *Thomas* could have influenced some stages of the synoptic gospels, and vice versa.[13] Ancient scribes, especially religious scribes, did not operate in a vacuum; in this respect, some modern scholars' ivory tower seclusion within academia might prove to be more extreme than a medieval monk's scriptorium.

---

10. It is possible that Justin knew John's gospel, but ignored it, just as Justin certainly must have known of Paul, but completely ignored his writings and theology.

11. Cf. Andrew Gregory, "The Third Gospel? The Relationship of John and Luke Reconsidered," in John Lierman (ed.), *Challenging Perspectives on the Gospel of John* (Tübingen: Mohr Siebeck, 2006), 109-22.

12. See Eldon Jay Epp, "The Multivalence of the Term 'Original Text' in New Testament Textual Criticism," *The Harvard Theological Review*, vol. 92, no. 3 (July, 1999), 256.

13. See Gregory J. Riley, "Influence of Thomas Christianity on Luke 12:14 and 5:39," *The Harvard Theological Review*, vol. 88, no. 2 (April, 1995), 229-235.

All three synoptic gospels as well as *Thomas* seem to have influenced one another, to have interacted with each other, each constituting what DeConick has labeled an expanding or "rolling corpus," borrowing a term from McKane.[14] All four canonical gospels as well as *Thomas* are to be dated similarly over a growing period of time, and all exhibit both early and late elements, resulting from substantial changes to the various compositional layers of their texts. They represent interweaving, expanding, breathing, living documents; redaction criticism will be unable to untangle these intertwining knots without destroying literary beauty and integrity, for such literary links are interwoven with each other like veins in a living body. According to Luomanen, at least a part of the *Thomas* sayings might be "directly based on a Jewish-Christian gospel harmony," or *Thomas* and the "Jewish-Christian fragments" might share a "common harmonizing predecessor."[15] It is on account of ancient reciprocal literary complexity that Luomanen is compelled to stress that his assertion covers only some of the *Thomas* logia, rather than the document as a whole.

Epp has described modern textual critics such as Westcott-Hort, Metzger, and Kurt and Barbara Aland as reductionist as well as anti-traditional in their methodologies. For example, Epp quotes Hort's law: "Where there is variation, there must be error in at least all variants but one."[16] The search for a reputed single "original text" is in fact the result of a reductionistic historicist approach, and it is anti-traditional inasmuch as it rejects a diversity of textual traditions which were held as valid and authoritative in the ancient churches. A few examples would be, as Epp points out, the "dual ver-

---

14. April D. DeConick, "The Original Gospel of Thomas," *Vigiliae Christianae*, vol. 56 (2002), 180.

15. Petri Luomanen, "Eusebius' View of the 'Gospel of the Hebrews'," in Jostein Ådna (ed.), *The Formation of the Early Church* (Tübingen: Mohr Siebeck, 2005), 278.

16. Eldon Jay Epp, "The Multivalence of the Term 'Original Text' in New Testament Textual Criticism," 250.

sions" of *Luke's* gospel and *Book of Acts*, namely, the B and D versions which are marked by "extensive textual variation." Additionally, "tradition provides various endings" to the *Gospel of Mark* in order "to adjust for the perceived abruptness" of *Mark* 16:8.[17] Additional examples are Jesus' saying on marriage/divorce and the *Pater Noster*, both of which varied regionally throughout the churches, reflecting diverse valid local traditions. The *Pater Noster*, for example, "has six main forms in the manuscript tradition," and the saying on marriage and divorce shows so much variation in the manuscripts that "the recovery of a single original saying of Jesus [on marriage and divorce] is impossible."[18] With regard to the *pericope adulterae* (*John* 7:53-8:11), scribes felt free to delete it from *John* or to displace it elsewhere, for example, into *Luke's* gospel.[19] Epp asks which forms or versions of *Luke-Acts*, the *Pater Noster*, the Markan endings, etc. were/are canonical?[20] His point is that all the various forms reflect valid, binding, local traditions. Modern text critics are anti-traditional in their desire to reduce such living diversity to a single authoritative frozen "original" form, for as Epp observes, they reject what was "once authoritative scripture" in both the ancient and medieval periods, and even beyond.[21] The text critics are also anti-traditional in that they as a rule either ignore or reject important Patristic evidence. As Epp notes, sources as early as Justin Martyr quote *Matthew* 19:17 in the following form: "And he [Jesus] said to him, 'Why do you ask me about what is good? One is good, my father in heaven.'"[22] The phrase "my father in heaven" was deleted from the surviving manuscript tradition out of theological embarrassment; yet despite the multiple attestations of this form in the Fathers, the modern

---

17. Ibid., 269.
18. Ibid., 265.
19. Ibid., 269.
20. See ibid., 275.
21. See ibid., 274.
22. Ibid., 261.

*The Matrix of Orality and Textuality*

text critics completely ignore it simply because it is not attested in *later* New Testament manuscripts.

A core presupposition of the modern text critics is that Christianity is primarily a religion of the written text rather than of the spoken word. The same applies to much of scholarship on Islam, for according to a common misunderstanding the Qur'an is essentially a written text, whereas in fact the Qur'an was first received as a spoken, oral transmission. To return to our main topic, Epp notes that there are "some 300,000 variant readings in the New Testament manuscript tradition."[23] Modern text critics see these as "corruptions," when in fact they largely represent the diversity of valid local ancient traditions.

Although he does not mention it, Epp's approach incidentally restores credibility to the Council of Trent's endorsement of the Latin Vulgate, because one can now understand that "canonical" and "authoritative" does not equate to "original reading" or "original text," whether that be "original Greek" or the "original" version/s of the Latin Vulgate. Yet even with the Latin translation of the scriptures we face a plethora of ancient pre-Vulgate divergent readings, representing regionally and individually held binding, authoritative texts. The same critique can be applied to DeConick's concept of an "original" *Gospel of Thomas*, which while admittedly useful on an historical plane is of lesser value for the service of theology and metaphysics if a chronological "later" is interpreted as necessarily implying a "theologically" less original or authoritative version or "development."

All in all the undeniable New Testament manuscript evidence clearly sustains Parker's assertion that for the early churches, "it was more important to hand on the spirit of Jesus' teaching than to remember the letter.... [T]he material about Jesus was preserved in an interpretive rather than an exact fashion."[24] The variations between the four canonical

---

23. Ibid., 277.
24. Quoted in ibid., 265.

gospels themselves are proof that the spirit and not wording is essential; and to a significant degree this gospel characteristic reflects the literary fluidity of Jewish targumic praxis, not to mention the freedom with which the Septuagint Greek translators handled the Hebrew Biblical texts, and then in turn the freedom with which the Masoretes handled the even earlier Hebrew texts of their period. The sacred text long remained fluid, and different theological schools, both Jewish and Christian, produced a rich treasury of scriptural variant readings, yet all the traditional schools of interpretation were held to be authoritative among their respective adherents.

In much of the Rabbinic writings all forms of traditions relating to specific questions are collected, often without a stated bias in favor of any one school or scriptural textual variant over another. Similarly in Islamic *tafsir* and *hadith* collections all variants and opinions are generally recorded and preserved. The same applies to the gospels. In light of all these cases of co-existing diversity we may ask which scriptural readings and traditions are "original"? Our answer is that all of the traditional forms are "original," for although historical reality was by no means ignored in the antique world, "historicity" in the modern sense was never the primary category of concern for either ancient Judaism or nascent Christianity. The underlying eternal and esoteric significance of events was more important than the bare historical phenomenon in itself.[25]

Jewish tradition speaks of variant readings in the Torah which are traced back to this or that Rabbi; one such technique is known as *tiqra*: "do not read thus, but read thus." Sanhedrin 110b gives us a typical example of *tiqra*: "*Isaiah 26:2, '*Open the gates, that the righteous nation which keeps truth may enter in'; read not 'which keeps truth' (*shomer emunim*),

---

25. As Schuon has observed, myth can communicate truth more effectually than mere historical reportage. See Frithjof Schuon, *Gnosis: Divine Wisdom*. Translated from the French by G. E. H. Palmer. (Pates Manor, Bedfont, Middlesex: Perennial Books, 1990), 18-22.

but 'which says Amen' (*she-omer amen*)". What is implied here is not that a Rabbi's copy of the Torah actually read differently from the standard version, but that the Rabbi interpreted the text in such or such a way, based on considerations of gematria, allegory, etc. The same applies to the well-known phenomenon of variant readings in the Qur'an; contrary to the claims of many academic western Orientalists these were primitive interpretations of an already fixed text, not primitive textual variants. Which of the traditional variants were considered original? All of them, because nascent Islam was not concerned with an "original" *historical* reading, neither at the Qur'anic level, as the various versions attest, nor at the level of the *ahadith*, which exhibit the same types of oral and exegetical fluidity as do Jesus' sayings in the gospels. Even according to a non-traditional scholar such as Wansbrough, the "'companion' codices" as well as the "'regional' codices" (*masahif al-amsar*) "are largely fictive. Of genuinely textual variants exhibiting material deviation from the canonical text of revelation, such as are available for Hebrew and Christian scripture, there are none."[26] However, the fact that the early Islamic authorities presented these traditions as such proves that their concept of textuality was fluid and that all traditional schools of exegesis were equally respected as such.

The traditional seven approved readings of the Qur'an demonstrate that at least in some sectors of early Islam oral diversity predominated over monolithic textuality even with regard to Islam's sacred text. This reflects the metaphysical tenet that there is not an identity but a continuity between the written and recited Qur'an and its celestial archetype. It is of the celestial archetype, not of its written or even recited analogue, that it is said the words of God are inexhaustible, as in Qur'an *sura* 31:27: "And if all the trees on the earth were pens, and if the seas were *ink and the seas were* expanded sevenfold, *the ink would be depleted before* the words of God would

---

26. John Wansbrough, *Quranic Studies. Sources and Methods of Scriptural Interpretation* (Amherst, NY: Prometheus Books, 2004), 203, 45.

be finished; surely God is mighty, wise." This undifferentiated infinity is also hinted at in the fact that many of the earliest Qur'ans were written without diacritical markings, which encouraged diversity of variant readings, interpretations, and recitations. That the variants are limited to seven is a valid traditional safeguard, but this does not imply that the possible meanings of the text are not infinite. According to a *hadith*, there are 70,000 veils of the Qur'an, just as "the Torah has 70 faces."[27] Ibn al-'Arabi teaches that each time one reads a Qur'anic *aya* (verse) one should understand it differently; there is no one meaning to the sacred text. This agrees essentially with the Buddhist doctrine of non-essence, which is more or less paralleled in Islamic mysticism, as for example when Seyyid Haydar Amuli writes in his *Asrar al-Shari'ah* (*Mysteries of the Shariah*), in the section on divine Unity (*tawhid*):

> The statements of all the Gnostics, moreover, mirror the same truth: "Nothing exists but God, his names, his attributes and his actions. Thus everything is him, by means of him, from him, and to him." Just as the waves vanish back into the sea and the drops of rain dissolve into the ocean in spite of our mental perception of them as distinct existent entities because, in actuality, the waves and drops of rain have no separate existence at all, so the real existence is solely that the sea and the waves are in a condition of mutual destruction and vanishing.... Therefore the one who witnesses the Real, and who sees the creation and its manifestations for what they in truth are, realizes that the creation and all phenomena are actually non-existent.... In truth, nothing exists but the Real.... God alludes to this when he says, "When you see the mountains you think they are solid, yet they shall vanish as the cloud vanishes" (Qur'an *sura* 27:88).

The Babylonian Talmud does not normally choose between competing traditions, pronouncing that one is "right"

---

27. Cited in Gershom Scholem, *Kabbalah* (NY: Meridian, 1974), 172.

and the other "wrong"; there is some of the latter procedure in the Jerusalem Talmud, but there as well we find an overall respectful preservation of all sides of religious questions. The Babylonian Talmud is typified by a tolerance, acceptance, and respect for a diversity of truth articulations. By contrast, the Jerusalem Talmud conforms more to the pattern of Scholasticism, to an Aquinas, for example, who assembles all opinions and then pronounces in favor of one. Boyarin argues that the Babylonian Talmud has adopted a Christian apophatic approach, and this is a possibility, but we do not share Boyarin's negative attitude towards apophasis in general.[28] Rather than always being necessarily shallow or non-intellectual, apophasis on the contrary can by means of extremely subtle and profoundly dialectical contemplation reconcile diverse faith interpretations and traditions which at first sight may appear dogmatically irreconcilable. Apophasis can demonstate that at an interior level some contradictories may coincide, at least to a certain degree. Thus apophatic thought may serve to nurture and support a co-existence of diverse faith interpretations and traditions.

At least theologically considered, there is ultimately no need to choose between valid textual variations of scripture, for as Gregory the Great writes in his *Moralis in Iob*, 20.I.I, *Scriptura sacra cum legentibus crescit*, that is, "Sacred scripture increases with those reading it." Cognate to the concept of a valid variety of variant readings of sacred scripture and a legitimate co-existence of competing theological and metaphysical propositions, is the question of divergence with regard to the establishment of a sacred canon of authoritative books. And here we find the same diversity as with scriptural variant readings. The different churches have different canons, such as the Roman Catholic, Eastern Orthodox, Protestant,

---

28. See Daniel Boyarin, "Hellenism in Jewish Babylonia," in Charlotte Elisheva Fonrobert and Martin S. Jaffee eds., *The Cambridge Companion to the Talmud and Rabbinic Literature* (Cambridge: Cambridge University Press, 2007), 347.

and Ethiopian Churches. The latter canon in fact includes the *Book of Enoch* in its Old Testament, and by adopting such works as the *Shepherd of Hermas*, its New Testament canon is quite different from the canons of all other churches.

## 2. Overcoming the Historicist Paradigm

In continental scholarship the principle has been advanced that Jewish sources can assist in the interpretation of Christian texts, even if the Jewish works in question were codified in written form well after the time of the composition of the New Testament writings. In order for scholarship to broaden its acceptance of this procedure's legitimacy, it would be necessary to overcome various assumptions inherent in historicism. We can understand something of what this entails by summarizing the issue from Vermes' essay entitled "Jewish Literature and New Testament Exegesis: Reflections on Methodology." Vermes begins this illuminating piece by noting that scholars such as Fitzmeyer believe that Jewish literature, e.g., the Targumim, which are dated later than the New Testament, are not of value for the interpretation of Christianity's sacred texts.[1] Scholars like Fitzmeyer, who tend to downplay the importance of Rabbinic literature, seem not have mastered such literature in the first place; for example, Vermes gives an example of Fitzmeyer confusing the Mishnah with the Talmud and the correct languages of certain texts.[2]

Vermes presents various possible alternatives that may be invoked to explain the genesis of parallel texts. For example when there is a parallel between Rabbinic literature and a New Testament passage, there are two choices which exegetes traditionally choose from: Either the Rabbinic text influenced the New Testament, or the New Testament influenced the Rabbinic text. While Vermes is skeptical of the sec-

---

1. Geza Vermes, *Jesus in His Jewish Context* (Minneapolis: Fortress Press, 2003), 71.
2. Ibid., 72.

ond alternative, the recent work of Boyarin, Liebes, and others, has demonstrated that such has upon occasion been the case.[3] There is a further third possibility that two texts may resemble each other simply out of coincidence. Finally there is a fourth option which is quite reasonable and is fortunately increasingly adopted by exegetes, namely, that two similar texts may independently reflect early Jewish traditions which were in general circulation.[4]

Vermes gets to the heart of the matter when he asks why is it that scholars are preoccupied with the Rabbinic literature as a tool for the possible interpretation of the New Testament instead of the reverse, that is, why isn't the New Testament utilized as a tool for understanding the vast corpus of Rabbinic literature?[5] The answer is that most New Testament scholars are "churchmen" who hold the New Testament as "central," while Judaism and all other ancient currents of thought are of interest only for any possible assistance they might afford in understanding the Christian scriptures.[6] Since all religions are unique in their own providential ways, such an attitude is understandable on its own level. Nevertheless, Vermes may be justified when he advocates that Christian scholars endeavor to view the New Testament as one particular manifestation of ancient Judaism among others, and that Jewish scholars overcome any "lingering subconscious dislike" of Christian material, and to recognize that the Christian scriptures are a manifestation of an ancient Judaism of the Second Temple

---

3. See Daniel Boyarin, "The Gospel of the *Memra*: Jewish Binitarianism and the Prologue of John," *Harvard Theological Review* 94 no. 3 (2001), 243-84; see also the following three works of Yehudah Liebes: "The Shofar Blast Angels and Yeshu'a Sar ha-Panim," in *ha-Mistiqah ha-Yehudit ha-Qedumah* [=*Mehqerey Yerushalayim be-Mahshevet Yisra'el* vi: 1-2] (1987), 171-95; *Studies in the Zohar*. Translated from the Hebrew by Arnold Schwartz, Stephanie Nakache, Penina Peli (Albany, NY: State University of New York Press), 1993; "Who Makes the Horn of Jesus to Flourish," *Immanuel*, no. 21 (Summer 1987), 55-67.

4. See Geza Vermes, *Jesus in His Jewish Context*, 77-78.
5. Ibid, 78.
6. Ibid., 78-79.

period. However, Vermes would qualify that the Christian scriptures are Jewish if the "accretions" of a Hellenistic nature are stripped from them; but this is questionable in the light of the more recent research of Boyarin which demonstrates that Hellenism had been integrated within Rabbinic Judaism already in the ancient period.[7] In any event, Vermes' proposed paradigm would make the New Testament relevant to Jewish scholars on the one hand, and on the other hand the New Testament would no longer "occup[y] the center of the stage"; this necessitates that both Jewish and Christian scholars study Judaism "as a whole," including Judaism's "Christian" components.[8]

Vermes' approach solves "the chronological difficulty," or what we may call the reductionist historicist model, and unveils the Christian scriptures "as organically bound up with" Judaism.[9] Vermes gives a concrete example of his proposed methodology by referring to Jesus' teaching on divorce in *Matthew* 5:32. If we assemble the parallels from the Bible (Hebrew and Greek), the Dead Sea Scrolls, Josephus, and the Rabbinic literature, we can discern their commonalities as well as distinctives, and in an "effect" that is "reciprocal," the Christian scripture "authenticates" the later Rabbinic literature's reference to the theological strife between Hillel and Shammai on this question, which is traditionally dated to the first century.[10] In the end, Christian history cannot be fully written without being contextualized within the borders of Judaism's larger history, insofar as Christianity emanated from a Jewish matrix. Conversely, an account of Judaism would not be complete without integrating the record of

---

7. See the following two works of Daniel Boyarin: "The Gospel of the Memra: Jewish Binitarianism and the Prologue of John," and "Hellenism in Jewish Babylonia," in Charlotte Elisheva Fonrobert and Martin S. Jaffee eds., *The Cambridge Companion to the Talmud and Rabbinic Literature* (Cambridge: Cambridge University Press, 2007), 336-63.

8. Geza Vermes, *Jesus in His Jewish Context*, 79.

9. Ibid., 80.

10. Ibid.

Christian tradition within the broader framework of Jewish history, especially in the post-Biblical periods.[11]

As one example of a work which would have benefited significantly if it had adopted the Vermes paradigm, we might mention Segal's classic *The Two Powers in Heaven*,[12] which suffers from a self-imposed limitative historicism in its exclusion of later *hekhalot* literature in a quest to find first-century or earlier "Jewish" confirmatory evidence for Paul's spiritual-mystical transformation experience. On the positive side, we can give a few examples of American scholars who use later sources to understand earlier writings. Orlov cites the medieval *Zohar* numerous times in order to interpret the ca. first-century Jewish text of *2 Enoch*. In one case he presents, the *Zohar* actually helps solve a philological perplexity, the name *Adoil* in *2 Enoch* 24, which has long challenged scholars. The various interpretations that have been offered for the meaning of *Adoil* include "hand of God," "light of God," "his eternity; his aeon," "Hades + El," and even "Adonai-El." But as Orlov shows, the key to solving the puzzle lies in *Zohar* I,17b, where we find the term *El-gadol*, "the Great God." The *2 Enoch* text specifically calls Adoil "the great one." The problem in an ancient text is thus solved by means of a judicious consideration of a later medieval text.[13]

Before presenting a second example, we note how Pagels in an audio CD lecture hesitates to explain the esoteric components of the *Gospel of Thomas* as reflecting Jewish mysticism, since, according to her, the latter (in the forms paralleled in *Thomas*) is documented only in later medieval sources (in the *hekhalot* literature, for example).[14] In contrast to Pagels, DeConick does not hesitate to ascribe much of the esoteric fea-

---

11. Ibid.
12. Alan F. Segal, *Two Powers in Heaven: Early Rabbinic Reports about Christianity and Gnosticism* (Leiden: Brill, 1977).
13. Andrei A. Orlov, *The Enoch-Metatron Tradition* (Mohr Siebeck, 2004), 198-99.
14. Elaine Pagels, *The Gospel of Thomas*. Audio CD. (Boulder, Colorado: Sounds True, 2006).

tures of *Thomas* to ancient Jewish mysticism; she documents, as has been common since the pioneering work of Scholem, that the later *Merkabah* texts are rooted in ancient Jewish mystical and apocalyptic currents of the Second Temple period.[15] According to DeConick, because many (admittedly not all) of the central ideas in medieval Jewish mystical texts are rooted in ancient traditions, these later texts "are valuable" for understanding and elucidating the "interface" between Christianity and ancient Judaic esoteric trajectories.[16] This contrasts with Pagels' limitative historicist approach which claims that the "Christian" *Thomas*' esoteric features cannot be said to represent parallel ideas found in later Jewish mystical documents. Such historicism prevents scholars from seeing that *Thomas* itself might be an ancient example of the very Jewish mysticism which they think does not appear until the medieval period. Implicit in such thinking is also an assumption that *Thomas* is "Christian" in a mode that possesses little if any relationship to ancient Judaism. In any case, with regard to DeConick, we recognize the positive benefits of a Vermes-like paradigm that integrates early Christian literature within the category of ancient Judaism.

Many American scholars are still more firmly entrenched in limitative historicist presuppositions than their continental colleagues, but generally in America Christian scholarship of the New Testament, patristics, and early church history, has for well over a century used Jewish textual parallels for the interpretation of Christian sources, based on the recognition that the Church historically emerged from Judaism, and indeed constituted in its historical beginnings one form of Second Temple Judaism. More recently, Jewish scholarship (for example Talmudic scholar Boyarin, whom we have already mentioned more than once) has begun referring to nascent Christian sources as a tool to be employed in the in-

---

15. April DeConick, *Seek to See Him. Ascent and Vision Mysticism in the Gospel of Thomas* (Leiden: E. J. Brill, 1996), 28ff.
16. Ibid., 31.

terpretation of primitive Jewish texts, again recognizing that Christianity began as a form of ancient Judaism.

The next stage in this process involves the integration of Islamic studies into the above paradigm, which will require the overcoming of several prejudices within the various faith communities of all three Abrahamic religions. Although we will deal with this stage involving the integration of Islamic materials in the study of Judaism and Christianity in a later chapter, it will be appropriate at this point to explain the overarching theological and indeed metaphysical justification for such a paradigm. This conceptual structure is erected on the foundational thesis that the three Abrahamic religions constitute three branches of a single archetypal tree. As a consequence, all three trajectories are genetically and organically related. At different times throughout history, different branches have developed on the tree; yet all branches, regardless of chronological considerations, may mutually illuminate meanings inherent in the other branches' traditions, since all flow from the same life source. The branches are admittedly different, each being unique. Yet viewed as a whole, the tree is one, and even the distinctives flow from the same source as the convergences. As we will have occasion to illustrate throughout this study, later Islamic texts can at times shed light upon earlier Jewish or Christian texts and traditions, while earlier Jewish or Christian texts may reveal anticipations of later Islamic conceptions and articulations.

# 3. Ancient Jewish Esoteric Trajectories

In this chapter we trace the main conceptual outlines of ancient Jewish mysticism. *Hagigah* 11b divides esoteric matters into four branches; 1): the teachings concerning forbidden sexual relations; 2): the teachings concerning the secrets of creation; 3): the teaching concerning the secrets of the *merkabah* (chariot) throne of God; 4): the teachings concerning cosmogonic secrets. Despite this fourfold division, Jewish mysticism is in general dominated by the second and third branches listed above. First is *ma'aseh bereshit*, literally the "work of creation," which involves the various modes of God's self-manifestation or revelation. This category pertains to such matters as the ten divine utterances (nine explicit, one implicit) of the phrase "let there be!" in the *Genesis* 1 account of creation understood as ten emanations called the *sefirot*. *Ma'aseh bereshit* may be called the Lesser Mysteries, and these may overlap with and include the fourth category of potentially perilous cosmogonic secrets, as described in *Hagigah* 11b: "Whoever looks into four matters, it were better if he had not been born: what is above, what is below, what is before (creation), and what is after (i.e., apocalyptic secrets)."

The other main category is *ma'aseh merkabah*, the "work of the chariot," or throne mysticism, which relates to the mysteries of God's very essence and nature. *Merkabah* mysticism involves the secrets of the divine hypostases, and therefore pertains to such matters as the Primordial Divine Human (*Adam Qadmon*) and the *shi'ur qomah* ("extent of the measure") which involves speculations on the vast cosmic dimensions of the body of the hypostatic Image or Glory of God. The *merkabah* mysticism is held to be more secret than *bereshit* (creation) mysticism, since the latter delves into cosmogonic matters, but the former treats of more arcane theosophical realities. *Hagigah* 11b dictates: "One may not expound the *ma'aseh bereshit* in front of two listeners, and of the *merkabah* not in front of one listener, unless this one be a sage who understands of his own knowledge." The same passage warns in this context: "And whoever does not guard the honor of his creator, it were better if he had not been born." As we shall learn, this warning alludes to the grave danger of compromising or even losing one's belief in the divine Unity after having a *merkabah* vision in which *two* divine thrones appear; such visions are related to the so-called "two powers heresy" which we discuss below.

Both the lore of creation and of the throne can exhibit protological and eschatological features, secrets pertaining to sacred beginnings and endings, both on an individual and on a cosmic scale. Additionally, throne mysticism texts may also stress the present eternal Now of the unseen, supernal world. Spirits standing behind the forces of nature, angelic hosts of the heavens, God seated upon the divine throne, all of these may be witnessed by the mystic through the medium of the traditional symbolisms.

The ancient Palestinian Rabbinic gnosis shared the same essential themes as the Jewish Alexandrian gnosis, but the former did not necessarily derive from the latter, especially not in all respects, and the possibility of mutual influence would be natural to assume. The Hebrew and Aramaic Rabbinic literature adopted Greek loan-words pertaining to esoteric matters; in *P. Targum Genesis* 28,12 we find *iqonin* (= Greek *eikonion*, 'icon') and *Bereshit Rabbah* 68,18 contains *misterin* (= Greek *musterion*, 'mystery'). There are a number of such Greek loan-words throughout Rabbinic literature, but this phenomenon does not necessarily imply that the Rabbis "borrowed" their esoteric concepts from Hellenistic philosophy; rather it suggests that Palestinian and Diaspora Hellenistic Jewish circles were in intimate contact regarding esoteric matters. When we read the Greek *Corpus Hermeticum*, we are struck by the pervasive Jewish influence on these texts. Obviously, Hebrew and Aramaic speaking Jews of Palestine and Greek speaking Jews of Alexandria, for instance, were sharing esoteric ideas, but to argue on this basis that Palestinian Judaism's mysticism arose as the result of such Hellenistic contacts is to reduce a vital and mutual relationship between religious peers to little more than an academic preoccupation with historically determined "influences." Just as many of the earlier Orientalists were prejudiced against Islam to the point that they felt compelled to trace virtually all of the profoundly mystical components of Sufism to non-Islamic sources, such as Buddhism or Neoplatonism, for example, similarly much of scholarship still tends to trace the bulk of Jewish Kabbalism's intriguing aspects to Hellenistic sources assimilated by Diaspora Judaism. Regarding the relationship between the Jews of ancient Palestine and Alexandria there is no need to deny the genius and originality of either group. In any case, in their larger metaphysical outlines, both Palestinian and Alexandrian Jewish mysticism would have in all likelihood descended from even more ancient common Jewish sources.

The Lesser Mysteries of *ma'aseh bereshit* pertain to the secrets of emanation, whereas the Greater Mysteries of *ma'aseh merkabah* pertain to the Divine as such; but why are the mysteries of the divine essence designated by the term 'throne' (or 'chariot')? The *merkabah* throne functions as an allusion to the Divine as manifested in the form of a human who sits upon the celestial throne, as was most famously witnessed by the prophet Ezekiel (cf. *Ezekiel* 1:26-27). This implies a theomorphic nature of humanity, that is, humanity is a manifestation of God, which is the ultimate significance of the creation of humanity in the "image" of God (*Genesis* 1:26-27).

Since the *merkabah* throne involves the manifestation of God in human form, the Lesser and Greater Mysteries necessarily overlap in certain respects, and indicative of this interpenetration is the fact that the Torah's creation account in *Genesis* 1, which explicates the sefirotic Lesser Mysteries, also contains the teachings of the Greater Mysteries relating to humanity's creation in the image of God, the same theomorphic image which in *Ezekiel* 1 sits upon the divine throne pertaining to the Greater Mysteries. But that the Greater Mysteries concentrate on the *merkabah* throne alludes to the necessity of an ascent in order to *regain* the image that was established in the primordial beginning. The mysteries of the androgynous dimension of God, alluded to in *Genesis* 1:26, have to do with the nature and essence of God, and therefore also pertain to the Greater Mysteries. (God created humanity in the divine image, but because God created humanity "male and female," God must consequently be both male and female simultaneously, that is, God's nature must be androgynous).

In *De Sacr.* 62 Philo uses the terms Lesser and Greater Mysteries, and there can be little doubt that these correspond generally to the Palestininan *ma'aseh bereshit* and *ma'aseh merkabah* respectively: "In reference to which, those persons appear to me to have come to a right decision who have been initiated in the lesser mysteries before learning anything of these greater ones." According to Philo, among the most secret doctrines of Judaism is that of two immeasurable powers who accompany God, producing a supernal triadic configuration of the divine Unity. Philo illustrates this point in *De Sacr.* 59-60 with the story of Abraham's three guests:

> When God, being attended by two of the heavenly powers as guards, to wit, by authority and goodness, he himself, the one God being between them, presented an appearance of the figures to the visual soul; each of which figures was not measured in any respect; for God cannot be circumscribed, nor are his powers capable of being defined by lines, but he himself measures everything.... Now it is very good that these three measures should, as it were, be kneaded together in the soul, and mixed up together, in order that so the soul, being persuaded that the supreme being is God, who has raised his head above all his powers, and who is beheld independently of them, and who makes himself visible in them, may receive the characters of his power and beneficence, and becoming initiated into the perfect mysteries, may not be too ready to divulge the divine secrets to any one, but may treasure them up in herself, and keeping a check over her speech, may con-

ceal them in silence; for the words of the scripture are, "To make secret cakes"; because the sacred and mystic statements about the one uncreated Being, and about his powers, ought to be kept secret; since it does not belong to every one to keep the deposit of divine mysteries properly.

Among the Jewish esoteric traditions which overlap both the Greater and Lesser Mysteries is the doctrine of the hypostatic Lady Wisdom, a figure first encountered in *Proverbs* 8. The Hellenistic Philo's doctrine of the Sophia-Logos is ultimately to be traced back to such Biblical origins; the presence of Hellenistic components in Philo's thought should not be denied, but neither should they be exaggerated. That there are wide structural parallels between the Palestinian and Alexandrian Philonic mysticism suggests not that Palestine has borrowed from Alexandria, but that Alexandria has preserved (if even in transformed modalities) the same ancient Biblical mysteries cultivated and maintained faithfully in Palestine; that is, the Rabbis of Palestine and Philo have not influenced each other to the point of *creating* their respective esoteric traditions, but rather both have been mutually informed by Israel's more ancient Biblical heritage, especially by means of the supremely arcane passages of *Genesis* 1, *Ezekiel* 1, the *Song of Songs*, and *Proverbs* 8.

The fact that Philo's feminine Sophia and masculine Logos seem at times to be synonymous can be explained on two bases: 1) Sophia-Logos pertain to the androgynous dimension of God; 2) In Hebrew or Aramaic both Wisdom (*Hokhmah*) and Word (*Milta*) may be grammatically feminine. As a consequence of this second consideration, in Philo's metaphysical portrait Sophia is revealed simultaneously both as the supernal Mother and as the "daughter of God." In *De Ebrietate* 30-31, Philo teaches that Lady Wisdom is the spouse of God with whom he united in order to bring forth creation:

> At all events we shall speak with justice, if we say that the Creator of the universe is also the father of his creation; and that the mother was the knowledge of the Creator with whom

God uniting, not as a man unites, became the father of creation. And this knowledge having received the seed of God, when the day of her travail arrived, brought forth her only and well-beloved son, perceptible by the external senses, namely this world. Accordingly wisdom is represented by some one of the beings of the divine company as speaking of herself in this manner: "God created me as the first of his works, and before the beginning of time did he establish me." For it was necessary that all the things which came under the head of the creation must be younger than the mother and nurse of the whole universe.

In *De Cherub* 48-50, Philo explicitly calls God "the husband of Sophia" and clearly assigns this doctrine to the Greater Mysteries of Judaism:

(48) Now I bid you, initiated men, who are purified, as to your ears, to receive these things, as mysteries which are really sacred, in your inmost souls; and reveal them not to any one who is of the number of the uninitiated, but guard them as a sacred treasure, laying them up in your own hearts, not in a storehouse in which are gold and silver, perishable substances, but in that treasurehouse in which the most excellent of all the possessions in the world does lie, the knowledge namely of the great first Cause, and of virtue, and in the third place, of the generation of them both. And if ever you meet with any one who has been properly initiated, cling to that man affectionately and adhere to him, that if he has learnt any more recent mystery he may not conceal it from you before you have learnt to comprehend it thoroughly. (49) For I myself, having been initiated in the great mysteries by Moses, the friend of God, nevertheless, when subsequently I beheld Jeremiah the prophet, and learnt that he was not only initiated into the sacred mysteries, but was also a competent hierophant or expounder of them, did not hesitate to become his pupil. And he, like a man very much under the influence of inspiration, uttered an oracle in the character of God, speaking in this manner to most peaceful virtue: "Have you not called

me as your house, and you father, and the husband of your virginity? (*Jeremiah* 3:4), showing by this expression most manifestly that God is both a house, the incorporeal abode of incorporeal ideas, and the Father of all things, inasmuch as it is he who has created them; and the husband of wisdom, sowing for the race of mankind the seed of happiness in good and virgin soil. For it is fitting for God to converse with an unpolluted and untouched and pure nature, in truth and reality virgin, in a different manner from that in which we converse with such.

According to Philo's *Alleg Int.* II,86 Lady Wisdom was the first entity "quarried" out of the divine powers. Philo then specifies that the Word of God occupies "the second place." It is not clear if by this he is implying the synonymity of Wisdom and Word, or if he is stating that after God and his spouse Wisdom that it is the Word which occupies the next rung in the supernal realm:

> For the abrupt rock is the wisdom of God, which being both sublime and the first of things he quarried out of his own powers, and of it he gives drink to the souls that love God; and they, when they have drunk, are also filled with the most universal manna; for manna is called something which is the primary genus of every thing. But the most universal of all things is God; and in the second place the word of God. But other things have an existence only in word, but not in deed, being in temporality equivalent to that which has no existence.

In *De Fuga* 50, Sophia is called the "daughter of God":

> For you will find the house of wisdom a calm and secure haven, which will gladly receive you when you are anchored within it. But *Bethuel* in the sacred scriptures is called wisdom; and this name, being translated, means "the daughter of God;" and the legitimate daughter, always a virgin, has received a nature which shall never be touched or defiled, both

on account of her own orderly decency, and also because of the high dignity of her Father.

In the fragment of Philo's *De Prov.* quoted by Eusebius, the Word is called a "second God":

> Why, then, does he use the expression, "In the image of God I made man" (*Genesis* 1:27), as if he were speaking of that of some other God, and not of having made him in the likeness of himself? This expression is used with great beauty and wisdom. For it was impossible that anything mortal should be made in the likeness of the most high God the Father of the universe; but it could only be made in the likeness of the second God, who is the Word of the other; for it was fitting that the rational type in the soul of man should receive the impression of the Word of God, since the God below the Word is superior to all and every rational nature; and it is not lawful for any created thing to be made like the God who is above reason, and who is endowed with a most excellent and special form appropriated to himself alone

In his *Quis rerum* 205-206 Philo explains that the Word is neither created nor uncreated, but occupies an ontological status in between these two. The Word is furthermore "archangelic," which agrees with the Jewish-Christian or Ebionite Christology we will explore in a later chapter:

> (205) And the Father who created the universe has given to his archangelic and most ancient Word a pre-eminent gift, to stand on the confines of both, and separated that which had been created from the Creator. And this same Word is continually a suppliant to the immortal God on behalf of the mortal race, which is exposed to affliction and misery; and is also the ambassador, sent by the Ruler of all, to the subject race. (206) And the Word rejoices in the gift, and, exulting in it, announces it and boasts of it, saying, "And I stood in the midst, between the Lord and you" (*Numbers* 16:48); neither

being uncreate as God, nor yet created as you, but being in the midst between these two poles....

Based upon all of the above passages, it would seem that the Mother-Daughter Sophia and the archangelic Logos are the two immeasurable celestial powers to which Philo refers in his treatment of Abraham's three guests.

Certain "Gnostic" dimensions of Philo's doctrine of creation are sometimes overlooked. In *De Opificio* 73-75 Philo asserts that the maker of the imperfect components of creation could not have been God. Whatever is imperfect must be the work the divine assistants:

Some things again are of a mixed nature, like man, who is capable of opposite qualities, of wisdom and folly, of temperance and dissoluteness, of courage and cowardice, of justice and injustice, in short of good and evil, of what is honourable and what is disgraceful, of virtue and vice. (74) Now it was a very appropriate task for God the Father of all to create by himself alone, those things which were wholly good, on account of their similarity with himself. And it was not inconsistent with his dignity to create those which were indifferent since they too are devoid of evil, which is hateful to him. To create the beings of a mixed nature, was partly consistent and partly inconsistent with his dignity; consistent by reason of the more excellent idea which is mingled in them; inconsistent because of the opposite and worse one. (75) It is on this account that Moses says, at the creation of man alone that God said, "Let us make man," which expression shows an assumption of other beings to himself as assistants, in order that God, the governor of all things, might have all the blameless intentions and actions of man, when he does right attributed to him; and that his other assistants might bear the imputation of his contrary actions. For it was fitting that the Father should in the eyes of his children be free from all imputation of evil; and vice and energy in accordance with vice are evil.

In *Alleg Int.* I,41, Philo repeats this doctrine of creation by lower powers by invoking the formula that whereas all things are created "through" God, not all things are created "by" God. In this passage, Philo seems to teach that the imperfect things were created by God through the agency of the hypostatic Logos ("the reasoning power"):

> For of all created things some are created by God, and through him: some not indeed by God, but yet through him: and the rest have their existence both by him and through him. At all events Moses as he proceeds says, that God planted a paradise, and among the best things as made both by God and through God, is the mind. But the irrational part of the soul was made indeed by God but not through God, but through the reasoning power which bears rule and sovereignty in the soul....

This Philonic doctrine, *mutatis mutandis*, would seem to lead in a straight line to the demiurgical concept found in Jewish Christianity and in so-called classical Gnosticism.

It is noteworthy that the same Sirach who warns against the mysteries (3:21-23; there is no reason why he could not be referring here to the two principal divisions of Palestininan Jewish mysticism), also presents the most exalted esoteric doctrine of *Hokhmah* (chapter 24), who is "exoterically" wedded to the Torah (for Sirach identifies Lady Wisdom as appearing on earth as the Mosaic Law). *Sirach* 24 indicates that *Hokhmah* speculation continued to be productive and advanced in Palestinian Judaism, and thus there is no reason to ascribe the substance of Philo's Sophia doctrine to Hellenistic "influences," although he certainly employs Hellenistic terminology in his discussions of Sophia. Already according to the Hebrew scriptures God created the cosmos by the divine Wisdom (*Proverbs* 8), who is inseparable from the Word, for she manifests herself as the Torah (*Sirach* 24), so that the Wisdom and Word are always joined together. One must again remember that in Aramaic *Milta* is feminine. This is one reason why in Christianity the Mother and Son, or Holy Spirit and Word are inseparable. The triad of Father,

Mother, and Son found in Philo is precisely mirrored in the Jewish-Christian gnosis, which coincides in this respect with the classically Gnostic texts, since in its basic contours Gnosticism is a phenomenon emanating from Jewish mysticism. Within Judaism, the Father, Mother, Son triad plays a central role in the *Zohar*. Islam also knows of this triadic mystery of the Father, Mother, and Son, as witnessed by Jili in his *al-Insan al-Kamil*.

To return to the topic of *merkabah* mysticism, this is based essentially on *Ezekiel* 1. The four Living Ones, or Living Creatures, are actually single creatures with four faces, or *hypostases*; this may be related to the term *elohim* which is both ontically one and yet grammatically plural. The *ofanim*, the wheels, are animated, and the underlying idea here might be that the Spirit-Mother was in the wheels. Above the creatures with four heads was a throne on which a human form was seated. This Spirit which is repeatedly referred to may be the female cherub which, according to Rabbinic and Kabbalistic sources, was situated atop the Ark of the Covenant. Perhaps this feminine cherub was named Shaddai, which means 'the breasted one'. *Ezekiel* 10:10: "The four had one likeness, like a wheel inside a wheel"; this verse might shed light on what "wheel inside a wheel"[1] may essentially mean, namely, that they were many yet one. This may well be related to the triadic divine Unity alluded to by Philo. In Ezekiel's vision we seem to have: 1) The Unseen, that is, God as the divine Essence (this is why qualifying phrases such as "as it were" and "like unto" are frequently repeated); 2) the Human form seated atop the throne; 3) the feminine Mother Spirit dwelling below the throne.

---

1. With the figure of a wheel within a wheel, compare the finger making a circular motion in the Islamic salat. The thumb and middle finger form a stationary circle, while the forefinger rotates in the form of a circle counterclockwise. These may refer to the static divine essence (pertaining to *al-Rahman*) and to the active divine manifestations (pertaining to *al-Rahim*).

A central problem ancient Judaism experienced with the mysteries was the antinomian tendencies of some schools which in the name of allegory relaxed Torah and *halakhah* requirements for Jews. This is the same problem Judaism had with Pauline Christianity, in contrast with Jacobean or Jamesian Jewish Christianity. As Philo explains, the laws are like the body, and the allegorically based mysteries are like the soul, and one cannot have the body without the soul, nor can one have the soul without the body. The antinomians wanted the soul alone. With regard to Judaism in its insistence on *halakhah*, and of Islam in its insistence on *shariah*, we must must keep two facts in mind: First, Islam, like Pauline Christianity, also relaxed certain portions of the Torah and *halakhah*; for example, while the *shariah* forbids the consumption of pork, it nevertheless allows shrimp and rabbit, which are both forbidden to Jews in the Torah. Second, there are some well-known antinomian-sounding Islamic *ahadith*, such as, "All is predestined, so do as you wish." In this respect (which is admittedly not its historically dominant tendency), Islam agrees more with the antinomian aspect of Pauline Christianity than with Judaism and Jacobean Jewish Christianity.

Whereas all three Abrahamic religions developed detailed *halakhah*, canon law, and *shariah*, at the same time essentializing interpretations of all three legal systems also developed. In Judaism the essence of the Law was synthesized down to the love of God and neighbor; in Christianity, Jesus repeats this Jewish stance, which incidentally is affirmed by Aquinas who in his *Summa theologiae* criticizes the multiplication of canon laws; and in Islam the idea arose that *dikhr* of God, the contemplative remembrance of God, is the purpose of all *shariah*, indeed of all action and thought in general. Yet from a sound comparative esoteric perspective, certain aspects of a religious Law must not be simplistically bypassed, but rather, at the appropriate stage/s, surpassed.[2] If we look at the Jaco-

---

2. See Reza Shah-Kazemi, *Paths to Transcendence according to Shankara, Ibn Arabi, and Meister Eckhart* (Bloomington, Indiana: World Wisdom

bean church we see an exoteric emphasis upon the Torah and *halakhah*, but secretly we discover within this same community an esoteric gnosis as unveiled in the Nag Hammadi Jacobean texts. The same applies to Islam; outwardly we see an emphasis upon *shariah*, but secretly we see the traditions of Sunnite Sufism and Shi'ite gnosis. Yet these two dimensions, the outward and the inward, are not related as contradictories, but rather as complementarities and contrasts, as body to soul, as Philo explained.

While it is correct to say that Aristotle, Plato, and Hermeticism have each exercised tremendous influences in Jewish, Christian, and Islamic mysticism, it is often underemphasized that ancient Jewish conceptions on *unio mystica* may have influenced both Plotinus and the Syrian Numenius of Apamea; Idel even suggests that Rabbi Akiva may have influenced Numenius on the subject of the *unio mystica*.[3] Idel cites Rabbi Akiva's teaching on *unio mystica* based on an interpretation of *Deuteronomy* 4:4 which portrayed the "cleaving to God" as "literally (*mamash*) cleaving."[4] Idel does not cite any particular saying of Numenius, but we would refer to Porphyry' observation concerning Numenius' teaching on the "unification and indistinguishability of the soul with its source."[5] Such ancient Jewish traditions as reflected by Rabbi Akiva would seem to have pre-dated both the Hellenistic Philo and the contemporary Palestinian rabbis.

Rather than maintaining that Philonic thought has influenced a text such as the *Gospel of Thomas*, it would be more natural to assume that both Philo and *Thomas* reflect various common ideas that were circulating within Judaism in the

---

Books, 2006).

3. See Moshe Idel, *Kabbalah: New Perspectives* (New Haven and London: Yale University Press, 1988), 39.

4. Ibid., 38.

5. See the Greek text of Porphyrius *ap. Stob. ecl.* I,41,25 cited in Kenneth Sylvan Guthrie, *Numenius of Apamea, the Father of Neo-Platonism: Works, Biography, Message, Sources, and Influence* (London: George Bell and Sons, 1917), page 53.

first century of the Common Era. But since it is probable that not only the Hellenistic Philo but also the Palestinian Rabbi Akiva has influenced Numenius, there is really no reason why one should assume that *Thomas'* Hermetic-like components could not have originated in Palestine. During Second Temple Judaism there was an interpenetration of esoteric traditions between Hellenistic Jewish thought and Palestinian Jewish thought, so that restricting the provenance of ideas to certain geographic areas becomes essentially problematic and at some point even artificial. DeConick has astutely observed that scholars have been misinterpreting Jewish mysticism for Gnosticism; we would add that with regard to the esoteric layers of the *Thomas* gospel, scholars (like Quispel and DeConick) have been misinterpreting Jewish Palestinian Hermeticism for Jewish Alexandrian Hellenistic Hermeticism. As a consequence of the actual historical conditions of mutual exchange of esoteric ideas, there is really no fundamental reason why one could not trace back the core of *Thomas'* esoteric logia to a Palestinian or Syro-Palestinian provenance.

Stroumsa has presented evidence that Aher was a Sethian Gnostic.[6] Stroumsa mentions that the Rabbis may have been aware of certain Gnostic beliefs, especially since some were present in the area, such as the Archontics of Palestine.[7] The fact that the Babylonian Talmud reveals that Aher's heresy was the result of his vision of Metatron's supernal throne indicates the purely Palestinian Jewish nature of his gnosis. We would stress, however, that such Palestinian Gnosticism is a *Jewish* phenomenon, and precisely the type of esoteric thought from which Jewish-Christian gnosis emerged, which is attested by the essential role that Metatron traditions played at the formative stages of Jewish-Christian Christology.[8] Recall also that

---

6. Gedaliahu G. Stroumsa, "Aher: A Gnostic," in Bentley Layton (ed.), *The Rediscovery of Gnosticism*. Vol. 2: *Sethian Gnosticism* (Leiden: E. J. Brill, 1981), 808-18.

7. Ibid., 814.

8. See Gedaliahu G. Stroumsa, "Form(s) of God: Some Notes on Metatron and Christ," *Harvard Theological Review*, vol. 76, no. 3 (1983), 269–

according to Liebes' research, Jesus is mentioned along with Metatron in one of the Jewish prayers of the shofar blast.[9] This raises two startling possibilities: Since such an Ebionite influence on the Jewish liturgy is unthinkable past the first century CE, this implies that 1) the original Jerusalem church formulated its Christology with reference to Metatron, and conversely 2) that the Rabbinic doctrine of Metatron existed already in the first century CE.

To a certain extent, even esoteric Pharasaic mysticism shared various of the gnostics' beliefs, but the Rabbis had to openly distance themselves from such esoteric positions; dissimulation is not at all an uncommon praxis in the history of mysticism. Regarding Idel's suggestion of contact between Numenius and Rabbi Akiva, this leads us to observe that Numenius' belief in a higher God, whom he calls 'the Standing One',[10] and a lower creative demiurge called a 'Second God' (in agreement with Philo's usage), seems to be hinted at in Rabbi Akiva's reputedly "earlier" interpretation of two supernal thrones in the text of *Daniel* 7, that is, one throne for God, one throne for the Messiah (cf. TB. *Sanhedrin* 38a; 67b), for which Rabbi Akiva received censure from Rabbi Yose in *Hagigah* 14a: "Akiva, for how long will you treat the Divine Presence as profane!"[11] Similar ideas are associated with the further Tanna Rabbi Eleazar ben Azarya (cf. TB *Hagigah* 14a), concerning which Odeberg observes: "It is evident that the controversy related in TB. Hag. 14a, Sanh. 38a, 67b, touches a subject that was, from some cause or other, rather delicate,

---

88, and Jarl Fossum, "Jewish-Christian Christology and Jewish Mysticism," *Vigiliae Christianiae*, vol. 37 (1983), 260-87.

9. Yehudah Liebes, "The Shofar Blast Angels and Yeshu'a Sar ha-Panim," in *ha-Mistiqah ha-Yehudit ha-Qedumah* [=Mehqerey Yerushalayim be-Mahshevet Yisra'el vi: 1-2] (1987), 171-95.

10. See the Greek fragments of Numenius on the Standing One in Kenneth Sylvan Guthrie, *Numenius of Apamea, the Father of Neo-Platonism: Works, Biography, Message, Sources, and Influence*, 33.

11. Hugh Odeberg, *3 Enoch or the Hebrew Book of Enoch* (London: Cambridge University Press, 1928), 35.

i.e. closely connected with views abhorred as heretical."[12] In any event, despite Rabbi Yose's censure of Rabbi Akiva, or even precisely because of it, it seems probable that Akiva's interpretation may be somehow genetically related to Numenius' dyadic terminology.

Boyarin has correctly assessed the situation behind this ancient controvery by explaining that later Rabbinic authorities "suppressed" Akiva's belief in a hypostatic Memra by assigning to this concept the pejorative term of "the heresy of 'Two Powers in Heaven,'" a belief which at one time had been a perfectly orthodox position held by a "multitude" of Palestinian and Disapora Jews.[13] The fact that despite this suppression, the basic ideas of the two powers continued to surface in the *hekhalot* literature, which is eminently Rabbinic,[14] indicates that the suppression of the two powers concept had more to do with a public, exoteric stance involving dissimulation for the purpose of protecting the faithful from the very real dangers of esoteric truths than with an essential condemnation of the idea as such.

We give here the relevant fragments from Numenius on the Standing One and the Second God:

20. Evidently the First God is the Standing One, while on the contrary, the Second is in motion. The First God busies himself with the Intelligible, while the Second One busies himself with the Intelligible and the Perceptible.

21. Don not marvel at this my statement, for you will hear of things still far more marvelous. In contrast to the motion characteristic of the Second God, I call that characteristic of

---

12. Ibid.
13. Daniel Boyarin, "The Gospel of the Memra: Jewish Binitarianism and the Prologue of John," *Harvard Theological Review* 94 no. 3 (2001), 254. Boyarin refers to a piece he was then composing with a tentative tile "The Heresy of Rabbi Akiva: Two Powers in the House of Study."
14. Cf. P. S. Alexander, "The Historical Setting of the Hebrew Book of Enoch," *Journal of Jewish Studies*, vol. 28 no. 2 (1977), 173-74.

the First God, a standing still, or rather, an innate (motion). From this (First God) is shed abroad into the universe the organization of the world, eternity, and salvation.[15]

Numenius' title for the higher God, the Standing One, coincides with the famous (or infamous) self-designation of Simon Magus, the archetypal heretical Gnostic who called himself the Standing One. The Syro-Palestinian nature of this term is indicated not only by Simon's Samaritan origin, but also by the role the term (with a different meaning of course) played in Jesus' teachings (both in the canonical gospels and in *Thomas*) and in the early church.[16] The term "standing ones" is common in ancient Jewish sources, mainly denoting the angels; lastly, the term continued to be productive in Islamic Sufism.[17]

We should also mention that according to Origen, Numenius once presented an allegorical interpretation of a "story about Jesus." Origen does not tell us which "story" this was, but we would identify it tentatively with the following fragment preserved in Eusebius, and we would further propose that this might actually be none other than an allegorical interpretation of Jesus' parable of the sower:

> The relation between the farmer to the sower is exactly that between the First God and the Creator. For this (Creator) is himself the seed of every soul, and sows (himself) in all the things which are allotted to him. The Lawgiver plants, distributes, and transplants in each of us that which has been sown from there.[18]

---

15. Ibid., 32.
16. See David Wenham and A. D. A. Moses, "'There Are Some Standing Here....' Did They Become the 'Reputed Pillars' of the Jerusalem Church? Some Reflections on Mark 9:1, Galatians 2:9 and the Transfiguration," *Novum Testamentum* vol. 36, no. 2 (1994), 146-63.
17. See Muhammad ibn al-Hasan an-Niffari's *Book of Standings* (*Kitab al-Mawaqif*).
18. See Kenneth Sylvan Guthrie, *Numenius of Apamea, the Father of Neo-*

Could Numenius have known this parable from the *Gospel of Thomas* (logion 9) rather than from one of the canonical gospels? We would suggest that a philosopher such as Numenius might be more interested in a sapiential collection of esoteric logia such as represented by *Thomas* than in the canonical gospels which reflect the genre of biography rather than philosophy or esoteric maxims.

Concerning ancient Palestinian Jewish sources for later Gnostic-Kabbalistic concepts, something akin even to the Lurianic doctrine of *tiqqun*, the restoration of the divine sefirotic structures, may be seen underlying Rabbi Akiva's statement: "If it had not been written explicitly in the scripture, one would not be able to say it, that which Israel said to God: 'You have redeemed yourself'; as if one could think of such a thing!"[19] This tradition obviously has an overlooked relevance for the interpretation of the Jewish-Christian teaching on Jesus as the "redeemed redeemer," or "saved savior." As we noted above, Rabbi Akiva was in fact rebuked by Rabbi Yose for insisting that there were two thrones in heaven. Therefore we should probably detect a polemical tone underlying *Berakhoth* 61b's notice that Rabbi Akiva died while uttering, "The Lord is one," which was followed by the *Bath Qol*: "Happy are you, Rabbi Akiva, that your soul departed with that word *one*."

A related Jewish Rabbinic esoteric mystery is alluded to in the following three passages:

*Pirqe Aboth* 1,14: Rabbi Hillel: If 'I' (God) do not own myself, who owns me, and I am alone, what am I, and if not now, when?

*TB Sukka* 53a: They used to tell of Hillel the Elder that when he rejoiced with the joy of the festival of [the house of] water-

---

*Platonism: Works, Biography, Message, Sources, and Influence*, fragment 24, page 24, and fragment 28, page 30.

19. Idel gives a competent, but less forceful rendering of this *Mekhilta* passage in Moshe Idel, *Kabbalah: New Perspectives*, 226.

## Ancient Jewish Esoteric Traditions

drawing he said thus: 'If 'I' is here, all is here, and if 'I' is not here, who is here?'

*M. Sukka* 42: Every day (of the festival of Sukkoth) they used to go round the altar saying: 'O, Lord, save, O, Lord, deliver!' but R. Yehuda used to say: *'Ani wa-hu* (I and he) do save!'

Odeberg, from whom we cite these three passages (slightly modified), gives the following explication of these enigmatic utterances:

> The underlying meaning of R. Hillel's and R. Yehuda's words (which has been obscured by the Rabbinical tradition) seems to be based on the mystical belief that the Salvation was to be brought about through the union of the Holy One and his *Shekhinah* (his abode or presence on earth, e.g. in the Temple). Through men's sin the Holy One and his *Shekhinah* have been separated, (result: the Temple destroyed). R. Yehuda's dictum is easiest of explanation: Let the union of 'I' (= the *Shekhinah*) and 'He' (= the Father in Heaven, the Holy One) bring about the Salvation! Hillel's words again would express some inner dialectical process in the Divine mind regarding the separation of the Godhead from his earthly abode.[20]

Thus already in the Rabbinic sources we find a doctrine related to the restorative *tiqqun* involving a union between God and the feminine *Shekhinah*. These ancient conceptions reverberated later in the *Zohar*'s identification of the divine first person pronoun, 'I' with the Holy Spirit (see *Zohar* II:228a and IV:236b).

---

20. Hugo Odeberg, *The Fourth Gospel Interpreted in its Relation to Contemporaneous Religious Currents in Palestine and the Hellenistic-Oriental World*, (Uppsala/Stockholm: Almqvist & Wiksells Boktryckeri-A.-B., 1929), 331-32.

# 4. The Reality and Nature of the Esoteric Teachings of Jesus

Parallel to the question of the priority of diverse textual variants over a reputedly historical single "original text," which we explored in chapter one, stands the modern scholarly obsession with the quest of the historical Jesus, which often similarly distorts and obscures a priority of meaning over isolated historical event. For instance, what is generally regarded as the latest canonical gospel, *John*, is the most interpretative gospel, and this quality leads scholars to deny the possibility that the author of *John*'s gospel could have been what he claimed, namely, an eyewitness to Jesus. But this scholarly posture ignores the fact that a follower of any dominant spiritual master, such as Jesus surely must have been, will from the beginning understand their master from the viewpoint of a profound spiritual interpretation. Indeed, one could conceivably argue that the more insightful and interpretative a gospel is, the more likely it is that it was written, directly or indirectly (e.g., by having access to immediate material), by an eyewitness. How could one personally follow Jesus of Nazareth, or any other spiritual master or sage, and relate his teaching in a cold, detached, matter-of-fact style? Accordingly, not only would the earliest gospels show the same verbal reformulation, adaptation, and divergence we see between synoptic passages in Rabbinic literature in general, but in the case of Jesus, we would expect to see his teaching interpreted from the beginning in the light of his followers' attempts to understand and unveil perceived eternal significances latent or implicit in even the simplest of their master's statements.

Thus it may well be that the *Gospel of John* stands under the towering impact of Jesus' personal presence, even over the distance of perhaps more than seven decades. For a follower of a spiritual sage, the concern to uncover the eternal significance which lies concealed behind the master's sayings and deeds must naturally be predominant. Just as *Luke* reformulates the words of Jesus for the sake of his Gentile audience,[1] a similar process of reformulation in *John*'s gospel is evident in that Jesus speaks in this latter text with a distinctive vocabulary and in a hieratic tone essentially absent from the synoptic gospels. This is because John is primarily interested in presenting Jesus' teaching according to the categories of spiritual significance more than according to historical modalities. By reading the three letters of John in the New Testament, one readily sees that this evangelist has employed his own vocabulary in presenting Jesus' teaching in his gospel. The importance of meaning in contrast to isolated event may be illustrated by the fact that the actual event of Jesus' ascension would have gone undetected by a photographic camera, for we would be dealing here with a transcendent reality which could not be confined within spatial and temporal boundaries, though it would certainly be related in some way to the domains of *tempus* and *locus*.[2]

Whereas Jesus' unique vocabulary and hieratic tone in *John*'s gospel are virtually absent from the synoptic gospels, the *Thomas* gospel, by contrast, occupies a position intermediate between the synoptics on the one hand and *John* on the other. In the case of *John*, Jesus' hieratic tone in this gospel cannot be explained by saying that whereas the synoptics record Jesus' public exoteric words, *John* records Jesus' esoteric, private teachings. Such a claim confuses the hieratic with the esoteric, and is in any event untenable because the *Gos-*

---

1. Luke, for example speaks of cellars in houses, of bailiffs, and of mustard-seed planted in gardens, none of which makes sense in Palestine, but all of which accurately describe the evangelist's Hellenistic culture. See Joachim Jeremias, *Rediscovering the Parables* (NY: Charles Scribner's Sons, 1966), 18.

2. On the priority of meaning over history, see Frithjof Schuon, *Gnosis: Divine Wisdom*, 18-22.

*pel of John* plainly has Jesus delivering his hieratic-sounding teachings *publicly* not only to the accepting crowds, but to his most virulent opponents as well. John is therefore reformulating the words of Jesus in a hieratic tone in order to reach his intended audience more effectively. By contrast, Thomas' gospel consists of a mixture of exoteric parables and aphorisms, often paralleled in the synoptic gospels, and esoteric sayings that more or less, but sometimes not at all, resemble Jesus' words in the synoptic or Johannine gospels.

Although the *Thomas* gospel begins with the note that "these are the secret sayings of Jesus," this does not necessarily mean that all the sayings were spoken in private, for the *Thomas* gospel includes many parables which, according to the synoptic gospels, were delivered in public. Thomas means to imply that the reader must try to reach to the inner meaning of the sayings he records, and it is obvious that some sayings will require more reflection than others; for example, a number of the parables are more straightforward than other more enigmatic pronouncements, although even an outwardly simple parable may conceal deep, hidden spiritual implications requiring perhaps an equal amount of pondering than other more "clearly" esoteric sayings, if we may use such a figure of speech.

The thrust of John's gospel is public, to make plain to the world the spiritual significance of Jesus and his words which were hidden from the crowds during the time of his historical ministry. The thrust of *Thomas* is similar, in that his gospel proclaims the hieratically formulated teachings of Jesus, but it differs from *John* in that the interpretations of the sayings are not given, for each reader must seek out the meaning of the various logia, and furthermore, the *Thomas* gospel was not written to be published at large, but to be communicated to individual seekers. On the other hand, what may be esoteric in one setting may overlap with the "exoteric" domain in another. For example, the *Thomas* gospel in India would perhaps be less of a mystery than in Palestine or Syria. Now it is intriguing that quite ancient ecclesiastical traditions link Thomas with activities in India. The enigmatic sayings of the

*Thomas* gospel are in fact reminiscent of the Buddhist *koan*, an intentionally perplexing statement or question that is crafted to encourage the reader or listener to ponder paradoxes which may have no logical, rational solution. The Thomasine emphasis upon unity as such and the union and even transcendence of opposites reminds one of Hindu non-dualism, especially as enshrined in the *Upanishads*. For example, one could compare logion 108 with the Vedanta doctrine of non-dualism.

However, to invoke an influence of Hinduism upon *Thomas* is unnecessary in order to explain his esoteric themes, for we can find parallels to *Thomas* 108 within Jewish Kabbalism, for example in Abraham Abulafia's writings. However, even if the *Thomas* gospel were an inspired reformulation, or adaptation, of Jesus' teaching directed to a Hindu or Buddhist audience, Thomas could have availed himself of native Jewish mystical traditions, for these in turn already paralleled certain Hindu and Buddhist concepts. Because of the universally shared experiences of humanity, as well as the intrinsic reality of truth as such, parallels will and do inevitably exist across varying cultures and religions, though always accompanied by simultaneous divergences as well, divergences which are to be traced back to historical as well as metaphysical causations.[3]

These considerations lead us to the phenomenon of Gnosticism. If we call *Thomas* "gnostic," this does not have to imply that it is "late" or "unhistorical." Koester describes *Thomas* as "gnostic" in the sense of "esoteric."[4] He opposes to this the later more developed systems of classical Gnosticism; but we must speak of a line of continuity here, for later Gnosticism is undeniably to be categorized under the rubric of the esoteric. The Jewish apocalyptic literature, as well as the Dead Sea Scrolls, show us that esoteric thought was native to Palestine

---

3. On this paradigm, see Frithjof Schuon, *The Transcendent Unity of Religions*. Tr. by Peter Townsend (New York: Harper & Row, 1975).
4. See Helmut Koester, *Ancient Christian Gospels. Their History and Development*, 124-28.

before and during the time of Jesus. The later Jewish Kabbalism grew organically from these ancient sources. Fully developed medieval Kabbalism is not paralleled as such in the most ancient texts, but this is not necessary in order to posit that *Thomas* may contain evidence of ancient Kabbalistic elements in Jesus' teaching and in the earliest forms of Christian metaphysics. Scholars bound by historicist reductionism constantly aver that we cannot demonstrate that Jewish Kabbalism was in existence in the time of Jesus, and that therefore it is not possible to prove that gnostic elements may have been present in the historical Jesus' teaching. Apart from limiting Jesus' ideas to the domain of the historical, such claims are in part circular. That is, the argument proceeds as follows: Jewish texts paralleling ideas in *Thomas* stem only from the later medieval periods; ergo, *Thomas*' mysticism cannot be proven to derive from Jewish mysticism of the first or second century. But what if the *Thomas* gospel (and other similar Nag Hammadi texts) is precisely the ancient evidence being sought, yet ironically unrecognized for what it actually is?

DeConick has seen clearly through much of the distorting lenses of modern scholarship when she states that we have been mistaking Jewish mysticism for Gnosticism.[5] And yet in almost every instance where *Thomas* diverges from the canonical synoptic portrait of Jesus by exhibiting an esoteric attribute, DeConick assigns this to Alexandrian or Hellenistic influences, usually of a Hermetic complexion. In this she largely follows Quispel; yet his prize piece of evidence for Hermetic influence in *Thomas*, logion 67's reputed similarity to a Hermetic treatise's maxim, turns out, as we discuss at length in our textual-philological *Thomas* commentary, to be a false lead. Not only has the Hermetic maxim in question been often misrepresented as to its actual form (by means of selective, abbreviated citation), but logion 67 has a closer parallel in Palestinian Rabbinic literature (in *Nedarim* 41a).

---

5. See the discussion in April D. DeConick, *Seek to See Him. Ascent and Vision Mysticism in the Gospel of Thomas* (Leiden: E. J. Brill, 1996), 3-39.

The historical evidence for first-century Jewish mysticism is in fact not lacking. Various authorities have recognized that Paul's opponents in Corinth were of a mystical, esoteric, even "gnostic" orientation. And it appears that the Jesus traditions of Paul's opponents were of a similar esoteric orientation to those recorded in the *Gospel of Thomas*. Indeed, specific *logia* found in *Thomas* are apparently referred to and even cited by Paul (cf. *Thomas* 17 and *1 Corinthians* 2:9). The somewhat later *2 Clement* to the Corinthians also contains logia reminiscent of traditions paralleled in *Thomas* (*2 Clement* 5, 11, 12, 14 = *Thomas* logia 2, 17, 22, 19).[6] Nowhere does Paul or Clement condemn these Jesus sayings as inauthentic; only the exaggerated attitudes of certain readers and their particular interpretations of the sayings are assailed. This makes it highly unlikely that Jesus did not teach, at least upon occasion, an esoteric doctrine, for if such esoteric sayings of Jesus as were circulating in Corinth had been forgeries, the sayings would have been easily exposed and denounced as false by the Jerusalem apostles who had known Jesus, especially by those like Peter who had personal contact with the Corinthian church. Such esoteric sayings which circulated among the Corinthians admittedly could indeed have represented reformulations of Jesus' words, re-articulations crafted in order to bring out the inner significance of his pronouncements,[7] but since they

---

6. It is intriguing that the order of these parallels, with the exception of the final set, is the same in *Thomas* and *2 Clement*. But the last set of parallels is not as certain as the first three, for it has to do only with a general parallel theme, namely the pre-existence of Jesus (the saying in *Thomas* 19 was interpreted by Irenaeus as referring to the pre-existence of Jesus). Regarding a possible first-century dating for *2 Clement*, cf. Karl Paul Donfried, *The Setting of Second Clement in Early Christianity* (Leiden: E. J. Brill, 1974).

7. Peter explains in the *Deutero-Clementines* that although Jesus did not have sufficient time to teach concerning certain esoteric matters at length, nevertheless he adequately prepared his disciples to explicate such matters on their own. We have a distaste for the standard designation of this literature as the *Pseudo-Clementines*, for this implies that these documents have no historical or theological validity at all, and this is simply not the case.

were not condemned as forgeries by the apostles, nor assailed by Paul, they would have been circulating with the implicit approval of the highest authorities of the nascent churches.

Therefore when we read in the Jacobean Nag Hammadi texts that James taught classical gnostic doctrines such as a dual Sophia and a lower demiurge contrasted with a higher God, we should pause before entirely discounting the possibility that the historical James or his descendents could have taught such esoteric beliefs. Medieval Kabbalah knows both doctrines, even in orthodox texts such as the *Zohar*. The Gnostic doctrine of the two Sophias is paralleled in the Kabbalistic doctrine of the Upper and Lower *Shekhinah*. Scholem wanted to deny this parallel,[8] but when one reads the relevant texts, one cannot escape the parallels' transparently genetic relationship with each other. Scholem does admit the openly Gnostic character of the *Zohar*-based Lurianic doctrine of the origin of evil in the divine Pleroma which constitutes the manifestations of the divine nature: "The fact that such an unrecognized Gnostic theology was able to dominate the mainstream of Jewish religious thought for a period of at least two centuries must surely be considered one of the greatest paradoxes of the entire history of Judaism."[9] As with any major paradigm revision, paradoxes are bound to arise as new discoveries demand integration within the existing body of scholarly knowledge, and the increasing recognition that early Christian esoteric systems are often essentially manifestations of ancient Jewish mysticism deserves our closest attention.

At first glance there seems to be an unbridgeable gap between the simple yet profound utterances of the Rabbi Jesus as found in the synoptic gospels, especially in the Sermon on the Mount and the parables, and the esoteric depths of the

---

8. Gershom Scholem, *On the Mystical Shape of the Godhead, Basic Concepts in the Kabbalah*. Tr. from the German by Joachim Neugroschel (NY: Schocken Books, 1991), 174.

9. Gershom Scholem, *Kabbalah*, 143.

Jesus tradition in Corinth and Jerusalem in the time of Paul. But this gulf may simply be the result of an optical illusion produced by the predominance of Jesus' portrait in the synoptic gospels, which incidentally did not yet exist in Paul's time, although some of their sources certainly would have. And although later St. Irenaeus in his anti-Gnostic polemic denied that the apostles handed on a secret doctrine from Jesus, by contrast Paul contradicts this claim by clearly saying that he does indeed teach a secret doctrine to those capable of receiving it, to the "perfect" (*1 Corinthians* 2:6). He says this in the context of alluding to the esoteric Jesus traditions circulating in Corinth. Therefore he does not deny the validity and truth of the esoteric Jesus tradition as such; he only disapproves of an elitist mentality and of various false interpretations cultivated by some of the Corinthians who were in possession of Jesus' secret sayings.

It would seem, based on the above evidence, that certain Hellenists were indeed inclined to misinterpret the secret doctrines of Jesus in an elitist mode. Therefore it is not surprising to find Paul disapproving of Gentile Christians cultivating Jewish mysticism, which would have been naturally prevalent throughout the Jerusalem church (cf. *Colossians* 2:8). With the eclipse of Jewish Christianity, which was caused by Roman persecution of Jews (which included the Jewish Christians) and the rising numbers of Gentile converts to the churches, Christianity was destined to forget the Jewish esoteric component not only of the early Jerusalem church, but of Jesus himself. Its traces remained mostly among the descendents and heirs of the Jacobean church, namely, the Ebionites, whose *Deutero-Clementine* literature contains the later-attested Kabbalistic doctrine of the *sefirot*.[10]

---

10. Shlomo Pines, *Points of Similarity between the Exposition of the Doctrine of the Sefirot in the Sefer Yezira and Text of the Pseudo-Clementine Homilies. The Implications of This Resemblance.* Proceedings of the Israel Academy of Sciences and Humanities, VII 3 (1989).

Thus Weiss' opposition between the almost pastoral simplicity of Jesus' teaching with the involved metaphysics of Paul would seem to be the result of an illusion created by the predominance of the synoptic gospels.[11] Similarly mistaken is Vermes' reconstruction of the historical Jesus' teaching,[12] in which anything mystical has been excluded—as if esoteric thought had been unknown to first-century Palestinian Judaism, a notion which in any case was overturned long ago by the pioneering research of Scholem. Based on this misunderstanding, Vermes has no choice but to conclude that the *Gospel of Thomas* is "apocryphal" (intended pejoratively) and "often tainted with heretical ('Gnostic') ideas."[13] Based on Scholem's general confirmation of an ancient Jewish mysticism, there would seem to be no reason to question the synoptic paradigm according to which Jesus taught a simpler doctrine to the crowds and reserved an esoteric doctrine for his apostles in private (cf. *Mark* 4).

Of course, it is possible that Jesus' esoteric teaching was largely bestowed during the so-called resurrection appearances, and this might explain some of the differences of tone between the synoptics on the one hand and *Thomas* and *John* on the other. It is well known that the early Gnostics usually presented Jesus' esoteric teachings in the form of discourses delivered during resurrection appearances. The polarity between the exoteric synoptics and the exo-esoteric metaphysics of *John* is bridged, as we have already remarked, by *Thomas*. Whereas there seems to be little continuity between the synoptics and *John*, that is between their respective dogmatic and hieratically articulated teachings, what we find by contrast in *Thomas* is often an esoteric penetration into precisely Jesus' public, exoteric teachings as preserved in the synoptic gospels. Sometimes this is achieved by the particular sequen-

---

11. Johannes Weiss, *Paul and Jesus*. Tr. by H. J. Chaytor (London/NY: Harper & Brothers, 1909).

12. See Geza Vermes, *The Authentic Gospel of Jesus* (London: Penguin Books, 2004).

13. Ibid., xiii.

tial location of a saying in *Thomas*, which thereby assumes a more pronounced esoteric implication. For example, the saying "Let not your right hand know what your left hand does" in the synoptics has to do with the proper attitude of humility regarding almsgiving; by contrast, in *Thomas* the same saying takes on an esoteric implication by being placed after the saying: "I tell my mysteries to those who are worthy of my mysteries" (logion 62). Additionally there are several esoteric sayings in *Thomas* which possess only a remote similarity, or none at all, to various logia of the synoptic gospels. But in general, the presence throughout *Thomas* of parallels from the Sermon on the Mount and the synoptic parables creates the impression that there is a continuity between Jesus' exoteric and esoteric teachings, and that to a large extent the esoteric truths are verbally based upon the exoteric formulations. We are reminded of Meister Eckhart's simile of the necessity of breaking the exoteric dogmatic shell in order to arrive at the esoteric kernel of mystical insight.

It may very well be that the wording, concepts, and general esoteric ideas of Jesus were from the beginning known and shared by his family and disciples, so that the latter's reformulation of Jesus' esoteric words may by no means have been created out of thin air. For centuries many scholars have suspected a connection between the family of Jesus and the Jewish sect of the Essenes. In modern times, especially after the discovery of the Dead Sea Scrolls, many respected scholars have theorized that John the Baptist may have at one time belonged to the Qumran Essene community that produced the Dead Sea Scrolls.[14] Now, Jesus and some of his disciples, including John the Beloved, originally moved within the circle of John the Baptist's followers. Though not conclusive, there is much anecdotal evidence of connections between the ancient groups known as the Essenes, the Ebionites, the

---

14. For bibliographic references, see Israel Knohl, *The Messiah before Jesus. The Suffering Servant of the Dead Sea Scrolls*. Tr. by David Maisel (Berkeley / Los Angeles / London: University of California Press, 2000), 52.

Mandaeans (the Qur'anic Sabaeans who revere John the Baptist as a celestial figure), and the Samaritans. The relationships between the *Gospel of John* and the Essenic, Mandaean, and Samaritan literatures and traditions have been treated at length by various scholars. Many esoteric doctrinal aspects of these groups are known to be reflected in the Syrian Christian literature, such as the *Odes of Solomon*, and that the Syrian churches in turn share many traits with the Mandaeans and Manichaeans is also well known. The Syrian *Book of the Holy Hierotheos* by the monk Bar Sudaili, contains a variety of Gnostic and Jewish Kabbalistic elements. In folio 24a of the Coptic *Book of the Resurrection of the Savior by Bartholomew the Apostle*, the disciples call the Eucharist "the Treasury of Life," a centrally important Mandaean phrase.

The common scholarly objection that Jesus would not have been sympathetic to the Essenes because of their legalistic rigorism (which Christian theologians often over-exaggerate) as documented in the Dead Sea Scrolls is unconvincing, because Jesus' knowledge of Essenism could have been of a more general nature pertaining mostly to the public persona of Essenism. There is no reason to assume that Jesus had read the private writings of this sect, which would not have been as accessible then as they are now when anyone who wishes to may read the complete library of the Dead Sea Scrolls in a single handy volume. In general the Essenes presented the public images of pious asceticism and prayer, and Jesus could only have approved of these qualities. Christian scholars such as Daniélou argue that despite the outward resemblances between Jesus and the Essenes, on account of the simultaneous differences, there can be no essential connections between the two. But Daniélou is unable to bridge the gap thus created between Jesus and the early church in Jerusalem which according to Daniélou was undeniably permeated and drenched through and through with Essenism. The cleavage between Jesus and the Jerusalem church must be bridged and removed; this can be done by recognizing, as we discuss in a later chapter, that there is no essential difference between

James and Jesus, both of whom were Torah-observing Jewish mystics.

It is difficult to avoid the conclusion that the parallels between the esoteric components of *Thomas* and Mandaeism are far closer than with Philonic thought. Odeberg reached a similar conclusion regarding the *Gospel of John* by assembling an impressive array of textual evidence; his observations are worth citing:

> It is significant (1) that in the scanty sources of early Samaritan and Jewish Mysticism or Gnosticism we meet with a similar salvation-mysticism [as in the *Gospel of John*], (2) that we are actually able to demonstrate that there existed already in the first and second centuries CE, in the Judaism that moved within the folds of Rabbinic tradition, several circles of a salvation-mystical character, and (3) that some of these, in ideas and expressions, were more closely bound up with Mandaean mysticism than with any other known mystical religious formation outside Judaism. (This the present writer believes to have sufficiently demonstrated in his *3 Enoch*, Introduction, pp. 64-79).[15]

In the context of this chapter we must discuss the earliest sources of Jesus' teachings which have survived. Papias, a follower of "John the Elder," informs us that "each interpreted Matthew's logia as best as they could." For Papias, this refers to a reputed original Hebrew version of *Matthew* which was used and interpreted variously and rearranged in differing chronological orders by the canonical synoptic gospel authors. Scholars debate whether such a Hebrew original ever existed. Although it cannot be doubted that collections of Jesus' sayings existed in Aramaic (and we would argue even Hebrew), and that the apostle Matthew may indeed have com-

---

15. Hugo Odeberg, *The Fourth Gospel Interpreted in its Relation to Contemporaneous Religious Currents in Palestine and the Hellenistic-Oriental World*, 215-16.

piled such a collection, nevertheless what Papias is referring to is a reputed Hebrew version of canonical Greek *Matthew*. Papias' source of information is none other than John the Elder, who was the author of the *Gospel of John*. John the Elder is explaining to Papias why the teaching of Jesus sounds so different in his gospel than in the synoptic gospels, and also why the chronology in John's gospel differs so markedly from the chronology in the synoptics. John explains that Jesus' life was first written by Matthew in Hebrew, and that whoever translated this into Greek as the canonical *Matthew* changed the order of the Hebrew text, and Mark and Luke did the same, all doing the best they could. This implies that Greek *Matthew*, *Mark*, and *Luke* were not written by eyewitnesses of Jesus, but that they had at their disposal eyewitness accounts which they interpreted and set in the best chronological order they could manage. John the Elder is emphasizing the superiority of his gospel as the only account written by an eyewitness.[16]

The original Hebrew or Aramaic collection of Jesus' sayings by Matthew in all probability first consisted mainly of material such as we find in the Sermon on the Mount, and the many parallels to sayings from the Sermon on the Mount in early Christian works may testify to the popularity of this small compendium, which has also been incorporated into *Thomas*; DeConick has indeed reconstructed a central literary layer of *Thomas* that coincides with much of the Sermon on the Mount.[17] Further parallels to this *Matthew* compendium are found in works such as the *Didache*, in an early pre-Diatessaronic Jewish-Christian harmony used by Justin, and in the *Gospel of the Hebrews*.

According to Luomanen, the *Gospel of the Hebrews* was originally written in Greek, and then later translated, perhaps only partially, into Aramaic-Syriac or Hebrew, so that

---

16. Cf. Richard Bauckham, *Jesus and the Eyewitnesses*, 412-37.
17. See April D. DeConick, "The Original Gospel of Thomas," *Vigiliae Christianae*, vol. 56 (2002), 167-99.

the *Gospel of the Hebrews* and the *Gospel of the Nazarenes* are merely two versions of a single original gospel.[18] We are not convinced that the *Gospel of the Hebrews* was written originally in Greek, for it could have existed in a dual Greek-Aramaic version from the very beginning. The *Gospel of the Ebionites* is nothing other than a further recension of the *Gospel of the Hebrews*, which would have varied locally, just as did the canonical gospels. We do not agree with Lührmann when he asserts that Jerome's *Gospel of the Nazarenes* was composed in Aramaic in the $4^{th}$ century as a recension of Greek *Matthew*.[19] The *Gospel of the Hebrews* is either in its first or later stages somehow related to the canonical gospels. Quispel claims the *Gospel of the Hebrews* was written in Egypt, but its conception of the Holy Spirit as a feminine celestial entity indicates a Semitic Syro-Palestinian origin.[20]

For Quispel, the *Gospel of the Egyptians* is the earliest literary product of the Egyptian Christians, and the text bears all the marks of Jewish Christianity. But as Hornschuh has emphasized, this particular gospel's title does not absolutely necessitate that it was actually written in Egypt, and in fact the term "Egyptian" was a pejorative term among Greek speakers even in Alexandria, so that the title *of* or *according to the Egyptians* would have to have been assigned to this writing by someone outside of Egypt.[21] Originally this gospel would not

---

18. Petri Luomanen, "Eusebius' View of the 'Gospel of the Hebrews'," in Jostein Ådna (ed.), *The Formation of the Early Church* (Tübingen: Mohr Siebeck, 2005), 268.

19. Diter Lührmann, *Die apokryph gewordenen Evangelien. Studien zu neuen Texten und zu neuen Fragen* (Leiden/Boston: Brill, 2004), 247.

20. See Petri Luomanen, "'Let Him Who Seeks, Continue Seeking': The Relationship between the Jewish-Christian Gospels and the *Gospel of Thomas*," in J. Ma. Asgeirsson, A DeConick and R. Uro (eds.), *Thomasine Traditions in Antiquity: The Social and Cultural World of the Gospel of Thomas*. Nag Hammadi and Manichean Studies 59 (Leiden: E. J. Brill, 2006), 123-27.

21. M. Hornschuh, "Erwägungen zum 'Evangelium der Ägypter', insbesondere zur Bedeutung seines Titels," *Vigiliae Christianae*, vol. 18, no. 1 (March, 1964), 6-13.

have been called *of the Egyptians*, and it certainly would not have originally circulated under that name there. For Hornschuh it is likely that the title was imposed from Rome. There is an obvious relationship between the *Gospel of the Egyptians* and the *Thomas* gospel, and as DeConick has shown, the traditions shared between these two texts exists in *Thomas* in a more nascent form than in the *Egyptian* gospel.[22] In any case, the interrelationship between the traditions in the *Gospel of the Hebrews*, the *Gospel of the Egyptians*, and the *Gospel of Thomas* suggests that the *Egyptian* gospel is a Jewish-Christian text which preserves Syro-Palestinian traditions.

Another important source for Jesus' sayings is the *Didache*. Aldridge has shed intriguing light on the *Didache* and its relation to a work to which several Fathers allude, namely, the *Iudicium Petri*, the *Judgment of Peter*,[23] which bears some relation to the section in the *Didache* which scholars have long designated the *Two Ways*, following Rufinus' allusion to a document known as *Duae viae*. But we cannot agree with Aldridge's conclusion when he writes: "Clearly, Peter did not write the *Two Ways*. That work is of manifestly Jewish rather than Christian character, despite its preservation only in Christian sources."[24] As soon as one accepts the paradigm which sees Christianity and especially Jewish Christianity as an essentially Jewish phenomenon, then Aldridge's dichotomy here is revealed as fundamentally artificial. The evidence against his claim is precisely the *Two Ways*' "preservation only in Christian sources." We see no reason why the ancient *Judgment of Peter* could not be the *Two Ways*, the latter being from the first incorporated into the *Didache*, and there is no fundamental reason why the historical Peter could not have written the *Two Ways*; why would that be so extraordinary? This argumentation, incidentally, would explain the odd use of *vel*

---

22. April D. DeConick, *Seek to See Him. Ascent and Vision Mysticism in the Gospel of Thomas*, 177.
23. Robert E. Aldridge, "Peter and the 'Two Ways'," *Vigiliae Christianae*, vol. 53, no. 3 (August, 1999), 233-264.
24. Ibid., 263.

in Rufinus' phrase *Duae viae vel Iudicium secundum Petrum*, which indicates that the two works in question were distinct yet inseparable, and this can be explained if, as Aldridge obsrerves, the *Iudicium Petri* were an expansion of the *Two Ways* (*Duae viae*).[25] Peter would have composed (or dictated) the *Two Ways* in Aramaic and it would have been subsequently translated into Greek.

We suggest that the *Didache* includes the *Duae viae* which may have been composed (dictated) by the historical Peter, and that the supplemental material of the *Didache* preserves a core of first-century Syrian Ebionite traditions ultimately inherited via the Jerusalem church.[26] The manuscripts show that the text of the *Didache* underwent regular updating, so that certain features in the work are later than others (for example, 9:5's baptism "in the name of the Lord" is earlier than 7:1, 3's Trinitarian baptismal formula).[27] *Didache* chapters 9-10 do not pertain to the Eucharist as Passover, but to the regular and frequent agape feasts of the early churches. Jewish Christians held the Passover Eucharist only once a year, and only in Jerusalem. The Torah is explicit that only males who are circumcised may partake of the Passover meal. Therefore *Didache* 9's mention that only the baptized may partake of the Eucharist would refer to the *agape*, not the Passover. The call to repentance at the end of the meal (chapter 10) is appropriate given the chance that the unworthy might stray into such a religious feast.[28]

Other major sources for Jesus' sayings were recovered in the Nag Hammadi codices, and these include the *Gospel of Philip*, the *Book of Thomas the Contender*, the *Dialogue of the Savior*, and the *Apocryphon of James*. In an important essay,

---

25. Ibid., 245.
26. On the *Didache* as a document directed towards Gentiles being integrated into a Jewish-Christian community, see J. A. Draper, "Ritual Process and Ritual Symbol in 'Didache' 7-10," *Vigiliae Christianae*, vol. 54, no. 2 (2000), 121-58.
27. See ibid., 132.
28. Ibid., 134.

Stroumsa first refers to "the Gnostic Gospel of Philip," then notes that it "reflects ... some Semitic traditions"; he then clarifies that it "seem[s] that the text originated in a Jewish-Christian milieu, or among gnosticized Jewish Christians."[29] It seems as if Stroumsa is trying to acclimate his audience by creating a continuity between the two categories of Gnostic and Jewish Christianity, and that he uses the mediating category of "gnosticized Jewish Christians" in order to achieve this goal. This is a useful procedure given that many scholars seem perplexed when faced with the oddity of a Jewish or Jewish-Christian text which contains elements traditionally labeled "Gnostic." What is needed is a recognition that so-called gnosis was at home within Rabbinic Judaism, and that this phenomenon was merely inherited by Jewish Christianity.

Admittedly, not every Jewish Rabbi or Jewish Christian would have been inclined to gnosis or to mysticism, but to deduce from this that gnosis or esoteric, mystical elements were not at home within ancient Rabbinical and Jewish-Christian circles would be to argue against the general tendencies of the available evidence. In his review of Stroumsa's 1984 monograph *Another Seed*, Quispel writes: "Stroumsa has no hesitation whatsoever in presuming that Gnosticism is of Jewish origin."[30] Quispel notes that based on Stroumsa's findings, both Christianity and Gnosticism may be called Jewish heresies.[31] But the missing link that provides a fuller solution is Boyarin's observation, detailed in the previous chapter, that the belief in two powers was an ancient *orthodox* Jewish position, which the post-70 CE Rabbinic institutions suppressed through labeling the belief, and related concepts, as heresy.[32]

---

29. Stroumsa, "Form(s) of God: Some Notes on Metatron and Christ," 284.

30. Gilles Quispel, "Another Seed: Studies in Gnostic Mythology by Gedaliahu A. G. Stroumsa," *Vigiliae Christianae*, vol. 40, no. 1 (March, 1986), 97.

31. Ibid.

32. Daniel Boyarin, "The Gospel of the *Memra*: Jewish Binitarianism

Up to this point we have sufficiently examined the question of the possibility of an esoteric doctrine on Jesus' part; at this juncture we turn our attention to the question of the nature and content of that esoteric teaching. Although there are a number of texts that must be consulted in this regard, the single most important source in this respect is the *Gospel of Thomas*. Based on our reconstruction of Palestinian Jewish mysticism in Jesus' era, we would expect that Jesus' esoteric teachings would conform to the basic two branches of the *ma'aseh bereshit* and the *ma'aseh merkabah*, and when we turn to the *Thomas* gospel, this is precisely what we find represented. The *ma'aseh bereshit* and the related topics of what is above, below, the beginning, and the end, is attested terminologically in such *Thomas* logia as 18-19, which treat of both protological (pre-existence) and eschatological themes; indeed logion 18 equates the beginning and the end, which in effect implies the atemporal stasis of realized eschatology, as witnessed by logion 51, where Jesus states that the resurrection and the new earth have already come.

One of *Thomas*' central themes, the regaining of the prelapsarian state of androgynous innocence, is also simultaneously protological and eschatological. As for the theosophical secrets referred to by *Hagigah* 11a as "what is above and below," these are alluded to explicitly in logion 22, and logia 83-84s' theme of the celestial images also belong to the first branch of Palestinian mysticism, but to the *ma'aseh merkabah* as well, for the vision of one's celestial counterpart often preceded the *merkabah* ascent. As a consequence, the actual central theme of the *Thomas* gospel, namely, self-knowledge, or knowledge of one's true self as a pre-existent celestial counterpart, pertains to both main branches of first-century Palestinian mysticism. Additionally, the one who learns Jesus' teaching on the need for self-knowledge comes to realize that they are equal to him (logia 13, 108). In this respect the *Thomas* mysticism accords rather well with the *hadith* (narra-

---

and the Prologue of John," *Harvard Theological Review* 94 no. 3 (2001), 254.

tion of the Prophet of Islam) popular among Islamic Sufis: "Whoever knows oneself, knows one's Lord."

In the *Thomas* gospel it is ever the burden of Jesus to point his disciples to their own self-knowledge. Whenever the disciples show interest in knowing the nature or identity of Jesus, the master deflects this curiosity away from his own person, and urges his listeners to look within themselves. Even in logion 13 Jesus is not promoting speculation about his nature, but about *who or what he is like*. When Thomas responds that he cannot say what the rabbi is like, Jesus declares that he is not Thomas' teacher, for Thomas has become equal to Jesus; the same equality is announced in logion 108. Jesus knows that his true self is his celestial counterpart, and now Thomas has discovered his true identity in his own celestial image. In logion 24, when according to Callahan the disciples ask Jesus of what "type" he is (*tupos*, not *topos*, 'place'),[33] he does not answer their question, but rather directs the disciples' attention to their own inward selves by pointing out that "There is light in a person of light."[34] Consequently, Jesus is not presenting himself as "the Man of Light," that is, the Adam Qadmon. On the contrary, he is referring to the disciples' own inner divine sparks. That Jesus is not referring to himself is confirmed by the final part of the statement which warns against a person of light becoming darkness. In logion 43 Jesus admittedly laments that his hearers "do not know who I am from what I say to you," but what Jesus says here, as throughout the entire *Thomas* gospel, even though he speaks of himself, is designed to urge the listeners to knowledge of their own true selves, and not that of Jesus' celestial identity.

In logion 52, when the disciples speak of Jesus' importance as one who was spoken of by all the prophets, Jesus re-

---

33. See Allen Callahan, "No Rhyme or Reason": The Hidden Logia of the 'Gospel of Thomas," *The Harvard Theological Review*, vol. 90, no. 4. Jesus' Sayings in the Life of the Early Church: Papers Presented in Honor of Helmut Koester's Seventieth Birthday (October, 1997), 414.

34. Thomas Zöckler, *Jesu Lehren im Thomasevangelium* (Leiden/Boston/Köln: Brill, 1999), 244-52.

*Reality and Nature of the Esoteric Teachings of Jesus*

fuses such attention and upbraids the disciples for forsaking or disregarding God ('the Living One'; in *Thomas* Jesus is the *son* of the Living One, he never claims to be the Living One as such). In logion 79, a woman is so impressed with Jesus that she breaks out in praise of his mother; Jesus refuses such honor and gives all praise to his disciples who do the will of God. In logion 91 "they" want to know who Jesus is so that they may "believe in you." Jesus responds by saying that they do not "know the One who is in your presence," that is, God (and by implication God's feminine presence, *Shekhinah*). In logion 52, "the (Living) One who is in your presence" does not refer to Jesus, but to the God "in whom we live, move, and have our being" (*Acts* 17:28); the *Psalms* often present the traditional idea of Israel living in the presence of God, and it is against this background that we are to understand *Thomas*' term 'the Living One who is in your presence'.

In logion 91 Jesus is therefore refusing belief in him, for all belief must be directed instead toward the One God. As Jesus specifies in logion 100, "Give God the things that belong to God, and give me what is mine." Towards the end of the *Thomas* gospel, Jesus stresses the equality between him and those who drink his teaching on self-knowledge (logion 108). The gospel ends in 114 with Jesus declaring that every woman who acts with self-motivated courage will enter the kingdom of heaven. Jesus does not need to be the disciples' guide; he is there principally to point them in the right direction, that is, towards their own hearts, where they will discover their true identity in their pre-existent celestial counterparts. Therefore, even in logion 77 in which Jesus declares that he is the light, the real stress is not on this particular statement, but on what follows this, namely, the fact that everything in the end attains to the universal light. This is why logion 77 follows immediately after logion 76's story of the single pearl, which represents the value of self-knowledge; and for the same reason, logion 77 is soon followed by logion 79 in which Jesus refuses praise for himself, and applies it to the disciples instead.

The *Thomas* gospel presents an esoteric teaching of Jesus which concentrates on the individual, not the community.

Furthermore, Jesus in his esoteric approach is not interested in receiving praise from humans; he wants all praise and faith to be directed solely to God (and to the divine presence, the feminine *Shekhinah*). As in the ancient Palestinian Jewish mysticism, Jesus in his esoteric doctrine desires his listeners to seek and find their true identities in their pre-existent celestial counterparts, which pre-exist in the supernal *Shekhinah*. In short, Jesus' secret teaching is one not of faith in a divine messenger, nor of a worshipping community, but of an individual Self-realization.

## 5. Recovering the Esoteric James

In the previous chapter we noted how Christian scholars such as Daniélou, after analysing the relevant extant ancient sources, have arrived at a reconstruction of the nascent church under James, and beyond, as having been fundamentally marked by Essenic traditions. Daniélou, however, cannot accept that the historical Jesus would have had as much in common with Essenism as did the church under James, with its emphasis on Torah and Israel. Daniélou thus creates an unbridgeable gulf between a mystically inclined and open-minded Jesus and a strict and Torah-devoted James.

However, the first indication that Daniélou's conflicting portrait between Jesus and the early church is flawed is that after presenting extensive convincing similarities between Jesus and the Essenes, he then brushes aside all of this evidence and its implications with the claim that despite these similarities in diction as well as praxis, the actual inward meanings were different. It is certainly valid to insist that one must not exaggerate the parallels between Jesus and Essenism; parallels between Jesus and Pharisaism are also quite extensive. However, the central point in the present context does not revolve solely around the question of whether the early church was marked by Essenism. What most disturbs Daniélou is that the early church emphasized theological concerns differing from what he perceives as being Jesus' main emphases as portrayed in the canonical gospels (and also in the theology of the Catholic Church), and those emphases have to do with devotion to Torah and Israel, and this is so regardless of the question of Essenic influence.

The argument is often made that the extensive influx of Jewish converts to the Jerusalem church (cf. *Acts* 21:20) led to a "legalism" in thought, word, and deed, the very attitudes combated by Jesus during his earthly ministry, at least as portrayed in the canonical gospels. However, the gulf which exists in the minds of many believers and scholars between Jesus and the James who led the nascent Jerusalem church, can be bridged by recognizing that both James and Jesus were Jews who were simultaneously faithful Torah-observers and committed mystics; it is time to recognize that in Judaism there is no essential incompatibility between Torah observance and the cultivation of mysticism. In fact the canonical gospels themselves preserve evidence of a very James-like Jesus who insisted that until the entire cosmos passes away, nothing in the Torah will pass away (*Matthew* 5:17); who insisted that he came only for Israel (*Matthew* 15:24), and who called non-Jews "dogs" (*Matthew* 15:27). On the other hand, we find in the canonical *Epistle of James* several passages whose profoundly esoteric significations are generally overlooked. We will explore these passages in more depth below, but for now it will suffice to refer to *James*' attribution to God of a feminine dimension (1:18), and to *James*' Gnostic-Kabbalistic doctrine of two Sophias, that is, an Upper and a Lower Wisdom (3:15).

Several additional, but generally overlooked, sources can aid us in reconstructing an esoteric portrait of James the Just, as he was called in the early church. Before beginning our examination of the pertinent texts, we should remind the reader that the English name 'James' is in fact the Biblical name 'Jacob'; this is deeply important, for the early church would doubtless have made an association between James/Jacob the Just and the Jewish patriarch Jacob. In the *Prayer of Joseph*, quoted by Origen, we read:

> I, Jacob, who speak to you, and Israel, I am an angel of God, a ruling spirit, and Abraham and Isaac were created before every work of God; and I am Jacob, called Jacob by men, but my name is Israel, called Israel by God, a man seeing God, because I am the first-born of every creature which God caused to live.

When I was coming from Mesopotamia of Syria, Uriel, the angel of God, came forth, and said, I have come down to the earth and made my dwelling among men, and I am called Jacob by name. He was angry with me and fought with me and wrestled against me, saying that his name and the name of Him who is before every angel should be before my name. And I told him his name and how great he was among the sons of God: "Are you not Uriel my eighth, and I am Israel and archangel of the power of the Lord and a chief captain among the sons of God? Am not I Israel, the first minister in the sight of God, and I invoked my God by the inextinguishable name?"

The provenance of this text is still debated by scholars, many arguing that it is a strictly Jewish work, but the most likely scenario is that the *Prayer of Joseph* is of Jewish-Christian origin, as Resch argued.[1] However, the latter erred when he interpreted Jewish Christianity as a *Christian heresy* rather than as a phenomenon of *Jewish mysticism*. If we interpret the *Prayer of Joseph* as a Jewish-Christian work, then the curious title might be explained as an indirect allusion of sorts to James the Just's father, *Joseph*. And in turn, Joseph is an appropriate name for the father of James the Righteous, for the patriarch Joseph is called Joseph the Righteous in Kabbalah, and he bears the title Pillar of the World, *'amuda' de-'alma'*.

We would suggest that the ancient *Prayer of Jacob*, usually classified together with the so-called magical papyri, is also Jewish Christian rather than strictly Jewish. This prayer ends with the same angelic status of Jacob as found in the *Prayer of Joseph*: "Make me strong, Lord, fill my heart with goodness, Lord, as a terrestrial angel, as one who has become immortal, as one who has received this gift from you. Amen, amen!"[2] Bromiley writes that this prayer seems "to be thor-

---

1. See Alfred Resch, *Agrapha. Aussercanonische Schriftfragmente* (Leipzig: J. C. Hinrichs'sche Buchhandlung, 1906), 295-96.

2. On the *Prayer of Jacob*, see John Joseph Collins, *Between Athens and*

oughly Jewish with scarcely a trace of pagan elements."[3] The "pagan" component which most scholars see in the prayer is its reference to God as being seated upon the "serpentine gods." It seems to have gone unrecognized that this is thoroughly Jewish in both imagery and diction, for it refers to the seraphim, which are depicted in tradition as flying serpents of fire. The plural form "gods" merely presupposes the Hebrew word *elohim* in the Biblical sense of "angels." The image of God together with the cherubim and seraphim is frequent in the so-called magic papyri.[4] The image of God seated above the seraphim is ultimately based on the image of the angels surrounding the divine throne on the Ark of the Covenant.

Paul calls James (as well as Peter and John) a "pillar," and this alludes to his status as one of the "standing ones" who witnessed the Transfiguration,[5] which in Ebionite terms is the resurrection-ascension.[6] That James is a "pillar" also coincides with the already mentioned Kabbalistic title of the *Tsaddiq* as 'Pillar of the World', '*amuda' de-'alma*'. As Moshe Idel specifies, in Jewish esoteric traditions, the *Tsaddiq*, the

---

*Jerusalem: Jewish Identity in the Hellenistic Diaspora*; Hans Dieter Betz (ed.), *The Greek Magic Papyri in Translation. Including the Demotic Spells*. 2nd ed. Volume 1: *Texts* (Chicago, Illinois: University of Chicago Press, 1996), 261.

3. Geoffrey W. Bromiley, ed., *International Standard Bible Encyclopedia: K-P* (Grand Rapids, Michigan: Wm B Eerdmans, 1995).

4. See e.g., Marvin Meyer, Richard Smith, *Ancient Christian Magic: Coptic Texts of Ritual Power* (Princeton, NJ: Princeton University Press, 1999), in which we read of God sitting "upon the cherubim," with the seraphim "around him" (193); Yatael Yoel sits "over the cherubim of light" and "over the serpent ... in the abyss" (286); the God of gods "sits over the cherubim and seraphim" (315).

5. See David Wenham and A. D. A. Moses, "'There Are Some Standing Here....' Did They Become the 'Reputed Pillars' of the Jerusalem Church? Some Reflections on Mark 9:1, Galatians 2:9 and the Transfiguration," *Novum Testamentum* vol. 36, no. 2 (1994), 146-63. That the apostle James who witnessed the transfiguration was none other than James the *Tsaddiq* is confirmed by Paul; this has been providentially obscured in the canonical gospels based on exoteric concerns.

6. See chapter 8 in Samuel Zinner, *Christianity and Islam: Essays on Ontology and Archetype* (London: Matheson Trust, 2011).

Just One, who is the standing pillar, the *axis mundi*, is also associated with the angels, for Jewish tradition interprets the "standing ones" (*ha 'omedim*) as the angels.[7] Rabbi Ezra of Gerona writes of three pillars in his *Commentary on the Account of Creation*,[8] two sustaining the heavens and one sustaining the earth, and this is intriguing in the light of the triad of pillars constituted by James, Peter, and John. In the *Tiqunnei Zohar*, the *Tsaddiq* is the Son in the triad of Father, Mother, and Son.[9] According to Rabbi Todros Abulafia, heaven and earth and the pillar between them represent the *sefirot Tif'eret* (Beauty), *Malkhut* (Kingdom), and *Yesod* (Foundation) as the *Tsaddiq* who is Foundation,[10] and this reminds us of the *Gospel of Thomas* logion 12 which mentions "James the Just" and "the heavens and the earth." Other Jewish traditions specify that the pillar is present in all celestial palaces, that the saints ascend by means of the pillar, and that furthermore the pillar is the ladder of Jacob.[11] Could these themes shed light on the terminology of *Thomas* 12?: "Wherever you are, you are to go to James the Just," or more literally, "The place, wherever you go/are, you are to go up to *Jacob* the Just." Perhaps "the place" is the celestial palace where Jacob and his Ladder are situated.

Intriguingly, even the material Idel gathers on the Besht with regard to the *Tsaddiq* pillar seems to be relevant to the image of James the Just in the *Gospel of Thomas*, although surprisingly Idel never mentions this gospel's portrait of James in his study of the Pillar. In his famous celestial ascents, the Besht refers to such themes as three mysterious divine names, to a fountain (which Idel correctly suspects symbolizes the Besht's teaching),[12] and he mentions seeing the living and

---

7. See Moshe Idel, *Ascensions on High in Jewish Mysticism: Pillars, Lines, Ladders* (Budapest/NY: Central European University Press, 2005), 79.
8. Ibid., 84.
9. Ibid., 89-90.
10. Ibid., 91.
11. Ibid., 117, 178.
12. Ibid., 147; Idel notes that the Besht's disciples spoke of his teaching

the dead ascending to the Pillar in a back and forth movement. The Besht explains that if his contemporaries study, they too will be able to perform celestial ascents "and become like me."[13] Idel explains that the Besht's messianic concept was similar to Abraham Abulafia's inner messianism, which accentuates an inward renovation rather than an outward historical change brought about by the Messiah within the world order.[14]

We can at this point list the parallels between the Besht's experiences and *Thomas*: 1: The "pillar" to which the living and the dead ascend is reminiscent of James the *Tsaddiq* as cosmic pillar, up to whom the disciples go (*Thomas* 12); 2: The "three divine names" parallel the "three sayings" spoken privately to Thomas (*Thomas* 13); 3: The "fountain" is equivalent to the "bubbling spring" of Jesus (*Thomas* 13); 4: That the Besht's contemporaries may "become like me" parallels Jesus' statement in *Thomas* 13, "I am not your teacher," that is, the student is equal to the teacher, as in *Thomas* 108: "Whoever drinks from my mouth will be equal to me, and I will be equal to them, and the hidden things will be revealed to him." 5: The Besht's interior messianism parallels to a certain degree the realized eschatology of *Thomas* (e.g., logion 51). 6: The Besht's visions are paralleled by *Thomas* 15's allusion to celestial visions. The fact that logion 14 seems to have been displaced from logion 6 to its present position indicates that logia 12, 13, and 15 were originally placed sequentially together in the *Thomas* gospel, so that the parallels to the Besht's ascents would all occur in a single cluster of three logia joined sequentially.

According to the *Prayer of Joseph*, Jacob is an "angel, a ruling spirit," "the first-born of every creature," "the archangel of the power of the Lord." What conception is such an exalted status based upon? The *Gospel of Thomas* 12 reveals the

---

as a fountain of wisdom, *ma'ayan hokhmah*.
13. Ibid., 144-45.
14. Ibid., 148.

basis conclusively: "You are to go up to James the *Tsaddiq*, for whose sake the heavens and the earth came into being." This appears to be clear evidence of the antiquity of the Kabbalistic doctrine of the *Tsaddiq* as the foundation of the world, and that James is called the Just, the *Tsaddiq*, would seem to confirm this. Thus the Kabbalistic-Gnostic understanding of James as *'amuda' de-'alma'*, the cosmic pillar, dates to the earliest times of the Church, and is a Jewish-Christian, not a "Hellenistic" concept.

This celestial image of James is continued in the Nag Hammadi James documents, what we have called Jacobean texts. According to Funk, the two Nag Hammadi Jacobean apocalypses emanate from a Jewish-Christian exile community in Syria,[15] and there is no reason to contest this. However, Funk's dating of the first piece to post 150 CE because of it containing "a Valentinian liturgical formula" is open to question because even if the document is post-Valentinian, this might apply only to its final form. The original form may be earlier, especially when we take into account that much of Valentinian gnosis, like many other forms of related gnosis, is composed of Jewish mystical tradtions to a significant degree, directly or indirectly as the case may be.[16] Another scholar has suggested that the work was chiefly interested in the tragedy of 70 CE,[17] and this may give us a better clue as to its background than Funk's preoccupation with Valentinianism. Scholarship seems to have missed an important clue in the *First Apocalypse of James* (see below) which would indicate a date of circa 97 CE for the publication of this text, and this would place it in a category with similar Jewish-Christian lit-

---

15. Cf. Marvin Meyer, ed., *The Nag Hammadi Scriptures. The International Edition* (NY: HarperOne, 2007), 322; 332.

16. From these comments one may conclude that the concept of an "original" text is valid when "later" variations are not depreciated as theologically inferior solely on account of chronological considerations.

17. William R. Schoedel, "A Gnostic Interpretation of the Fall of Jerusalem: The First Apocalypse of James," *Novum Testamentum*, Vol. 33, Fasc. 2 (Apr., 1991), 153-178.

erature from around 100 CE which anticipated an apocalyptic event at that general time.[18] The teaching of the dual Sophia did not necessarily originate with Valentinus; as suggested by much of his gnosis, he appears somehow to have come into direct or indirect contact with Jewish or Jewish-Christian esoteric ideas, and indeed these may have been transmitted to him by teachers familiar with ideas paralleling those in works such as the *James* apocalypse. That the dual Sophia doctrine has early precedents is demonstrated by its attestation already in the canonical *Letter of James*, where we read of a Wisdom from above and below, and in light of our *Apocalypse*, it is not inconceivable that the ultimate origin of the doctrine came from the circle of James.

With regard to the second Jacobean *Apocalypse*, Funk dates it more generally to "a time in the second century," because of what he perceives as its knowledge of "Marcionite theology,"[19] which may again be contested on the principle that what is generally perceived as "Gnostic" theology may actually represent a modulation of earlier Jewish esoteric traditions. It is generally recognized that the church fathers were able theologians but at times bad historians; contrary to their claims, the heresies they examined often turn out to be more ancient than the heresy-hunting fathers believed or were led to believe. In any event, Valentinus and Marcion did not invent their ideas from out of thin air; their ideas must have had antecedents of varied forms.

Meyer claims the Nag Hammadi *Apocryphon of James* was written most likely in Alexandria, Egypt circa 200 CE.[20] This differs considerably from the better informed Kirchner, who concludes that it is a Syro-Palestinian document which may

---

18. Cf. the *Testament of Jacob* (from the *Three Testaments of the Patriarchs*), which was written ca. 100 CE by Elkaasite Jewish Christians; see David Flusser, *Judaism and the Origins of Christianity* (Jerusalem: Magnes Press, 1988), 238-40. Slightly later, see the Syrian *Epistle of the Apostles*.
19. Ibid., 332.
20. Ibid., 21.

be "as early as the second half of the 1st century."[21] Now that we have addressed the question of the dating of the Nag Hammadi Jacobean documents, we turn to a systematic overview of their contents.

*First Apocalypse of James* folio 26 refers to 72 heavenly vessels;[22] with this image we might compare the Jewish Kabbalistic concept of the *qellipot*.[23] In folio 27, Jesus tells James that he (James) will be the One Who Is, which is a direct rendering of the famous name of God, *Ehyeh asher Ehyeh*, 'I am that I am'. Folio 30 seems to portay James as the Paraclete, the "second teacher." In folio 31 the resurrected Jesus appears to James. These traditions may therefore be related to the resurrection appearance known from Jerome's quotation from the *Gospel of the Hebrews*, but the details here in folio 31 are more substantial and extensive than those known from the Jerome excerpt. Jesus explains in folio 31: "I am the one who was within me; at no time did I suffer in the least, and I was not distressed." Jesus explains that rather than him suffering, "a type" or "figure of the archons" was destroyed. Unfortunately the text becomes fragmentary at this point. The phrase "I am the one who was within me" is clearly paralleled in the concept of the Hidden or Esoteric Adam (*Adakas*, the inward dimension of the Kabbalistic *Adam Qadmon*) known from Mandaean texts. As Odeberg explains: "A peculiar character adheres to Adakas. This name, according to Lidzbarski, is shortened for *Adam kasia*, the hidden Adam. Adakas represents the inner man, the celestial or Divine essence in him,

---

21. Wilhelm Schneemelcher (ed.), *New Testament Apocrypha*. Vol. 1: *Gospels and Related Writings*. Revised Edition (Louisville/London: Jerome Clarke & Co., Westminster John Knox Press, 2003), 287.

22. See William R. Schoedel, "Scripture and the Seventy-Two Heavens of the First Apocalypse of James," *Novum Testamentum*, Vol. 12, Fasc. 2 (Apr., 1970), 118-129.

23. See Moshe Idel, *Kabbalah: New Perspectives*, 122-25; on the *sefirot* as vessels, see 141-44.

that part which belongs to, has emanated from, the world of light."[24]

In folio 33 and following, Jesus prepares James for his own arrest and departure, teaching him a dialogue to hold with the celestial gate keepers in a format similar to the *Gospel of Thomas* logion 50. In folio 35, Jesus begins a teaching on Achamoth (= Hebrew *Hokhmah*, 'Wisdom'), the supernal female; this first reads like an interpolation, inasmuch it interrupts the conclusion to the dialogue of questions, yet the theme is then expanded in a natural way that suggests the teaching on the female is original to the passage. Sophia is presented as the mother of Achamoth, and Jesus says that "I shall cry up to her mother," that is, to Sophia. In this paradigm, Sophia is the Upper Wisdom whose essence is entirely positive and full of light, while Achamoth is the Lower Wisdom whose nature is ambiguous.[25] However, that Sophia and Achamoth are not really two separate entities but two modes of a single metaphysical reality is demonstrated by folio 36's explanation, "Achamoth, which is translated 'Sophia.'"

We now encounter an extraordinary passage: "You are to conceal within yourself who I am and who the imperishable Sophia is, by whom you will be delivered, and whose children are all the children of the One Who Is." This teaching of Sophia is to be kept secret, and entrusted to Addai. "In the tenth year" Addai is to write down these mysteries; this seems to be a reference to ten years after the destruction of Jerusalem in 70 CE, therefore we would arrive at 80 CE. The writings will then be given to Levi, whose two future sons will inherit the teachings. The smaller of the sons will be greater,[26] and he is

---

24. Hugo Odeberg, *The Fourth Gospel Interpreted in its Relation to Contemporaneous Religious Currents in Palestine and the Hellenistic-Oriental World*, 84.

25. In this respect, Wisdom is beyond the categories of good and evil, encompassing aspects of both, like the Hindu *Maya*; cf. Frithjof Schuon, *Light on the Ancient Worlds*. Translated by Lord Northbourne; second edition (Bloomington, Indiana: World Wisdom Books, 1984), 76.

26. Compare *Hagigah*'s account of Hillel's most prominent disciples,

to begin teaching the secret doctrine after his 17th year. This would take us to ca. 97 CE, and we would propose this as the date of this text's redaction, which would certainly have been based on earlier Jerusalem and Syrian traditions. With regard to the name Levi, it is significant that this name occurs in the list of early Jerusalem bishops in Eusebius, and also in the *Epistle of James to Quadratus*, in which Levi is said to be a co-worker of James. Actually, Eusebius was mistaken in understanding Levi to be a successor bishop to James, for as van den Broek has clarified, Levi was in reality a contemporary co-worker with James, for the latter surrounded himself with a college of twelve assistants.[27]

Incidentally, it is not inconceivable that another of these twelve assistants, whose name Eusebius gives in the Greek form *Tobias* (in Hebrew *Thobiyah*, 'Yahweh's goodness'), may be none other than the Theboutis mentioned by Hegesippus as a contender against Simeon bar Clopas for the succession to James' throne after the latter's martyrdom in either 62 or 66 CE. Simeon's father Clopas was the brother of Joseph, spouse of Jesus' mother Mary. Simeon was therefore Jesus' first cousin, as was also Theboutis. Although it cannot be confirmed, we would leave open the possibility that this Theboutis might be the same individual as the priest Theboutis son of Jesus mentioned by Josephus. Hegesippus' source portrayed Jesus' cousin Theboutis as embittered at his failure to win the succession to James the *Tsaddiq*. Theboutis then began to corrupt the church with esoteric Jewish heresies, which was natural for him since he belonged to all seven of the Jewish sects. But it is quite preposterous that an individual in the first century CE could belong to multiple Jewish sects, especially to all

---

one who was smaller, the other taller.

27. See Roelof van den Broek, "Der Brief des Jakobus an Quadratus und das Problem der judenchristlichen Bischöfe von Jerusalem (Eusebius, HE IV, 5, 1-3)," in T. Baarda, A. Hilhorst, G. P. Luttikhuizen, A. S. van der Woude, eds., *Text and Testimony. Essays on New Testament and Apocryphal Literature in Honour of A. F. J. Klijn* (Kampen: Uitgeversmaatschappij J. H. Kok, 1988), 56-65.

of them simultaneously. The report therefore exhibits all the classic traces of dissimulation.

It must be remembered that the Jerusalem church at the time Hegesippus visited it to obtain this information about its history was no longer Jewish Christian, but in the control of a Hellenistic hierarchy who would no longer have understood esoteric Jewish ideas. From contact with the remnants of Jewish Christians, these Hellenistic authorities could have been aware of the former's esoteric propensities and they would not have hesitated, out of sheer ignorance, to label them as heretics. As a former Jewish scribe, James' assistant Thobiah would have been steeped in esoteric traditions (since the scribes held "the keys of gnosis"). It is not inconceivable that Thobiah, whose name means '*Yahweh*'s goodness', may have been seen as somehow close to James in nature, in view of a Biblical text which poetically portrays the two terms 'righteous' and 'good' as synonyms. *Hagigah* 12a, in the context of its discussion of the primordial light of the *Tsaddiq*, quotes *Isaiah* 3:10 in the following form: "Say to the *righteous* one that he is *good*." Rather than being an arch-heretic, Theboutis may have been a revered teacher of esoteric wisdom who later fell victim to the charge of heresy, just as all of Jewish Christianity was to be later demonized by the Great Church. There have been some Christian scholars who have wondered whether Theboutis was none other than the heretic Ebion (who in fact never existed), the supposed founder of the Ebionites. This is of course impossible, since Jesus and James were the founders of the Ebionites. Yet perhaps Theboutis-Thobiah, as an assistant to James, might have had the honor of being a consolidator of Ebionism, that is, of Jewish Christianity. All of this, naturally, must remain highly speculative, but at least the motivation prompting our speculation is the fact that Hegesippus' account concerning Theboutis is clearly characterized by traits which suggest a distortion of historical facts.

To return to our summary of the Nag Hammadi Jacobean text, in the *1st Apocalypse of James* folio 38 there is a reference to seven female disciples of Jesus, who seem to be compared to seven spirits, which include the spirits of thought, counsel, knowledge, fear, but the rest are missing because of the fragmentary text. However, this seems to be a clear allusion to *Isaiah* 11, which prophesies that seven spirits shall rest upon the Messiah. This seems to suggest that the seven female disciples are a sevenfold manifestation of the Spirit of the Messiah. This is an indication of the Semitic thought world of this Jacobean text, for the Spirit of the Messiah would be none other than the Holy Spirit, which in Judaism and consequently in Jewish Christianity was conceived of as the feminine celestial Mother. Since the Hebrew and Aramaic words for 'spirit' (*ruah, ruha*) are in general grammatically feminine, it would be quite natural to assimilate the seven women to the sevenfold Holy Spirit or seven holy spirits who rested upon the Messiah. There then follows a reference to Adonai which, however, might be an interpolation, since this subject seems to appear in the text without any apparent connection with what comes before or after it. The end of the apocalypse seems to suggest that James the Just was not arrested and executed, but another man of the same name. Whether or not this suggests a docetic understanding is not clear, but it parallels the account of Jesus' crucifixion in the the same *Apocalypse.*

With regard to the first *Apocalypse*, there are two possible "Gnostic" references to God in a negative sense; at the end of folio 31 and in folio 39, but both passages are fragmentary. Whether the recently discovered Codex Tehacos will shed further light on these passages remains to be seen. However, in the second *Apocalypse of James* there is cleaty present a doctrine of an Upper and a Lower Father, or God. It is difficult to determine if this paradigm was based on the Upper and Lower Sophia doctrine (perhaps the reverse could have been the case), but that there is a structural parallelism is readily apparent. That both doctrines are fully Jewish is demonstrated by their Kabbalistic analogues, namely the doctrine of the Upper and Lower Wisdom or *Shekhinah*, and the general Kabbalistic sefirotic system which speaks of the Divine as possessing an "other side," the side of evil; the integration of evil in God is a central metaphysical concept in the *Zohar*, Abraham Abulafia, and Isaac of Luria. In both traditions, the Gnostic and the Kabbalistic (which actually are different versions of a single overarching esoteric trajectory branching out diversely over space and time) the upper Father is utterly untouched by any negative connotations, so that the goodness of God as such is not compromised. The negative associations pertain solely to the creative demiurge; naturally, as Schuon has observed with reference to both a luciferian creative demiurge and the simultaneously good and evil Maya, "sentimental moralism finds it difficult to understand an ambiguity of that order."[28]

The juxtaposition of the two Fathers forms the centerpiece of the risen Jesus' revelation to James in this second *Apocalypse*. Just as in the first *Apocalypse* Sophia and Achamoth are actually dual aspects of a single entity, so in the second *Apocalypse* the transcendent Deity (Father) and the demiurge (God) may be simply dual aspects of the One God; this may be suggested by the opening of James' rather moving prayer as he dies by stoning in folio 62: "O my God and Father...." In general, this conception of God according to essence and according to creative activity agrees with both the Neoplatonic distinction between Being and Beyond Being, as well as the Hindu doctrine which distinguishes God without and with attributes (*Saguna-Brahman* and *Nirguna-Brahman*), which represents the Absolute and the Relative respectively. According to Ramakrishna, the seed of relativity inheres in the Absolute, and the seed of absoluteness inheres in relativity. One may also recall Meister Eckhart's distinction between the Godhead and God, as well as the distinction between the divine essence and the divine energies in Eastern Orthodox theology.

For Rabbinic Judaism as well as the early church fathers, who were generally theologians and not philosophers or metaphysicians, such philosophical distinctions could not but be misunderstood as compromising the divine Unity. This is illustrated by *1 Timothy*'s emphasis upon the divine

---

28. See Frithjof Schuon, *Light on the Ancient Worlds*, 76.

Unity in the midst of attacks on the perfectly orthodox Jewish doctrine of the sefirotic emanations ("aeons"). The Rabbinic literature similarly censures the idea of "two powers" in heaven which arose among Jewish mystics; yet as we have already observed, the doctrine of the two powers in heaven had been an ancient *orthodox* doctrine in Palestine and beyond. And it is precisely in the doctrine of the two powers in heaven that the origin of the so-called Gnostic doctrine of the negative creative demiurge is to be found, for as Idel explains, the ancient Jewish traditions referred to as "the two powers in heaven" have less to do with "dualism" as such than with an "attempt ... to transfer some anthropomorphic expressions from the supreme deity to a lower divine entity [such as Metatron], or an angel, which assumes the status of creator...."[29] James' doctrine of an Upper and Lower Father agrees in essence, therefore, with the entirely orthodox Jewish esoteric doctrine of the Greater and the Lesser Lord, that is, God and Metatron.[30]

In the second Jacobean apocalypse, the ascended Jesus also appoints James as his successor. James is presented in exalted terms, for Jesus tells him, "You are an illuminator and a deliverer.... The heavens bless you." James' understanding of Jesus (what some would call Christology) is revealed in folio 58: "He (Jesus) was the Holy Spirit and the unseen one who did not descend to earth; he was the Virgin...." This reflects the Jewish-Christian or Ebionite Christology which distinguishes between the man Jesus and the celestial pre-existent Christ, which was understood as the Holy Spirit, the celestial Virgin.

---

29. Moshe Idel, *Ascensions on High in Jewish Mysticism: Pillars, Lines, Ladders*, 85.

30. See Daniel Abrams, "The Boundaries of Divine Ontology: The Inclusion and Exclusion of Metatron in the Godhead," Harvard Theological Review, vol. 87 no. 3 (1994), 291-321; Daniel Abrams, "From Divine Shape to Angelic Being: The Career of Akatriel in Jewish Literature," *The Journal of Religion*, vol. 76, no. 1 (Jan., 1996), 43-63.

The same doctrine of the Upper and Lower Wisdom as encountered in the *First Apocalypse of James* is found in the canonical *Letter of James*:

> Who is wise and understanding among you? By his good life let him show his works in the meekness of Sophia.... [D]o not ... be false to Aletheia [Truth]. This Sophia is not such as comes down from above, but is earthly, unspiritual, devilish.... But the Sophia from above is first pure, then peaceable, gentle, open to reason, full of mercy and good fruits, without uncertainty or insincerity (3:13, 15, 17).

One is struck here by the phrase "wise and understanding," for these are the adjectival forms of the nouns of the two *sefirot* so centrally linked in Jewish mysticism, Wisdom and Understanding, in Hebrew *Hokhmah* and *Binah*. James' Upper and Lower Sophia correspond to the Kabbalah's Lower *Shekhinah*, who is the *sefirah Hokhmah*, and Upper *Shekhinah* who is the *sefirah Binah*.[31] The Upper and Lower *Shekhinah* are Mother and Daughter, precisely as are Sophia and Achamoth in the Jacobean apocalypses. *Aletheia* is an "aeon" in the classical Gnostic texts, and "aeon" corresponds in essence with the Jewish concept of the *sefirot*. In *James* 1:18 we read: "Of his own will he brought us forth by the Logos of *Aletheia* that we should be a kind of first fruits of his creatures." This us an extraordinary statement, for "brought us forth" means 'gave birth', which is a patently feminine imagery. When we understand that James would have been thinking in Aramaic as he composed or dictated this passage, we realize that *Logos* in Aramaic would be the grammatically feminine term *milta*; therefore in Aramaic the phrase *milta d-qushta* becomes the maternal womb by which God "gives birth to us." The phrase "God and the Father" in *James* 1:27 sounds a bit suggestive of a distinction between a supreme Father and a demiurgic God (cf. also *James* 3:9, "Lord and Father"). The *Letter of James* 3:1

---

31. Cf. Scholem, *Kabbalah*, 174.

refers to the "Perfect Human," which may be an allusion to the doctrine of the primordial Adam. *James* closes at 5:19 with a reference to the aeon *Aletheia*, Truth.

There exists another ancient work known as the *Ladder of Jacob*, preserved only in Slavonic, but apparently originally authored in Hebrew or Aramaic, and we would argue that scholars have incorrectly identified this work as an originally Jewish document containing supposed later Christian interpolations. The *Ladder of Jacob*, on the contrary, exhibits all the characteristics of a purely Jewish-Christian document in which the Patriarch Jacob and James (=Jacob) the Just may coincide at an implicit level. The document has certainly undergone various redactions, but it is, we would argue, essentially a primitive Jewish-Christian document. One example of redaction is the transformation of an originally *merkabah* vision into an apocalyptic vision. The man on top of the Ladder is the divine man, the *kabod* of *Ezekiel* 1:26-27, and not a demonic leader of the heavens or the earth, as is incongruently implied by the interpolation. Ultimately the celestial man at the top of the ladder is none other than Jacob (= James). We give here some representative selections from chapters 1 and 2; note that Jacob's prayer in chapter 2 bears several attributes in common with the *Prayer of Jacob* papyrus, and both the papyrus prayer and the selections below are replete with specifically *Jewish-Christian* elements:

> And lo! a ladder was set up on the earth, whose top reached unto heaven. And the top of the ladder was a face as of a man, hewn out of fire. Now it had twelve steps up to the top of the ladder, and upon each step up to the top were two human faces on the right and on the left—twenty-four faces seen to their breast, on the ladder. But the middle face was higher than them all, which I saw made of fire, to the shoulder and the arm, very terribly, more than the twenty-four faces. And as I looked, behold, the Angels of God ascending and descending thereon but the Lord was set above it, and he called me, saying: Jacob, Jacob. And I said: Here am I, Lord.

And when I heard it from above, fear and trembling fell upon me, and I rose up from my dream. And while the Voice of God was yet in mine ears, I said: How dreadful is this place! this is none other but the house of God, and this is the gate of heaven. And I set up the stone that was under my head for a pillar, and poured oil on the top of it, and I called the name of that place the house of God. And I prayed to God and said: Lord God of Adam, of thy creature, and Lord God of Abraham and Isaac my father, and of all whose ways are right before thee, thou that sittest mighty upon the Cherubim and upon the throne of the majesty, of fire and full of eyes, as I saw in my dream; that holds the Cherubim with four faces, that bears the Seraphim full of eyes, that bears the whole world under his arm, and is borne of none. Thou hast established the heaven for the glory of thy name. Thou hast spread out upon the clouds of the heaven the heaven that flieth (resteth ?) under thee, that under it thou mayest move the sun and hide it in the night lest it be held for God: thou hast ordained the way for the moon and the stars, and her thou makest to wax and wane, but for the stars, thou bast commanded them to pass over, lest these also should be supposed gods. Before the face of thy majesty the six-winged Seraphim fear, and hide their feet and their face with their wings, and with the others they fly, and sing. Highest, with twelve faces, many-named, fiery, lightning-formed, holy one! Holy, Holy, Holy, Yao Ya-ova, Yaoel, Sabakdos, Chabod, Sabaoth, Omlelech, Elaber, Ame(?) S'me Barech, eternal king, strong, mighty, very great, long-suffering, Blessed One, that fillest heaven and earth and the sea and the abyss and all aeons with thy glory. Hear my song wherewith I have praised thee, and grant me my petition for which I pray to thee, and show me the interpretation of my dream. For thou art strong and mighty and glorious, a holy God, the Lord of me and of my fathers.

The Jewish-Christian work mentioned by Epiphanius, *The Ascents of James*, very likely stems from the same circles that may have produced the original layers of the *Ladder of Jacob*. The *Ascents of James* has likely been incorporated into the *Deu-*

*tero-Clementine* literature.³² Stories of James' physical ascent up the Temple stairs could not but have led to speculations about James' *merkabah* experiences, and because *merkabah* mysticism was both Temple-inspired and Temple-centered, it may very well be that the title *Ascents of James* refers to James' visionary ascents. It may indeed be that Paul's reference to "a man" who fourteen years previously had been "caught up to the third heaven (*2 Corinthians* 12:2) is not a self-reference, but an allusion to James. Two facts speak in favor of this alternative. First, in verse 5, Pauls clearly states: "On behalf of this man I will boast, *but on my own behalf I will not boast....*" Second, the figure of fourteen years curiously coincides with the phrase "after fourteen years" in *Galatians* 2:1, referring to when Paul went to Jerusalem *to meet James*.

The Jacobean Gnostic traditions may possibly be further reconstructed from the *Book of Thomas the Contender*, if, as Schenke holds,³³ it was originally written as an epistle from "The Contender," that is, the patriarch Jacob. But whereas Schenke sees this hypothetical *Epistle of Jacob the Contender* as a pre-Christian Jewish document, we would suggest that the Jacob in question might be James the Just, for the early Jerusalem church would have viewed James the Just precisely as coinciding with the Biblical patriarch Jacob. Our suggestion may be supported by the fact that in this *Contender* document, at least in the form in which it is presently extant, we find several of the esoteric Jewish-Christian Jacobean themes known indirectly from *1 Corinthians*, the evidence of which has led scholarship to detect the use in Corinth of an esoteric collection of Jesus' sayings, which Paul considered to have been misused in an elitist fashion by the Corinthians.

---

32. We again avoid the pejorative label "Pseudo-Clementines," which is used by scholarship in general to discredit any historical and factual passages in the Clementines that might suggest they were indeed written by the descendents of the original Christians of the Jerusalem church led by James the Just.

33. See Wilhelm Schneemelcher (ed.), *New Testament Apocrypha*. Vol. 1: *Gospels and Related Writings*. Revised Edition, 237.

*The Gospel of Thomas*

We will here delineate some of the parallels between the *Contender* document and Pauline allusions, especially in the two epistles to the Corinthians. In the opening of the *Contender*, Jesus in folio 138 stresses to Thomas the need for self-knowledge, and Jesus declares that Thomas knows he is "the Knowledge of Truth" (cf. *Hebrews* 10:26; *1 Timothy* 2:4; *2 Timothy* 3:7). A form of logion 67 of the *Thomas* gospel is given which ends with the observation that those who know themselves know "the depth of all" (cf. *1 Corinthians* 2:10, "the depths of God"). Folio 138 contains repeated references to children and beginners in contrast to the "perfect," which is reminiscent of *1 Corinthians* 2:6 and 3:1. Folio 138 continues with the statement that when the light comes, the darkness will vanish, and what every person has accomplished will be manifest (cf. *1 Corinthians* 4:5). Folio 140 speaks of "teaching for the perfect" (cf. *1 Corinthians* 2:6), who are those "perfect in all wisdom" (cf. *James* 1:4-5), which is coupled with an allusion to *Psalms* 1:3. *Contender* folio 140-141 gives a variant of *Thomas* logion 2. Folio 141 speaks of the passing away of the fleshly vessel and the superiority of the invisible over the visible (cf. *2 Corinthians* 4:18, 5:1). Only a short time remains before the visible creation will pass away (cf. *1 Corinthians* 7:31). Folio 141 contains the phrase "thinking they are wise" (cf. *Romans* 1:22). According to folio 142, Jesus' sayings are ludicrous to the world (cf. *1 Corinthians* 2:14). Folio 143 refers to those who live in bondage but believe they are free (cf. *Galatians* 2:4: 4:3, 9; 5:1). Based upon a comparison of these *Contender* passages and their Pauline parallels, it would seem more natural to conclude that the traditions underlying the *Contender* have exercised an influence on Paul rather than vice versa. This is especially the more natural conclusion because the *Contender* contains no elements reflective of a Pauline theology, and merely a certain degree of diction is shared between the two.

Indeed, one might be tempted to entertain the possibility that the *Epistle of the Contender* may have been in actuality an epistle of James to the Corinthians, from which they derived many of the ideas referred to by Paul throughout *1 Corinthi-*

*ans*. Paul even uses the term "contender" or "athlete": "Every athlete exercises self-control in all things. They do it to receive a perishable wreath, but we an imperishable" (*1 Corinthians* 9:25); this follows shortly after a possible allusion to the famous vegetarianism of James the Just (cf. *1 Corinthians* 8:13). The theological picture that emerges from the *Contender* epistle is that through self-knowledge one can rule over the lower self and its disordered desires and attain to the state of *Malkhut*, reigning over the Pleroma, and thus finding rest, or union with the divine.

We will conclude our reconstruction and recovery of the esoteric James by reviewing the *Apocryphon of James*. The text opens with the note that it is a secret book of James written in Hebrew (which does not necessarily mean 'Aramaic'). The early folios give a teaching of Jesus concerning spiritual deficiency and fullness, which ends with the exhortations "Be filled with spirit," and be "lacking" in the "reason" which is "of the soul" and which indeed "is the soul." This may be understood with reference to the canonical *Epistle of James* 3:15-17, which distinguishes between the Upper Sophia and the Lower Sophia, and which describes the Lower negative Sophia with the Greek word *psuchike*, "psychical," which roughly means literally, 'soulish' in a pejorative sense. The *Apocryphon of James* is therefore alluding to the dual Sophia doctrine, designating the Upper Sophia as the Spirit (*ruha*) and the Lower Sophia as the Psyche (*nefesh*).

In folio 5, Jesus promises James that the Father "will love you" and "make you equal to me." In folio 6, Jesus intensifies this motif: "Become even better than I am. Be like the son of the Holy Spirit." This is quite reminiscent of the *Gospel of the Hebrews*' statement from Jesus concerning "My mother, the Holy Spirit." In folio 7, this theme is continued: "Be eager on your own, and if you can, pass even beyond me." Folio 9 gives us a Jewish-Christian Christology which brings the above quoted statements into further relief: "Understand what the great light is. The Father does not need me; a father is not in need of a son, for it is the son who needs the father."

According to folio 8, faith is the first quality of the word, "the second is love, the third is works, and from these issue life." Jesus gives the following parable to illustrate this point: "The word is like a grain of wheat. When a person sowed it, he had faith in it, and when it sprouted, he loved it.... Only after he worked was he saved.... This is how you can gain the kingdom of heaven for yourselves. If you do not attain it through gnosis, you will not be able to find it." This passage accords well with James' teaching on faith and works in his canonical epistle. In light of the *Apocryphon*'s emphasis on gnosis and works, there is no real parallel here to the Pauline emphasis on love and faith.

Neither is the *Apocryphon*'s emphasis on the cross representative of Pauline theology, for in the *Apocryphon* the cross is understood as salvific only when one takes it as an example to be imitated: "Be seekers of death." This is then followed by the statement already given above regarding becoming better than Jesus and by becoming like the Son of the Holy Spirit. There seems to be a nascent form of a belief in the Upper and Lower Father: Folio 11: "Or perhaps you think the Father is a lover of humans?" Folio 14: "Whoever receives life and believes in the kingdom will never depart from it, not even if the Father should wish to banish him." A transparent Jewish aspect of the *Apocryphon of James* is that in this extensive text of 16 folios, the name 'God' is spoken explicitly only 4 times (or 5 if we accept a possible textual emendation in folio 6). But in fact, only two of these instances may be original, for the other two occurrences are found in the phrase "kingdom of God," which does not conform to the overall usage in the *Apocryphon*, which instead gives the form "kingdom of heaven" 9 times. This avoidance of speaking the name of God is historically accurate for Jesus' lifetime, and for the same reason the name God is avoided throughout the *Gospel of Thomas*, occurring in only a single logion (100).

To recapitulate our findings, it may be concluded that the esoteric image of James the Just which we have reconstructed agrees in its overall essentials with what it is known of ancient Palestinian Judaism with its esoteric doctrines concerning the sefirotic-emanational mysteries of creation, the theosophy of the *merkabah* throne, the doctrine of an Upper and Lower Sophia, as well as an Upper and Lower Lord (the Lesser YHWH being Metatron). James was a faithful Torah-observant Jew as well as a gnostic initiate; between these two categories, representing the exoteric and esoteric planes respectively, there need be no inherent contradiction.

At this point we would refer to Strouma's important observation that the famous 2nd-century Gnostics developed esoteric themes which originated from within Jewish Christianity, and not from primarily Hellenistic sources.[34] When the church fathers began their attack on these Gnostics, the Jewish-Christian ideas they had integrated into their system were fated to assume the appearance of heresy, a sort of guilt by association.[35] However, one must emphasize that when the attack against Gnosticism began, the Great Church had already been estranged both from Judaism and from Jewish Christianity and its esoteric ideas. In any event, with the downfall of Gnosticism within the church came the downfall of Jewish Christianity within the confines of the Great Church; the esoteric arcana would then be replaced with the mystical theology of Augustine and those who followed in his steps.[36] And between mystical theology and esoteric metaphysics there exists a substantial qualititative distinction.

---

34. Guy G. Stroumsa, "From Esotericism to Mysticism in Early Christianity" in Hans G. Kippenberg and Guy G. Stroumsa (eds.), *Secrecy and Concealment: Studies in the History of Mediterranean and Near Eastern Religions* (Leiden: E. J. Brill, 1995), 298.
35. Ibid., 299.
36. Ibid., 300ff.

## 6. Jewish Esoteric Traditions in 2nd-Century "Gnosticism"

In previous chapters we have noted the importance of Syria as an area where Jewish-Christian traditions were transplanted from the Jerusalem mother church. Recent research has established that Jewish Christians from Palestine introduced Christianity to Egypt as well.[1] The basic model of initiates passing through various celestial palaces and gates by means of appropriate passwords, a paradigm known from Jewish, Christian, and Mandaean mystical literature, has its earliest parallels in ancient Egypt, as Quispel has noted.[2] The same applies to the concept of emanationism.[3] Christianity remained diverse in Egypt, with Gnostics, Catholics, and Jewish Christians living together in peace until the reign of Bishop Demetrius, who exerted pressure for ecclestical uniformity between 189-232 CE.[4] The pre-Demetrius prevalence of respectful diversity among Jewish Christians and Catholics in part explains how Valentinus and others, many of whom were labeled heretical only after their deaths, were able to absorb a number of Jewish esoteric ideas, transmitted mainly through Jewish Christians of Alexandria, who taught that the Messiah is the divine Name (*Iao*).[5]

Although Valentinus was branded as a heretic at some point before his death, he must not be judged solely by later

---

1. For references, see Roelof van den Broek and Cis van Heertum (eds.), *From Poimandres to Jacob Böhme: Gnosis, Hermetism and the Christian Tradition* (Amsterdam: Bibliotheca Philosophica Hermetica, 2000), 322-23.
2. Ibid., 216-17.
3. Ibid., 244.
4. Ibid., 249.
5. Ibid.

standards. There were many theological ideas which were considered perfectly orthodox in their own day, but which came to be perceived as heretical by later standards, and this would apply to almost all of the ante-Nicene church fathers on the subjects of Christology and the nature of the Holy Spirit. None of the early Fathers, for instance, conform to the later precisions of orthodoxy as established at the Nicene council and beyond. Valentinus was in fact highly respected in Rome and almost became a bishop, and there is nothing which should force one a priori to doubt the honesty or possibility of his claim to have been a student of Theudas, a disciple of Paul. Valentinus' birth is usually placed at about 100 CE, but there is really no reason why it could not be pushed back earlier into the late first century, since his career seems to have concluded about 165 CE, and Polycarp, disciple of John the Elder, had died at a quite advanced age perhaps only about a decade previously. Moreover, the name Theudas is curiously reminiscent of Syrian Jewish-Christian traditions, and this might explain the many Jewish (actually, Jewish-Christian) Kabbalistic elements in the Valentinian system.

Traditional scholarship over-emphasizes the Hellenistic aspects of Valentinus' thought; we therefore now turn to an examination of the possible Jewish components found in his metaphysics. First, in the Valentinian system, *Logos* and *Zoe* (Word and Life) emit ten emanations, whereas the celestial Son of Man and *Ecclesia* (Church) emit twelve emanations. These numbers correspond precisely to the ten *sefirot* and the twelve tribes of Israel, which the Kabbalists add together in order to arrive at the number of the 22 letters of the Hebrew alphabet. In the later Valentinian school of Ptolemy we encounter a doctrine of two Sophias, precisely paralleled in the Kabbalah's Upper and Lower *Shekhinah*, the Upper being wholly righteous, the lower being morally ambiguous. The Jewish-Christian Ebionite distinction between the celestial Savior and the earthly Jesus also seems to be reflected in Valentinian thought. The Valentinian system's references to concepts such as the Father's measure, size, or extent are all reminiscent of the ancient *shi'ur qomah* traditions. For Valentinus, Sophia is the last of the aeonic emanations, precisely as *Shekhinah* is the final *sefirah* in Kabbalah.

According to Ptolemy, all the aeons were "Words," which is exactly paralleled in the Kabbalah's teaching that the ten *sefirot* correspond to God's ten words of creative command in the *Genesis* creation account (nine explicit commands, one implicit). The Valentinian use of gematria in the Greek name *Iesous* is also indicative of typical Kabbalistic procedures. Although gematria was by no means confined to Jewish circles, in light of the other extensive specifically Jewish parallels in Valentinus' thought, it is more natural to associate his practice of gematria with Judaism than with Hellenism. As the *Zohar* teaches that *Hokhmah* made the emanation *Elohim* (*Binah*, "Understanding"), so the Valentinian Ptolemy teaches that Sophia is exalted above the demiurge. Naturally qualifications must be made with regard to various details, but the overall general paradigms seem sufficient to indicate a strong Jewish, or better, Jewish-Christian component within Valentinianism, and we would suggest that the best candidate for transmission of these ideas to Valentinus would be Theudas.

Since it is quite likely that the Nag Hammadi *Gospel of Truth* was written by Valentinus, we should comment on it somewhat. Its Jewish-Christian character is especially apparent in its divine Name Christology. We note that the word 'God' occurs in this document only once, and this is strongly suggestive of the traditional Jewish avoidance of the name of God. There is a heavily Syrian Jewish-Christian complexion to this text; if this tendency had been mediated to Valentinus via Theudas, this then might imply that the latter may have been of Syrian origin. According to the *Gospel of Truth* 17, the obvious flaws in creation do not in actuality exist, for the mutable creation itself, in contrast to the immutable Father, can be said to be non-existent; therefore the flaws in creation are no dishonor to God. In such an approach, which possesses curious parallels in both Neoplatonism and Hindu *Vedanta*, the purity, goodness, and Unity of the Divine as such is safeguarded. In folio 18 we find a point curiously paralleled in

Philo: "Oblivion did not emerge into existence *from* the Father, even if it did come to *because* of him."

The image of the hypostatic Book in folios 19-23 is deeply Jewish Christian in tone.[6] In folio 23 we encounter a list of emanational attributes associated with the supernal pleroma, many of which curiously coincide, to varying degrees, with the Kabbalistic *sefirot*, such as Wisdom, Knowledge, Forbearance, Crown, Glory, Love. Folio 24 reflects the Syrian Jewish-Christian idea that the feminine bosom of the Father is the Holy Spirit; Jewish-Christian as well is the triad of Father, Mother (= Holy Spirit), and Son: "... into the Father, into the Mother, Jesus of the unending sweetness." Folio 27's language may indicate knowledge of the traditions concerning pre-existence found in the *Gospel of Thomas* logion 19, and this is yet another Syrian feature of the *Gospel of Truth*: "... those come into existence ... before they come into existence." Folios 38-39 present the Jewish-Christian doctrine of the Son as the Name of the Father. This passage implies that the Father's essence is unnamable, for his essence cannot be named; therefore, "the Son is his name."

When we work our way back in time from Valentinus, we encounter Basilides, whose teaching may have been known to the former. Basilides was already teaching in Alexandria before the 130s CE, so that there is really no reason not to place his birth sometime in the first century, which makes possible his claim to have been taught by one Glaucias who had functioned as an interpreter for St. Peter. Scholarship is inclined to emphasize the Stoic complexion of Basilides' thought. We wish here to point out some possible Jewish-Christian elements within his system, which would most logically be traced back to Glaucias. As with Valentinus and Theudas, and Basilides and Glaucias, who did not receive their esoteric doctrines directly from Jewish circles, but through

---

6. On the Jewish-Christian components of the hypostatic Book imagery in the *Gospel of Truth*, see Jean Daniélou, *The Theology of Jewish Christianity* (Chicago, Illinois: Henry Regnery Company, 1964), 202-24.

Jewish-Christian channels, so the "Gnostic" Markos would have received his strikingly Jewish esoteric ideas through the medium of Jewish-Christian teachers.[7]

Basilides' denial of Jesus' death (paralleled incidentally in the the Qur'an and throughout Islamic traditon) is typically Ebionite, and his claim that Jesus laughed at the crucifixion reflects the Jewish-Christian tradition of Isaac's laughter at the *aqedah*.[8] The Basilidean portrayal of Jesus' polymorphic abilities is also Jewish Christian[9] (as well as being parralelled in Islamic sources). Basilides' knowledge of the Hebrew text of *Isaiah* 28:10 can be best explained by knowledge mediated via the bi-lingual interpreter Glaucias. From this Biblical text Basilides (or Glaucias) derived the Savior's mystic name *Kaulakaua*, "line upon line" (*kau la-lau* in Hebrew). This may allude to the concept of measurement, and thus could be related to the *shi'ur qomah* concepts. Basilides' followers claimed that they were "no longer Jews," yet neither were they "Christians," and this would be a rather precise description of Jewish Christians caught between nascent Rabbinic Judaism and the then emerging Catholic Christianity. Typically Jewish are the Basildeans' use of angelic names employed during the ascent through the various heavens. Ebionite is also Basilides teaching that Jesus was fully human, and that only God is pure, as established and necessitated by *Job* 14:4 (and probably also Jesus' own statement: "Why call me good? There is none good but my Father who is in heaven").

Scholem suggests the possibility that medieval groups such as the Cathars may have had links with ancient Manichaeism, and that ancient Manichaean, Mandaean, and Jew-

---

7. On Markos' indirect reception of Jewish ideas, cf. Stroumsa, "Form(s) of God," 281.

8. Cf. G. G. Stroumsa, "Christ's Laughter: Docetic Origins Reconsidered," *Journal of Early Christian Studies*, vol. 12, no. 3 (2004), 267-88.

9. Cf. G. G. Stroumsa, "Polymorphie divine et transformations d'un mythologème: l' 'Apocryphon de Jean' et ses sources," *Vigiliae Christianae* vol. 35 (1981), 412-34.

ish gnosis may have reached medieval Europe.[10] Scholem left open this possibility on account of the lack of specific evidence. We have gained a better understanding of these interrelationships, however, in the wake of Idel's groundbreaking work, which strengthens the case for a knowledge of Manichaean traditions among medieval Jewish Kabbalists, which was first suggested by Scholem. This link is important in light of the specifically personal Jewish-Christian background of Mani, which became known with the discovery of the Cologne Mani codex. Idel specifies that the relevant evidence applies to Castile, the home of the Aramaic *Zohar*, and not to Provence or Catalunia.[11] Idel notes that Aramaic was not the typical "tool of expression of European Jewry."[12] In the medieval period Christian literature in Syriac-Aramaic was in circulation among some Jews. As Idel notes, a Syriac *Book of Wisdom* is cited by Nahmanides; Idel fails to specify that this was none other than the Syriac Peshitta translation of the Greek Septugint's *Book of Wisdom*.[13] Nahmanides, in fact, quotes not only the Christian Syriac Peshitta translation of the *Book of Wisdom*, but also *Judith* as well as *Bel and the Dragon*. At an earlier period, it is uncontested that the Peshitta version of *Proverbs* had been known to the author/s of the *Targum* of the Hagiographa.[14]

Some medieval Jews therefore obviously had access to Christian documents. As Idel notes, the Manichaean image of the column of light is uncannily paralleled throughout the *Zohar*.[15] And the later Lurianic theosophy is also uncannily

---

10. Gershom Scholem, *Origins of the Kabbalah* (Philadelphia, 1987), 16, 192-93. For further references, see Lawrence Zalcman, "Christians, Noserim, and Nebuchadnezzar's Daughter," *The Jewish Quarterly Review, New Series*, vol. 81, no. 3/4 (Jan. - Apr., 1991), 424-25.
11. Moshe Idel, *Ascensions on High*, 126.
12. Ibid., 125.
13. See Alexander Marx, "An Aramaic Fragment of the Wisdom of Solomon," *Journal of Biblical Literature*, vol. 40 (1920), 57-69.
14. Cf. John Day, *Wisdom in Ancient Israel* (Cambridge: Cambridge University Press, 1995), 183.
15. Moshe Idel, *Ascensions on High*, 123-24.

proximate to the Manichaean idea concerning the redemption of light-sparks and the pentadic Perfect Man; as Idel writes, the "similarity ... is astonishing."[16] Interestingly, *Zohar* I:99b mentions access to "books of wisdom" from the east which contained astrological rites and other similar exotic elements; could this be an allusion to Manichaean manuscripts? Idel mentions further Manichaean elements in orthodox medieval Kabbalism, namely, in the *Zohar* and in Lurianic Kabbalah.

A more complete picture emerges in the studies of Liebes who has highlighted evidence of Ebionite-like compositions as having been in the possession of medieval Kabbalists.[17] Idel similarly refers to the possibility of "Jewish-Christian" texts circulating among Jewish Kabbalists.[18] Liebes notes, as has Green, that the *Zohar* has integrated various Christian Trinitarian concepts, which were predictably exploited by medieval and Renaissance Catholic thinkers.[19] However, neither of these authors points out that the trinity in question which is reflected in the *Zohar* is by no means the "Father, Son, and Holy Spirit" of the Great Church, but is instead the "Father, Mother, and Son" of ancient *Jewish Christianity*. Unmentioned by Idel, Liebes, and Green are also the parallels between Jewish-Christian traditions relating to the integration of evil into the very divine structure which are attested in the thought of Abraham Abulafia,[20] the *Zohar*, and Luria. Such a concept can be traced back to Jewish-Christian gnosis in general and to the Ebionite doctrine of Christ and Satan as the two hands of God known from the *Deutero-Clementine* literature. This same Ebionite *Clementine* literature contains

---

16. Ibid., 129-30.
17. See Yehudah Liebes, *Studies in the Zohar*. Translated from the Hebrew by Arnold Schwartz, Stephanie Nakache, Penina Peli (Albany, NY: State University of New York Press, 1993), 241.
18. Moshe Idel, *Messianic Mystics*, 87.
19. Yehudah Liebes, *Studies in the Zohar*.
20. See throughout Robert Sagerman, *Ambivalence toward Christianity in the Kabbalah of Abraham Abulafia*. Ph.D. dissertation, Department of Hebrew and Judaic Studies New York University, May 2008.

precisely the same sefirotic conception as does the *Sefer Yetsirah*, down to several minutiae, as Pines has demonstrated.[21]

Green suggests that the *Zohar*'s Lady *Shekhinah* is patterned after the medieval Christian theology of the Virgin Mary.[22] But again, it is not so much the Catholic understanding of the Virgin Mary as the Mary of Jewish-Christian gnosis that parallels the Kabbalistic *Shekhinah*, for the corporate dimension shared by the latter two is noticeably largely absent from the Great Church's Mariology. For example, the two Jewish-Christian documents *Revelation* (chapter 12) and the *Shepherd of Hermas* (*Visions* 1-3) both portray the Virgin as a corporate entity which merges images of Sarah, Lady Zion, Ecclesia, Mary, and the Holy Spirit.[23] The corporate aspect of the Kabbalistic *Shekhinah* lies in the fact that she is also called *Kneset Israel*, the sense being that she is the celestial counterpart of the earthly *Kneset Israel*. This is in turn equivalent to the Valentinian celestial Lady Ecclesia as counterpart to the earthly church.

Astoundingly, Liebes has also documented traces left by first-century Jewish Christians in the traditional Jewish liturgy which persists to the present day, including an actual positive reference to Jesus in one of the *shofar* prayers.[24] The picture that is obtained from all this recently gathered evidence is one in which Jewish-Christian esoteric traditions, individuals, and writings continued to circulate among non-Christian Jews from the ancient period all the way into the medieval Kabbalistic era. This explains many of the similarities shared between the medieval Jewish Kabbalah on the one hand,

---

21. Shlomo Pines, *Points of Similarity between the Exposition of the Doctrine of the Sefirot in the Sefer Yezira and Text of the Pseudo-Clementine Homilies. The Implications of This Resemblance.*

22. Arthur Green, *A Guide to the Zohar* (Stanford, California: Stanford University Press, 2004), 95.

23. On this symbology in the *Shepherd of Hermas*, see J. Massingberd Ford, "'Thou Art Abraham' and Upon This Rock," 298.

24. Yehudah Liebes, "The Shofar Blast Angels and Yeshu'a Sar ha-Panim."

and ancient Jewish-Christian esoteric traditions on the other. They are all of a piece and mutually illuminate each other; even the qualifications and modulations the traditions underwent often reveal the underlying interconnections between the various streams of traditions. Judaism and Christianity, especially Jewish Christianity, may be viewed as branches of a single Abrahamic tree. It is to the *third* branch of this Abrahamic tree that we next direct our attention, namely, Islam.

# 7. From Jewish Christianity to Islam

In a previous chapter we summarized Vermes' paradigm which advocates a scholarly integration of ancient Jewish and Christian literary sources in order to enable and facilitate a mutually enlightening understanding of texts emanating from both of these faith traditions. Unfortunately Vermes stops two-thirds of the way. In order to arrive at a more complete understanding of what may be called Abrahamism, Islam may and must be integrated as the third branch of the Abrahamic faith/s within the inclusive structure proposed by Vermes. The use of Islamic sources in order to interpret Christian and Jewish texts (and vice versa) is only beginning, and many promising signs are already surfacing. Besides a growing body of essays and literature on commonalities shared between Islam and Judaism, even regarding mutual influences between the two at the levels of *kalam* and of mysticism, scholars of Judaism and Christianity are beginning to show an increased interest in Islamic studies, especially in the Jesus *ahadith* collections in Sunnite and Shi'ite sources.[1]

---

1. See Marvin Meyer, "'Be Passersby': *Gospel of Thomas* 12, Jesus Traditions, and Islamic Literature," in J. Ma. Asgeirsson, A DeConick and R. Uro (eds.), *Thomasine Traditions in Antiquity: The Social and Cultural World of the Gospel of Thomas.* Nag Hammadi and Manichean Studies 59 (Leiden: E. J. Brill, 2006), 256-71; April D. DeConick, *The Original Gospel of Thomas in Translation*, throughout; Gilles Quispel, "The Muslim Jesus," in *Gnostica, Judaica, Catholica* Collected Essays of Gilles Quispel (Leiden: Brill, 2008), 627-64; Shlomo Pines, *The Jewish Christians of the Early Centuries of Christianity according to a New Source. The Israel Academy of Sciences and Humanities Proceedings*, vol. II. No. 13 (Jerusalem, 1966); G. G. Stroumsa, "Christ's Laughter: Docetic Origins Reconsidered," *Journal of Early Christian Studies*, vol. 12, no. 3 (2004), 288.

The extensive parallels between nascent Islam and early Jewish branches of Christianity associated with James the Just and the early Jerusalem church are also receiving increasing scholarly attention. Over the last century or so it has become a standard practice for New Testament scholars to present Jewish literary evidence when trying to understand obscure New Testament passages. The same assimilation of Islamic evidence for understanding Christian texts should be pursued, for the bridges that exist between the three Abrahamic faiths, on account of their common origins, may illuminate each other in surprising ways. Despite the fact that the three Abrahamic faiths are three separate and distinctive branches, these admittedly quite diverse branches nevertheless emanate from what may be described as a single Abrahamic tree.

The faith and texts of each of the three Abrahamic branches can mutually illuminate the faith and texts of the others. Because of the many organic connections subsisting between these three Abrahamic religions, similar thought patterns and faith practices can be discerned throughout the course of their emergent historical growth/s. The recognition of such an organic relationship may empower scholarship to transcend some of the narrow confines of historicist methodology, since invoking a process of historical "cause and effect" is not always necessary in order to explain similarities shared between various faiths connected organically in a living way. Certain trajectories will flower at their own natural times on each branch, manifesting simultaneous similarities as well as dissimilarities based on innate as well as extrinsic conditions.

In this chapter we focus on Jewish Christianity's nature as a bridge to nascent Islam, as well as pointing out further parallels between Jewish Christianity and Jewish mysticism. And it is in Jewish-Christian mysticism, with its "Gnostic" depths, where we detect profoundly overlapping common characteristics with not only Jewish mysticism (e.g., the *Zohar*, the system of *sefirot*-emanations, *merkabah* mysticism, *shi'ur qomah*, etc.), but also with Islamic mysticism among all its main branches, including Sunnite Sufism, Shi'ite gnosis, and Ismailism.

In approximately the fourth to sixth centuries, a large contingency of Jewish Christians eventually entered the Nestorian church, and in this way indirectly established a presence in the Arabian peninsula. Hawting explains that the rock inscriptions in the Negev desert researched by Nevo represent "a form of Judaeo-Christianity not identifiable with Judaism, Christianity or Islam."[2] Hawting does not recognize the significance of this "Judaeo-Christianity" as possible evidence for a specifically Ebionite presence in pre-Islamic Arabia. Nevo specifies that of the Negev inscriptions, those from Sde Boqer from the mid-first century AH form a separate group which he labels "Judaeo-Christian texts," one of which reads, in a prayer for forgiveness: *amin rabb-l-alamin rabb Musa wa-'Isa*, that is "Amen, Lord of the worlds, the Lord of Moses and Jesus."[3] Although Nevo saw the Sde Boqer texts as "scarcely identifiable" with any "defined sect," on the basis of the textual contents we would identify this "Judaeo-Christianity" as precisely the form of Jewish Christianity known as Ebionism. Addmittedly, early Jewish Christianity was pluriform, and this diversity must not be overlooked. However, neither must one diminish the significance of the fact that the Ebionites were the original constituency of the Jerusalem church under James, from whom all later main branches of Jewish Christianity descended. In order to emphasize this connective and unifying fact, we have chosen to use the terms Ebionite and Jewish Christian as synonyms, without by any means implying that we overlook the diversity which existed within Jewish Christianity.

In an effort to explain the predominantly Jewish character of Ethiopian Christianity, Ullendorf has reconstructed the various phases of Jewish settlement in ancient South Arabia. Ullendorf reminds us that in Biblical times the Hebrew King-

---

2. G. R. Hawting, *The Idea of Idolatry and the Emergence of Islam. From Polemic to History* (Cambridge: Cambridge University Press, 1999), 40.

3. Yehuda D. Nevo, "Towards a Prehistory of Islam," *Jerusalem Studies in Arabic and Islam*, vol. 17 (1994), 108-41.

dom encompassed the Sinai peninsula, and the Old Testament refers to Jewish presence and activity both in Arabia and South Arabia. The majority of Jews in ancient Arabia arrived there after the harrowing events of 70 CE, and later by the early second century CE large Jewish settlements existed in Arabia. In the following centuries before the rise of Islam it appears that entire Arabian tribes had converted to Judaism.[4] The Jewish influence led to various replacements of pagan concepts, such as the rise of the name *Rahmanan* for God (witnessed to in numerous inscriptions), which was "clearly derived from Judaic conceptions."[5] Shortly before the beginning of the seventh century, under Persian occupation, the formerly growing Christian power in Arabia was decisively undermined; yet both Jewish and Christian groups opposed to Rome were more than tolerated by the Persian authorities, yet all three collective influences, Persian, Jewish, and Christian, "soon disintegrated" with the rise of Islam.[6] All in all, the evidence gathered by Ullendorf proves that Judaism "was strongly entrenched" in Arabia before the emergence of Islam, and Judaism's presence in Arabia was "considerable" and even assumed "astonishing proportions."[7]

The Judaism of pre-Islamic Arabia, although generally of an archaic pre- and non-Talmudic nature, was rich in Haggadic lore, and the pervasive heritage of the Arabian Jewish Haggadah and Midrash is transparent in the early Islamic *tafsir* and *hadith* authorities such as Baidawi, Bukhari, Tabari, and Zamakhshari, to name only a few.[8] From pre-Islamic Arabia Jews had settled in Ethiopia, bringing their pre-Talmudic form of Judaism with them, and their descendents are known as the Falashas, the so-called Black Jews of Ethiopia. Ullendorf traces the heavily Jewish character of Ethiopian

---

4. E. Ullendorf, "Hebraic-Jewish Elements in Abyssinian (Monophysite) Christianity," *Journal of Semitic Studies*, vol. I, no. 3 (July 1956), 220-21.
5. Ibid., 222.
6. Ibid., 223.
7. Ibid., 223-24.
8. Ibid., 224.

Christianity to the influence of Falasha Jews who converted to Christianity after the missionizing activity of the Syrian Frumentius.[9]

Here we must interject to remark that whereas no doubt some Falashas did indeed convert to Christianity under Frumentius, this is insufficient, *contra* Ullendorf, to explain the essentially Jewish nature of Ethiopian Christianity, which could not have developed as such if it arose under the "orthodox," non-Judaic Frumentius. A better explanation may perhaps lie in the Ethiopian oral tradition which traces church origins there back to the first century. We can accept this claim without basing it on *Acts* 8:26ff. Rather than being founded as a result of Philip the evangelist's missionary activity, it would be historically more likely to trace Ethiopian Christianity back to Ebionites who together with their Jewish compatriots may have fled the destruction of Jerusalem in 70 CE. Such a centuries-long presence of Jewish Christians in Ethiopia would explain why Frumentius was not able to alter the Ethiopian church's fundamentally Jewish character. According to this paradigm, the Jewish character of the Ethiopian church would not have been created by the Falasha converts, but instead would have been merely confirmed and strengthened by their influx. The Ethiopian oral tradition of first-century origins would finally offer scholarship an explanation for the Ethiopian church's possession of the *Book of Enoch* and other similar so-called Jewish sectarian literature, especially Essenic texts. The Ethiopians' interest in the *Book of Enoch* cannot be explained by the standard historical model which argues that the Ethiopian church in the post-Frumentius period had been guided by the See of Antioch in producing its version of the Greek scriptures. The standard model furthermore claims that it was not until ca. 500 CE that a Ge'ez translation of the scriptures was undertaken under the impetus of the Eastern Mediterranean "Nine Saints," who were all of an "orthodox"

---

9. Ibid., 227.

Christian and not a Judaic character.[10] That the Ethiopian Church was created by Mediterranean and Antiochene representatives cannot be reconciled with the Ethiopian Old Testament canon which includes the Essenic[11] books of *Enoch* and *Jubilees*, the Jewish-Christian *Ascension of Isaiah*, nor with their unique version of the New Testament which contains 35 books, including the Jewish-Christian *Shepherd of Hermas*.[12]

Before returning to Ullendorf's historical reconstruction, we pose the question: Could the Jewish Christians who may have fled Jerusalem in 70 CE first have settled in Arabia before eventually resettling in Ethiopia? We have a specific reason for asking this, which we will make explicit below. Regarding Christianity in pre-Islamic Arabia, whose presence reached "over wide areas of the Arabian peninsula," this was represented mostly by Monophysite and Nestorian communities, which, however, as Ullendorf notes, possessed a "general Semitic character."[13] Ullendorf offers no explanation for this Semitic component of Arabian Christianity, and since Nestorianism is an Eastern, not a Semitic branch of the Christian faith, the lack of an explanation for the Semitic complexion of Arabian Nestorianism appears as a glaring deficiency in Ullendorf's model. The most natural solution is presented by Pines, who gathered evidence which indicates that Jewish Christians in Arabia, branded as heretics, entered Nestorianism in significant numbers in order to preserve their Jewish-

---

10. Ken Perry, ed. *The Blackwell Companion to Eastern Christianity* (Malden, MA/Oxford: Blackwell Publishing, 2007), 119, 128.

11. We do not imply that the Essenes wrote *Enoch* and *Jubilees*, only that these texts seem to possess various connections with this group, and that, as Gabriele Boccaccini concludes, Qumran, where *Enoch* was a favorite book, was a "successor to the community or communities that authored ... the Enochic texts." See Gabriele Boccaccini, ed., *Enoch and Qumran Origins: New Light on a Forgotten Connection* (Grand Rapids, Michigan: Wm. B. Eerdmans, 2005), 12.

12. See Ken Perry, ed. *The Blackwell Companion to Eastern Christianity*, 128.

13. E. Ullendorf, "Hebraic-Jewish Elements in Abyssinian (Monophysite) Christianity," 224-25.

Christian faith clandestinely.[14] From where did these Jewish Christians originate? Again, the most natural answer would be that they had the same origin as countless other Jews of Arabia, namely, they had settled in Arabia in the wake of the tragic events in Jerusalem in 70 CE.[15]

Once more, it would be most natural to conclude that just as many of these Arabian Jews eventually made the further move to Ethiopia, so a large contingent of Jewish Christians who had settled in Arabia after 70 CE later relocated to Ethiopia, precisely when has unfortunately been lost in the mists of vanished history. But we can surmise that their compatriots in faith who chose to remain behind in Arabia eventually found refuge in the Nestorian communities, and their numbers were sufficient to actually bestow and maintain a Semitic stamp on the "Eastern" churches in Arabia. As Pines notes, many of these clandestine Jewish Christians were later absorbed into Islam, whose Christology actually quite closely coincides with the non-Pauline, non-Hellenistic Christology of the Jewish Christians.[16] With regard to the Jewish Christians who resettled in Ethiopia, although in the centuries following Frumentius they were deeply influenced

---

14. See Shlomo Pines, *The Jewish Christians of the Early Centuries of Christianity according to a New Source*, 37-39.

15. Christianity is not documented in Arabia until the 3rd century; cf. Ken Perry, ed. *The Blackwell Companion to Eastern Christianity*, 1. This, however, poses no great obstacle to a proposal of an earlier Christian presence on the Arabian peninsula, for the later references all refer to Christians of an "orthodox" character with an institutional ecclesiastical organization; any form of Jewish Christianity would have been ignored by the Great Church as "Judaism." As throughout human history, the "minority" was marginalized and left few, if any, direct traces of their existence. Their indirect traces, however, are substantial enough to work out a reconstruction of their existence, especially their bestowal of a Semitic stamp upon Eastern Nestorianism in Arabia. Further evidence is found in the Semitic elements in the Jesus *ahadith* perservered in part by early Jewish-Christian converts to Islam.

16. See Shlomo Pines, "Notes on Islam and on Arab Christianity and Judeo-Christianity," *Jerusalem Studies in Arabic and Islam*, vol. 4 (1984), 135-52.

by non-Hebraic "orthodox" Christianity, they have nevertheless managed to retain the essentially Jewish character of their Ebionite ancestors.

Similarly, the Semitic components of Christianity in Arabia, especially as documented indirectly in the Qur'an (e.g., reference to a belief in Mary as a celestial entity, which is a Syro-Palestinian tenet of the Jewish-Christian 'Nazaraeans'[17]), cannot be explained by the presence of the documented Eastern forms of Christianity in Arabia, such as the Nestorians and Jacobites. A more sufficient explanation would be the early presence in Arabia of Jewish Christians who later influenced the Eastern Nestorians in a Semitic mode. The Qur'an refers as well to a docetic belief in both Jesus and Mary, when it stresses that both had to eat (*sura* 5:75). Docetism is alien to the Nestorians and Jacobites, but was an ancient component of the Jewish-Christian gnosis. The Qur'an itself supports a docetic understanding of the crucifixion (*sura* 4:157-58).[18]

On the basis of the above reconstruction, founded mainly on Ullendorf and Pines, we can trace two branches of the Arabian Ebionite heritage, one in the present-day Ethiopian churches and the other in nascent Islam. Through the Islamic branch, Jewish-Christian gnosis was to spread further organically throughout the ages in the various sectors of Islam. As Quispel has noted, the Ismailis are "very much indebted to the Jewish Christians and the Jewish Gnostics," that is, the Mandaeans, from southern Iraq.[19] The Mujiriyya, who influenced the early Shi'ites, have strong connections to the Mandaeans and other Gnostics.[20] As Quispel remarks, the

---

17. See François de Blois, "Nasrānī (Ναζωραιος) and ḥanīf (εθνικος): Studies on the Religious Vocabulary of Christianity and of Islam," 13-15.

18. Cf. Henri Corbin, "Divine Epiphany and Spiritual Birth in Ismailian Gnosis," in *Man and Transformation*. Papers from the Eranos Yearbooks. Bollingen Series XXX, vol. 5 (New York: Pantheon Books, 1964), 69-160.

19. G. Quispel, "Kosmologie und Heilslehre der frühen Ismaʿiliya: Eine Studie zur Islamischen Gnosis by Heinz Halm. Review," *International Journal of Middle East Studies*, vol. 12, no. 1 (August, 1980), 111-112.

20. W. F. Tucker, "Rebels and Gnostics: Al-Muġīra Ibn Saʿīd and the

Hermetic gnosis was circulating in Iraq before the Harranian Sabians. The ultimate origins of this and of Shi'ite gnosis go back to the Jewish mystics of Palestine (from among the Pharisees and Essenes). This Jewish Gnosticism was brought into the churches not only by Valentinus and Origen,[21] but had been present from the earliest days of Christianity, for the Ebionites under James the Just were, to put it simply, Jewish Gnostics. This same Abrahamic Gnosticism is present in Islam, though not always necessarily via historically determined channels, given the possibilities of naturally arising independent archetypal paradigms.

Abu Mohammed Ali of Cordova (b. 994), more commonly called Ibn Hazm al-Zahiri, writes indignantly in his *Book of Religions and Denominations*, fol. 72ro.: "All Rabbanite Jews are destined to be united in the wrath of God and his curse. They pray on the night of Kippur, which is the tenth of Tishri in October. Then rises Ansatrin [scribal error for *Metatron*] which according to their opinion signifies the "minor Lord" (far from God such heresy)."[22] These comments overlook the fact that there are Islamic esoteric traditions that parallel the Jewish concept of Metatron as the "Lesser Lord."[23] There is, for example, a *hadith qudsi* which records: "I am *'Arabi* without the *'ayn*, and *Ahmad* without the *mim*," that is, "I am *Rabb*, and I am *Ahad*," "I am Lord and I am One." This *hadith qudsi* is at times cited in Sufi circles as a saying of the Prophet; for example, Schuon applies to the Prophet the two sayings, "I am Ahmad without *mim*" and "I am an Arab [*'Arabi*] without

---

Muġīriyya," *Arabica*, tome xxii, fascicule I (1975), 33-47.

21. G. Quispel, "Die islamische Gnosis: Die extreme Schia und die 'Alawiten by Heinz Halm. Review," *Vigiliae Christianae*, vol. 37, no. 4 (Dec., 1983), 408-409.

22. Quoted in Hartwig Hirschfeld, "Mohammedan Criticism of the Bible," *The Jewish Quarterly Review*, vol. 13, no. 2 (Jan., 1901), 232.

23. Scholem was doubtless correct when he suggested the Mandaean *Iurba* is none other than *Yu-Rabba*. See P. S. Alexander, "The Historical Setting of the Hebrew Book of Enoch," *Journal of Jewish Studies*, vol. 28 no. 2 (1977), 162.

'*ayn*," and he also cites a further *hadith*: "Whoso hath seen me hath seen God."[24] Even Metatron is known among Sufis, who call him Sayyidna Mitatrun, that is, "Lord Metatron."[25] Furthermore, the Jewish intention in designating Metatron as the "Lesser Lord" is not to comporomise the divine Unity, but specifically to safeguard it, that is, the term is a means of specifying that Metatron is in fact not the supreme Lord, but a "lesser" reflection or image of God.

There is a rather important *hadith* from Ibn Abbas recorded in Suyuti: "I saw my Lord in the form of a beardless youth (*amrad*)."[26] Ritter has collected the various versions of this *hadith*. Hammad ibn Salama's version of this *hadith* reads that the beardless youth was "in the most beautiful form" (*fi ahsani suratin*), seated "upon a throne of grace" (*'ala kursiyyi'l-karamati*), and surrounded by a golden carpet. The same author gives another variant, which states that the Prophet's feet were "in greenery," that he was wearing "golden shoes," and had a golden veil (*firash*) over his face. A third variant refers to a green robe. Dhahabi records that the Prophet saw "God" (all other versions we are aware of specify "Lord") as a beardless youth covered with "a veil of pearls," and again the divine feet were "in greenery." Ibn Jurayj records 'A'isha's version, according to which the youthful form sat upon a throne, and the divine feet were in greenery "of glittering light." Suyuti gives yet another version that speaks of "the Lord of the worlds" rather than simply "Lord," dwelling in a *hazira min al-quds*, a sacred garden (Ritter translates this as "a heavenly garden"), and instead of the Lord being seated

---

24. Frithjof Schuon, *Treasures of Buddhism* (Bloomington, Indiana: World Wisdom Books, 1993), 106.

25. *Sayyidna Mitatrun* is equivalent to the Holy Spirit (*al-Ruh*) as creative demiurge in Frithjof Schuon, *Dimensions of Islam*. tr. by P. N. Townsend (London: George Allen and Unwin, 1970), 112.

26. For a modern quotation, see Shaykh al-'Alawi, *The Knowledge of God: A sufic commentary on al Murshid al-Mu'in of ibn al-'Ashir*. Edited by 'Abd as-Sabur al-Ustadh; translated by 'Abd al-Kabir al-Munawarra and 'Abd as-Sabur al-Ustadh (Norfolk, UK: Diwan Press, 1981), 237-38.

upon a throne, we find the equivalent royal image of his wearing a crown that "dazzled the eyes."

There are related *ahadith*, such as: "Be careful when you look at beardless youths, for their facial features are like God's facial features."[27] "God's dwelling place is between the cheeks of beardless youths." "Look for the Good among those beautiful of face." "There are three things which bestow a gleam to the eye: beholding greenery, beholding water, and beholding a beautiful face." "To gaze upon the Ka'ba is worship.... To gaze upon one's parents is worship. To gaze upon greenery is worship; and to gaze upon a beautiful face is worship."[28]

As Ritter notes, according to the various versions of the beardless youth *hadith*, the Lord's hair is described variously as "abundant," "curly" (*ja'dan amrada*), "frizzy, wooly" (*qatat*). However, Amdi reports the belief of certain sectarians, the *mujassima* or anthropomorphists, who teach that the divine form is that of an "old man with grey hair and a grey beard (*shaykh ashmat al-ra's wa'l-lihya*)." Ritter fails to note that this version is of the highest significance for the question of the genetic relationship between nascent Islamic esoteric traditions and Jewish mysticism, for Amdi's report agrees precisely with the image of God as the "Ancient of Days" or "Head of Days" as seen by the prophets Daniel and Enoch. In *Daniel* 7:9, we read that the "Ancient of Days took his seat; his raiment was white as snow, and the hair of his head like pure wool; his throne was fiery flames, its wheels were burning fire." In verse 13, Daniel sees "one like a son of man" come "to the Ancient of Days and was presented before him." In *1 Enoch* 46:1 we read: "And there I saw One who had a head of days, and his head was white like wool, and with him was another being whose countenance had the appearance of a

---

27. Our translation; the Arabic is given in Hellmut Ritter, *The Ocean of the Soul: Men, the World, and God in the Stories of Farid al-Din 'Attar*. Tr. by John O'Kane with editorial assistance of Bernd Radtke (Leiden: Brill, 2003), 459.

28. Ritter collects these, 466ff; we offer our own renderings from the original versions.

man, and his face was full of graciousness, like one of the holy angels." In the following verses this "man" is called "the Son of Man." In *1 Enoch* 71:10 we find: "And with them [the angels] the Head of Days, his head white and pure as wool, and his raiment indescribable." Then verse 14: "And he [the Head of Days]²⁹ came to me and greeted me with his voice, and said unto me: 'You are the Son of Man, and righteousness abides over you, and the righteousness of the Head of Days forsakes you not.'" This is in fact the first record of Enoch's transformation into the supra-angelic Metatron.

The imagery of the Muslim sectarians who described the form of God as that of an "old man with grey hair and a grey beard" agrees precisely with both Daniel's image of the Ancient of Days, whose hair was "like pure wool," and with the Kabbalistic preoccupation, based upon an expansion of Daniel's imagery, with the esoteric significances of the divine beard of the Ancient of Days. Before continuing we must present the Shi'ite parallel to the Lord as beardless youth *hadith*. Kulayni, *Al-Kafi*, H 266,10, 3, records a *hadith* from 'Ali al-Rida, where we find the following version: "The Prophet Muhammad saw his Lord in the form of a fully grown young man thirty years old." The belief of Hisham ibn Salim and Sahib al-Taq and al-Maythami is then referred to, namely, that God "is hallow down to his navel, and the remainder is solid." The Imam responds that God is different from any imagery that can be imagined. The Imam then clarifies that with regard to the Prophet seeing "his Lord in the form of a fully grown young man thirty years old," the Messenger of God actually "beheld the greatness [or Glory] of his Lord." The Imam is then asked, "Who was the one whose feet was in the greenery?" This presupposes the traditions found in Sunnite sources cited above from Ritter. The extraordinary answer of the Imam as to the identity of the one with his feet

---

29. "He" here is the Head of Days, and not, *pace* R. H. Charles, an "angel"; see R. H. Charles (ed.), *Apocrypha and Pseudepigrapha of the Old Testament*, vol. 2 (London: Oxford University Press, 1913), 237.

in the greenery is: "He was the Prophet Muhammad; when he gazed upon his Lord with his heart, he [i.e., his Lord] placed him in the Light like that of the hujub, so he could see what is inside the hujub. Some of God's light is green, some red, some white, some other colors." The Imam here is interpreting the "Lord" which the Prophet saw as the Glory of God, that is, the manifestation of God in human form. This agrees precisely with early Jewish mystical concepts regarding the Primordial Human as the Glory of God, that is as the manifestation of God in the mode of the hypostasis of the *Kabod*, the divine Glory. In all of the versions of the Lord as beardless youth *hadith*, the one whose feet were in the greenery is clearly the same being as the Lord who appeared as a beardless youth. Therefore, when the Imam boldly identifies the one whose feet was in the greenery as the Prophet, the Imam is identifying the Prophet of Islam as the hypostatic Glory of God. In essence, the Prophet saw his own celestial counterpart. Abraham Abulafia in his *Hayei ha-Olam ha-Ba* (*Life of the Future World*) teaches that the mystic sees his self as the God who appeared in the form of a human seated upon the divine throne, as in *Ezekiel* 1:26. Abulafia seems to allude to *Ezekiel* 1:26 to explain the phenomenon of the visionary human form, which is the "human form attributed to the Creator."[30]

We can now recognize the broad outlines of the Islamic esoteric conceptions involved in the Lord as beardless youth *hadith* and related *ahadith*. God as "old man with grey hair and a grey beard (*shaykh ashmat al-ra's wa'l-lihya*)" is the counterpart of the opposite image of the Lord as a beardless youth. These two correspond to the Danielic-Enochic Ancient/Head of Days and the Son of Man. But both of these coincide as a single entity, namely as Metatron who is both ancient and young. In Abulafia's *Hayei ha-Olam ha-Ba*, 148, the Hebrew word *na'ar*, youth, and the Arabic word *shaykh*, old man, are

---

30. For the Hebrew text see MS Oxford-BL 1582.

said to be numerically equivalent, and the two terms are referred to Metatron.[31]

No doubt, the "abundant hair" emphasizes the aspect of youth, *na'ar*. The other Islamic themes associated with the *hadith* in question are throne, throne of grace, the golden carpet, feet in greenery of glittering light, golden shoes, golden facial covering, a green robe, a veil of pearls, a celestial garden, and a dazzling crown. The components of feet, shoes, and face are reminiscent of Kabbalistic interest in the divine body, the *shi'ur qomah*. The robe is reminiscent of the divine raiment in *Daniel*. The term "grace" is paralleled in *Enoch* 46:1 where of the Son of Man it is said that "his face was full of graciousness." The divine crown, *Keter*, is a central symbol in Kabbalism. According to *shi'ur qomah* speculations the body in question is that of the Glory of God, that is, of the hypostatic Glory, and not of God as such. This Glory is also called the divine "form" or "image," and it can be no coincidence that the *hadith* in question speaks of the "form" of the Lord. Early Jewish-Christian Christology was founded upon equivalent esoteric Jewish conceptions regarding the hypostasis of the divine Form or Image.[32] And that with only a single exception the *hadith* versions speak of "Lord" and not "God" in the form of a beardless youth further strengthens the suggestion that ultimately an equivalent of Metatron is being alluded to, for Metatron is the "lesser *Lord*." He is simultaneously youth and elder; in other words, the Son of Man is the mirror image and form of the Ancient of Days. That is, the Son of Man is

---

31. The text has been variously interpreted; cf. G. G. Stroumsa, "Polymorphie divine et transformations d'un mythologème: l' 'Apocryphon de Jean' et ses sources," *Vigiliae Christianae* vol. 35 (1981), 422-23; Moshe Idel, *The Mystical Experience in Abraham Abulafia* (Jerusalem: Magnes/ Albany: State University of New York Press, 1988), 122.

32. See the pioneering work of Jarl Fossum, "Jewish-Christian Christology and Jewish Mysticism," *Vigiliae Christianiae*, vol. 37 (1983), 260-87, and G. G. Stroumsa, "Form(s) of God: Some Notes on Metatron and Christ," *Harvard Theological Review*, vol. 76, no. 3 (1983), 269–88.

the Ancient of Days,³³ or the manifestation of the Ancient of Days in human form. According to Rabbinic sources, *Exodus* 15:3's reference to the Lord as "the man of war" meant that God had appeared at Sinai in the form of a youth; in contrast, *Exodus* 20:2's statement "I am the Lord your God" meant that God had the form of an old man. The Samaritans interpreted the Youth alluded to in *Exodus* 15:3 as their central mediating angel Kabbalah, or Kavalah, who is equivanlent to the Jewish Metatron.³⁴

Odeberg cites an extraordinary passage in which Simon the Righteous claims to have annually seen God in the form of an old man in a white garment, which seems to be an obvious allusion to the Ancient of Days figure from *Daniel*:

*TY Yoma* 42c: (cf. *TB Yoma* 39b): Forty years long did Simon the Righteous (about 300 B.C.E.) serve Israel in the office of High Priest. The last year [of his service] he said to them: 'In this year I shall die'. They said to him: 'Whence do you know?' He answered: 'Every year, at the time when I entered the Holy of Holies (i.e. on the day of atonement) an aged one clad in white garment and cloak entered with me and went out with me. This year he entered with me but did not go out with me'. They asked R. Abbahu [to explain this]: "Lo, it is written (*Lev.* 16:17): 'There shall be no man in the tabernacle of the congregation', not even those of whom it is written (*Ezek.* 1:10): 'the likeness of their face is the face of a man'; he said to them: 'If someone says that it was (the son of) a man, I on the contrary maintain that it was the Holy One."³⁵

---

33. The possibility that the Ancient of Days and the Son of Man might be the same entity is explored in Loren T. Stuckenbruck, "'One Like a Son of Man as the Ancient of Days' in the Old Greek Recension of Daniel 7,13: Scribal Error or Theological Translation?" *Zeitschrift für die neutestamentliche Wissenschaft und die Kunde der älteren Kirche*, Band 86 (1995), 268-76.

34. See Jarl Fossum, *The Name of God and the Angel of the Lord: Samaritan and Jewish Concepts of Intermediation and the Origin of Gnosticism* (Tübingen: Mohr, 1985).

35. Hugo Odeberg, *The Fourth Gospel Interpreted in its Relation to*

When John in his *Revelation* combines the imagery of Daniel's Son of Man and Ancient of Days into the single figure of the ascended Jesus, he is operating fully within Jewish monotheistic parameters: 13) "I saw ... one like a son of man, clothed with a long robe and with a golden girdle round his breast; 14) his head and his hair were white as white wool, white as snow; his eyes were like a flame of fire, 15) his feet were like burnished bronze." This passage assimilates imagery not only from *Daniel* 7, but also from *Daniel* 10:5-6 which describes the glorious body of "a man clothed in linen." This "man" is in fact a mysterious angelic figure who is, as Jeffery concludes, "superior to Gabriel and Michael...."[36] Based on *Revelation* 1, we would suggest that the most likely identification of the angelic figure of *Daniel* 10 is none other than the Son of Man of *Daniel* 7, and that he coincides with Enoch-Metatron. According to a repeated formula in Shi'ite *ahadith*, the Holy Spirit "is a Spirit greater than Michael or Gabriel." This is none other than Metatron, who although he is greater than Gabriel, may nevertheless also be identified with Gabriel inasmuch as Gabriel may upon occasion operate as a manifestation or emanation of Metatron. This is the sense in which Gabriel is designated the Holy Spirit in Islamic tradition. Thus Gabriel is not the Spirit as such in a reductive or restrictive sense. As an emanation of the Holy Spirit, the appearance of Gabriel is also marked by the ineffable majesty of his supernal source, and this is why some Islamic interpreters, such as Ibn al-'Arabi, have concluded that it was God, rather than Gabriel, who appeared to the Prophet in *sura* 53:1-18 and *sura* 81:15-23.[37]

---

*Contemporaneous Religious Currents in Palestine and the Hellenistic-Oriental World*, 277.

36. R. H. Charles and A. Jeffery as quoted in Louis F. Hartman and Alexander A. Di Lella, *The Book of Daniel. The Anchor Bible* (Garden City, NY: Doubleday, 1978), 279.

37. See Ibn 'Arabi, *Journey to the Lord of Power. A Sufi Manual on Retreat.* Tr. By Rabia Terri Harris (Rochester Vermont: Inner Traditions International, 1989), 59.

We learn from Islamic writers who specialized in documenting the beliefs and practices of what they perceived as deviant Islam that certain sectarians or Sufis would "see a beautiful form," and that they would bow to it as though God dwelt in it.[38] This practice was actually quite widespread among the early Sufis, and was known as the "prostration of the lovers" (*sajda-yi 'ashiqan*) and as "playing the witness" (*shahid' bazi*). As Pourjavady explains, this practice was justified by the belief that metaphorical love, *'ishq-i majazi*, could be the first step to true love, *'ishq-i haqiqi*, on account of the *wahdat al-wujud*, or oneness of being.[39] In other words, since there is a metaphysical continuum or ontological continuity between creatures (beings) and God (Being as such), love for the created can function as a link to love for God. Pourjavady documents that the "prostration of the lovers" and "playing the witness" were common practices in Tabriz, the home of the famous Shams-i Tabrizi, who played such a central role in the inspiration of Rumi's poetry. Reports of Ahmad al-Ghazali "playing the witness" in Tabriz are abundant, and this particular individual was none other than the brother of the great Muslim theologian Imam al-Ghazali.

Pourjavady remarks that Aflaki quotes Rumi to the effect that God would appear to Shams-i Tabrizi in the form of a woman,[40] an anecdote to which Ritter also refers,[41] and this is intriguingly reminiscent of the Jewish and Jewish-Christian belief in the maternal celestial Holy Spirit. Rumi advocated the practice of the "prostration of true lovers" to the "*qutb* of the age," that is, to whatever human happened to be the central spiritual *axis mundi* of a given era.[42] As eccentric as this

---

38. Cf. Ritter, 459ff.
39. Nasrollah Pourjavady, "Stories of Ahmad al Ghazali 'Playing the Witness' in Tabriz (Shams-i Tabrizi's Interest in Shahid-bazi)," in Todd Lawson (ed.), *Reason and Inspiration in Islam* (London: I. B. Tauris, 2005), 216.
40. Ibid., 214.
41. Ritter, 462, 491.
42. Pourjavady, 214.

practice may seem to the average Muslim today, it essentially accords with the Qur'anic accounts which repeatedly refer to God's commandment to the angels to prostrate before the newly created Adam and to worship him (or more accurately 'it', since according to the *Genesis* text at this point Adam was still the androgynous Perfect Humanity, when Eve dwelt within Adam). This particular Qur'anic theme may indeed shed light on a curious passage in the *Letter to the Hebrews* 1:6: "And again, when he brings the first-born into the world, he says, 'Let all God's angels worship him.'" The "first-born" may here refer to Adam. The *Gospel of Thomas* logion 15 may be pertinent here as well: "When you see the one not born of woman, fall on your face and worship. That one is your father." This might refer to the common father of humanity, Adam, yet not the common earthly Adam, but the celestial Adam as the hypostatic Glory of God. The phrase "one not born of woman" would seem to make better sense as an allusion to Adam than to God, of whom it seems rather strange to describe as "one not born of woman." On the other hand, Adam is human, and yet he is not born of a woman. The Islamic prostration of true lovers and the story of the angelic worship of Adam, each of which involves the worship of humans as a revelation of God may help us to set the worship of Jesus in nascent Christianity into its original context, which is fully Jewish and monotheistic.

The *hadith* concerning the Lord as a beardless youth parallels essential themes of Jewish *merkabah*-throne mysticism. There are additional Islamic traditions that point in this direction: "The Prophet asked Harithah: 'What is the reality of thy faith?' He answered: 'I have inclined my soul away from this world, I have fasted by day, and kept vigil at night: and it is as though I behold the throne of my Lord coming forth, and as if I behold the people of Paradise visiting one another, and the people of Hell at enmity with one another.' …. The Prophet also said: 'If any man wishes to behold a servant whose heart God has illumined, let him look upon

Harithah.'"[43] Although without an explicit mention of the divine throne, there is a tradition of 'Umar seeing God: "A man greeted him while he was circumambulating the Kaaba, and he did not answer him. The man complanined of this to some of his friends; and 'Abdullah said: 'We were beholding God in that place.'"[44] In a *hadith* related by Kulayni we read of a weekly *merkabah*-like ascent of the Shi'ite Imams: "Every Friday eve the spirits of the prophets and their dead and living representatives in your midst are allowed to ascend to heaven and walk around the throne seven times and to offer two cycles of prayer behind each of the columns of the throne. Afterwards the spirits of the prophets and their representatives are restored to their bodies and they wake up full of joy, and the representative in your midst wakes up with an exponential increase in knowledge."

Various *ahadith* document that the Prophet of Islam had direct exposure to Jewish *merkabah* mystics. In one tradition, the Prophet asks the Jew Ibn Sa'id what he sees in a vision: "The Apostle of God said to Ibn Sa'id: 'What do you see?' He said, 'I see a throne upon the water, around it *al-hayyat*'." As Halperin notes, *al-hayyat* is obviously a reference to the Hebrew term for the "living creatures" from *Ezekiel* 1's *merkabah* vision.[45]

According to Kabbalistic sources, in the sixth celestial palace there is what is known as a test of waters, during which one sees what looks like the presence of immense waters, but the visionary is warned not to say, "Water, water," for what one is seeing is instead pure marble. This test is precisely paralleled and described in Qur'an *sura* 27:44, which narrates the queen of Saba's entrance into the palace of Solomon:

---

43. Abu Bakr al-Kalabadhi, *Kitab al-Ta'arruf li-madhhab ahl al-tasawwuf. The Doctrine of the Sufis*. Translated by Arthur John Arberry (London: Cambridge University Press, 1935), 7-8.
44. Ibid., 123.
45. Cf. David J. Halperin, "The Ibn Sayyad Traditions and the Legend of al-Dajjal" *Journal of the American Oriental Society*, vol. 96, no. 2 (April-June, 1976), 217.

"She was asked to enter the lofty palace; and when she saw it, she thought it was a lake of water, and she (tucked up her skirts), uncovering her legs. He said: This is but a palace paved smooth with slabs of glass. She said: O my Lord, I have indeed wronged my soul. I do (now) resign myself with Solomon to the Lord of the Worlds."[46]

Esoteric matters pertaining to the second main category of ancient Jewish mysticism, the *ma'aseh bereshit*, are also present in Islam, especially with regard to the themes of the supernal feminine. To introduce these themes, we may begin by observing that the Prophet of Islam is called *ummi*, which is usually rendered "illiterate." In part *ummi* suggests *umm*, 'mother', so that *ummi* may denote a child still at home with its mother, a child who has not yet separated from its mother to attend school to learn its "letters." The New Testament also describes Jesus' apostles as illiterate (*agrammatoi*, Acts 4:13), but this does not strictly mean they could not read or write, but that they did not possess a formal higher education, and indeed the Greek term *agrammatoi*, which literally means 'unlettered', is more accurately rendered in modern English as 'uneducated'. Similarly, the Prophet of Islam could not have been totally illiterate, for this would be impossible for a successful business man such as he was; it is well known that certain *ahadith* imply the Prophet did not lack all reading or writing skills. Implicate in the Arabic term for illiteracy, *ummi*, is also the idea of being spiritually "childlike," as in the *Gospel of Thomas* 22. Also, a child is inarticulate, not yet having learned to speak on its own. It must acquire this skill in large part from its mother. For Islamic theology, the Prophet did not possess his own words, for he spoke the words of God. In his humanity he was illiterate; in his spirit, he was the divine Pen. His celestial mother in this respect was the *Umm*

---

46. An identification of this Qur'anic account as pertaining to *merkabah* mysticism's celestial palace water test is found in C. R. A. Morray-Jones, *A Transparent Illusion: The Dangerous Vision of Water in Hekhalot Mysticism: A Source-Critical and Tradition-Historical Inquiry* (Leiden: Brill, 2002).

*al-Kitab*, the Mother of the Book, about whom we will have more to say below.

Adam, although uneducated, eloquently gave names to all the beasts (*Genesis* 2:19); for the Kabbalist this will contain a reference to the living creatures of *Ezekiel* 1, the angelic attendants of the divine throne. The Qu'anic account of Adam's bestowal of names may suggest that he was in possession of the angelic names; *sura* 2:31, 33:

> And he taught Adam all the names, then showed them to the angels, saying: Inform me of the names of these, if you are truthful.... He said: O Adam! Inform them of their names, and when he had informed them of their names, he said: Did I not tell you that I know the secret of the heavens and the earth? And I know what you disclose and what you conceal.

According to Shi'ite exegesis, the names that were given to Adam were the names of the pre-existent celestial Imams. The creature known as Buraq, literally, "the flashing, gleaming one," upon which the Prophet of Islam is said to have ascended to the heavens, in fact derives its name from *Ezekiel* 1, the basis of all Jewish *merkabah* ascent mysticism; *Ezekiel* 1 represents the only passage in all the Bible where the Hebrew word *baraq* (= Arabic *buraq*) is found. In Tabari's biography of the Prophet we read that two angels descended and inserted *Sakina* (= *Shekhinah*) in the form of a white cat into the heart of the Prophet. In Qur'an *sura* 48:4 the *Sakina* similarly enters hearts, and the *aya* ends with a mention of "the heavenly hosts," that is, the angels, implying that *Sakina* is an angelic or supra-angelic entity. This points to *Sakina*'s status as coinciding in some sense with the Holy Spirit and the Mother of the Book. "He it is who sent down *Sakina* into the hearts of the faithful that they might add faith unto their faith. God's are the hosts of the heavens and the earths, and God is Knowing, Wise." In contrast to *sura* 3:7 where the phrase *umm al-kitab* is used in the exegetical sense of "Authority of the Book" (Arabic *umm* here is used in the sense of the Rabbinic Hebrew *em* 'mother' with the meaning 'authority'),[47] in *sura* 43:4 the term *umm al-kitab*, because it is assigned two divine names, must be understood in a quite different sense, namely, as a title for God. The other Qur'anic occurrence of the term *umm al-kitab* is found in *sura* 13:39, where it is usually understood in the sense of "archetype of the Book," but *sura* 43:4 would seem to indicate that a hypostatic archetype is involved here, and not a mere linguistic metaphor.[48] In this case the *umm al-kitab* would correspond to the Kabbalistic *ha-shah ha-'elyonah*, the Supernal Lady, who is none other than the well-known primordial hypostatic Lady Wisdom (Hebrew *hokhmah* = Arabic *hikma*) known from the Jewish scriptures (cf. *Proverbs* 8; *Sirach* 24; *Wisdom* 7; *Baruch* 3-4), who was also understood to be the pre-existent hypostatic Torah who appears on the earthly plane as the written Torah.

Other Islamic aspects mirroring the *ma'aseh bereshit*, in this instance the doctrine of the primordial *sefirot*, may be detected in the very first Qur'anic *sura*, *al-Fatiha*, "The Opening," which contains a precise parallel to the classic Rabbinic and Kabbalistic descriptions of the contrast between Mercy (*Hesed/Rahamim*) and Wrath (*Din*). Ayat 1 and 3 refer to the Merciful and the Compassionate, *al-Rahman*, *al-Rahim*, and that the divine mercy prevails over wrath is indicated by the fact that *ayat* 1 and 3 precede the mention in *aya* 4 of "judgment," *din*, the Arabic word agreeing precisely with the Hebrew word *din*. The final *aya*, 7, mentions the bestowal of the divine favor, blessing, or grace (*'an'amta*; the noun form is *ni'mata*), which closely corresponds semantically to Hebrew *hesed*, and only thereafter does there follow a reference to God's wrath (*ghadab*), which corresponds semantically more with Hebrew *din* than with Arabic *din*. The *Fatiha* ends on a note of mercy prevailing over wrath, for if we read *ghay-*

---

47. Cf. W. Bacher, *Die exegetische Terminologie der jüdischen Traditionsliteratur*, vol 1 (Leipzig, 1899), 119-21; L. Zunz, *Die Gottesdienstlichen Vorträge der Juden* (Frankfurt, 1892), 338.

48. Consider Ibn al-'Arabi's divine statement: "'My Book is nothing other than My Essence" (*Al-Futuhat al-makkiyya* ch. 411).

*ril maghdubi* rather than *ghayral maghdubi* (both options are found in the traditions), *aya* 7 speaks positively of "those whom you have blessed, upon whom wrath does not rest, and who go not astray," and not negatively as in most, but certainly not all, translations, "those whom you have blessed, not those upon whom wrath rests, and who go astray."[49] The opposition in the *Fatiha* between the divine *din* (Judgment) and *rahma* (*al-Rahman*), parallels the central Kabbalistic doctrine of the intradivine conflict between *din* (Judgment) and *rahamim* (Mercy), the latter predominating over *din*, precisely as in the Qur'an and in *ahadith*.

Moreover, the mention of King (*malik*) in *aya* 4 is reminiscent of the important *sefirah Malkhut* ('Kingdom') in the Kabbalah, which is paralleled by the significant role that Arabic *Malakut* plays in Sufi metaphysics. We should mention that the phrase "Lord of the Worlds" (*rabbi-l-'alamin*) in *aya* 2 is a well-known, even quite standard Jewish title for God which is found throughout ancient and medieval Aramaic and Hebrew literature, and the Arabic phrase *rabbi-l-'alamin* bears linguistic marks of having perhaps originated from Aramaic (Hebrew *'olam*, plural *'olamim* = Aramaic *alma*, plural *almin*). The Jewish term passed into ancient Christian Kabbalistic (i.e., Gnostic) literature as "the Lord of all the aeons" (see e.g., *Pistis Sophia* I:32, 34). Similarly the Arabic term *al-Rahman* was held among traditional Muslim authorities such as Mubarrad and Tha'lab to have entered Arabic from the Hebrew word *Rahmana*, 'the Merciful'. None of these correspondences between the Qur'an and Judaism should come as a surprise, for after all the Qur'an presents itself as a confirmation and renewal of the earlier revelations given through Moses and Jesus.

---

49. M. A. S. Abdel Haleem translates this phrase as "those who incur no anger," and astutely comments that "the verb here is not attributed to God." Cf. *The Qur'an*. A new translation by M. A. S. Abdel Haleem (Oxford: Oxford University Press, 2005), 3.

Regarding apocalyptic matters, which also generally pertain to the *ma'aseh bereshit*, a further Islamic theme clarified by esoteric Jewish traditions is the figure of 50,000 years in Qur'an *sura* 70. This accords exactly with the well-known Jewish idea of the cosmic time cycles of 50,000 years, consisting of 7 periods of 7,000 years each, totaling 49,000 years, which in turn are followed by a 1,000 year apocalyptic Sabbath.[50]

We would emphasize that not all similarities between Jewish and Islamic mystical traditions are to be explained by historical influences, although when there is evidence of such contact, there is no reason to deny it.[51] The central reason that historical influence and contact need not be invoked in every case is the genetic, organic relationship which exists between all three of the Abrahamic faiths, which makes it possible that quite similar ideas and practices may arise and flourish in both place and time independently of each other. Similarities may arise on account of the common trunk of the Abrahamic tree; distinctives may arise on account of the diversity of branches.

---

50. See Scholem, *Kabbalah*, 120-21.
51. Frithjof Schuon, *Spiritual Perspectives and Human Facts*, tr. by P. N. Townsend (Pates Manor, Bedfont, Middlesex: Perennial Books, 1987), 76.

PART II

A Reconstruction of Early
Jewish Christianity and Gentile
Church History and Thought

# 1. Reconstructing the Jerusalem Church's Ebionite Faith through an Indirect Reading of the Pauline Corpus

In this chapter we will attempt an historical reconstruction of the theology and metaphysics of the Jerusalem church under James the Just by means of systematically examining the letters of Paul. The relevant evidence in Paul's writings is of two categories: 1) direct, where he names James or other authorities in Jerusalem as his theological antagonists; 2) indirect, where in a theological dispute his opponents remain unnamed, but where a contextual reading suggests that Paul is referring to James or other Jerusalem authorities. For readers who may be unsettled to learn that such a polarization existed between Paul and James, we must recall that this enmity is documented already in the New Testament, above all in *Galatians* 2, where Paul has a face-to-face confrontation with Peter over the theology of James. Paul often refers to his Ebionite opponents as "Jews," but once we realize that he means the Jewish Christians, the historical picture emerges into clearer relief. This opposition between Paul and James is not unknown even among the later church fathers. Victorinus writes, for example, in his *Commentary on Galatians*: "But clearly Paul was not able to learn anything from James, for the latter possessed a different view of the Gospel.... James was not an apostle, and he may even have been in heresy. Now Paul does record that he saw James: 'I saw the novelty that James was spreading around and preaching, but because

I knew and spurned his blasphemy, you Galatians should also reject it.'"[1]

If we approach this matter theologically, one could view the polarization, which both ran deep and involved bitter recriminations emanating from both sides, as reflecting providential tensions that are in essence reconcilable on certain levels. Paul, for instance, when referring to his theological opponents in *Philippians* 2:17-18, nevertheless states that he rejoices that at least they proclaim Christ, and he is inwardly satisfied with that. As an example of how theology and metaphysics can at times ameliorate even the bitterest of dogmatic clashes, we refer to Schuon's justification of Luther's strong condemnations of certain legitimate Catholic traditions and beliefs. Enlightening also for the Jacobean-Pauline conflict would be Schuon's model for interpreting the conflict between the early Shia and Sunnis, in which neither side constituted an "intrinsic heresy."[2]

Catholic, Orthodox, and Protestant Christians raised under the dogmatic need for harmonization between Paul and the twelve apostles might find it difficult to concede conflict between these two camps. This is in part the case because exoteric dogma is designed to shield the average believer from esoteric concepts that may present a real danger of elitism if improperly understood. The conflicts between James and Paul also have to do with providential polarizations which ensure that diverse traditions will be preserved. Just as Catholics and Protestants have hurled harsh polemics against each other, including such slogans as "doctrines of demons," "Antichrist," etc., and yet both churches can be authentic manifestations of the body of Christ, so despite Pauline and

---

1. Victorinus here may either be paraphrasing *Galatians* or preserving an earlier more polarized version of the *Galatians* passage than has otherwise survived.

2. See Frithjof Schuon, *Christianity/Islam: Essays on Esoteric Ecumenism*, tr. by Gustavo Polit (Bloomington, Indiana: World Wisdom Books, 1985), 28-29, 49; and Frithjof Schuon, *Islam and the Perennial Philosophy*, tr. by J. Peter Hobson (World of Islam Festival Publishing Co., 1976), 105-06.

Jacobean Christians' calling each other similar names, this does not mean that either group was false to the truth or to Jesus' teachings. Paul could no more tolerate the Jacobean Christians' devotion to Lady Wisdom than Protestants could tolerate Catholic devotion to Mary, yet the Jewish Christians' devotion to Sophia no more detracted from their devotion to Jesus than does the Catholic devotion to Mary. And the Jewish Christians were no less devoted to the Messiah than was Paul. The conflict between Paul and James is as difficult to reconcile as is the conflict between Protestantism and Catholicism, or between the Shia and the Sunnis, and the chief difficulty lies in the fact that only by a dialectical metaphysics can two seemingly absolute contradictories be harmonized in essence, and to a certain degree in details as well.

The following picture of the Ebionites and their beliefs emerges from Paul. They possess an "eloquent wisdom" (*1 Corinthians* 1:17; cf. 2:1). The "Jews," that is, Jewish Christians, "demand signs" (*1 Corinthians* 1:22) that is, miracles such as Jesus performed. In *1 Corinthians* 2:6-16 Paul uses key metaphysical Ebionite terms, but reinstrumentalizes them, adopting the outward vocabulary but strategically changing their inward meaning; as J. Reiling shows, Paul here is using his opponents' terminology related to the "searching" and "investigation" of "the spirit" into "the depths of God" (*ta bathe tou theou*) and of divine mysteries of Wisdom which are known to the "perfect" (*teleios*) and to the "pneumatic" person (*pneumatikos*) as opposed to the "psychical" person (*psuchikos*) who cannot know the mysteries of the Spirit or of God.[3] Paul here is using the Ebionites' own vocabulary in order to reinterpret the concepts in a Pauline sense. It is of the utmost significance that this passage contains the much-discussed citation from an unknown scripture in verse 9: "But

---

3. J. Reiling, "Wisdom and the Spirit. An Exegesis of 1 Corinthians 2,6-16," in T. Baarda (ed.), *Text and Testimony. Essays on New Testament and Apocryphal Literature in Honour of A. F. J. Klijn* (Kampen: Uitgeversmaatschappij J. H. Kok, 1988), 200-11.

as it is written, 'What no eye has seen, nor ear heard, nor the human mind conceived, God has prepared for those who love him'"; (as Reiling documents, the words "for those who love him" are Paul's addition to the original quotation).⁴ This "scripture" is found as a saying of Jesus in the *Gospel of Thomas* logion 17, in a form lacking the Pauline interpolation "for those who love him," but with an additional phrase, "what no hand has touched." This suggests the possibility that the Corinthians possessed a collection of Jesus sayings which contained this particular logion; Paul quotes the saying in order to divest it of the Corinthian Ebionite interpretation. This is indeed Paul's almost universal modus operandi, namely to refer to logia of Jesus without identifying them as such, and this usually occurs in polemical contexts where Paul considers that the logia are being misinterpreted or misused by his opponents, such as in *2 Corinthians* 1:17-18, where, as Wenham demonstrates, Paul alludes to a saying of Jesus preserved in *Matthew* 5:37, a logion also cited in the *Letter of James* 5:12.⁵ Wenham further shows that the Paul's wording of this logion agrees more in some particulars with *James* 5:12's version than with *Matthew* 5:37's. For Wenham this means that we have three independent versions of this logion, with Paul and James just happening to share features lacking in *Matthew*.⁶ We suggest an alternative explanation; as Wenham explains, Paul cites this logion in response to an attack made against him that he was inconsistent and "two-faced," a "yes and no man." Paul is arguing that "his word *is* true and trustworthy!"⁷ But we might ask whether Paul here is quoting the logion in a version associated with James the Just, whose famous *Epistle* seems to disagree with Paul's teaching concerning faith and works. In other words, was it James who had suggested that Paul's word vacillated between "yes" and "no"? In any

---

4. Ibid., 204.
5. David Wenham, "2 Corinthians 1:17,18: Echo of a Dominical Logion," *Novum Testamentum*, vol. 28, fasc. 3 (July, 1986), 271-279.
6. Ibid., 271-72.
7. Ibid., 274.

event, Paul is generally reluctant to cite Jesus logia explicitly as such.⁸ The reason for this will be his insistence that it was the celestial Lord and not the earthly Jesus who taught him his version of the gospel, so that he has no interest in knowing about Jesus "according to the flesh," which as we will see below operates as a polemic against James and the Twelve who knew Jesus personally in the flesh.

In the next relevant *Corinthians* passage, 3:11, Christ is described as the only foundation of the Church; this is a strategic allusion to the traditions preserved in *Matthew* 16:16ff. where Jesus presents Peter as the foundation of the Church. *1 Corinthians* 3:22's reference to Paul, Cephas, and other apostles refers to the Jerusalem authorities' denial that Paul was an apostle of equal status to the Twelve. In 9:2 Paul says, "to others I am not an apostle," a reference to the lower dignity of apostleship assigned to him by Jerusalem.⁹ In 3:22 Paul seeks to "equalize" the situation, as he does in 4:6 where he castigates those who are "in favor of one against another," and in a defensive tone in 15:10 Paul even says that he is the greatest of all the apostles. Continuing with *1 Corinthians*, in 4:10 the

---

8. Among various exceptions are *1 Corinthians* 7:10 and 9:14 which refer to Jesus' teaching on divorce and on an apostle's right to financial support for his work. In *1 Thessalonians* 4:15 "the word of the Lord" may refer to general scriptural apocalyptic promises rather than specifically to a saying of Jesus. With regard to Paul's quotation of a saying of Jesus in *Acts* 20:35, this lies outside the Pauline corpus, and having been written by Luke, he would have had authorial freedom to reword Paul's speech for various reasons such as for the sake of clarity, for synopsis, etc., redactional practices common in traditional literature. What indicates that Luke is rephrasing Paul's original words here is that he has Paul say "the words of the Lord Jesus," whereas in the letters written directly by Paul, when he clearly or indirectly refers to words of Jesus he generally uses the formula "the Lord" (as in *1 Corinthians* 7:10, 9:14, and possibly *1 Thessalonians* 4:15), rather than "the Lord Jesus," which for the historical Paul may have implied too close of an association with Jesus "according to the flesh," which for the apostle to the Gentiles has negative connotations on account of the overriding centrality of the spirit-flesh dichotomy in Pauline theological thought.

9. The portrayal in *Galatians* does not imply Jerusalem supported Paul without reservations.

Ebionites consider themselves to be wise in Christ, strong, and are held in honor. Ebionites have countless guides (4:15), a reference to the Jerusalem authorities. In 4:16 Paul admonishes the Corinthians to be imitators of him, which implies an avoidance of following Jerusalem's guides. In 6:12 Paul quotes the Ebionite dictum: "All things are lawful for me," and in 6:13, "Food for the stomach, the stomach for food."[10] This is reminiscent of James' designation of the Torah as the "Torah of Freedom." In his *Commentary on Isaiah*, Jerome records the following statement from the *Gospel of the Hebrews*: "The full fount of the Holy Spirit descended upon him. For the Lord is the Spirit and where the Spirit of the Lord is, there is liberty." *Descendet super eum omnis fons spiritus sancti. Dominus autem spiritus est, et ubi spiritus Domini, ubi libertas.* Jerome clearly presents the second sentence as well as the first as a quotation from the Aramaic *Gospel of the Hebrews*; Paul may therefore be alluding to this traditional saying or concept in *2 Corinthians* 3:17. Most scholars leave out the second sentence from their collections of fragments of the *Hebrews* gospel, presuming it to be an explanatory gloss by Jerome. In any event, Jerome's Latin does not accurately reproduce what the Aramaic would have read, for the Holy Spirit that has descended upon Jesus in the *Gospel of the Hebrews* is clearly depicted as a feminine celestial entity, which the same gospel elsewhere calls the "Mother" of Jesus. Therefore, the statement that followed in the Aramaic would have to read: "For the *Lady* is the Spirit, and where the Spirit of the *Lady* is, there is liberty." Because *spiritus* is masculine in Latin, Jerome was forced to change the feminine gender of the Aramaic term for 'Lady' (feminine 'Lord') to the masculine Latin form *dominus*, 'Lord', rather than feminine *domina*, 'Lady'.

In the relevant *Corinthians* passages Paul is arguing against the freedom preached by the Ebionites, which is an esoterically based freedom which does not contradict the heart of the

---

10. Cf. Michael D. Goulder, *Paul and the Competing Mission in Corinth* (Peabody, Massachusetts: Hendrickson Publishers, Inc., 2001), 154.

Torah, whereas for Paul only the Messiah brings liberation, and that in the mode of an abrogation of the Torah. *1 Corinthians* 6:12-13 deals with food, but food in verse 13b is associated with the theme of immorality; what is the connection? The dynamic presupposed here is that the Ebionites took a practical approach to food with their asceticism,[11] whereas Paul sees this liberal practicality as contrary to asceticism. That a law-centered religion can simultaneously emphasize the legitimacy of enjoying the good things of the earth, even to the point of apparent libertinism, is illustrated by Islam. The Qur'an often enjoins the faithful to enjoy food and the "good things" God has supplied, and certainly some might perceive the following *hadith* from Abu Hanifa's *Musnad* as exhibiting overtones of libertinism: "Do what you wish, for everyone is disposed to that for which he has been created."

In *1 Corinthians* 6:16, the theme of the two becoming one, from *Genesis* 2: 24, may be an allusion to the same Ebionite theme found, for example, throughout the *Gospel of Thomas* (e.g. logion 22), which accords with the general Ebionite teaching on the return to the prelapsarian Paradise. In *1 Corinthians* 7:1 Paul refers to the Ebionites' teaching which advocates celibacy and the "sinfulness" which can be associated with marriage. As Jews, the Ebionites could not have condemned marriage in itself; what is involved here, therefore, is the pre-Christian Jewish emphasis upon married couples either temporarily or permanently refraining from sexual union after experiencing a divine theophany. The best example of this is the Rabbinic traditions which state that after seeing God, Moses became a permanent celibate. The evidence for the advocacy of celibacy within Judaism has received increasing scholarly attention in recent years. In pre-Christian Judaism, life-long celibacy was unknown; among the Essenes, one became a celibate only after having raised a family,[12] which

---

11. Cf. the *hadith* transmitted from Abu Dharr in Muslim: "One who satisfies his appetites lawfully gains a [divine] reward."

12. On this model of Essenic celibacy see Gabriele Boccaccini, *Beyond*

is paralleled in Hinduism, where one may retire to the forest to live a celibate, solitary life only after raising a family. Later in the Syrian church, the Ebionite tradition was continued, as Vööbus has amply documented.[13] The Syrian requirement for celibacy indicates that the Ebionites held conversion to Jesus as functionally equivalent to Moses' theophany which marked his adoption of permanent celibacy.

As Horsley has argued, the celibacy of the Corinthians was based on the idea of the believer being married to the celestial Lady Wisdom,[14] an idea that likely had been brought to the Corinthians by the Jerusalem Ebionites. We disagree, however, with Horsley's claim that the idea of marriage with Sophia is to be limited to Hellenistic Judaism, because the marriage with *Hokhmah* is present already in the Hebrew scriptures (which later manifests itself in the Kabbalistic doctrine of the union of the feminine *Kneset Israel* and *Shekhinah* with the divine masculine sefirotic potencies), and traditions of celibacy and asceticism are documented also in the Rabbinic literature. In any event, as the recent research of Boyarin has revealed, it is impossible to make a complete distinction between ancient Hellenistic and Palestinian Judaism, given the interpenetration of cultures. Yet Horsley is correct when he explains that the Corinthians believed that their particular spiritual leader, whether it was Peter or someone else, had baptized them into Sophia.[15] This will not appear so strange when we recall the equivalency of Wisdom and the Holy Spirit already in pre-Christian Judaism (e.g., *Wisdom* 1:4-5). We trace the Corinthians' belief in Sophia back to the Jerusalem Ebionites; contrary to Horsley, if the Alex-

---

the Essene Hypothesis: *The Parting of the Ways between Qumran and Enochich Judaism* (Grand Rapids, Michigan: Wm. B. Eerdmans, 1998), 38ff.

13. A. Vööbus, *Celibacy: A Requirement for Admission to Baptism in the Early Syrian Church. Papers of Estonian Theological Society in Exile*, 1 (Stockholm, 1951).

14. Richard A. Horsley, "Spiritual Marriage with Sophia," *Vigiliae Christianae*, vol. 33, no. 1 (March, 1979), 30-54.

15. Ibid., 47.

andrian scripture expert Apollos taught a Sophia doctrine at Corinth, he would not have created this teaching there;[16] at most he would have confirmed the Ebionite doctrine on Lady Wisdom as the Holy Spirit. Also, the "bridal chamber" motif known from the Jewish-Christian gospels of *Philip* and *Thomas*, will likely have been connected to the ascetic idea of marriage with Sophia.[17]

Paul himself advocates celibacy within marriage in view of the impending apocalyptic disaster (*1 Corinthians* 7). In *1 Corinthians* 9:5 Paul refers to Peter and the Lord's brothers as having "sister wives," that is, celibate wives, who accompany them in their apostolic missions, possibly implying that these wives shared in the apostolic ministry, which would agree with the evidence for Jewish Christianity's institution of a female diaconate with a sacerdotal character equal to that of the male diaconate, based on the fact that men are representatives of the male Messiah, while women are representatives of the feminine Holy Spirit.[18] This practice Paul finds dangerous for the Gentile Christians, and accordingly in *1 Corinthians* 14:33-35 he refers to a general practice, "in all the churches of the saints," that forbids women to speak; yet this custom was obviously not completely universal, for Paul in combating the practice shows that it was an existing tradition. By "all the churches of the saints" Paul mostly likely means the generality of the Gentile congregations only, for the opposite practice prevailed in Jewish-Christian synagogues.

*1 Corinthians* 12:3 reveals that Jewish Christians proclaimed that "Jesus is separated," *anathema*, which should not be rendered "Jesus is cursed"; *anathema* literally means something set aside either for destruction or for the use of the sacred services of the Temple. *Anathema* is thus semantically related to the Hebrew term *qodesh*, 'sacred', 'consecrated', and the positive sense of *anathema* must be the one intended by Jewish

---

16. Ibid., 48.
17. Ibid., 52.
18. Cf. the Syriac *Didascalia Apostolorum* 2, 26, 4.

Christians in this context. In fact this interpretation of *anathema* finally provides a simple yet satisfactory explanation of the previously perplexing reference in *Didache* 16 to Jesus who will save the world as *up' autou tou katathematos*, which is usually translated as some form resembling "the Curse," but which will be properly rendered as "the Separated One," or "the Consecrated One," "the One set apart." And this usage likewise confirms the *Didache*'s Jewish-Christian provenance. Draper is correct to see in the *Didache*'s *up' autou tou katathematos* a Jewish-Christian tradition, but his conclusion that it was framed in response to Paul's remark in *Galatians* misses the mark; it is more closely related to *1 Corinthians* 12:3, which represents an authentic Ebionite Jerusalem Christology.[19]

To "separate" Jesus in this context parallels the later Catholic conception of the two natures of Jesus, which although they are united, nevertheless retain distinction strictly speaking, for the created humanity of Jesus cannot be said to be uncreated and eternal like the eternal hypostasis of the Word of God, known as the eternal Son. The Jewish-Christian Christologies expressed a similar paradigm, but in wholly Jewish categories of thought and metaphysical articulation. What Aquinas implies by his teaching that the divine nature of Christ did not die on the cross, the Ebionites expressed by saying that the Christ or Spirit departed from Jesus, or "forsook" him (without pejorative connotations) on the cross (or at some point shortly before). In any case, in the light of *1 Corinthians* 12:3 the prevailing view that "separationist" Christologies arose rather late in the early church must be abandoned.[20] *1 Corinthians* 12:3 simply refers to the Ebionite separationist Christology, and does not imply that those who shouted "Jesus is separated" were speaking in anger, as Goulder mistakenly supposes.[21]

---

19. J. A. Draper, "Torah and Troublesome Apostles in the Didache Community," *Novum Testamentum*, vol. 33, fasc. 4 (Oct., 1991), 370-71.

20. Cf. Darrell D. Hannah, "The Ascension of Isaiah and Docetic Christology," *Vigiliae Christianiae*, vol. 53 (1999), 169.

21. Michael Goulder, "A Poor Man's Christolgy," *New Testament Studies*,

From *1 Corinthians* 14 we learn that the Ebionites spoke in "the tongues of angels," but "without interpretation." This in all likelihood refers to the Jewish Kabbalistic practice of the *merkabah* ascent, during which Hebrew and Aramaic forms of angelic names were recited in order to gain access through the various celestial mansions or palaces, the *hekhalot*. The Jewish Christians who spoke Hebrew or Aramaic understood these ecstatic utterances and so had no need to "interpret" these angelic statements. Paul wants this practice to cease, not as a condemnation of the ritual in itself, but for the sake of the Gentiles who attend the services, and who cannot understand Hebrew or Aramaic. Therefore he stipulates that charismatic "tongues" should be interpreted for the sake of the Gentiles who may be present.

Jewish Christians did not share Paul's eschatological outlook of an impending disaster, at least not in the same sense, for the Ebionites possessed a realized eschatology. When the Jewish Christians in their Eucharistic celebration prayed "Maranatha, anathema!"[22] "O Lord, come for judgment," which was a prayer to God and not to Jesus, this was understood to be answered at every Eucharist, whereas for Paul the Eucharist may have indicated a mystical presence of Christ among the congregation, but not in the sense of a realized eschatology. The Jewish-Christian realized eschatology derives from Jesus traditions reflected in such sources as *John* 5:25, "Amen, amen I say unto you, that the hour comes, and now is, when the dead shall hear the voice of the Son of God, and they that hear shall live," and the *Gospel of Thomas* 51, "His disciples said to him: 'When will the day come when the dead will rest? And on what day will the new world come?' He said to them: 'What you are looking for has already come, but you do not

---

vol. 45 (1999), 346.

22. This prayer is in all likelihood a vocative form of *1 Enoch* 1:9, quoted also in *Jude* 14:1, "The Lord comes ... to execute judgment." See Matthew Black, "The Maranatha Invocation and Jude 14,15 (1 Enoch 1.9)," in B. Lindars ed., *Christ and the Spirit in the New Testament* (Cambridge: Cambridge University Press, 1973), 189-96.

see it.'" For the Ebionites this concept of realized eschatology implied that the resurrection (the rest, or repose, of the dead) had already come, and so the future resurrection was of no metaphysical concern, for only the present moment, the eternal Now, was of salvific significance. As the Jewish-Christian *Gospel of Philip* explains, "If one does not first attain the resurrection, he will not die." Resurrection in this sense comes before death, not after. This explains the extended discussion in *1 Corinthians* 15 in which Paul attacks those who deny the resurrection. These are not "Greeks" who deny the physical resurrection in favor of the belief in the immortality of the spirit or soul only, but rather the realized eschatology of the Ebionites is the issue, who in fact did not deny the resurrection as such, but rather preached that the resurrection had been realized in Jesus' ascension to God; Paul himself grants a certain degree of validity to this posture when he refers in this discussion to Christ as the "first fruits" of the resurrection.

For Paul the urgency of the belief in the resurrection relates to the necessity of the belief in the resurrection of Christ. But for the Ebionites Jesus was not raised from death, because the Ebionites did not believe that Jesus had died on the cross; they believed that he had been rescued before death, since the binding of Isaac had been a central prototype of Jesus as affixed on the cross. At the beginning of his discussion on the resurrection, Paul points out that he had received the tradition that Jesus had died for our sins, was buried, and rose on the third day. He received this tradition, however, not from the Jerusalem authorities, not from James or the Twelve, but from the Hellenistic church at Antioch.[23] The church at Jerusalem with the Twelve and James the Just at its head had no concept of Jesus' death as a sacrifice which voided the necessity of the Temple sacrifices, no more than the early Jewish

---

23. Cf. Gilles Quispel, "Paul and Gnosis: a Personal View," in Roelof van den Broek and Cis van Heertum (eds.), *From Poimandres to Jacob Böhme: Gnosis, Hermetism and the Christian Tradition*, 288.

idea that the blood of martyrs brought purification for the sins of Israel implied any rejection of the Temple sacrifices. *Acts* reveals that the Apostles continued attending the Temple services, including those that included sacrifices; *Acts* 3:1, for example, has the Apostles going to the Temple at "the hour of prayer, at the ninth hour," which is the hour of public prayer including the *Tamid* sacrifice of a male lamb. *Acts* 21 has Paul undertaking a vow which required several forms of sacrifice for sins in the Temple. As James D. G. Dunn implies, it is easier and more natural to believe that the Apostles and the Jerusalem church simply did not preach an understanding of Jesus' death as voiding the Temple sacrifices than to believe that all the Apostles and the entire church had been "Judaized."[24] The view that Jesus' death required the end of the Temple sacrificial system did not originate with the Apostles, but rather with the Hellenists of *Acts* 6-7, as Dunn points out. The Hellenists spoke only Greek and were not indigenous to Jerusalem, but had merely resettled there. These Hellenists, originally led by the later martyr Stephen, were persecuted and spread to Damascus and Antioch, where Paul was introduced to the formula that Jesus had "died for our sins."[25] It is of course natural that Paul did not require animal sacrifices for the Gentiles, for this agrees with the Rabbinic teaching of Rabbi Jochanan ben Zakkai: "In the way that sin-offering atones for Israel, so righteousness atones for the people of the world" (*Baba Bathra* 10b).

The three days concept is a liturgical-symbolic motif, for the original belief was that Jesus ascended to God from the cross, and one sees glimpses of this theme in Paul when he quotes Palestinian hymns, such as the canticle in *Philippians* 2 which equates the cross with the victorious ascension to God. From the cross God raised Jesus to Paradise, and from Paradise in the transfigured state of resurrection, Jesus appeared several times to the Apostles; thus these appearances were not

---

24. Ibid., 178.
25. Ibid., 181.

merely "visions," but real appearances, yet not crassly physical, but appearances of a being in the resurrected state. Jesus indeed suffered the nails on the cross, yet not to the point of death, just as in the case of Isaac, who had been truly bound by ropes, but who had escaped death at the last moment.

The Jewish Christians could even speak of an actual death of Jesus, but always dialectically in the sense of death *in semblance*, even if this qualification was not always stated explicitly. Jesus had been slain and died in the same sense that Isaac had been bound, and some Jewish traditions even held that Isaac had died in sacrifice.[26] Since this belief directly contradicts the clear testimony of the Torah, in all likelihood Isaac's "death" would have been understood seriously but not literally. We suggest that the binding of Isaac was interpreted as a type of sacrificial death,[27] and that his untying was interpreted as a type of the resurrection. *Bereshit Rabbah* 56 says that Abraham carried the fire wood for the sacrifice of Isaac as a cross on his shoulders: כזה שהוא טוען צלובו על כתפו. This has a bearing on two points. First, Jewish tradition could (at whatever time is beside the point in this context) portray the sacrificial wood of Isaac as a cross, and this makes it possible that the Ebionites could naturally have applied Isaac as a type of Jesus' crucifixion, thus reinforcing the docetic interpretation of Jesus' cross. Second, the phrase "to carry one's cross" is a Semitic idiom, so that where it appears in the gospels, it is to be taken in only a general sense, and not as an allusion to the crucifixion of Jesus. We find this idiom in *Matthew* 10:38, 16:24; *Mark* 8:34; and *Luke* 9:23, 14:27; the version in *Thomas* is found in logion 55, and the presence of this idiom in *Thomas*

---

26. Gedaliahu G. Stroumsa, "Christ's Laughter: Docetic Origins Reconsidered," 282-83.

27. Similarly, Paul says in *Romans* 4:19 that before the birth of his son, Abraham was not discouraged by the fact "that his own body was dead." See the discussion in J. Massingberd Ford, "'Thou Art Abraham' and upon this Rock," 294. This is just one example of a metaphorical use of the theme of death.

demonstrates that in this text it in no way of necessity refers to a knowledge of or belief in Jesus' death, *pace* DeConick.[28]

The saying from *Bereshit Rabbah* 56 also confirms Stroumsa's thesis concerning the *aqedah*'s application to Jesus' crucifixion and its docetic understanding. Stroumsa's thesis can be further strengthened when we recall that both the *aqedah* and Jesus' crucifixion took place on a mountain, Moriah and Golgotha respectively. The Ebionites would no doubt have seen in this shared detail a further reason for linking the two incidents, and they could easily have conceived of Jesus' deathless crucifixion quite literally a "living sacrifice," that is, a deathless sacrifice. Such conceptions indeed seem to have given rise to the dialectical expressions within Jewish Christianity according to which Jesus both suffered and did not suffer on the cross, with the specification that "Christ" did not suffer in the least on the cross, but rather laughed at Death.

In *1 Corinthians* 15:19 we learn that the Ebionites teach that "only those of us who are alive presently have hope," but the presupposition here is that the present generation *are* the resurrected. Such ideas were based on Jesus traditions such as are recorded in the *Gospel of Thomas* logion 11, "those who are alive will not die." Again, to show that Paul concedes a certain degree of validity to the Ebionite position is indicated by his hope in *1 Thessalonians* that the present generation will live to see the *parousia*. In any event, in *1 Corinthians* 15:29 Paul asks how one can deny the resurrection and at the same time perform baptisms on behalf of the dead. First we refer to the Mandaean practice of masses for the dead in order to clarify the nature of what Paul here alludes to. As for the question of how the Ebionites could believe in a realized eschatology (which Paul portrays as a "denial" of resurrection),[29] and perform baptisms for the dead, we must note that the fact that

---

28. See the discussion in chapter 9 in Samuel Zinner, *Christianity and Islam: Essays on Ontology and Archetype*.

29. This indicates that at least some of the Corinthians had not fully understood the Ebionite concept.

they performed such baptisms demonstrates that they did not deny the reality of resurrection carte blanche. There is no inconsistency here, for the Jewish Christians practiced baptisms for the dead on the model of Jesus and the Apostles, who were believed to have descended to the dead and baptized them. According to widespread Jewish-Christian traditions, Jesus descended to Sheol from the cross to baptize the dead, and this baptism constituted their resurrection on Good Friday as Shem Tob's *Hebrew Matthew* narrates (Greek Matthew interpolates the "after three days" motif). The *Shepherd of Hermas* documents the Jewish-Christian belief that the Apostles also descended into Sheol after their deaths. First of all, the Apostles descent to Sheol after their death is a specifically Jewish-Christian belief; secondly, *pace* Daniélou,[30] those whom the Apostles baptized in Sheol are not the "Old Testament" saints, for these were held to have been already baptized and raised by the Messiah. Those to whom the Apostles preached were either Christians and/or their believing or unbelieving relatives who had died on the one hand after the resurrection of the saints on Good Friday or on the other hand before the death of the Apostles. Thirdly, and again *pace* Daniélou, those baptized by the Apostles in Sheol experienced not only the liberation of their souls, but also a physical resurrection, as an analogue to the physical resurrection of the Jewish saints on Good Friday. This posed no theological difficulty for the Ebionites, for they would have understood that both groups of the resurrected were raised from the dead in transfigured bodies, and that they do not live in that state on this present earth, but in the hidden Garden of Eden, where Enoch, Elijah, and Ezra also presently reside in an immortal state. The fact that the theological issue of what is to happen to the faithful who die after the Apostles' death does not arise for Hermas indicates that this passage of the *Shepherd of Hermas* was in all probability written in the immediate post-Apostolic age, and so would represent one of the earliest sections of the

---

30. Jean Daniélou, *The Theology of Jewish Christianity*, 237ff.

work. We should add, however, that the evidence from *1 Corinthians* indicates that the Ebionites practiced this baptism for the dead while the Apostles were still living.

For the Ebionites, the suffering (not unto death in its full sense) of Jesus on the cross did not cancel the need for the continuing sacrifices for sin which were a part of the Temple services required by the Mosaic Torah, which states that for Jews these are to be eternal commandments. Thus the *Book of Acts* plainly states that the Apostles after Jesus ascent continued praying in the Temple and making the various sacrifices for sin according to the Torah (cf. *Acts* 2:46; 21:23ff.). This provides us with a transition to *2 Corinthians*, to which we now turn to continue a reconstruction of Ebionite belief and practice. In *2 Corinthians* chapter 1 Paul places heavy accentuation upon the theme of his own personal sufferings, which includes his battles with the Jewish Christians, and via his doctrine of the mystical body of Christ, according to which the Church's sufferings exist on a continuum with Christ's, Paul projects his own personal sufferings onto his theological portrait of Christ, and it is in this dynamic that we may in part discern the beginnings of the development of Paul's doctrine of the cross. For Paul, the immediacy of his own sufferings contributes to the concept of the *simplicity* of his doctrine of the cross, in distinction to the Ebionites, who in verse 13 are said to write things that cannot be read or understood, that is, they write deep mysteries, which accords with Paul's quotation of an Ebionite dictum in *1 Corinthians* 8:1: "All of us possess *gnosis*."

In chapter 3:1 we learn that the Jerusalem authorities issue letters of recommendation, in the sense of accreditation, so that they can prove that they are official representatives of the Apostles of Jesus. In 3:6ff. Paul attacks these letters of accreditation by comparing them to the Torah, which he also attacks as a form of bondage. When in verse 3:14 Paul says that "when they read the Torah there is a veil over their faces," he is referring to the Ebionites. Based on the evidence from Jerome, it is possible, as we previously saw, that Paul in 3:17 then quotes the Ebionites' own traditions which later found their way into the *Gospel of the Hebrews*; in this case Paul will be strategically quoting the Ebionites' scriptures against them. In 5:16 Paul reveals that his opponents are those who knew Jesus in the flesh, that is, they knew him personally; these can be none other than the twelve apostles and their extended circles. Paul polemicizes against this by asserting that he has a superior knowledge of Christ based on the spirit rather than on the flesh. In 8:4 Paul alludes to the financial offering for the poor in Jerusalem, the *Ebionim*. He then polemicizes against this group by arguing that although Christ was poor, he became rich: "For you know the grace of our Lord Jesus Christ, that though he was rich, yet for your sake he became poor, so that by his poverty you might become rich" (8:9). Similarly in verse 15: "As it is written, 'He who gathered much had nothing over, and he who gathered little had no lack.'"

In 10:7 Paul argues that his apostleship is equal to that possessed by the Jerusalem authorities: "Behold what is before your eyes. If any one is confident that he is Christ's, let him remind himself that as he is Christ's, so are we." This may even be a direct reference to James. In any event, Paul opens this polemical statement with an apparent quotation from a Jewish-Christian saying of Jesus preserved in the canonical gospels and in the *Gospel of Thomas* logion 5: "Know what is in front of your face." (Cf. also logion 91: "He said to them, 'You read the face of the sky and of the earth, yet you have not recognized the one who is in front of you, and you do not know how to read the moment"). In *2 Corinthians* 10:12 Paul anonymously refers to James and the Twelve as "those who commend themselves," who are guilty of "boasting." The Ebionites preach "another Jesus" and "a different gospel" (11:4); they are "hyper-apostles" (11:5ff.), even "false apostles, deceitful workmen, disguising themselves as apostles of Christ" (11:13). In verse 22 Paul's opponents are identified as "Hebrews, servants of Christ," but Paul considers himself "better than them" because he suffers more than they do (verse 23). These thinly veiled attacks on James and the Twelve are quite reminiscent of the Shi'ite ability "to reject ... certain venerable personages for the same reason that Islam rejects" the Church's Christology.[31] These conflicts between Paul and the Twelve also parallel the later paradigms of denunciations and recriminations between the Catholic and Protestant communities.

In *2 Corinthians* 12:2 Paul alludes to "a man" who 14 years earlier had been assumed to the third heaven. This is generally interpreted as a self-reference to Paul. However, if Paul is referring to James, then this passage would be more closely aligned with the overall context of the previous chapters. The ancient Ebionite work called the *Ascents of James* may refer simultaneously to his climbing the Temple's stairs as well as to his *merkabah* ascents to heaven (recall that *merkabah* and *hekhalot* mysticism developed as Temple-centered practices),[32] and in this case James would have had a reputation for his heavenly experiences, and it would be against these that Paul polemicizes here in *2 Corinthians* 12. That this person referred to as "a man" is not Paul seems to be indicated by verses 5ff. where Paul seems to imply that he has more visions *than his opponents*. He has so many visions, in fact, that God sends him "a thorn in the flesh, a messenger of Satan, to harass me." We would suggest that this thorn and messenger of Satan is none other than James.[33] In verse 11 Paul then avers that he "is not inferior to these hyper-apostles," which might rein-

---

31. Cf. Frithjof Schuon, *Islam and the Perennial Philosophy*, 105.

32. Consider, for example, that in *Hekhalot Rabbati*, 225-228, Rabbi Nehuniah's *merkabah* ascent takes place in the precincts of the Jerusalem Temple. The pioneering work of Margaret Barker has also identified the Temple setting of Jewish *merkabah* traditions. Cf. Margaret Barker, "Enthronement and Apotheosis: The Vision in Revelation 4-5," in P. J. Harland and C. T. R. Hayward (eds.), *New Heaven and New Earth: Prophecy and the Millennium. Essays in Honour of Anthony Gelston* (Leiden: Brill, 1999), 217-27.

33. One should recall in this context that among Jews to call a person "Satan" is not as pejorative as among Christians, for in Hebrew the word satan may merely mean an "opponent," as when Jesus in the *Gospel of Matthew* called Peter "Satan" and told him to "get out of my sight" (in the older versions, "Get thee behind me, Satan").

force the suggestion that the thorn and messenger of Satan is one of these hyper-apostles. This can be strengthened even further by referring to 11:13-14, for in verse 13 Paul refers to the "false apostles" who are "deceitful workmen, disguising themselves as *apostles* of Christ." He then comments in verse 14: "And no wonder, for even Satan disguises himself *as an angel of light*." The term 'angel' of course can be understood as 'messenger', which coincides with the meaning of the word 'apostle'. In 13:3, Paul states that the Corinthians to whom he is writing "desire proof that Christ is speaking in me"; the letter therefore ends on a note reminding us of the Jerusalem opposition which the Corinthians were following obediently, and which contested Paul's full apostleship.

Our interpretation of the "hyper-apostles" and "false apostles" in *1* and *2 Corinthians* will be confirmed as we turn now to the *Letter to the Galatians*, where Paul's opponents are explicitly identified by name, that is, as "James," "Peter," and "John," who constituted the Jerusalem leadership. In chapter 1, Paul pronounces "anathema" against those who "preach a gospel contrary" to his (1:9), which he received not from man, but by a revelation; this language is a polemical allusion to the tradition preserved in *Matthew* 16:16ff., according to which Peter received a revelation, "not from flesh and blood," but directly from God. This is the first sign of competition with Peter that we find preserved in this particular epistle. In 2:2 Paul refers to "those of repute" in Jerusalem, who are "false brethren" (2:4), who are "reputed to be something—what they were makes no difference to me" (2:6), and in verses 8-9 he identifies these as "James, Cephas [= Peter], and John." Verse 12 speaks of "certain men" who "came from James," whom Paul vigorously attacks. These men from James have caused the Galatian believers to "observe days, and months, and seasons, and years" (4:10), an obvious reference to the Torah and the Jewish feasts; this in itself reveals that the Jerusalem church continued observing all the Jewish feasts. In 4:14, Paul apparently alludes to the Ebionite angelic Christology when he writes, "you . . . received me as an angel of God, as Christ Jesus." Paul does not necessarily agree with this belief; he may merely use it strategically against the Galatians in a polemical context. 5:10 refers in the singular to "he who is troubling you," and this would seem to be James, who is behind all of Paul's problems. According to 6:12, the Jewish Christians who advocate circumcision are not persecuted like Paul is. For Paul, only those who are persecuted and suffer for their preaching are preaching the cross and are authentic apostles. This lack of persecution of the Jewish Christians by Jews is to be attributed to the fact that the Jewish authorities in Jerusalem accepted the Ebionites as fellow Jews, and the Ebionites saw themselves as faithful Torah-observing Jews as well.

The *Letter to the Romans* was written just before Paul's journey to Jerusalem, as described in *Acts* 21, which ended in his arrest; he was apparently prepared for such an event. In *Romans* he presents his overall dogmatic system including faith rather than works, spiritual circumcision, and his "spiritual Jews" or "true Israel" concept, all of which were in tension with the Ebionite theology and esoteric metaphysics. For the period after his arrest, we have the so-called Pastoral Letters, *1* and *2 Timothy* and *Titus*.[34] In these the esoteric, even Kabalistic, components of the Ebionite opponents of Paul at times come into rather clear relief. *1 Timothy* 1:4 speaks of myths, genealogies, and speculations, which given the Jewish background of Paul's Ebionite Jewish-Christian opposition, will refer to the genealogies of the Kabbalistic emanations (*sefirot, aeons*), each of which bears a name or title, and each of which possesses hypostatic dimensions, such as Lady *Hokhmah*, or *Sophia*; these same individuals desire to be teachers of the Torah (1:7), which indicates that the matters spoken of in verse 4 are part of the esoteric, Kabbalistic exposistion of the Jewish Torah, and not any form of "Hellenistic Gnosticism." The specifically Jewish nature of the opposition is also confirmed in *Titus* 1:10 where it is called "the party of the circumcision,"

---

34. For the purposes at hand the debate on the Pauline authorship of these epistles is not centrally relevant.

who exercise themselves in Jewish "myths" (*Titus* 1:14); finally *Titus* 2:9 is an exhortation to "avoid stupid controversies, genealogies, dissensions, and quarrels over the Torah," another clear reference to Jewish Kabbalistic and perhaps also *halakhah* matters. In *1 Timothy* 4:3 we learn that Paul's opposition forbids marriage and requires adherence to kosher food laws. This accords again with what is known of the practice of celibacy among the Torah-observing Ebionites. In 4:7 Paul repeats his opinion about 1:4's esoteric doctrines by writing of "godless and silly myths," which for Paul represent a form of knowledge (*gnosis*) which is falsely so-called (6:20). We receive further details on his opponents' esoteric systems in *2 Timothy*; in 2:14 he disparages their disputing about words, which will allude to Kabbalistic gematria, wordpuns, the sefirotic personification of words, *in nuce*: word mysticism, which is also what Paul condemns in 4:4 where he writes of those who "wander into myths." 2:17-18 contains a censure of the doctrine that the resurrection has already occurred, which as we have seen is a classical Ebionite tenet based on the resurrection of the saints on Good Friday. Here Paul ascribes the propagation of this doctrine to a certain Hymenaeus and Philetus, who curiously play no significant role in later patristic heresiology.

Goulder has identified several allusions to Jewish-Christian beliefs and practices in the Pastoral letters.[35] *1 Timothy* 6:15 stresses that no one *has* seen God and that no one *can* see God: "The blessed and only Sovereign, the king of those who reign and lord of those who rule, he who only has immortality, dwelling in light unapproachable, whom no man has seen, nor can see." 1:17 insists on the invisibility of God, and this implies that God cannot be seen: "Now to the King of the aeons, imperishable, invisible, the only God." Both of these verses stress the divine Unity, "the blessed and *only* Sov-

---

35. Michael Goulder, "The Pastor's Wolves: Jewish Christian Visionaries behind the Pastoral Epistles," *Novum Testamentum*, vol. 38, fasc. 3 (July, 1996), 242-256.

ereign," "the *only* God." Both verses also mention lower celestial beings, "those who reign ... those who rule," "the aeons."[36] The accentuation on the invisibility of God is an indirect attack on the Jewish and Jewish-Christian practice of *merkabah* mysticism. The "aeons" and the celestial lords and rulers are the angelic powers witnessed during the *merkabah* ascent; the aeons are also related to the doctrine of the *sefirot*. Why is the unity of God stressed in the two verses? Goulder suggests that here it is being implied that the Jewish-Christian doctrine of the aeons compromises monotheism, at least in the eyes of the Pastoral letters.[37] Certain Kabbalists have suggested this as well concerning the doctrine of the *sefirot*; for example, Abulafia once wrote that some versions of the *sefirot* were worse than the Christian belief in the Trinity. But that the Jewish-Christian doctrine of the aeons is fully monotheistic can be demonstrated by remembering that Philo held that the Logos, which for him was equivalent to Sophia, was a sort of "second God," which reminds us of Metatron's title of "lesser Lord."

*Timothy* is also very likely alluding to the Ebionite distinction between God as Essence (which the Ebionites called "the unknown Father," "the unknown God") and God as manifestation (the God of Revelation; the demiurge, Creator), which they based upon Jesus' sayings such as "no one knows the father but the son" (*Matthew* 11:27).[38] This same distincton is alluded to in the Jewish-Christian *Gospel of Philip*: "And the Lord would not have said 'My Father who is in Heaven' [*Matthew* 16:17], unless he had had another father, but he would have said simply 'My father.'" This saying has been incorrectly interpreted as implying that Joseph was the natural father of Jesus, but what is presupposed here is instead the Ebionite

---

36. See ibid., 246-47.
37. Ibid., 256.
38. The Ebionites attacked the heretical distortion that made the unknown God and the revealed God into two separate Gods, rather than as one God viewed from two different interpretative angles. See the *Clementine Recognitions* 2, 47-48.

distinction between the Unknown Father and the Revealed Father. The God of Revelation or Manifestation of course involves the hypostatic aeons or *sefirot*,[39] and the Ebionites would have held that the celestial Christ or Holy Spirit were to be counted among these divine emanational aeons, whereas for *Timothy* this would threaten the uniqueness of Jesus Christ. For the Ebionites, however, this did not threaten the primacy of Christ, for they held that he was the *highest* of all celestial powers, the *unique* archangel, a belief which agrees with Philo's doctrine of the Logos as archangel and cherub.

Goulder has identified several strategic allusions to Jewish and Jewish-Christian esoteric traditions in *Ephesians*.[40] When we move onto *Philippians*, in 3:2 Paul uses quite harsh language for his long-time Jewish-Christian opponents: "Watch out for the dogs, watch out for the evil-workers, watch out for the mutilators of the flesh." This of course is a reference to circumcision, as well as a reversal of the standard Jewish designation of the uncircumcised as 'dogs', a usage employed by Jesus in the *Gospel of Matthew*. By contrast, Paul counts the Torah and his Hebrew background "as trash" (verse 8), and desires righteousness based on faith in Christ, not on the Torah (verse 9), that he may "attain the resurrection from the dead." That we have here a polemic against the Ebionite realized eschatology which held the resurrection to be a present fact is confirmed by the following verse 12: "Not that I have *already obtained this* [i.e., the resurrection] or that I am already *perfect* [a title of the *Ebionim*]...." According to verse 17, his opponents are "enemies of the cross of Christ," which is extraordinary language to use of one's fellow believers in Jesus unless one is aware of the longstanding conflicts between Paul and the Jerusalem Church, the latter having seen no central theological significance in the cross, as can be plainly seen

---

39. We have already pointed out that the Ebionites taught virtually the same *sefirot* doctrine as contained in the classic Jewish Kabbalistic text *Sefer Yetsira*, as has been demonstrated by Shlomo Pines.

40. M. D. Goulder, "The Visionaries of Laodicea," *Journal for the Study of the New Testament*, vol. 43 (1991), 15-39.

from the *Letter of James*' complete silence on the cross or any clear reference to Jesus' death. By the term "enemies of the cross" Paul means, "enemies" to Paul's particular doctrinal interpretation of the cross formulated for the sake of Gentiles, rather than for the sake of Jews or Jewish Christians. Of the Jewish Christians Paul goes on to say that "their end is destruction," that is, damnation, and "their god is their belly," and their "minds [are] set on earthly things" (verse 19), which hearkens back to his criticism of the Ebionites' "libertinism" with regard to food in his letters to the Corinthians.

In *Colossians* 2:8 Paul attacks those who use "philosophy and empty deceit, based on human tradition, based on the elemental spirits of the cosmos, and not based on Christ." This refers to the wisdom (philosophy) of the Jewish sages, which Paul says has to do with elemental cosmic spirits; these are the angels of the *merkabah* and *hekhalot* mysticism. In verse 11, Paul polemicizes against circumcision, which for the Gentiles has been replaced with baptism. Christ defeated the angelic "principalities and powers," and Paul implies that this is one reason why Christians should not interact with angels in the *merkabah* ascent, for in Christ's own ascent he conquered and rose above all angelic forces. In verse 16 Paul reveals that his opponents passed judgment on the Colossians based upon "questions of food and drink," i.e., kosher requirements, and "with regard to a festival or a new moon or a Sabbath," which demonstrates that the Jewish Christians observed the Sabbath and other Jewish feasts. The Jewish Christians "insist on self-abasement and worship of angels" in the context of "visions" of a "sensuous mind"; this transparently involves the *merkabah* and *hekhalot* mysticism which requires asceticism and humility accompanied by visions of ascent through the celestial palaces guarded by angels which must be respectfully treated (what Paul labels "*worship* of angels").

In 4:10-11 Paul informs us that there are only three Jewish Christians, "men of the circumcision," who support him in his apostolate, but two of these may be Hellenistic Jews, as their names might suggest: Aristarchus and Mark. The third is "Jesus who is called Justus," that is, "Jesus the Just." This latter name is indeed curious; in Hebrew it would be rendered *Yeshuah ha-Tsaddiq*, therefore, Jesus the *Tsaddiq*, which is reminiscent of "James the Just."

Already in the earliest of Paul's letters, *1 Thessalonians*, in a controversial passage which many scholars consider an interpolation, he fiercely attacks "the Jews" for killing Christ; but by verse 5 the possibility appears that these "Jews" may actually be Jewish Christians, for they are "hindering us from speaking to the Gentiles that they may be saved." Paul enigmatically then concludes this passage with: "But God's wrath has come upon them at last." This would make sense as a reference to the tragic events of 70 CE, but that was still almost two decades in the future, *1 Thessalonians* having been written ca. 53 CE. What wrath fell upon Jews at the time of this letter's composition? We are at a loss to determine this; however, if "the Jews" are the Jewish Christians, then Paul could be referring to one of the early persecutions of the Jewish Christians in Jerusalem as related somewhere in the *Book of Acts*. In *2 Thessalonians* 2:1ff. we learn that someone had circulated a letter in Paul's name advocating an eschatologically realized *parousia*. Paul vigorously denies that he had propagated this letter or doctrine. No such letter survives, so it may be that the letter in question was actually *1 Thessalonians* misinterpreted by someone who read Paul's eschatological hope to be alive at the arrival of the *parousia* as being in agreement with the Ebionite realized eschatology.

Toward what he perceives as the approaching end of his life, *2 Timothy* 1:15 has Paul lament: "You are well aware that all who are in Asia have turned away from me." This is an extraordinarily informative statement which requires an explanation. Historically viewed we must ask what could have caused all Christians of Asia to reject Paul, who here is writing "in chains" after his arrest? The knowledge of such universal Asian rejection is something well known: "You are *well aware* that *all* ... have turned away from me." In answering this question it would be wise to avoid unbridled speculation; rather we should be guided by available written evidence. We suggest that *Acts* 21 and its following chapters may provide us with several of the necessary clues. Based on these chapters we know that not only the Jews but also the Jewish Christians of Jerusalem sought the arrest of Paul. When Paul was arrested, instead of accepting martyrdom, he avoided such a fate by invoking Roman citizenship. The Jerusalem leadership could hardly be expected to defend Paul after avoiding martyrdom by invoking Roman citizenship; additionally, the purpose of Paul's visit to Jerusalem was to deliver to James a large financial offering collected from all the Pauline churches for the sake of the *Ebionim* in Jerusalem. Apparently Paul was arrested before he delivered this offering to James. Now, to purchase Roman citizenship was a quite expensive transaction, and a rumor may have spread that Paul used the offering to purchase Roman citizenship. The fact that the Jerusalem authorities, that is, James and the Twelve, did not defend Paul would have "spoken" volumes to the churches throughout the Holy Land as well as in Asia.

The composition of the *Books of Acts*, with its conciliatory and harmonizing tone (compared to *Galatians* and the Pauline corpus in general) between Paul and Jerusalem, would have been written precisely in order to rehabilitate Paul in the eyes of the Asian churches after his arrest and death. Since Luke seems to betray knowledge of Josephus, his gospel may have been written shortly before the *Epistle of the Apostles* and the letters of Ignatius of Antioch. Ignatius shows no sign of knowledge of Luke's *Gospel* or *Acts*. The *Epistle of the Apostles* may have actually introduced the *Gospel of Luke* to Syrian churches. The rehabilitation required several decades to take effect, which is confirmed by Justin Martyr's complete avoidance of the person and writings of Paul. The only way the *Epistle of the Apostles* can rehabilitate Paul is to place in the mouth of Jesus a prophetic legitimization of Paul. Clement of Rome refers approvingly to Paul; *1 Clement* is traditionally dated to sometime in the 90s, but could have been written as early as the mid 70s.[41] But Clement's opinion of Paul was not

---

41. Kurt Erlemann dates *1 Clement* to the "last quarter of the first century."

necessarily shared by the entire church of Rome. The more or less contemporary *Shepherd of Hermas* demonstrates that the Roman church also had members who show no Pauline influences in the least, and that these individuals were respected and accepted as prophets whose writings later almost became canonical books; indeed, in Ethiopia the *Shepherd of Hermas* is a part of the New Testament canon.

To understand more fully Paul and his interactions with the Ebionites it will be necessary to supply more specific historical background data. Paul's first missionary journey took place in 45-47 CE,[42] and he undertook this journey as a functionary of the church at Antioch. This missionary journey seems to have polarized the conflict between Paul and Jerusalem, for in the following year, 48, the Apostolic Council headed by James was convened in Jerusalem in order to resolve the bitter disputes that had been raging about the status of Gentile believers in Jesus. The implementation of the Apostolic Decree issued under James in *Acts* 15 was rejected by Paul, as he himself informs us in *Galatians* 2 when he accuses Peter to his face (in 48, not 50 CE, *pace* Quispel) of hypocrisy under pressure from James' emissaries who delivered the decree to the Antiochene church. This led to Paul's break with the church at Antioch, and he departed on his second missionary journey which lasted 50-53 CE, and which ended at Corinth, from where he wrote his earliest known letter, to the *Thessalonians*.

What is crucial to observe here is that all of Paul's letters were written after he had proclaimed complete apostolic independence, and that his writing career began only after the break with Peter and Antioch over the issue of James. This accounts for the continual negative animus against the Jewish Christians in the entirety of the Pauline corpus. Paul's final

---

See Kurt Erlemann, "Die Datierung des ersten Klemensbriefes—Anfragen an eine Communis Opinio," *New Testament Studies*, vol. 44, no. 4 (1998), 591-607.

42. See the chronology established in Quispel, *Poimandres*, 302.

letter before his arrest in 56 CE, is to the *Romans*; since the Roman church was an important community with contacts in Jerusalem, Paul's letter to this church was written in order to pave the way for his journey to Jerusalem where he was to deliver the financial offering to James. *Romans* represents Paul's last attempt in freedom to argue his case for his version of the gospel. After his arrest, his letters reveal that he was abandoned, virtually excommunicated, by the Jerusalem and Asian churches.

We can imagine that what the delegation from James said at Antioch which drove Paul away from that church and separated him from both Peter and Barnabas must have derived its power and persuasive force from the very highest authority for even Pauline Christians, namely, the words of Jesus. We could hazard to guess that the delegation reminded the audience, in the name of James, that Jesus had said he came only for the lost sheep of the house of Israel, and that he had plainly stated that nothing would pass from the Torah until the end of the world, and that included the Sabbath observance, for had not Jesus said (*Matthew* 24, *Mark* 13) to pray that the eschatological crisis would not fall on a Sabbath, which would prevent one from traveling past the allowed distance on the Sabbath? This, incidentally, shows that even for Jesus there were situations when the principle of the Torah exceeded the value of life.

The whole thrust of such a speech by the Jacobean delegation would therefore not have been to impose further burdens on the Gentiles, but rather to reinforce Torah observance among Jewish Christians, and of course to enforce the Apostolic Decree upon Gentiles. But if the Gentiles of the church of Antioch would not accept the Jerusalem Decree regarding the prohibition against meat sacrificed to idols, then a separate Eucharist would have to be held for the Jewish Christians. The reason for this is that at this time, the Eucharist was held in the context of a full meal, known as an *agape*, or feast of love, an apostolic practice which curiously passed out of use in the early church. Peter would have been attending the common Eucharist with Gentiles, believing in good conscience that the meat was kosher and not sacrificed to idols. Somehow word got back to Jerusalem which revealed that Paul did not accept the Decree, which necessitated a delegation be sent to protect Jewish Christians from Torah and *halakhah* violation. In addition to citing the above words of Jesus, the delegation would no doubt have forcefully pointed out that Paul at the council had agreed to the Apostolic Decree.

In his *Letter to the Galatians*, Paul of course says nothing of these matters; he concentrates instead only on what he considers theological essentials, and he neglects to include Peter's self-defense. In any event, the Antioch church for the time being was won over to James, and Paul departed on his first truly independent missionary journey. Later he was to attempt to return to Jerusalem and James, but from *Romans* 15:31 it is clear that Paul recognizes the danger inherent in this move when he asks the Romans to pray for him "that I may be delivered from the unbelievers in Judaea," which refers to the Jewish Christians, not to the Jews outside the church, for there was no conflict between the church in Jerusalem and Judaism at this time; "and that my service for Jerusalem may be acceptable to the saints," that is, that the Jerusalem church authorities would accept the financial offering he would bring with him. It appears as if the offering was not delivered, the arrest of Paul intervening beforehand.

## 2. Reconstructing the Jerusalem Church's Ebionite Faith through the Jerusalem Pillars Peter and John

*Acts* 15 and the *Letter of James* give us James' position on the matter of Pauline Christianity in relation to the issue of Jewish Christianity. Since in this monograph we have already sufficiently analyzed the Jabobean traditions enshrined in these two texts, in this chapter we concentrate on the writings of the other two Jerusalem pillars, namely, Peter and John. The position of Peter is preserved in the Deutero-Clementine literature, which is sharply anti-Pauline. The conflicting evidence in *2 Peter* 3:15, which refers to "our beloved brother Paul" and "the wisdom given him," as well as to his letters, in which "there are some things ... hard to understand, which the ignorant and unstable twist to their own destruction," this may indicate a reconciliation between the Petrine and Pauline positions, yet it should be stressed that a number of fully orthodox ancient church fathers rejected *2 Peter* as a document authored by the historical apostle of that name. In any case, *2 Peter* 3:15 is a general statement without details, whereas the Deutero-Clementines lay out specific points of conflict between Paul and Peter. In the end, the Deutero-Clementine literature agrees with James' stance as known from *Acts* and the *Letter of James*. Regarding the two epistles of Peter, *1 Peter* has Pauline overtones, stressing the suffering of Jesus; in stark contrast to this, *2 Peter* does not contain a single mention of Jesus' death, and this epistle is full of Jewish-Christian traditions and terminology as well.

The account of Peter's vision at Cornelius' house as narrated in *Acts* 10 is generally misinterpreted in a Pauline sense. But Peter's own interpretation in *Acts* 11 clearly demonstrates that what is meant by the vision's contents was not that Peter could now eat food forbidden by the eternal Law of Almighty God—there is never a scene in *Acts* where Peter does anything remotely like this—but that the presence of unclean animals does not contaminate pure animals if the latter come into contact with the former. Peter's interpretation clearly reveals that the food in the vision was an *allegory* with the message that he should abandon his reservations about entering a Gentile's house, because the Gentiles who believe in Jesus do not render a Jew unclean. After retelling the vision, he does not say in *Acts* 11 that he ate a non-kosher meal, but rather: 11) "At that very moment [when the vision ended] three men arrived at the house in which we were, sent to me from Caesarea. 12) And the Spirit told me to go with them, making no distinction [between Jew and Gentile believers]." And when at the Apostolic Council in *Acts* 15 Peter refers to the same incident, he does not speak of *foods* that were purified or cleansed, but of *Gentiles* who were cleansed by their faith; *Acts* 15:9: "and he made no distinction between us [Jews] and them [Gentiles], but cleansed their hearts by faith."

Thus when Peter had been eating with Gentile believers in the church at Antioch, he was eating kosher food, but at the same table with Gentiles, which he knew did not render him unclean. The reason he withdrew from the *agape* meal with the Gentile believers after the delegation from James arrived was most likely that Jerusalem had learned that Paul did not feel obligated to implement the Apostolic Decree, which forbade the Gentile believers from the eating of meat sacrificed to idols (demons). Peter would have presumed that the meat had been kosher, purchased at the local Jewish butcher, because the Apostolic Decree would have practically required this even of Gentiles, for meat from the Antioch square would have been sacrificed to idols. Without the assurance that the meat met the requirements of the Apostolic Decree, which agrees with general Rabbinic rulings, Peter would have been obligated in conscience to withdraw from the table with Gentiles. This incident led to the famous face-to-face confrontation between Paul and Peter. Later St. Augustine and St. Jerome would strongly disagee with each other regarding the incident. St. Jerome, following general Catholic theology, believed that both Peter and Paul were infallible apostles, so that the confrontation had necessarily been feigned as such for the sake of instructing the onlookers. St. Augustine, rightly following his common sense, found Jerome's claim absurd, and asserted that Jewish Christians should be allowed to follow the Torah and Gentile Christians should be free of the Law, which incidentally is precisely what the Apostolic Decree and Rabbinic law advocates. To this Jerome became rather uncharitable and lashed out at St. Augustine, claiming that Jewish Christians are neither Jews nor Christians, and launched into an unnecessarily insensitive tirade.

The common misinterpretation of Peter's vision usually rests on an equally erroneous interpretation of Jesus' teaching on food and purity in *Mark* 7:15: "There is nothing outside the person which can defile them if it goes into them; but the things which proceed out of the person are what defile the person." Since Jesus is speaking to Jews, the food which "goes into" them would naturally be ritually clean. In other words, what Jesus is saying is that what a Jew eats does not result in ritual impurity, since Jews eat only ritually pure food; impurity is caused only when the food leaves the person in the latrine. *Mark* 7:18-19: "… 'whatever goes into a person from outside cannot defile him, since it does not enter his heart but his stomach, and so passes out, thus purging all foods." The last phrase in Greek, *katharizon panta ta bromata*, is consistently mistranslated on account of the Pauline presuppositions of modern translators as "Thus he declared all foods clean." This is a clear distortion of the Greek, which simply refers to the purging of food as excrement; thus the phrase is not a comment by the gospel writer, but is a continuation of the words of Jesus. Jesus' point is that just as food that comes from within does not make a person ritually impure until it exits in the form of excrement, so when sin proceeds outward from the heart (an analogue here to the stomach), it renders one unclean.

Some modern theologians claim that Paul never advocated that Jewish Christians abandon the Torah, only that Gentile believers should be free of Torah and *halakhah*. These theologians assert that Paul never ceased seeing himself as a faithful Jew, that he never left Judaism. Such points are often stressed by modern so-called Messianic Jews. Paul's own letters, by contrast, make such claims untenable, especially *Galatians* 1:13 where Paul speaks of his "former" adherence to "Judaism." The *Book of Acts*, which emphasizes the points of harmony in the early church, never includes a single word of conflict between Paul and Jerusalem without overlaying such with a harmonistic, pacifying layer. Paul's own letters, however, are filled with sharp statements that leave no doubt in the matter. Yet both presentations may be justified from a metaphysical perspective which recognizes various underlying commonalities of the heart in the Pauline and Ebionite versions of faith.

As far as the third Jerusalem pillar is concerned, John in his *Apocalypse* is equally direct in supporting, in the name of the ascended heavenly Christ, James' position. Once we understand the deep conflict that was raging between Pauline and Jacobean Christianity before, during, and after the time when John wrote his *Revelation*, then we can begin to find the necessary hermeneutical and historical keys to understand its description of the condition of the churches at that time. *Revelation* 2 and 3 contain seven short letters written to various churches by John in the first person voice of the heavenly Christ. *Revelation* 2:14 and 20 attacks the practice in the churches of eating food sacrificed to idols. There is, however, only one person in the New Testament who publicly endorsed the eating of meat sacrificed to idols, and that is Paul in *1 Corinthians*. In both verses of *Revelation* 2:14 and 20 this practice is linked with the theme of "immorality." What specific form of immorality is not given, but if we turn to *1 Corinthians* again, where Paul, although allowing celibacy, argues against the Ebionite encratism based on marriage to Sophia, we can confidently suggest that by "immorality" John refers to the Pauline rejection of Ebionite celibacy in the Asian churches.

Confirmation of this interpretation comes from *Revelation* itself, which in 14:1-5 refers to the 144,000 saints "who have not defiled themselves with women, because they are virgins." The implication is that those who are not virgins are "defiled" by women; this is pure encratism. When Daniel C. Olson objects to a literal understanding of this verse as "incompatible" with the remainder of the New Testament, he overlooks the fact of the diversity of views within the New Testament. Neither does Olson refer to the centuries-long requirement of celibacy for baptism in the early Syrian church, a praxis which emanated from the Jerusalem mother church; he only refers to "the ascetics and monks" that later established themselves as "a permanent fixture in the Chuch."[1] But the early Syrian celibates were not of the same category of traditional monasticism as known in the Great Church, for the latter does not require universal celibacy nor forbid marriage. Olson is correct, however, when he argues that the passage in *Revelation* 14 is based on the *Book of Enoch*'s story of the celestial Watchers who mated with human women and thus defiled themselves. But Olson does not draw the conclusion that encratite celibacy was justified precisely because these celibates viewed themselves as living an angelic life, or as in the words of Jesus (to which Olson refers), they considered themselves as "equal to the angels," for they were now "sons of the resurrection" (*Luke* 20:36), on the basis of the Ebionite realized eschatology. Finally, Olson asserts that John would not stress a literal celibacy of the 144,000 "when he ignores" celibacy elsewhere in *Revelation*.[2] But in fact John does stress celibacy elsewhere, namely in his condemnation of "immorality" in chapters 2 and 3, but this is usually overlooked by exegetes ufamiliar with the Ebionite practice of marriage to Sophia in the early apostolic churches.

---

[1] Daniel C. Olson, "'Those Who Have Not Defiled Themselves with Woman': Revelation 14:4 and the Book of Enoch," *Catholic Biblical Quarterly*, vol. 59, no. 3 (July 1997), 492-510.

[2] See ibid., 493.

We see already in *1 Timothy* 4:3 that it was Jewish Christians, those who were promoting kosher dietary *halakhah*, "who enjoin abstinence from foods" and who "forbid marriage." It is impossible that the encratite ban on marriage could have been so widespread in the early church if the practice had not had apostolic endorsement. It is interesting that what *Mark* places in the future, "when they shall rise from the dead they shall neither marry nor be given in marriage," *Luke* 20:34-35 states as a present reality: "The sons of this world marry and are given in marriage; but they that are accounted worthy to attain to that world and to the resurrection from the dead do not marry nor are given in marriage."[3] The evidence from Aphrahat on the Syrian churches' universal requirement of celibacy for baptism; the two epistles of Clement on virginity; Ignatius' attack against Jewish-Christian celibates; Ephrem's avoidance of condemning Marcion's rejection of marriage; as well as Ephrem's and other orthodox fathers' use of the encratitic *Acts of Thomas*; all of this constitutes strong evidence on just how widespred celibacy was in the early churches, which again indicates a basis in the earliest apostolic traditions.

*Revelation* 2:14 calls the practice of eating meat sacrificed to idols and immorality "the teaching of the Nicolaitans." Tradition holds that these are followers of Paul's colleague Nicolaus, who according to *Acts* was a Jewish prostelyte of Antioch, who became one of the seven deacons or leaders of the Hellenistic wing of the church in Jerusalem. Brox argues that the Nicolaitans merely used the name of the deacon Nicolaus in order to legitimize themselves. The evidence from the church fathers is divided, some of them agreeing with Brox's stance, others clearly accusing the historical deacon Nicolaus of fall-

---

3. See F. Crawford Burkitt, *Early Eastern Christianity* (London: John Murray, 1904), 120. As Burkitt points out, Luke knows only of the "resurrection of the righteous" (*Luke* 14:14); Burkitt failed to cite *Philippians* 3:11, in which Paul also presupposes a resurrection only for the just: "that if possible I may attain the resurrection from the dead."

ing into grave heresy.[4] But it seems unusual that a faithful Nicolaus would not be exonerated in *Revelation*. In any case, although the church fathers always characterize the Nicolaitans as libertine Gnostics, there is a more likely and more historically probable explanation, namely, that Nicolaus merely shared Paul's ruling on the permission to eat meat sacrificed to idols, and did not require celibate devotion to Sophia as did the Ebionites. If our interpretation is correct, then some of the conflicting patristic data concerning Nicolaus would be explained. For example, he is accused of both libertinism and encratism. But if he was a Pauline Christian, he could have been a celibate, who nevertheless advocated marriage and rejected Jewish-Christian celibate encratite Sophia marriage.

One notices that the Apostolic Decree in *Acts* 15:20 also links together the "meat offered to idols" and "immorality." As Quispel reminds us, Codex Bezae, which contains the version of *Acts* in use at Antioch ca. 100 CE reveals that the "ritual prescriptions" of the Apostolic Decree had been allegorized from "meat offered to idols" to a general ban on "idolatry," and that in fact, this Decree "was never implemented in Antioch."[5] The Decree against eating meat sacrificed to idols and against immorality (as understood by Ebionites as a transgression against celibate devotion to Sophia, required not because of an impending eschatological disaster, but on the basis of a realized eschatology) was simply rejected by Paul, and Nicolaus, who may have returned to his native Antioch to work with Paul in the Hellenistic church there, simply shared Paul's views. A blatant rejection of the Decree of James, who ruled with Peter and John, would have naturally led to John's indignation over the matter, and this is likely what we see in *Revelation* 2:14 and 20. In fact, John's seven letters reveal a mortal combat taking place between Pauline

---

4. Norbert Brox, "Nikolaos und Nikolaiten," *Vigiliae Christianae*, vol. 19, no. 1 (March, 1965), 23-30.

5. Quispel, in *Poimandres*, 289.

and Jacobean understandings of the gospel. The entire *Book of Revelation* was given to John for distribution to the seven churches named in *Revelation* 2 and 3. This suggests that the spread of Paulinism sparked the propagation of *Revelation*. However, it should be stressed that not Paul but only a certain brand of Paulinism is prophetically attacked in the name of the celestial Christ in *Revelation*. And this is theologically justified given the metaphysical legitimacy of the Judaic character of Jewish Christianity, which ironically never insisted that Pauline Christians be bound by the Jewish *halakhah*.

Beginning in *Revelation* 2, we learn of false apostles in Ephesus, where there is a growing sense of complacency, but at least they are opposed to the Nicolaitans, who are the Pauline Christians advocating the eating of meat sacrificed to idols. The church of Ephesus was of course originally a Pauline church. In the church at Smyrna, the members are "poor," that is, *Ebionim*, yet some there claim to be Jews, yet are not; this would refer to Pauline Christianity's concept of the Gentiles as the "true Israel," they are instead a synagogue of Satan. Therefore, this verse is far from representing a traditional Pauline anti-Semitism, for on the contrary, it is opposing precisely just such ideas. In the church at Thyatira there is a prophetess teaching immorality and the eating of meat sacrificed to idols, again a clear reference to the Paulines; the faithful, however, have not learned "what some call the deep things of Satan," these are perhaps the Pauline "mysteries" involving what they consider "the depths of God" (cf. *1 Corinthians* 2), which for Paul would involve the abandonment of the Torah. In the Sardis church only a few are faithful, that is, there are only a few Jewish Christians, the others are all Paulines. In Philadelphia there is intense persecution, or pressure against the faithful by the would-be synagogue of Jews, that is, the Paulines who consider themselves to be the true Israel. The picture is one of a beleaguered minority of Jacobean Christians under pressure to adopt Pauline Christianity. With regard to the believers in Laodicea, they do not care about the conflict between Pauline and Jacobean positions. Thus they consider themselves rich, but they are in reality poor, in a pejorative sense unrelated to the sense of the Jacobean *Ebionim*. In *Revelation* chapters 2 and 3 the repetition of the name of Satan is of interest. In *Corinthians*, Satan may allude to James; in *Revelation* Satan may allude back to Paul; 'Satan' means 'adversary'. It is no wonder that the pro-Paul Martin Luther wanted to expunge *Revelation* from the Biblical canon, not to mention the *Letter of James*. Again we must stress that such inter-religious conflicts may best be understood with reference to Schuon's enlightening explanations regarding the providential character of the conflicts between Protestantism and Catholicism in Christianity and between the Sunnites and Shi'ites in Islam.

The Great Church, the Pauline variant of Christianity, which is the Church of the Gentiles, by sheer force and weight of numbers was destined to overshadow Jewish Christianity. There is no room for triumphalism here, for the overwhelming success of Gentile Christianity was in part facilitated by th Romans' near extermination of Jews, which included Jewish Christians, under Titus in 70 CE and later during the time of the Bar Kochba revolt. That the remnants of Jewish Christianity were able to integrate themselves into nascent Islam constitutes a providential triumph for Jewish Christianity.

## 3. A Reconstruction of Ebionite Faith in the Diaspora. The Late 1st and 2nd Centuries, and Beyond

The ancient first-century Syrian document known as the *Didache* constitutes one of the most important primary sources for a direct reconstruction of Jewish-Christian traditions outside the New Testament. The *Didache*'s usage of the terms "Jesus" and "Christ" is quite revealing. Neither of these names occurs until the prayers of chapters 9-10. In chapter 9 we find twice the phrase "thy son Jesus," and once "Jesus Christ," and in chapter 10, "thy son Jesus" once. But when we examine these two chapters, it becomes quite evident that chapter 9's reference to "Jesus Christ" is a secondary revision to the text, reflecting later liturgical developments. This can be demonstrated on the following grounds: Chapter 9's doxology "for thine is the glory and the power through Jesus Christ for ever and ever" is an expansion of the authentic reading of the parallel in chapter 10, which lacks any reference to Jesus or Jesus Christ: "for thine is the glory and the power for ever and ever." Incidentally, all references to Jesus as "Son" in chapters 9-10 may be alternatively rendered as "servant." One also notes that in these two chapters, as throughout the *Didache*, all prayer is directed solely to God, never to Jesus. As for the term "Christ," it is found only once, in chapter 12, in a condemnation of idle people who take advantage of the community's charity, and who are thus "trafficking upon Christ." In the immediately preceding sentence, the term "Christian" occurs, but it may be a later addition to the text, which in turn might call into question the term "Christ" that soon follows. In any case, there is not a single sure instance of the term "Jesus Christ" in the entire *Didache*, and the name Jesus occurs only within the context of prayer, which is directed, however, solely to God. This is a clear marker that the text is Jewish Christian.

Chapter 3's injunction, "The accidents that befall you, you shall receive as good, knowing that nothing is done without God," is of a piece with the traditions known concerning Rabbi Akiva. Chapter 4, "you shall not say that anything is your own," alludes to the Ebionite's community of goods (cf. *Acts* 2). In the same chapter, the emphasis on the "fear of God" is equally Rabbinic and Ebionite. Chapter 6 prohibits eating meat sacrificed to idols (*contra* Paul' position in *1 Corinthians* 8). Chapter 8's references to fasting on the fourth and sixth days is a later addition, replacing the Jewish-Christian fast days of the second and fifth days of the week. Chapter 13 reveals that the community has priests and even chief-priests, who receive mandatory tithes of all goods. Chapter 14 requires the keeping of Yom Kippur and sacrifices.[1] Finally, Jesus is called *anathema* in chapter 16, a Jewish-Christian usage meaning "the Consecrated One."

The same general phenomenon of avoidance of the name "Jesus" is exhibited by the 42 Syriac *Odes of Solomon*. In these Jewish-Christian hymns there is not a single occurrence of the name "Jesus." One instead reads of "the Son" (3:7; 7:15; 19:2, 8; 23:22), "the Son of the Most High" (41:13), "the Son of Truth" (23:18), "the Messiah" (41:15), "His Messiah" (9:3; 41:3), "Lord Messiah" (17:17; 24:1; 39:11), "the Man" or "Son of Man" (12:12; 36:3; 41:12), "Son of God" (36:3, apparently in an angelic sense; 42:15). Before we summarize the Jewish-Christian components of the *Odes*, we will note that in the quite extensive document known as the *Shepherd of Hermas*, the longest of all the so-called Apostolic Fathers, again there is not a single occurrence of the name "Jesus"; neither is the word "Christ" to be found even once, which is reminiscent of

---

1. See Neville L. A. Tidwell, "Didache XIV:1 (ΚΑΤΑ ΚΥΡΙΑΚΗΝ ΔΕ ΚΥΡΙΟΥ) Revisited," *Vigiliae Christianae*, vol. 53, no. 2 (May, 1999), 197-207.

the absence of the title "Christ" in the *Gospel of Thomas*. The first reference in *Hermas* to Jesus occurs in the second vision's phrase "his son"; "son of God" is the usual title for Jesus in *Hermas*. But for Hermas, the term "son of God" is not used in the Hellenistic sense which implies divine generation, but in the Biblical metaphorical sense of "angel." Behind Hermas' usage of "son of God" also lies the concept of "servant of God." Not only the content of *Hermas* is Jewish Christian, but the structure as well, for the book is composed of 5 Visions, 12 Commandments, and 10 Parables. The pair of 12 and 10 is well known in Kabbalah as signifiying the 22 letters of the Hebrew alphabet. The 10 *Hermas* Parables allude to the 10 Mosaic commandments, whereas the 12 *Hermas* commandmandments refer to the twelve tribes of Israel. The 5 *Hermas* visions of course represent the five books of the Torah.

These curious Jewish-Christian naming practices must be explained case by case. In texts that mention "Jesus" but not "Jesus Christ" (e.g., the *Gospel of Thomas, Didache, Barnabas'* underlying source/s), this practice may be explained by the Ebionite separation of Jesus from Christ, which emphasizes that the Christ, or Holy Spirit, descended upon Jesus and was united with him, departing again at or shortly before the cross. In texts that totally suppress the name Jesus (*Hermas, Odes of Solomon*), a different, but related Jewish-Christian metaphysical motivation is operative. In this instance, the answer lies in the Jewish divine Name mysticism which was inherited by Aramaic Jewish Christianity. Just as these Ebionites piously avoided speaking the name of God (Jesus's praxis in the *Thomas* gospel is an eminent example of this), so they likewise avoided explicit mention of the name of Jesus because they believed that Jesus had been clothed with the ineffable name of God. We find the explanation for the suppression of the name "Jesus" in the Jewish-Christian *Gospel of Philip* 54,5-13: "There is only a single *name which is not spoken* in the world, the name the Father gave the Son. This is the name above everything, it is the name of the Father. For the Son would not have become a father if he had not put on the name of the Father. Those who possess this name understand it, *but they do not speak it.*" The practice is further explained in 56,3f.: "'Jesus' is a concealed name; 'Christ' is a revealed name." The name "Jesus" was therefore concealed, hidden, and reverentially suppressed and avoided, for Jesus had in effect been *transformed into the unspeakable divine Name*, that is, the Tetragrammaton. With regard to the *Gospel of Thomas*, one might ask why Jesus avoids the explicit mention of God, but the various logia are introduced by the formula "*Jesus* said." The explanation for this may be gathered from the *incipit* which specifies that this is an *esoteric, hidden* gospel intended solely for intiates, and in such a context the sacred name "Jesus" would be safe from profanation.

There is a curious statement in the *Odes of Solomon* 41:15: "The Messiah in truth is one." This may be understood in the light of the *Gospel of Philip* 59,11-18: "'Father' and 'Son' are single names, 'Holy Spirit' is a double name." The statement in *Ode* 41:15 will mean that the Messiah is one, that is, not two, the two being "Jesus" and "Christ." In other words, the celestial Messiah is the "Christ," not the earthly Jesus, which is precisely why Jesus is never called "the Christ" in the *Gospel of Thomas*. The *Odes* make a clear distinction between Jesus (who is never mentioned by name) and "the Messiah," and this division is as clear as Aquinas' later distinction between the two natures of Jesus Christ. In the *Odes*, Jesus refers to the Messiah as if the latter were a different entity than Jesus, which is similar to the canonical gospels' sayings of Jesus concerning the coming of the Son of Man on the clouds of heaven. In the canonical gospels Jesus never explicitly identifies himself with the celestial Son of Man, referring to this celestial entity only in the third person; yet to separate Jesus and the Son of Man is unthinkable. The solution to the puzzle is that these canonical sayings presuppose the Ebionite distinction between the human Jesus and the celestial angelic Son of Man who is the preexistent Messiah, or in *Hermas*' terms, who is "the preexistent Holy Spirit" who united with Jesus as a reward for his righteous conduct.

To identify the passages in the *Odes* where Jesus refers to the Messiah as an entity other than himself will require one to ignore Charlesworth's two misleading editorial blurbs placed throughout the text, "Christ Speaks," "The Odist Speaks." In all instances where Charlesworth attributes a part of an ode to Christ, we must recognize that the ode *in its entirety* is spoken solely by Christ (or Jesus). Such a procedure will clear up a number of both textual and exegetical enigmas in the *Odes*, as well as enable us to recover several important Ebionite articles of belief. Textual: for instance, in *Ode* 15:9, Charlesworth claims that the Odist "confuses the terms which came to mean 'divine Word' and 'human word'...."[2] But he makes this argument only because he refuses to see that verse 9 is spoken by Jesus, because in verse 6 the speaker states: "I repudiated the way of error, and approached him (God) and received salvation from him in abundance." Charlesworth, perhaps unable to see how Jesus could ever have needed to "repudiate error,"[3] fails to see the Ebionite emphasis here on the humanity of Jesus, which is the basis of the Ebionite doctrine of the "redeemed redeemer." *Ode* 25 contains no editorial statement "Christ Speaks" by Charlesworth; however, this ode in its entirety is spoken by Jesus, including verse 11: "And I became the Lord's through the Lord's Name," which presupposes the Jewish and Ebionite esoteric divine Name mysticism involving the hypostatic Image of God.

*Ode* 29 is another piece spoken entirely by Jesus, which is obvious from a verse such as number 8: "And He bestowed upon me the scepter of his Power that I might crush the devices of the Gentiles." But we read in verse 6: "For I believed in the Lord's Messiah, and pondered that He is the Lord." Here we have another instance of the Ebionite distinction between the created Jesus and the preexistent Christ. In *Ode* 12:12 we read: "For the dwelling place of the Word is a man." Here Jesus the man is not the Word as such, but the Word dwells *in him*. *Ode* 41 is yet again to be entirely assigned to

---

2. James Hamilton Charlesworth, *The Odes of Solomon*, 69.
3. The repudiation of error by no means necessarily implies a previous adoption of error.

*A Reconstruction of Ebionite Faith in the Diaspora*

Jesus, and not to be cut up into three distinct sections as Charlesworth does. In verses 11-15 Jesus is therefore referring to his own celestial counterpart when he refers to "His Word," "the Savior," "the Son of Man," "the Son of the Most High," and Jesus speaks even verse 15: "The Messiah in truth is one." Such a theological paradigm need not upset modern Christians, for one can recall that even according to traditional Catholic theology, strictly speaking Jesus is not the eternal Son, but rather the eternal uncreated Son, who is the preexistent Logos, was hypostatically united with the created human nature of Jesus. In the terms of the Solomonic *Odes*, because the Word, the Christ, dwells in the man Jesus, on account of that indwelling, Jesus and Christ are simultaneously separate yet united.

In *Ode* 41 the man Jesus can say that he was begotten by the pleromatic riches of God, and that "the Father of truth ... possessed" Jesus the man "from the beginning." However, even if the phrase "from the beginning" refers to the theme of pre-existence, it would be the pre-existence of Jesus the human, and thus would not strictly equate Jesus with the pre-existent Christ. But in light of verse 8, the "possession" of verse 9 and the "begetting" of verse 10 may actually refer to Jesus' historical birth. This Jesus is to be distinguished from verse 14's "Word that was in him (the Father) before time."

To identify additional central Jewish-Christian features of the *Odes of Solomon*, the Ebionite provenance of these hymns must be taken seriously. Once we do this, we can easily recognize that not only is baptism prominently alluded to in these texts, but also the physical rite of circumcision is dominant as well, and this explains the frequent symbol of the crown, which is present from the very first line of *Ode* 1, for the crown would in this context at least indirectly allude or presuppose the corona which is exposed during circumcision. When an adult prostelyte was circumsized, baptism followed as soon as healing was accomplished (usually about a week), and this explains why in the *Odes* the theme of the crown usually precedes the imagery of baptismal water. If one examines the *Odes* impartially and without anti-Jewish bias, the allusions to circumcision (as well as a number of other Jewish components) will be quite readily recognizeable. *Ode* 11 especially conforms to the traditions relating to circumcision; after circumcision (verses 1-3), baptism follows (verses 6-8), and then, just as Abraham experienced a celestial vision after his circumcision, so here a *merkabah* vision of Paradise begins (verse 16), whose account contains a celestial hymn of praise, as is standard in *hekhalot* accounts (verses 18-19).

In the *Odes*, circumcision is called the "seal" (4:7-8), the "sign" (29:7). In 27:2, the upraised arms may signify the letter *shin*, denoting the name *Shaddai* which is inscribed on the phallus by circumcision.[4] *Ode* 39:7-8 contains a rather clear allusion to circumcision: "the sign on them is the Lord," that is, the Tetragrammaton which is inscribed on them by circumcision, and with this sign they safely "cross in/with the name of the Lord," "And you shall cross without danger"; 42:1. The frequent "crown" (5:12; 9:11; 11:16; 20:7) is, as remarked above, eminently compatible with the rite of circumcision. In 42:20, "I placed my name upon their head," here the "name," which by implication is the Tetragrammaton, is equivalent to the crown of circumcision. This raises the possibility that the very first line of the *Odes*, 1:1, and the very last line of the *Odes*, 42:20, may contain allusions to circumcision. The *Odes* exhibit a positive attitude towards the Torah, which is given the title "Love" (41:6; this is not a "replacement" of the Torah with love, but clearly an equation of Torah = love). Jesus is the servant of God (29:11), created by his Mother the Holy Spirit (36:5); Jesus as a man was given the name of the angelic Son of God, who is exalted above the highest of the angels (36:3-4); Jesus is separate from Christ or the Messiah (41:3, spoken by Jesus: "We receive life by his Messiah," *contra* Charlesworth who claims Jesus begins speaking only in verse 8); Jesus came for the redemption and instruction not of the

---

4. Cf. Elliot Wolfson. "Circumcision and the Divine Name: A Study in the Transmission of Esoteric Doctrine," *The Jewish Quarterly Review, New Series*, vol. 78, no. 1/2 (Jul. - Oct., 1987), 77-81.

Gentiles, but of his nation Israel, to fulfill the promises to the patriarchs (31:12-13). Prostelyte baptism may be alluded to frequently (4:10; 6:11, 18; 30:1-7; 35:1-2); *unio mystica* and equality, often with erotic imagery as in the *Song of Songs* is attested (3:7; 12:9-10; 14:2; 34:3), as is the related theme of immortalization (3:8-9; 5:14).

Typically Jewish Christian is the practice of imprecatory prayer (5:4-9), as well as a positive animus towards the Jerusalem Temple (6:8). The *shiʿur qomah* concept is reflected in 7:3; 17:15-16. No "sacrifice" of Jesus is referred to (*contra* Charlesworth, 7:10, "sacrifice," *thusia* is a misreading for "Being," *ousia*). Jesus was saved and redeemed (7:15-16; 8:21; 17:1; 25:12; 29:5; 42:18); the faithful preexist (8:13; 23:2-3). The "seal upon their faces" (8:13) may allude to the covenant of the tongue or mouth, which is the Torah, in contrast to the covenant of the foreskin.[5] Similarly among the Dead Sea Scrolls, the *Manual of Discipline* 10:10 refers to the covenant of Torah recitation: "When day enters, and when night enters, I will enter into the covenant of God; with the departure of evening, and with the departure of the morning, I will recite his statutes."

The Odes emphasize righteous works (11:20) and praises of the celestial Mother the Holy Spirit (6:7; 13:2). God is the mirror image of humanity (13:1). An accentuation is placed upon "rest," presupposing a positive attitude regarding Sabbath observance (3:5; 11:12; 15:3; 16:12; 20:8; 28:3; 30:2; 35:4, 6; 36:1; 37:4; 38:4). Jewish-Christian themes of celibacy (38:9-22); *merkabah* chariot mysticism (38:1), and hypostatic Name mysticism are present (15:8; 18:1; 25:11; 33:13; 39:13, the faithful "adore his name," that is the name of the "Lord Messiah," which refers to the name of the Father bestowed upon the Son, not to the name "Jesus" strictly speaking; 41:15, again, the name of the Messiah is the name of the Father, not "Jesus"). The divine mysteries are now revealed (16:8-9); all things subsist within the divine Being (16:18); God dwells in

---

5. Elliot Wolfson, "Circumcision and the Divine Name: A Study in the Transmission of Esoteric Doctrine," 96.

the faithful (32:1). The Word is self-originate (32:2; this contradicts the Hellenistic teaching of Philo and the *Corpus Hermeticum*, but agrees with Mandaean teaching, as we detail in our textual-philological *Thomas* commentary).

According to the *Odes*, Jesus did not die on the cross (28:8; this is spoken by Jesus, "the Spirit which is within me ... cannot die because it is life," that is, the Christ or Spirit dwelling in him since his baptism is not subject to death. A docetic "death" is confirmed by 28:10, 17-18; 42:10, 17); no "resurrection" of Jesus is referred to (*contra* Charlesworth, 17:13 must not read "resurrection," but "prayer"). The divine breath has been breathed into the faithful (18:15); the Holy Spirit is the celestial Mother (19:2, 4); the celestial Virgin, the Holy Spirit dwells in the faithful (33:8). Priests sacrifice in the community (20:1-3; they do not sacrifice "according to the flesh," this means not according to "the world," and thus does not necessarily imply a denial of physical sacrifices). The "cross" in the *Odes* reflects not the Pauline doctrine of the cross, but is a beam of wood that forms a bridge over the waters of death, which are crossed safely by the circumcised (39:7-10, 13). The wood may refer to the wood of Isaac's *aqedah*. If the *Odes'* wood alludes to the cross, this will be a docetic cross inseparable from the wood of the *aqedah*.

We note here an uncanny resemblance between *Odes of Solomon* 42:10 and Qur'an *sura* 4:157. *Ode* 42:10: "And I was not rejected although I was reckoned to be so; and I did not perish, although they thought it of me." Qur'an 4:157: "They did not kill him, nor did they crucify him, although it was made to appear to them as such." Charlesworth is confused by *Ode* 42:10's "docetic nuance" followed "clearly" by "the *descensus ad inferos*."[6] The solution is to take seriously the Jewish-Christian provenance of the *Odes*, which necessitates that the idea underlying this passage is that Jesus (or perhaps the Christ) descended to hell *alive*, for as the *Odes* elsewhere teach, the Messiah cannot die, 28:8, "the Spirit which is within me ...

---

6. James Hamilton Charlesworth, *The Odes of Solomon*, 147.

cannot die because it is life," and in O*de* 42:17, the dead speak to Christ in hell: "For we see that our death touches you not."

In the entirety of the massive *Clementine Homilies*, the name "Jesus" is found only 25 times (compare this to 170 times in much shorter *Gospel of Matthew*), "Jesus Christ" only three times, and another two times we read that "Jesus must be revealed to be the Christ" (2,17) and "Jesus, who with you is called the Christ" (spoken by the heretic Simon, 18,4). The term "Christ" is present roughly 40 times, and is therefore noticeably more frequent than "Jesus." In the *Recognitions*, which are generally viewed as having undergone extensive revisions in an orthodox direction, we find "Jesus Christ" four times (2,19; 2,46; 7,23; 10,70), "Christ Jesus" twice (1,45; 1,62), but also instances where Jesus is identified with the Christ (1,44; 1,60; 1,63; 1,68; 1,73). All in all, the text contains the name "Jesus" about 39 times, therefore more than in the *Homilies*, but still nothing approaching *Matthew*'s 170 instances of "Jesus."

The *Clementine Homilies* 7,8 contains a mini Jewish-Christian catechism which is noticeably theocentric rather than Christocentric:

> And this is the service He has appointed: To worship Him only, and trust only in the Prophet of truth, and to be baptized for the remission of sins, and thus by this pure baptism to be born again unto God by saving water; to abstain from the table of devils, that is, from food offered to idols, from dead carcases, from animals which have been suffocated or caught by wild beasts, and from blood; not to live any longer impurely; to wash after intercourse; that the women on their part should keep the law of purification; that all should be sober-minded, given to good works, refraining from wrongdoing, looking for eternal life from the all-powerful God, and asking with prayer and continual supplication that they may win it.

*Homilies* 11,20 contains the first reference to the cross, but without the doctrine of atonement or expiation in a Pauline sense, but in an exclusively imitative sense of mortification:

For the Teacher himself, being nailed to *the cross,* prayed to the Father that the sin of those who slew him might be forgiven, saying, "Father, forgive them their sins, for they know not what they do." They also therefore, being imitators of the Teacher in their sufferings, pray for those who contrive them, as they have been taught.

The *Epistle of Barnabas* exhibits a curious mixture of knowledge of Jewish traditions not usually known to non-Jews and anti-Jewish polemic. One must carefully distinguish between these two dimensions when discussing *Barnabas.* One element of this epistle that seems to reflect Jewish-Christian tradition is its avoidance of the term "Jesus Christ." There appears to be only one instance of the term "Jesus Christ" in the entirety of this extensive text, namely, in chapter 2's phrase "the new law of our Lord Jesus Christ." But in light of the avoidance of "Jesus Christ" elsewhere, this may have arisen as an interpolation, just as Codex Sinaiticus reveals that the phrase "our Lord Jesus Christ" at the opening of chapter 1 was originally "our Lord."[7] This means that the phrase in chapter 2 may simply constitute an imitation of an interpolation in chapter 1. Codex Sinaiticus' reading of chapter 1's "our Lord" has to be the authentic reading, for no Christian would have deleted "Jesus Christ" from the passage.

After the New Testament, one of the most significant extensive sources for an indirect reconstruction of classical Ebion-

---

7. As for the remainder of *Barnabas,* chapter 4 speaks of "the beloved Jesus." Chapter 6 has one instance of "Jesus." Chpater 7 thrice contains the phrase "the type of Jesus," but in the first instance Codex Sinaiticus has "the type of God," which is, however, then emended to "the type of Jesus." In chapter 8, we find "Jesus" twice; but in the first instance Codex Sinaiticus has "the law is Christ Jesus" instead of the standard reading "the calf is Jesus." In chapter 9 we find "Jesus" three times, in chapter 11 once. In chapter 12, "Jesus" is given five times, and "Christ" three times. Chapter 14 once has "the Lord Jesus," and in chapter 15 there is one occurrence of "Jesus."

ite belief and practice is constituted by the letters of Ignatius of Antioch.[8] By examining the beliefs of Ignatius' opponents, we see that they coincide with those of Paul's Jewish-Christian opponents. We find Ignatius' opponents occupied with "fables" (*Magnesians* 8), the same Jewish fables we read of in *Titus* 1:14 and 3:9. In *Trallians* 4 Ignatius implies that he has more visions, than his opponents, of "heavenly things and the arrays of angels and the musterings of the principalities, things visible and things invisible," which Goulder correctly interprets as a strategic allusion to Jewish *hekhalot* mysticism.[9] Goulder also correctly interprets Ignatius' warning against separate Eucharistic meetings as alluding to Jewish-Christian Eucharistic services which did not allow Gentile Christians to attend,[10] which was in fact the praxis implicitly required by the Apostolic Decree issued under James in *Acts* 15. From *Magnesians* 9 we learn that the Ebionites observe the Sabbath. *Smyrnaeans* 2 reveals that the Ebionites teach a docetic passion of Jesus.

There is conflicting evidence in the church fathers' writings on the question of the theological posture the various Jewish-Christian congregations took with regard to Jesus' virgin birth. Since the Qur'an's comments on Christian beliefs agree overwhelmingly with Semitic and Jewish-Christian theological orientations, the fact that the Qur'an propounds Jesus' virginal conception suggests that this belief did not originate solely in the Hellenistic congregations. A possible solution to the issue could be that the Ebionites did not deny the virginal conception as such, but that by rejecting the outward expression of the doctrine they were rejecting the doctrine's corporeal implications with regard to God as understood by pagan Gentile congregations. In view of these considerations it may be that the church fathers through a misunderstand-

---

8. See Michael D. Goulder, "Ignatius' 'Docetists,'" *Vigiliae Christianae* vol. 53 (1999), 16-30.
9. Ibid., 18.
10. Ibid., 20.

ing created an artificial distinction between the "heretical" Ebionites who supposedly rejected the dogma of the virginal conception in any sense and the reputedly more "orthodox" Nazarenes who accepted this dogma. In other words, the Nazarenes may in fact merely have been a group of Ebionites of the stripe represented by the author/s of the *Gospel of Philip* who strategically used the Pauline corpus in their missionary outreaches to Pauline Christians.

Similarly when the Qur'an denies Jesus' crucifixion, or more accurately, his death (at least in a definitive sense), it is in essence denying the Hellenistic understanding of the cross as held by Pauline Christianity. Similarly, the Mandaean rejection of Moses implies not so much a rejection of Moses as such, but a rejection of Judaism as represented symbolically by Moses. To phrase it theologically, the rejection has more to do with the historical manifestations of Judaism than with its celestial essence.

Irenaeus writes that the Ebionites possess *Matthew*'s gospel without a virginal conception narrative, and deduces from this that they have deleted the passage. But this, on the contrary, may indicate that the earliest versions of *Matthew* may not have contained an account of Jesus' birth. Like *Mark*, *Matthew* may originally have begun with the baptism story, and this conceivably might be why Jerome singled out this particular passage of the *Gospel of the Hebrews* for citation, namely, this account could have been the beginning of that particular gospel, perhaps reflecting some genetic connection with a Semitic language edition of *Matthew*.

Goulder's assertion that the Ebionite doctrine of the Holy Spirit is older than the angelic Christ belief is unnecessary,[11] for there is no reason why both formulations could not have

---

11. Michael Goulder, "A Poor Man's Christology," *New Testament Studies*, vol. 45 (1999), 336. Later Goulder corrected himself on this point, and traced the Ebionite belief in Christ as an angel back to primitive times, for he insists it is presupposed already by the time of the *Letter to the Hebrews*; cf. Michael Goulder, "Hebrews and the Ebionites," *New Testament Studies*, vol. 49 (2003), 397.

*A Reconstruction of Ebionite Faith in the Diaspora*

been present from the beginning of the church. Already in the *Parables of Enoch*, the Messiah is a celestial, not an earthly, entity. And Paul may be quoting the *Gospel of the Hebrews* when he writes that "the Lord [Christ] is the Spirit." In any event, Paul's use of the term "Spirit of Christ" presupposes a functional equivalence between the Messiah and the Holy Spirit. Similarly, Goulder's claim that the *Acts of John*'s idea of Jesus' "spiritual double" is later than the earlier Ebionite faith in the Spirit or Christ which entered into Jesus, is unwarranted,[12] for the idea of a spiritual double is rooted in concepts already prevalent in pre-Christian Judaism.[13]

In the *Shepherd of Hermas*, a celestial woman appears to Hermas holding a book; this is curiously paralleled conceptually in the Qur'anic image of the *umm al-kitab*, Mother of the Book. According to the *Gospel of the Hebrews*: "The full fount of the Holy Spirit descended upon him. For the Lord is the Spirit and where the Spirit of the Lord is, there is liberty." Above we emended Jerome's translation of the second statement to read: "For the Lady is the Spirit and where the Spirit of the Lady is, there is liberty." But another possibility is that the text as quoted by Paul identifies the masculine Christ with the feminine Spirit, so that Christ is the Holy Spirit. In support of this possibility is *Hermas*' teaching that "the Holy Spirit who spoke with you in the likeness of [the Lady] Ecclesia is the Son of God" (Similitude 9,1,1). For *Hermas* the pre-existent Son is the Holy Spirit; the historical Jesus is "the servant" of God. This perfectly parallels *2 Clement* 14's statement that the pre-existent female Lady Ecclesia "was manifested in the flesh of Christ," the pre-existent male; the pre-existent Lady Ecclesia "was spiritual, as our Jesus also was spiritual, but was manifested in the last days that She might save us." Clement here repeats that "Christ is the spirit."

---

12. Ibid., 339.
13. Cf. April DeConick, *Seek to See Him. Ascent and Vision Mysticism in the Gospel of Thomas*, 148–72.

*The Gospel of Thomas*

The most natural explanation for this gender fluidity might be the ancient doctrine of androgyny, and this is made explicit by *Clement* who introduces this section with a reference to the creation of Adam and Eve. *2 Clement* also sheds light on the origin of the concept of the Church as the body of Christ, for when Christ appeared on earth in the flesh, that flesh was the earthly manifestation of the celestial Lady Ecclesia, the Holy Spirit. However, in Jewish Christianity, the Holy Spirit united with Jesus at his baptism. According to Hermas *Similitude* 5, 6, Jesus was adopted by God as companion of the Holy Spirit as a reward for his righteous conduct. When we take into account that for Hermas the Holy Spirit (who is the Son of God) is the archangel Michael,[14] then we arrive at the Ebionite angelic Christology.

The *Gospel of Philip* contains several profound reflections on the Jewish-Christian doctrine of Sophia. In folio 52 we read that Hebrews have a mother, while Christians have a father and a mother. This may be related to folio 77: "Truth is the Mother, Knowledge (Gnosis) is the Father." In folio 55, the archons unknowingly do what they do by the will of the Holy Spirit. Furthermore, the Spirit is the celestial Mother, and as such Mary did not conceive by the Spirit. Folio 71 clarifies that the virginal conception was caused by "the Father of the Pleroma," and Jesus was born of "a bridegroom and a bride," suggesting the Father and Mother. Thus the conception is from the Father, and the birth delivery is from the Mother. This is followed by a reference to the two fathers of Christ; this does not contradict the Virginal conception, which is clearly upheld in folio 71.

In folio 59, we read of the three Marys, which is immediately followed by a saying on the upper and lower Holy Spirit.

---

14. This identification is denied by some theologians, but as J. N. D. Kelly observes on *Hermas*, "Both [the Son of God and Michael] ... are invested with supreme power over the people of God; both pronounce judgment on the faithful; and both hand sinners over to the angel of repentance to reform them." J. N. D. Kelly, *Early Christian Doctrines* (San Francisco, California: Harper & Row, 1978), 95.

Then follows a saying that evil forces have been tricked by the Holy Spirit into serving the saints (this is reminiscent of the demons serving Solomon in the construction of the Temple), illustrated by Jesus' words, "Ask your mother," suggesting that the Mother is the Spirit. Then comes a saying on Sophia who as pillar of salt is barren without children; the text then becomes fragmentary, but may contrast the barren Sophia with Wisdom as the Holy Spirit who is fruitful with many children. In folio 60 the Spirit leads her offspring astray, so that from a single Spirit "the fire is ignited and extinguished." Then follows a distinction between Wisdom, *Echamoth*, and *Echmoth*, which is Hebrew *'ekh-moth*, "like death,"[15] the latter being "the Lesser [little] Sophia." According to folio 63, "Wisdom designated as barren is the mother of the angels," which is followed by a reference to Mary of Magdala, suggesting that she is a manifestation of Sophia. As already noted, folio 77 explains that "Truth is the Mother, Knowledge (Gnosis) is the Father." In folio 68, we find a doctrine of two fathers, as in 75's allusion to the limitations of the demiurge. Folio 84 reveals that the demiurge, in the words of Meyer, can be "kinder and gentler ... not entirely diabolical."[16] This reminds us of Buckley's comments on the ambiguous Mandaean *Ruha*, of how scholars ignore her positve side, mistakenly portraying her as entirely evil.[17]

Folios 70-71 reflect an Ebionite understanding of Jesus' baptism. In folio 76, divine union "is a different kind of union. Even if we allude to these matters with the same words, there are other words [matters] that are transcendent to any word that is pronounced.... This cannot be comprehended by natural minds [literally, hearts of flesh]." Folio 79, "Blessed is the one who has never grieved a soul. Such is Jesus Christ," may be compared with Jerome's quotation from the *Gospel of*

---

15. See the comment in Marvin Meyer ed., *The Nag Hammadi Scriptures. International Edition*, 168.

16. Ibid., 185.

17. Jorunn Jacobsen Buckley, "A Rehabilitation of Spirit *Ruha* in Mandaean Religion," *History of Religions*, vol. 22, no. 1 (Aug., 1982), 60-84.

*the Hebrews* in *On Ephesians* 5:4: "And never be joyful except when you behold your brother with love," as well as in *On Ezekiel* 18:7: "'If a man has grieved the spirit of his brother' is placed among the greatest sins." Folio 82 forcefully insists on circumcision.

Meyer, not recognizing the predominantly Jewish-Christian complexion of the *Gospel of Philip* incorrectly labels folio 73,3-15 as "The Mystery of the Virgin Birth," when in fact the passage is about the Holy Spirit giving birth to Jesus at his baptism in the Jordan, which is related immediately prior to this section:

> Jesus manifested himself at the Jordan river as the fullness of the kingdom of heaven. The one who was conceived before the pleroma was conceived again. The one who had been anointed previously was anointed again. The one [already] redeemed redeemed others. It is necessary to declare a mystery. The Father of the Pleroma united with the Virgin who descended, and fire shone upon him [i.e., upon Jesus]. On that day he [Jesus] manifested the great bridal chamber, and in this manner his body came into existence. On that day he he exited the bridal chamber as one born of a bridegroom [the Father] and a bride [the Spirit Mother]. Thus Jesus established the pleroma in it [the bridal chamber], and it is appropriate that each disciple enter into their repose [in the bridal chamber]."

This refers to the Syrian tradition of the fire which shone on the Jordan at Jesus' baptism. We read of this in Tatian, and also in the *Gospel of the Ebionites*:

> After the people were baptized, Jesus also came and was baptized by John; and as he came up from the water, the heavens were opened, and he saw the Holy Spirit in the likeness of a dove that descended and entered into him, and voice from

heaven saying: "You are my beloved Son;[18] in you I am well pleased"; and again: "This day have I begotten you." And immediately there shone about the place a great light, which when John saw it, he said, "Who are you, master?" And again a voice from heaven saying unto him: "This is my beloved Son in whom I am well pleased." And then John fell down before him and said: "I beseech you, master, baptize me." But he prevented him, saying: "Let it proceed; for thus it is necessary to fulfill all things."

As in the *Gospel of the Hebrews*, the heavenly voice that speaks is the celestial Mother the Holy Spirit who gives birth to Jesus at his baptism.

The Syrian Narsai (born in the first half of the 5th century) in one of his spiritual poems recreates the scene of Jesus' baptism at the Jordan by employing the imagery of bridegroom, bride, and wedding day:

1. My spirit carried me to the Jordan,
And I beheld a wondrous event,
How the glorious bridegroom revealed himself
To perform the marriage with the bride, and to make her holy.
4. The bride is betrothed without knowing
Who the expected bridegroom is.
5. Then the bridegroom revealed himself
and came to John at the river.[19]

---

18. As is well-known, the Aramaic word *thalya* can mean either "child" or "servant," and the original sense of the passage above would have been "servant," given that the statement is an allusion to *Isaiah* 42:1: "Behold my servant, whom I uphold, mu chosen, in whom my soul delights; I have put my spirit upon him...." 'Servant' in Hebrew is *ebd*, cognate with Arabic *abd*. That 'servant' in Aramaic, *thalya*, also can mean 'child' enabled the Aramaic-speaking followers of Jesus to discern in the baptismal 'servant' the mystery of 'child', or 'son'. The fact that the concept and terminology of Jesus as 'son of God' was not in use in the earliest stages of the church's teaching suggests that it developed out of the earlier 'servant' ideology.

19. Our translation from the Syriac text in Franz Feldmann, *Syrische Wechsellieder von Narses. Ein Beitrag zur altchristlichen syrischen Hymnologie*

Narsai (or tradition before him) has transformed the original meaning of the imagery, according to which God and the Holy Spirit were bridegroom and bride, and transformed the bridegroom into Christ and the bride into the faithful. The evidence from *Philip* and *Narsai* may shed light upon *Thomas* logion 104, which refers to the bridegroom and the wedding chamber in the context of fasting and prayer: "They said to Jesus: Come, let us pray and fast today. Jesus said: What sin have I committed, or how have I been conquered? Instead, when the bridegroom has departed the wedding chamber, then let people fast and pray." Jerome quotes approvingly from the *Hebrews* gospel: "Behold, the mother of the Lord and his brethren said unto him: John the Baptist baptizes unto the remission of sins; let us go and be baptized of him. But he said to them: In what have I sinned, that I should go and be baptized of him? Unless perhaps this very thing that I have said is a sin of ignorance." (Ecce mater Domini et fratres eins dicebant ei: Ioannes baptista baptizat in remissionem peccatorum; eamus et baptizemur ab eo. Dixit autem eis: Quid peccavi, ut vadam et baptizer ab eo? Nisi forte hoc ipsum, quod dixi, ignorantia est). And then shortly thereafter Jerome approvingly quotes the words of Jesus from the *Hebrews* gospel again: "For in the prophets also, after they were anointed by the Holy Spirit, the word (matter) of sin was found." *Thomas* 104 and the passage from the *Hebrews* gospel are transparently related somehow. In light of *Philip*'s and Narsai's associating the theme of the bridal chamber with the baptism at the Jordan, we can deduce that *Thomas* 104 refers to the prayer and fasting which traditionally precedes baptism, and that the "they" of *Thomas* are the *Hebrews* gospel's "the mother of the Lord and his brethren," and because of the traditional association of the Jordan baptism with the bridal imagery, *Thomas* 104 was able to replace the explicit mention of the baptism with the bridal theme. Thus we regain another connection between *Thomas* and the *Gospel of the Hebrews*.

---

(Leipzig: Otto Harrassowitz, 1896), 11.

The account of Jesus' baptism and the fire over the Jordan in the *Gospel of Philip* continues: "Adam originated from two virgins, the Spirit and the Virgin Earth. Christ was born of a virgin to remedy to the fall that took place in the beginning." Given that the previous sayings relate to Jesus' birth from the Virgin Spirit at his baptism, this saying also should be consistently interpreted as referring to Jesus' baptism, not his birth from Mary. Jesus' baptism, not the cross, reverses the fall. Jesus was thus born, was made alive, at the baptism, long before the cross; it is against this background that we can understand folio 56: "The ones who say the Lord died first and then arose are incorrect, because he first arose and then died."

In contrast to *Thomas'* historically accurate usage of first-century Palestinian Jewish manners of avoiding direct reference to the name 'God', in the *Gospel of Philip* one finds over two dozen occurrences of the word 'God'. Incidentally, this alone indicates that the *Gospel of Philip*, which is undoubtedly a Syrian Jewish-Christian document, has nevertheless adopted a particular manner of speech to facilitate its being understood more readily by a diaspora Hellenistic Jewish community, which is self-obvious in light of *Philip*'s quotations from the Pauline corpus and the canonical gospels. Philip's strategy is to bring his readership to view such Greek literature through a more traditional Semitic prism, hence his correcting the neuter/masculine conception of the Holy Spirit to her proper feminine nature (55,23-33), as well as an obvious insistence on the practice of circumcision: "When Abraham became capable of seeing what he was [destined] to see, he circumcised the flesh of the foreskin, teaching us that it is necessary to destroy the flesh" (82,26-29). The reference here is to the Jewish tradition that circumcision enables one to see the vision of God. In the lines that follow *Philip*'s saying on circumcision, the reference to the ax that is laid at the root of the trees (cf. *Luke* 3:9) may simultaneously function as an allusion to the knife of circumcision.

A further important indication of the essentially Jewish-Christian origins of the *Gospel of Philip* has generally gone unnoticed; the gospel is named after "Philip the apostle" in folio 73,8-19. There Philip twice clearly refers to Jesus as the "offspring" of Joseph. It would seem to be no coincidence that when Philip the apostle is first introduced in the *Gospel of John* 1:45, he speaks to Nathanael and refers to "Jesus of Nazareth, *the son of Joseph*." In verse 48 Jesus speaks to Nathanael: "Before Philip called you, when you were under the fig tree, I saw you." Similarly in *Philip* folio 73,8-19, Philip refers to a "garden" (literally, 'paradise') of *trees* planted by Joseph; "garden" of course reflects idiomatic Hebrew and our passage should thus be translated "Joseph the carpenter planted an *orchard*," just as the *Song of Songs* 6:11 should be rendered "orchard of nuts" rather than "garden of nuts." Nevertheless, the use of the literal word "garden" serves as an allusion to the Garden of Eden with its tree of life. According to some Rabbinic traditions, the tree of life in paradise was a *fig tree*. In any case, Philip's explicit and repeated references to Jesus as the offspring of Joseph confirms the Ebionite character of the apostle Philip's faith. This rejection of the virginal conception of Jesus, however, does not necessarily imply that Philip, like other Ebionites, literally rejected the supernatural character of Jesus' conception *en toto*. Rather, what it implies is a rejection of the non-Jewish and Hellenistic interpretation or understanding of the virginal conception as being too perilously close to pagan ideas regarding the divine as quasi-corporeal, and this is precisely the same misunderstanding that is attacked in the Qur'an, as we have previously explained.

In *John* 12:20-21, Philip functions as an intermediary between Greek-speaking Jews, who had come to worship in Jerusalem, and Jesus. This is paralleled by the *Gospel of Philip* which serves a communication reaching out to Hellenistic Jewish-Christian communities. Philip the Evangelist, known from the *Book of Acts*, may be none other than the apostle Philip; in any event, Philip the Evangelist, according to *Acts* 21:9, had four celibate daughters who were all prophetesses. Their celibacy clearly marks out the Philip household as Jewish Christian; and this is confirmed by the following verses (10-11) which relate that the Judaean prophet Agabus came to Philip's residence and confronted Paul, announcing to him that "the Jews" would have him arrested in Jerusalem. "The Jews" refers to the Jewish Christians of Jerusalem, which is proven explicitly in verses 20-21. Nowhere does this text say that Agabus was a Pauline proponent, in fact it would seem that he was a Jewish Christian who was confronting Paul rather than necessarily protecting him through a forewarning.

# 4. From Jerusalem to Syria: The Esoteric Heritages of James and Thomas

The research of scholars such as Quispel has led to a paradigm shift in early Christian history which has enlarged the older picture of early Christianity which was pictured as mainly consisting of the western Catholic and eastern Orthodox churches, to include a further third branch of Christianity, namely, the ancient Syrian churches.[1] Whereas Miller criticizes Koester for identifying Gnosticism as the main component of early Syrian Christianity, Miller creates an unnecessary dichotomy when he nevertheless correctly stresses the Jewish character of Syrian Christianity into the 4$^{th}$ century.[2] The fact is that early Syrian churches were simultaneously Jewish and Gnostic because the Syrian gnosis represented primarily a modulation of Jewish esoteric traditions. The early Syrian Christianity was generally non-Pauline, and did not emphasize Jesus' crucifixion, and although it at times spoke of the crucifixion, it did not explicitly assign to it any redemptive significance. Accordingly, baptism was not understood as a mystical participation in the death and resurrection of Jesus. Some branches of the Syrian church, especially as represent-

---

1. See April D. DeConick, *The Original Gospel of Thomas. With a Commentary and New English Translation of the Complete Gospel*, 4ff.; also G. Quispel, "Gnosticism and the New Testament" *Vigiliae Christianae*, vol. 19, no. 2 (Jun., 1965), 65-85.

2. Troy A. Miller, "Liturgy and Communal Identity: *Hellenistic Synagogal Prayer 5* and the Character of Early Syrian Christianity," in David B. Capes, April D. DeConick, et al. (eds.), *Israel's God and Rebecca's Children Christology and Community in Early Judaism and Christianity. Essays in Honor of Larry W. Hurtado and Alan F. Segal* (Waco, Texas: Baylor University Press, 2007), 345-58.

ed by the Ebionites, were in open tension with St. Paul, as the Clementine literature testifies.

Ignatius of Antioch tried to reintroduce Pauline theology in Asia Minor at a time when such had been mostly absent since shortly before Paul's demise, as indicated by the latter's statement, "All in Asia have forsaken me," which occurred after the Jerusalem Temple incident involving James the Just (see *Acts* 21). Pauline theology was virtually absent from the churches towards the end of the first century CE and the tough tone Ignatius takes indirectly witnesses that the churches he wrote to largely entertained different ideas than his own. After his so-called martyrdom,[3] consistent Pauline theology remains absent from the Syrian churches for a few more centuries. Pauline theology had never been present in Edessa; rather Paul, like Ignatius, was associated with Antioch, but had been ostracized after the Jerusalem incident referred to in the *Letter to the Galatians*. The fact that some of the churches Ignatius writes to, such as Ephesus and Rome, accept Paul does not imply that all the churches were Pauline at the time, or that Ephesus or Rome were fully Pauline. Certainly Rome and Polycarp of Smyrna were sympathetic to Paul, yet the fact that Ignatius warns these churches' leaders against Jewish Christianity so forcefully indicates its prevalence in these regions also.

The *Epistle of the Apostles* was written sometime early in the second century, but certainly most of its contents reflect first-century traditions. It was then revised both sometime before 125 and again before 150 CE, when two predictions concerning the *parousia* were interpolated into the text, as we shall demonstrate below. Scholarship is divided on the geographic provenance of the *Epistle of the Apostles*, some arguing for Egypt, some for Asia Minor. But the weather conditions described in the text do not accord with Egyptian patterns, and the Asia Minor hypothesis is based primarily on the mention

---

3. We qualify this because as is known, it was possible for him to win a release from the Roman authorities, but he consciously refused this option.

of Cerinthus, the opponent of John the Elder of Aisa Minor. We would alternatively posit a textual origin in Syria, since John's gospel, which has deeply influenced our unknown author, was most likely composed in Syria. The author was a scribe and preacher, and an avid collector of materials. Cerinthus was probably still alive, and had certainly been active for some time. The author's ideas could have been general or geographically specific, and he was one of those responsible for helping create a new exoteric or dogmatic "orthodoxy." Despite this drive toward orthodoxy, the extant documentation demonstrates that the orthodoxy of ca. 100 CE was later to be assessed as heterodox by Irenaeus. For example the *Epistle of the Apostles'* story of the child Jesus learning and teaching the mystical letters at school, the idea that Christ was the angel Gabriel, etc., were all condemned by Irenaeus. In any event, this document idicates that angelic Christology was pervasive in the early days, confirming the picture given even in Irenaeus' *Proof of the Apostolic Preaching* of an angelic pneumatology, not to mention the *Shepherd of Hermas*.[4] Another sign of our author's orthodoxy which would later be branded heretical is the notion that the Son is the Father, reminiscent of the later Sabellianism, which according to the Fathers was taught in the *Gospel of the Egyptians*. But the idea here is not the same as later Sabellianism, for in our document the idea that the Son is the Father has nothing to do with ideas of divine hypostases, but rather with the reality of the *unio mystica*, in which all the faithful also share. The doctrine of Sabellianism has ancient Jewish-Christian roots, and originated in esoteric traditions concerning the Name of God. Metatron bore the Name of the Lord, just as Jesus received the Tetragrammaton (cf. *Philippians* 2). As the Jewish-Christian *Gospel of the Truth* explains:

---

4. See Charles A. Gieschen, *Angelomorphic Christology. Antecedents and Early Evidence* (Leiden/Boston/Koln: Brill, 1998).

Now the Father's name is 'the Son'. It is he who first gave a name to the one who emerged from him, who was himself, and he begot him as a son. He bestowed upon him his name, which belonged to him.... The name belongs to him; the Son belongs to him. It is possible for him to be seen. But the name is invisible, for it alone is the secret of the invisible, which approaches to ears that are utterly filled with it by him. For truly the Father's name is not spoken; it is manifest through a son.

This doctrine is already apparent in the canonical *Gospel of John* 14:8-9: "Philip said to him, 'Lord, show us the Father, and it will be sufficient for us'. Jesus said to him, 'Have I been with you for so long, and yet you still do not know me, Philip? Whoever has seen me has seen the Father; how can you say, 'Show us the Father'?'"

Jewish-Christian theology split into two camps over the Unity of God, one side emphasizing Jesus' humanity in order to preserve the divine Unity, the other emphasizing his "divine" nature but simultaneously rejecting the Hellenistic doctrinal formulation of three divine "persons"; but this "trinitarian" modalism did not equate "Jesus" with God, but rather the celestial Christ or Son was interpreted as a divine theophany which indwelt the earthly creature Jesus. Yet both of these positions were founded on traditional Jewish esoteric concepts.

The commonalities shared by the *Epistle of the Apostles* and the *Apocryphon of James* go back to Syrian traditions which accepted or tolerated Paul, but only insofar as he submitted to James and the twelve apostles. The cross is accepted in the *Epistle of the Apostles* and in the *Apocryphon of James*, but in neither document does it bear any Pauline soteriological significance. The emphasis lies on the *unio mystica*, and on the individual attainment of salvation through gnosis. The cross is an example of the need for perseverance and a symbol of death only in the sense of the mystical death which is equivalent to a realization of the *unio mystica*. We read in the *Apocryphon of James* after an exhortation to the apostles to seek death: "For the kingdom belongs to the ones who put themselves to death. Become better than I; make yourselves like the Son of the Holy Spirit." The *unio mystica* is even more explicitly formulated by Jesus in the *First Apocalypse of James*: "And then you will attain 'He-Who-Is'. And you will no longer be James; rather you are the 'One-Who-Is.'"

These doctrines are of Jewish-Christian origin, and included the idea of the *unio mystica* along with the concept of the Holy Spirit. This mystical union of the triad (not "Trinity") of Father, Mother, and Son can be traced back to Judaism's doctrines of the Father, the Mother the Holy Spirit, and the Messiah. The same order is seen in *1Peter* 1:2: "chosen and destined by *God the Father* and sanctified by *the Spirit* for obedience to *Jesus Christ*...." 1 *Peter*'s concept of the Holy Spirit as celestial Mother is supported also by 2:2, which refers to the "pure *logikon* milk," that is, pure milk of the Logos, which for a Hebrew or Aramaic speaker could be grammatically feminine, *milta d-qushta*, thus explaining why Peter can assign feminine imagery to the Word. Another indication of the Semitic thought of *1 Peter* is the transition from "babes" in 2:2 to "stone" and "stones" in 2:4-5 which is reminiscent of the common Rabbinic association between *ben*, 'son', and *'eben*, 'stone'.[5] The same association between feminine divine imagery and the Word occurs in *James* 1:18: "Of his own will he brought us forth by the word of truth...." "Brought us forth" in Greek here is *apekuesen*, which literally describes a *woman* giving birth to a child. James is clearly saying that the Word of Truth is the celestial Mother who gives birth to the faithful. Again, the Greek word *Logos* is understood not as a masculine but as a feminine celestial entity, which again shows that the author is thinking in Aramaic, of the feminine *milta*, rather than the targumic masculine *memra*, which is equivalent to the *Shekhinah* in Rabbinic tradition.

---

5. Cf. J. Massingberd Ford, "'Thou art Abraham' and upon this Rock," *The Heythrop Journal*, vol. vi, no. 3 (July 1965), 297. Curiously, Massingberd Ford does not refer to the Hebrew word *'eben*, only to *sur*.

The Jewish-Christian formula "Father, Mother, Son" resurfaces throughout the so-called Gnostic literature, as in the *Apocryphon of John*, where Jesus proclaims: "I am the Father, I am the Mother, I am the Son," in the *Epistle of the Apostles*, in the *Book of the Resurrection of the Savior by Bartholomew the Apostle*, the latter declaring: "Thou art the Father, Thou art the Son, and Thou art the Holy Spirit" (folio 22b), and continues in Mani, who although he has been influenced by the Pauline Church's "Father, Son, Spirit" formula nevertheless simultaneously preserves the Jewish-Christian "Father, Mother, Son" sequence known from his youth.

Further "Gnostic," that is, Jewish-Christian, elements in the *Apostle of the Epistles* include the doctrine of the archons and the genre of the post-resurrection discourse, although for Jewish Christians the resurrection was in fact the ascension, for like Isaac, Jesus had been rescued before death could take hold of him. A further indication of its Jewish-Christian "Gnostic" complexion is its many similarities to the Nag Hammadi *Apocryphon of James* and the *Dialogue of the Savior*, both of which are post-resurrection discourses characterized by speeches of Jesus which repeatedly alternate between approval and disapproval of the apostles, as well as the theme of the future generations of believers. Also noteworthy is the *Epistle of the Apostle's* inclusion of a doctrine of ten *sefirot*, divided into five positive and five negative attributes, precisely as in classical Kabbalah. Even several of the names of the ten virgin-*sefirot* coincide with the classical names of the *sefirot*. The Ethiopic and Coptic versions exhibit variation in the manuscripts, and we therefore reproduce both recensions below, although the variants are clearly of a synonymous nature arising most likely from alternative translational possibilities. We present the corresponding Kabbalistic *sefirot* to the right of each column:[6]

---

6. We present an in-depth analysis of this passage, as well as several other ancient Christian parallels to the sefirotic system, in Samuel Zinner, *The Mother of the Book: Images of the Supernal Feminine. Volume I: Essays*

| Ethiopic | Coptic |
|---|---|
| 1. Faith | 1. Faith |
| 2. Love = *Hesed* | 2. Love = *Hesed* |
| 3. Joy | 3. Grace = *Hesed* |
| 4. Peace | 4. Peace |
| 5. Hope | 5. Hope |
| 6. Insight = *Da'at/Binah* | 6. Knowledge = *Da'at/Binah* |
| 7. Knowledge = *Da'at* | 7. Wisdom = *Hokhmah* |
| 8. Obedience | 8. Obedience |
| 9. Endurance = *Nezah* | 9. Forbearance = *Nezah* |
| 10. Mercy = *Rahmamim* | 10. Mercy = *Rahmamim* |

In the Ethiopic version of the *Epistle of the Apostles* chapter 13 we find a reference to the *shi'ur qomah* traditions, where passing by the angels Jesus possessed "the measure of the wisdom of the Father who sent me." Similarly in Coptic chapter 17: "I am fully in my Father and my Father is in me in regard of the likeness of the form and the power and the fullness and the light and the full measure and the voice."

From the Johannine tradition our Syrian author has integrated the doctrine of the mutual indwelling of the Father, Son, Spirit, and believers, and in this mode understands the union of the Father and Son as one. This is not Trinitarian doctrine, but the metaphysics of the *unio mystica*, which is also paralleled in Islam, *mutatis mutandis*. In the two *parousia* predictions, Jesus' return is interpreted as the "coming of the Father," but that these two predictions could be interpolations is suggested by the fact that the ending of the document interprets "the coming of the Father" as Christ's ascension "after three days and three hours," not after 100 or 125 years. This ascension scene parallels the one found in the final section of the *Apocryphon of James*, and both include a

---

on Mandaean and Christian Gnostic Traditions (Casablanca, Morocco: Unpublished Monograph, 2009).

reference to the theme of parables. The ascension in these two documents also closely parallels the ascension at the end of the Coptic *Book of the Resurrection of Christ by Bartholomew the Apostle*, folio 14b:

> When the Savior took us up on the Mount [of Olives], the Savior spoke unto us [in a language] which we did not understand, but straightway He revealed it unto us. [He said unto us ], *Atharath thaueath*. And [straightway] the Seven Firmaments [were opened] ... our bodies saw, and we looked and we saw our Savior. His body was going up into the heavens, and His feet were firmly fixed upon the mountain with us. He stretched out His right hand and sealed us, the twelve. And we ourselves also went up with Him into the height, into the tabernacle of the Good Father, into the seventh heaven.[7]

Before proceeding, we should remark that *Book of the Resurrection of Christ by Bartholomew the Apostle* is one of the most explicit Christian analogues to the classical Jewish *merkabah* and *hekhalot* literature that survives from antiquity. As such, this document has been sorely neglected, and it could shed light not only upon the development of *merkabah* and *hekhalot* in Christianity, but in Judaism as well, since this document predates most of the Jewish analogues in question. Not only does *Bartholomew* exhibit repeated *merkabah* visions, but it also includes seven hymns of the angels, thus perfectly paralleling the *hekhalot* paradigms of angelic hymns. Of course all these elements appear in Christian mode, including the trisagion in folio 10a: "He is holy. He is holy. He is holy, the King, the Son of God, the Son of the King, and his Good Father,[8] and the Holy Spirit. The earth is full of the mercy of the Lord and his loving-kindness." In folio 11a-b we find the following

---

7. E. A. Wallis Budge, *Coptic Apocrypha in the Dialect of Upper Egypt* (London: Oxford University Press, 1913), 202.

8. Compare the term "Good Father" in the Cyril *Gospel of the Hebrews* fragment.

description of Adam and Eve which is reminiscent of Jewish and Jewish-Christian traditions:

> Now Adam was four score cubits in height, and Eve was fifty cubits....[9] There was a girdle of pearls [round about his loins], and a great multitude of angels [were singing to him] songs of heaven. [Rays of light shot] forth out of [his] eyes of diamonds which were like unto [the splendor] that I saw in the tabernacle of the Father. And characters and signs were written upon his forehead, the which flesh and blood were unable [to read]. And the Names] of the Father, and the Son, and the Holy Spirit were written upon his body in seven [symbolic signs?]. And the thongs of the sandals which were on the feet of the father shone brighter than the sun and the moon twice seven times. Eve herself was adorned with the adornments of the Holy Spirit, and the Powers and the Virgins sang hymns to her in the celestial language, calling her 'Zoe', the mother of all the living.

In folio 18b we find a vision given to Siophanes, the son of Thomas, of the twelve thrones of the apostles; again we are struck by the *merkabah* and *hekhalot* symbolism:

> And straightway Michael took me to the place which they call the "tabernacle of the Father," and I saw your twelve thrones which are [made of] pearls of light, your twelve thrones which are set with real stones (i.e. stones of price), and topazes and emeralds, which light up brilliantly the whole city of Christ. And I saw also twelve white robes lying upon the thrones of the spirit (?) ; and there were also twelve trees which were laden with fruit at all times, and each one overshadowed one of the thrones; and there were twelve eagles, each with the face of a man, and their wings were outstretched, one pair of wings over each throne; and a name of the Twelve Apostles

---

9. This is strikingly reminiscent of Elchasai's vision of the gigantic male Son of God and feminine Holy Spirit.

was inscribed upon each one of the thrones; and there were twelve veils, drawn over the thrones, to each throne a veil; and there was a canopy set with precious stones spread over the upper part of each throne ; and a thousand angels sang hymns (?) [before] each throne.

The following tradition in this manuscript is especially intriguing, namely, where Thomas says: "I rejoiced and was glad in my heart, and I summoned the multitude into His marriage chamber" (folio 20b). This is noteworthy on account of its reference to the theme of the marriage or bridal chamber, an image found also in the *Gospel of Thomas* logia 75 and 104. On account of all the above considerations we suspect that this *Bartholomew* work is ultimately Syro-Palestinian in its core; a revision naturally took place after the work was translated into Coptic, both during its circulation among Egyptian Jewish Christians and then among Egyptian "orthodox" Christians.

Like the Syrian Ignatius of Antioch, the author of the *Epistle of the Apostles* was a pro-Pauline Syrian, and was thus aligned with the Hellenistic Antiochine wing of Jewish Christianity in Syria. Like Ignatius—possibly even before him—he was fighting an uphill battle against what he considered to be the "heterodox" majority. To "legitimize" Paul, he must go to such great lengths as creating a prophecy by Jesus concerning Paul. Yet it is possible that this Pauline section is an interpolation; at most the author supports Paul as a venerable Christian, but not as a theologian, for he is not influenced by Pauline theology in the least. This again might indicate the Pauline section is an interpolation. Regardless of where the document was written, whoever wrote or interpolated this passage has "commended" Paul "for the first time" to a Jewish-Christian community where Paul had "played no role," as Detlef G. Muller expresses it.[10]

---

10. Muller posits a composition in Egypt; see Wilhelm Schneemelcher (ed.), *New Testament Apocrypha*. Vol. 1: *Gospels and Related Writings*. Revised

The *Epistle of the Apostles* helped spread what were to become the four canonical gospels, but did not limit itself to these four gospels, indeed it freely reshaped all of the gospels with a targumic-like fluidity and freedom. It may even be that the *Epistle of the Apostles* was designed as a "harmony" and substitute of the multiple gospels, a sort of forerunner to Tatian's later less creative *Diatesseron*.

The literature of the Jewish Christians displays an emphasis upon the humanity of Jesus, but it does not, contrary to some scholarly claims, deny a celestial aspect to Christ. The doctrines of the two aspects, earthly and celestial, exist simultaneously, just as orthodox Sunnite Islam emphasizes the humanity of the Prophet while at the same time affirming the Sufi doctrine of the *Nur Muhammadi*, the pre-existent light of Muhammad. According to a well-known *hadith*, the Prophet explained that he was already a *nabi* when Adam was yet but mere clay, before God breathed the divine Spirit into him and made him an animated, living being. According to the Sufis this *Nur Muhammadi* was passed down from generation to generation in a long line of Prophets, culminating in the earthly Muhammad. The poet Rumi extends the passage of the *Nur Muhammadi* past Muhammad to Ali, and then even further to al-Hallaj. The paradigm of a pre-existent prophetic substance transmitted from Adam is paralleled in the Ebionite doctrine of the True Prophet.

If we ask where the doctrines and basic orientation of Syrian Christianity came from, we need look no further than the original Jerusalem church under James the Just, the "brother" of Jesus. Quispel and others have forcefully presented a case for the founding and nurturing of Syrian Edessan Christianity from Jerusalem,[11] and Syrian tradition assigns a central role in the establishment of their church to the apostle

---

Edition (Louisville/London: Jerome Clarke & Co., Westminster John Knox Press, 2003), 251.

11. See April D. DeConick, *The Original Gospel of Thomas. With a Commentary and New English Translation of the Complete Gospel*, 4ff.

Thomas, and the almost universal scholarly recognition that the *Gospel of Thomas* received its standard form in Syria, specifically in the eastern branch dominated by Edessa, rather than the western branch dominated by Antioch, is of critical significance for the reconstruction of the earliest Syrian theology and for understanding the *Gospel of Thomas*. The history of the Syrian church is in fact mirrored in the order of logia 12 and 13 of *Thomas*. Logion 12 praises James as the leader of the apostles, and then logion 13 praises Thomas as more insightful than Peter and Matthew. The latter logion clearly intends to imply that Peter's and Matthew's presentation of the teaching and person of Jesus is unsatisfactorily confined to the exoteric domain, whereas Thomas recognized the esoteric depths of Jesus and his teaching. Jesus is more than "a wise philosopher," that is, a learned rabbi, and "a righteous angel." Jesus is more than this, for he is a manifestation of the primordial light (cf. logion 77), just as Muhammad was more than the righteous Final Messenger, for he was also a manifestation of the primordial Light, the *Nur Muhammadi*. Yet Thomas' emphasis is that the disciples are to come to the self-knowledge that they too are the cosmic light (logion 24); the same paradigm holds true for the *Nur Muhammadi* concept, for according to a *hadith*: "Whoever knows one's self knows their Lord." Thus, according to logia 12 and 13 James was the leader par excellence and Thomas was the teacher par excellence of hidden wisdom. Thus there is no need to interpret the two logia as stemming from two different time periods, for Thomas is not presented as a leader who replaces James. Nevertheless, James was a leader before Thomas established the church in Syria.

The esoteric orientation of Syria stemmed from the Jerusalem church, with James at its head. If we compare the canonical *Letter of James* with the three Jacobean texts of Nag Hammadi, we see a curious pattern that reminds us of the double nature of his "brother" Jesus' teaching. The *Letter of James* to a large extent contains parallels to the Sermon on the Mount, the crucifixion and resurrection of Jesus are nowhere mentioned, and in general the letter possesses a simple and seemingly exoteric tone. The difference between this and the Nag Hammadi Jacobean texts is as wide (indeed wider) as that between the teaching of Jesus as found in the synoptics on the one hand and *Thomas* and *John* on the other. The cause of this distinction is that the canonical *Letter* is James' public doctrine (with esoteric doctrines not completely absent, to be sure), whereas the Jacobean Nag Hammadi texts contain what are purported to be the esoteric, secret teachings of James.

*Grosso modo* it may be said that the early Syrian church represents in its thought the Jerusalem Jewish Christianity of James and the original apostles of Jesus, whereas the western Catholic and eastern Orthodox branches, although incorporating various traditions of the apostles, nevertheless assimilate these to the overarching Pauline paradigms, for after all, these two churches are the heirs of Paul's labors among the Gentiles. These two churches, being in essence the inheritors of Paul's efforts among the Gentiles, had little understanding of early Jerusalem or Syrian Christianity with their Semitic flavor, and ironically denied their apostolic status, having as little sympathy for it than it did later for Islam. We mention Islam in this context because Islam's presentation of Christian ideas accords more with the Semitic, Jacobean, Ebionite trajectories than with those of the predominantly Pauline churches. Shlomo Pines argues persuasively that Jewish Christians found in Nestorianism a refuge from persecution by fellow Christians. In turn, it appears that in all likelihood, a large contingent of Jewish Christians entered Islam, both openly as such and under the guise of Nestorianism.[12] We should also mention that the Syro-Malabar Church of India, which claims descent from the apostle Thomas, lost the entirety of its indigenous Christian literature under pressure from Roman authorities who saw it as tinged with Nestorianism. It is very likely that before its Romanization in theol-

---

12. Shlomo Pines, *The Jewish Christians of the Early Centuries of Christianity according to a New Source*, 38-39.

ogy and liturgy, the Thomas Christians may have exhibited an essentially Semitic complexion like that of early Arabian Christianity.

# 5. Models of Early Christologies

## PART I
## The *Gospel of the Hebrews*: Jerome and Cyril

When one turns to an examination of Islam's understanding of Jesus the Messiah, one is struck by several concords with Jewish-Christian theology. First there is a simultaneous emphasis upon the humanity of Jesus and an affirmation of his celestial aspect, for not only was he, as a human being, created by God's creative word of command, "Be!", but he is also the Word and Spirit of God, although these two titles are understood not as divine, but as celestial categories. In any event, neither did Jewish Christianity consider Jesus divine in the Nicaean sense. Next, the Qur'an denies the crucifixion of Jesus while affirming his ascension or assumption to God. The Qur'an asserts in Arabic something which agrees almost word-for-word with a Coptic Gnostic text (itself translated from Greek) on Jesus' seeming crucifixion: "They punished me [with death], yet I did not really die, rather only in appearance" (*Second Discourse of Great Seth*; cf. Qur'an *sura* 4:157: "They did not kill him or crucify him, but he/it was made to appear so to them"). Just as Jewish Christianity either denied the crucifixion, ignored it, or at least failed to assign any redemptive value to it, it consequently spoke more of an ascension of Jesus to God than of a resurrection from the dead. When we turn to the *Gospel of Thomas*, rather than any resurrection of Jesus being referred to, one reads simply of "the living Jesus," which would mean, in the context of Jewish Christianity, that Jesus was never subject to death, that he ascended to God alive, and that he remains in this state of transcendent life. Nowhere does Thomas mention a crucifixion, death, or resurrection of Jesus. Nowhere does Thomas assign titles to Jesus such as "Son of God," "Lord," "Savior," or "God."

None of this means that Thomas does not have an exalted view of Jesus; indeed, on the contrary, for Thomas Jesus is ineffable (logion 13), he is the primordial Light (logion 77). But this is not to say that, in the words of the proposition attacked in the Qur'an, "God is the Messiah." For Thomas what is essential to know is not the inner nature of Jesus' person, but the pre-existent, primordial nature of the disciple (cf. log. 18-19). Accordingly, when the disciples ask Jesus in logion 24 concerning his person and status, he turns the question on its head as it were by deflecting the interest away from his person and nature back onto the person and nature of the enquirers. For Thomas Jesus is, admittedly, the primordial light (cf. log. 77), but in logion 24 Jesus teaches that the disciples' interest should be in self-knowledge, and without that, searching for a knowledge of Jesus' nature, status, or person, could in fact constitute a distraction from what is most essential to know, namely the directly inward realization of the Supreme Self. This explains Thomas' emphasis on self-knowledge. Similarly, the search for knowledge concerning secrets of the future (prophetic, apocalyptic, eschatological secrets) as well as knowledge of the sacred past, even the Jewish scriptural prophecies of the coming Messiah, these are all pronounced as distractions in *Thomas* (cf. logia 51 and 52). These statements can be explained by the fact that according to Thomas, for Jesus the one essential knowledge to be sought is self-knowledge. And even if Jesus is the primordial light, the disciples are similarly the light of the world, that is, the cosmic light. The heavens and the earth were not created on account of Jesus, but on account of James (logion 12), and the disciple who possesses self-knowledge, the world is not worthy of such an one (logia 56, 80, 111b). Jesus is not the rabbi, teacher, or master of his followers (logion 13; cf. *John* 15:5), for those who assimilate the doctrine of self-knowledge have become equal to Jesus, and Jesus has become like them (logion 108).

Logion 108 does not belong to the category of *unio mystica*, although it is related to such. Similar pronouncements are found not only in St. Paul (*Galatians* 2; *1 Corinthians* 6:16-17),[1] but also in the Jacobean writings, "But you yourself will be He Who Lives." And as Jesus said, "I am the Truth," so the Sufi al-Hallaj proclaimed, "I am the Truth (*al-Haqq*)." None of these saints were claiming to be God in the strict sense, but they were speaking from the perspective of the *unio mystica*, or in Sufi terms, *fana'* and *baqa'*, a passing away in God and a subsequent subsistence in the knowledge of union. This mystery is by no means a Sufi "innovation," but finds its genesis in the Qur'an itself. Among other passages, we can highlight *sura* 17:1: "Glorified be He who carried his servant by night from the sacred place of worship to the far distant place of worship, whose precincts we have blessed, that we might show him of our signs. Lo! He (God) is the Hearer, the Seer." According to this verse, God let his servant *see* the divine signs, yet the same passage insists that only *God* is the one who sees. The verse therefore would seem to presuppose the concept of *unio mystica*

In 1915 E. Wallis Budge published the Coptic text and English translation of an ancient work bearing the title "The Discourse on Mary Theotokos by Cyril, Archbishop of Jerusalem." The piece was not in fact written by St. Cyril, but it is of extreme value on account of its comments regarding the lost ancient *Gospel of the Hebrews*. Budge gives us a short summary of the relevant passage, which we will cite here in its entirety:

---

1. "'The two shall be one.' But whoever is united to the Lord becomes one spirit with him." "United," that is "cleave to," as in *Ephesians* 5 where Paul quotes the same *Genesis* text, "The two shall be one." The Greek of *1 Corinthians* 6:17 says literally, "But whoever cleaves to the Lord is one spirit." That Paul is here alluding to the *Shema*, the Jewish profession of faith, has gone unnoticed. "Hear, O Israel, the Lord your God is One Lord; and you shall cleave to the Lord your God with all your heart, strength, and life." Thus in *1 Corinthians* 6:16-17 Paul interprets the *Shema* according to the paradigm of *unio mystica*. This is similar to the Sufi interpretation of the first part of the Islamic profession of faith, "There is no god but God," that is, "There is nothing but God."

The Discourse on Mary Theotokos is interrupted at this point by a personal anecdote told by Cyril himself. A certain monk called Annarikhus, who lived near Gaza, and who had studied with great success the works of the heresiarch Bion (?) and Harpocratius (?), began to preach the lies and blasphemies of these men to the pilgrims who flocked to the shrines in the neighborhood. When Cyril learned what the monk's doctrines were he sent two messengers to the Bishop of Gaza, ordering him to send Annarikhus, together with his books of heresy, to him in Jerusalem. When he entered Cyril's presence, in answer to the archbishop's accusation that he preached false doctrine, Annarikhus declared that he only preached the doctrine of the Apostles and of Fathers such as Sator, Ebion, and Harpocratius. Pressed by Cyril to declare what this doctrine was exactly, the monk, on the authority of the *Gospel to the Hebrews*, asserted that: 1. When Christ wished to come upon the earth the Good Father committed Him to the care to a mighty *dunamis*, which was called Michael. This *dunamis* came down upon earth, and was called Mary, and Christ was in her womb seven months. In reply to Cyril's question if he took the Gospels literally, the monk said Yes, and then Cyril asked him where in the gospels did he find it stated that the Virgin Mary, the Mother of God, was a *dunamis*? The monk replied, 'In the gospel of the Hebrews', a work which he regarded as of authority equal to that of the Gospels of Matthew, Mark, Luke, and John. When Cyril had shewn him the absurdity of setting the 'misleading doctrine of the Hebrews' in the place of the doctrine of Christ, and proved to him by quotations from the New Testament and the 'Ancoratus' (*'Agkurotos*) of Epiphanius that the doctrine of the Jews can never be joined unto the doctrine of Christ, the monk admitted that he had made a mistake, and asked for Cyril's forgiveness. He then delivered up his books to Cyril, who burned them in the fire. This done Cyril began to expound his doctrine of Mary Theotokos, but the loss of a leaf from our manuscript makes our statement of it incomplete. At the end of his exposition he told Annarikhus that if he was willing to accept and to confess this doctrine he would receive him into his fold, and that if not he must leave the place. The monk then cursed the heresy of Bion (or, Ebion) and Harpocratius, and Cyril baptized him in the name of Saint Mary. Finally, Annarikhus went into a monastery in the Mount of Olives, and preached the doctrine acceptable to Cyril, denying that Mary was a *dunamis*.[2]

We reproduce next, *in extenso*, Budge's translation of the relevant folios of the document from the original Coptic text:

> All these things have I related to you, beloved ones, because of the godless heretics, who say that Mary is a "force" (or, abstract power). Behold, I have already pointed out to you in the words which I have addressed to you, saying that Mary was flesh like all other folk, and that the Lamb of God, Who took away the sins of the world, took flesh in her. And now I wish to relate to you an incident that happened to me. There was a certain monk who lived in the neighborhood of Maioma of Gaza, who had received instruction in the heresy of Bion and of Harpocratius his master, of whose books he obtained possession, and he expounded them publicly, and he became filled with blasphemies and with falsehoods, and he masqueraded with great pride and arrogance, and he deceived all the people who were in that neighborhood by his pretensions, through those who used to come to the holy places (Fol. 11a) there to pray. And the things which he proclaimed in his corrupt heterodoxy were repeated to me, and I sent two ministers to the Bishop of Gaza, and I said unto him, "I beseech thee to seek out on my behalf a certain monk who is in the neighborhood of Maioma, and do thou send him to me, together with his books." And when the bishop had received the letter and read it, he caused search to be made for that monk everywhere. And when they had brought him to the bishop he said unto him, "My son, rise up and go to Jerusa-

---

2. E. Wallis Budge, *Miscellaneous Coptic Texts in the Dialect of Upper Egypt*, vol. V (London: Oxford University Press, 1915), ixxviii- ixxvix.

lem to the archbishop. If thou dost not go he will send for thee and thy books. He knoweth about thy doctrine, and about thy preaching, and whose it is." And the monk replied, "I will take my books and I will go to him in Jerusalem." And the two ministers took him to Jerusalem to the archbishop, who said unto him, "We have heard, O brother, that thou art teaching a strange doctrine, and that thou art changing the voices of the Holy Gospels." The monk, [who was called] (Fol. 11b) Annarikhus, said unto him, "My teaching (or, doctrine) is not a strange doctrine, but is that of our Fathers the Apostles, and our own Fathers taught it everywhere as sound doctrine." And Apa Cyril said unto him, "Who were thy Fathers?" And the monk said, "Sator, and Ebion, who succeeded him." And the archbishop said unto him, "Thou hast become a disciple and hast made thyself a mule-like beast under the stupid yoke of the chariot of the Devil." And the monk said unto him, "Harpocratius used to cast out devils." And the archbishop said unto him, "Shew me by what means thou dost cast out devils, and in what way thou dost preach the Gospel, and what thou dost say concerning Christ and His Birth according to the flesh, and concerning His mother who brought Him forth, and concerning His death, which was full of salvation, and His resurrection from the dead after the third day." And that monk replied, "It is written in the [Gospel] to (Fol. 12a) the Hebrews that when Christ wished to come upon the earth to men the Good Father called a mighty 'power' in the heavens which was called 'Michael', and committed Christ to the care thereof. And the 'power' came down into the world, and it was called Mary, and [Christ] was in her womb for seven months. Afterwards she gave birth to Him, and He increased in stature, and He chose the Apostles, who preached Him in every place. He fulfilled the appointed time that was decreed for Him. And the Jews became envious of Him, they hated Him, they changed the custom of their Law, and they rose up against Him and laid a trap and caught Him, and they delivered Him to the governor, and he gave Him to them to crucify Him. And after they had raised Him up on the Cross the Father took Him up into heaven unto Himself."

## The Gospel of Thomas

And the Patriarch Cyril said unto the monk, "Who sent thee about to teach these things?" And that monk said unto him, "The Christ said, Go ye forth into all the world, and teach ye all the nations in My (Fol. 12b) Name, in every place." And Apa Cyril said unto him, "Dost thou take the Gospels literally?' And the monk said, 'Yea, absolutely, my lord Father." And the archbishop answered and said, "Where in the Four Gospels is it said that the holy Virgin Mary, the mother of God, is a 'force.'" And the monk answered and said, "In the [Gospel] to the Hebrews." And Apa Cyril answered and said, "Then, according to thy words, there are Five Gospels?" And that monk replied, "Yea, there are." And Apa Cyril answered and said, "What is the name of the fifth Gospel? for I should like to know whence this doctrine concerning Christ is derived, and to understand it. The Four Gospels have written above them: '[The Gospel] according to Matthew '; '[The Gospel] according to Mark'; '[The Gospel] according to Luke'; '[The Gospel] according (Fol. 13a) to John.' Whose is the fifth Gospel?" And that monk said unto him, "It is [the Gospel] that was written to the Hebrews." And Saint Cyril answered and said, "If thou speakest the truth, O brother, must we not then reject the teaching of the Christ, and follow the misleading doctrine of the Hebrews? God forbid! The Hebrews wish for doctrine of this kind greatly, so that they may cast a blemish upon our purity and honor, even as it was said by the Christ in times of old, 'Thou castest out devils by Berzeboul.' And is it not written, 'He who doth not confess that Jesus the Christ hath come in the flesh is a deceiver and an Antichrist, like thyself'? And again, 'Whosoever shall come unto thee, and bring a doctrine that is different from thine, receive him not into thy house, neither say unto him. Hail!' And again, 'If they were of us they would have been like unto us; they came forth from us, but they are not of us.' Which meaneth (Fol. 13b) that they utter the Name of Christ with their mouths only, and that they make a pretence in their hearts. They heap up wrath for themselves in the day of the Judgment of Truth and the wrath that is from Jesus the Christ. The doctrine of the Jews cannot be joined unto the doctrine of Christ. What connection can there be between the agreement of the [Gospel to the] Hebrews and the agreement of the Holy Gospels? But those heresies must spring up which Epiphanius describes in his work '*Agkurotos*, saying, 'The error in each one of them is different, but evil is implanted in them all.' And Annarikhus the monk said unto Apa Cyril, "The night cannot contend against the day, neither can darkness stand before the light. I am vanquished by thy great wisdom, and I know that I have made a mistake. Let thy fatherhood grant repentance unto me! And all these things which I have overthrown I will build up again. But take my books, and burn them in the fire, and my possessions do thou give to the poor. My heart followeth thy words and [those of] the Holy Gospel." And when I (i. e. Cyril) had burned his books, I said unto him, "Who ..." (Fol. 14a) [One leaf wanting] "He to Whom no form can be assigned was born [in the form of] a son. He was the Beginning, and He Who had no beginning was brought forth. Now there was a beginning to that humanity, but the Godhead had no beginning, and was without form. And no addition took place to the Trinity in such wise that the Trinity, which consisteth of Three [Persons], became Four [Persons]. One *sunodos* entered one who was of two natures, and one son was brought forth, a unity of the flesh without any diminution. For He was neither changed in His nature, nor reduced in His strength, nor was He separated from His Ancient Begetter, that is to say, the Beginning. But the oneness of the flesh of God received one Nature. As for the coming to us of the blessed Offspring God the Word, it is the miracle that was hidden in God from eternity, I mean the miracle of God Who made Himself man. An impenetrable mystery is the Nature that abolished the curse and destroyed the sentence of death, and taught us concerning 'the foundation, which had no beginning', of the Only-begotten One, Jesus the Christ, our Lord, the production, according to the flesh, of the womb of Saint Mary, the perpetual Virgin, in whose holy house we (Fol. 14b) are gathered together this day to commemorate the day of her death. If thou wilt confess these things with a true and sincere belief then we will prepare to receive thee into the fold of all the sheep of the loving Shepherd Christ. Have no doubt about the matter; thou must either follow the words which I have taught thee or thou must get outside this place." And Annarikhus opened his mouth and anathematized the heresy of Ebion and Harpocratius, saying, "Anathema be every heresy; the things which thou [Ebion] hast said unto me are not to be believed. And now, O my father, receive thou me into good fellowship with thyself." And when I knew that his mind had received the light I baptized him in the name of the Lady of us all, Saint Mary, whose day is this day. Finally he went to a monastery in the Mount of Olives, and he builded upon the foundation of the Apostles until the day of his death. I have now described unto you the whole of the story concerning the heresy of Ebion, who said, "Mary, the mother (Fol. 15a) of the Lord, is a 'force.'"[3]

There are several comments in order on this extraordinarily intriguing passage. Sator is the Satornil of Antioch, who flourished in the time of Trajan; Satornil was a disciple of Meander, a Samaritan of Capparetia, who in turn was a disciple of Simon. As for Ebion, he never existed, for the name is based on a misunderstanding of the Hebrew word *ebonim*, meaning, "the Poor Ones," the title of the first Aramaic-speaking Christians in Jerusalem under St. James the Just, the "brother" of Jesus. This immediately indicates that the attack on the Ebionite doctrine has more to do with a Hellenistic misunderstanding of Jesus' original doctrine in its native Jewish mode than with any intrinsic heresy on the part of the *Ebonim*. Carpocrates taught in Alexandria in the reign of Hadrian (110-138 CE).

The association of Mary and Michael in the *Gospel of the Hebrews* is intriguing in light of the fact that in Rabbinic sources, as J. Massingberd Ford expresses it, "whenever Michael appears the *Shekhinah* appears with him."[4] Furthermore, one

---

3. Ibid., 635-40; the Coptic original is supplied in ibid., 58-63.
4. J. Massingberd Ford, "A Possible Liturgical Background to the

notices that in the Cyril text, the Trinitarian formula is missing from the Great Commission account within the *Gospel of the Hebrews*, in accord with the Shem-Tob Hebrew version of Matthew 28, which in turn agrees with the shorter Eusebian reading.

Gedaliahu G. Stroumsa has presented evidence indicating that Trinitarian ideas had their origin in ancient Jewish esoteric traditions which understood the two cherubim atop the ark of the covenant as two divine hypostatic emanations which were identified respectively as the masculine Angel of the Lord and the feminine Holy Spirit, representing the divine Logos and Sophia, and that these were linked to the two divine names Lord (*Yahweh*) and God (*Elohim*).[5] In our judgment, this suggests that in the earliest times Jews gazed upon the ark of the covenant in the Temple and viewed it as the throne of God flanked by two angels on the right and left. Besides the Logos and Sophia, or Angel of the Lord and Holy Spirit, who were these two cherubim identified as? According to *2 Enoch* 24:1, Gabriel dwells to the left of God. This suggests he might be one of the two cherubim. Which angel dwells on the right side? In light of his significance in Jewish traditions, we would suggest that the second angel is none other than Michael. In the *Ascension of Isaiah*, Gabriel sits at the left hand of God, while the Messiah sits at the right hand of God, in accord with general New Testament imagery. According to Cyril's account of the *Gospel of the Hebrews*, the Virgin Mary was an earthly manifestation of the celestial angel Michael; according to the orthodox *Epistle of the Apostles* and the "Gnostic" (or better 'Kabbalistic') treatise *Pistis Sophia*, Jesus was an earthly manifestation of the celestial angel

---

Shepherd of Hermas," *Revue de Qumran*, numéro 24, tome 6, fascicule 4 (Mars 1969), 546.

5. See Gedaliahu G. Stroumsa, "Polymorphie divine et transformations d'un mythologème: l' 'Apocryphon de Jean' et ses sources," *Vigiliae Christianae* vol. 35 (1981), 412-34; and Gedaliahu G. Stroumsa, "Le couple de l'ange et de l'esprit: traditions juives et chrétiennes," *Revue Biblique* tome 88 (1981), 42-61.

Gabriel. What this suggests is that Mary and Jesus are assimilated respectively to the Angel of the Lord Gabriel and the Holy Spirit Michael. This is reminiscent of the Qur'anic description of the belief of the "Nazarenes" in a triad consisting of God, Mary, and Jesus, rather than of "Father, Son, Spirit" or even of "Father, Mother, Son."[6]

In *1 Enoch* 39:13 we read: "Those who sleep not bless Thee they stand before Thy glory and bless, praise, and extol, saying: Holy, holy, holy, is the Lord of Spirits; He filleth the earth with spirits." This is closely paralleled in *Isaiah* 6:3: "Holy, holy, holy is the Lord of hosts; the whole earth is full of his glory," which is spoken by the two seraphim who stand above the Lord. The fact that these seraphim stand "above" the Lord suggests that they are in fact divine hypostases who are not inferior ontologically to the Lord. This vision of Isaiah suggests that the two angels above the ark of the covenant were alternatively interpreted as seraphim rather than cherubim, and the majesty and terror produced by the sight and sound of these two seraphim are reminiscent of the same holy dread which the vision of God inspires. We are not convinced by Black's argument that *1 Enoch* 39:13 is a reformulation of *Isaiah* 6:3, and that "Lord of hosts" has been rephrased as "Lord of spirits"; for us, this simply indicates an unconscious bias in favor of canonical *Isaiah*. Moreover, a comparison of the two passages shows that "spirits" is equally parallel to "glory" and not exclusively to "hosts." As Margaret Barker has remarked, "The *Enoch* writings could be as old as anything in the Old Testament,"[7] and we would propose accordingly the possibility that the Isaian and Enochian forms of the *trisagion*

---

6. See de Blois, François. "Nasrānī (Ναζωραιος) and hanīf (εθνικος): Studies on the Religious Vocabulary of Christianity and of Islam," *Bulletin of the School of Oriental and African Studies*, University of London, vol. 65, no. 1 (2002), 13-15. See the Trinitarian discussion in chapter 2 of Samuel Zinner, *The Abrahamic Archetype: Essays on the Transcendent and Formal Relationships between Judaism, Christianity and Islam* (Cambridge, UK: Archetype, 2011).

7. Margaret Barker, *Enoch the Lost Prophet* (London: SPCK, 1988), 22.

represent independent formulations of an archaic triadic hypostatic contemplation of the ark of the covenant with the two angels resting above it.

We next turn to an examination of canonical and extra-canonical accounts of Jesus' baptism:

*Mark* 1:9 And it came to pass, in those days, Jesus came from Nazareth of Galilee, and was baptized by John in the Jordan. 10 And forthwith coming up out of the water, he saw the heavens opened, and the Spirit as a dove descending, and remaining on him.
11 And there came a voice from heaven: Thou art my beloved Son; in thee I am well pleased. 12 And immediately the Spirit drove him out into the desert.

*Matthew* 3:16 And Jesus being baptized, forthwith came out of the water; and lo, the heavens were opened to him, and he saw the Spirit of God descending as a dove, and coming upon him. 17 And behold a voice from heaven, saying: This is my beloved Son, in whom I am well pleased.

*Luke* 3:21 Now it came to pass, when all the people were baptized, that Jesus also being baptized and praying, heaven was opened; 22 And the Holy Spirit descended in a bodily shape, as a dove upon him; and a voice came from heaven: Thou art my beloved Son; in thee I am well pleased.

*Gospel of the Hebrews*: "And it came to pass when the Lord was come up out of the water, the whole fount of the Holy Spirit descended and rested upon him, and said unto him: My son, in all prophets was I waiting for thee that thou shouldst come, and I might rest in thee. For thou art my rest, thou art my first begotten son, that reignest for ever."
(Factum est cum ascendisset Dominus de aqua, descendit fons omnis Spiritus sancti, et requieuit super eum et dixit illi: Fili mi, in omnibus prophetis expectabam te, ut uenires, et requiescerem in te. Tu es enim requies mea, tu es filius meus primogenitus, qui regnas in sempiternum).

Before continuing we should point out that we find the same themes of resting and reigning joined together in both the *Gospel of the Hebrews* and in the *Letter to the Hebrews*. Because of the common themes and similar titles shared between these two documents we strongly suspect that the *Gospel of the Hebrews* (or traditions presupposed or preserved in the latter text) was in use by the same community addressed by the *Letter to the Hebrews*.

In the Mandaean *Book of John* we read: "Then *Ruha* made herself like to a dove and threw a cross over the Jordan. A cross she threw over the Jordan and made its water to change into various colours. 'O Jordan,' she says, 'thou sanctifiest me and thou sanctifiest my seven sons.'" The cross over the waters of baptism is paralleled in *Agathangelus* and in the *Acts of Gregory of Armenia* in an account of King Taridatios and Queen Ripsime, at whose baptism in the Euphrates a pillar of fire arose over the waters in which the sign of the cross appeared.[8] The *Book of John*'s "many colors" would seem to refer to the fire or light which appeared at the baptism of Jesus in several early Jewish-Christian sources, such as the *Gospel of the Ebionites*: "And straightway there shone about the place a great light." According to Justin, the *Praedicatio Pauli*, *Sybilline Oracles* 6:6-7 and 7:82-84, and the *Gospel of Philip* 71, 3-15, a fire appeared at the baptism. In an essay on these light and fire images Drijvers and Reinink, who fail to mention the relevant *Gospel of Philip* text, argue that the fire image is older than the light image, and that it was Justin's student Tatian who originated the light imagery at Jesus' baptism.[9] Their argument is unconvincing as well as unnecessary, for both images could have been present from the beginning, especially since in Semitic languages the words for "light" and "fire" are

---

8. See Alfred Resch, *Ausserkanonische Schriftfragmente* (Leipzig: J. C. Hinrichs'sche Buchhandlung, 1906), 226-27.

9. H. J. W. Drijvers, G. J. Reinink, "Taufe und Licht: Tatian, Ebionäerevangelium und Thomasakten," in T. Baarda (ed.), *Text and Testimony. Essays on New Testament and Apocryphal Literature in Honour of A. F. J. Klijn* (Kampen: Uitgeversmaatschappij J. H. Kok, 1988), 91-110.

virtually identical, e.g., Syriac *nura* and *nuhra* or Arabic *nur* and *nar*. Drijvers and Reinink are correct to see a connection between the theme of fire in Justin and parallel accounts and the word fire in John the Baptist's statement in the canonical gospels that the Messiah would "baptize with the Holy Spirit and with fire." They are mistaken, however, in arguing that Justin's fire image was necessarily created from John's saying. A more likely scenario emerges once we realize that Christians would not have created the fire image at Jesus' baptism, for it clearly implies that John the Baptist, not the Messiah, baptized in water, the Spirit, and fire. The image of fire here may have actually originated in *Daniel* 7:9's river of fire, in which, according to Jewish traditions, the angels would baptize themselves; this purification is necessary to render one ritually pure to receive the *merkabah* vision of God.[10] In fact, this element of fire (so prominent in *Ezekiel* 1), coupled with the notice that "the heavens were opened" (*Matthew* 3:16) at Jesus' baptism, which alludes to *Ezekiel* 1:1, "the heavens were opened," would seem to virtually confirm that Jesus' baptism involved a *merkabah* ascent vision.[11]

The tradition of the fire or light appearing at Jesus' baptism could likely have originated among Baptist circles who carried it over into Jewish-Christian literature, such as the *Gospel of the Ebionites*. The canonical gospels may have eliminated the image as part of their exoterically motivated anti-Baptist polemic. Even when this event was remembered, the "light" tradition became predominant in order to erase the allusion to the "fire" spoken of by John the Baptist in the canonical accounts, and in Greek-speaking communities the Semitic connection between the words light and fire would have been weakened, since *pur* and *phos* do not resemble each other phonetically, although *phos* can be understood directly as light or by extension as fire, which incidentally is anoth-

---

10. See David J. Halperin, "Origen, Ezekiel's Merkabah, and the Ascension of Moses," *Church History*, vol. 50, no. 3 (Sep., 1981), 273.

11. This is the interpretation of Origen; cf. ibid., 261-75.

er reason why the argument of Drijvers and Reinink seems forced when they posit an essential distinction between the fire and light traditions.

# 6. Models of Early Christologies

## PART II
## Transfiguration and Crucifixion

Besides his baptism, the other famous case of a heavenly voice in the presence of Jesus is that which occurred at the transfiguration. In the transfiguration case, like that of the baptism, the texts do not specify that God or "the Father" spoke on this occasion. Therefore Robert J. Miller errs when he states that "the [canonical] gospel tradition" interprets the voice as that "of God," in contrast to that of the Holy Spirit in the *Gospel of the Hebrews*.[1] Here we present the relevant evidence:

> *Mark* 9:7: And a cloud overshadowed them, and a voice came out of the cloud: This is my beloved Son; listen to him.

> *Matthew* 17:5: A bright cloud overshadowed them, and a voice from the cloud said: This is my beloved Son, with whom I am well pleased; listen to him.

> *Luke* 9:34: A cloud came and overshadowed them; and they were afraid as they entered the cloud. 35 And a voice came out of the cloud, saying: This is my Son, my Chosen, listen to him.

In the New Testament we find the following reference to the transfiguration:

---

[1]. Robert J. Miller, ed. *The Complete Gospels. Annotated Scholars Version.* Revised and Expanded Edition. Foreword by Robert W. Funk (Santa Rosa, California: Polebridge Press, 1994), 431.

*2 Peter* 1:16 For we have not by following artificial fables, made known to you the power, and presence of our Lord Jesus Christ; but we were eyewitnesses of his greatness. 17 For he received from God the Father, honor and glory: and the voice was borne to him from the majestic glory: This is my beloved Son, in whom I am well pleased. 18 And this voice we heard borne from heaven, when we were with him in the holy mount.

The idea that it was "God the Father" who spoke to Jesus at the transfiguration would seem to be based on the influence of *2 Peter*; however, this is a misreading of the latter text as well, for while it says that God the Father bestowed "honor and glory" on Jesus, nevertheless the "voice" itself is said to have descended from or by "the majestic glory" (*megaloprepous doxes*), which is a typical Jewish manner of referring not only to God, but also to the Holy Spirit, who is the *kabod*, the Glory of God. Therefore *2 Peter* does not necessarily identify the voice of the transfiguration as that of God the Father. Neither does the *Apocalypse of Peter*, written about the same time as *2 Peter*, ascribe the heavenly voice to God: "And behold, suddenly there came a voice from heaven, saying: This is my beloved Son in whom I am well pleased: [obey] my commandments. And then came a great and exceeding white cloud over our heads and bore away our Lord and Moses and Elias." Indeed *2 Peter* 1:21 confirms that divine speech is effected by means of the Holy Spirit, for "humans spoke from God moved by the Holy Spirit"; or as other variants read: "moved by the Holy Spirit holy people of God spoke." The heavenly voice at Jesus' baptism and transfiguration was not that of God "the Father," but of his Mother, the Holy Spirit.

Regarding the question of the transfiguration narrative as a resurrection account, Robert H. Stein's objections to *2 Peter* 1:16ff. being a resurrection account are not persuasive. For example, in one of his main arguments he attacks the idea that "honor and glory" *necessitates* a reference to the resurrection. Stein is correct in denying such a necessity. Yet he goes on to produce an unconvincing argument when he claims that the epistle's opponents rallied under the name of Paul, who could claim a resurrection appearance, so that in order to sustain Peter's priority *2 Peter*'s transfiguration account could not be a tradition of the resurrection.[2] But whoever the opponents were, the writer of *2 Peter* sees no competition with Paul (cf. chapter 3). Moreover, Stein's remark that the word "glory," *doxa*, is more descriptive of the *parousia* than the resurrection,[3] overlooks the possibility that the *parousia* itself may be conceptually inseparable from the resurrection on a theologically implicit plane.[4] The fact remains in the end that *2 Peter*'s rhetoric surrounding its transfiguration account requires that it presents at this point the central fundamental event in Jesus' career that bestows upon Christianity its central significance, namely the resurrection, which in Ebionite terms, however, coincides with the ascension.

It is not usually considered that *John* 19:26 constitutes the story of the succession to Jesus. Typologically the Woman may represent the Holy Spirit, whose son is Jesus; as in the *Gospel of the Hebrews*, according to which Jesus refers to "my mother, the Holy Spirit." Here in *John*, Jesus appoints the Beloved Disciple as his successor in an act tantamount to declaring that the Beloved Disciple is now the Son of the Holy Spirit; the Beloved Disciple is in fact the first manifestation of the promised Paraclete, the sending of whom requires Jesus' departure. The appointment of the Beloved Disciple as son of the Holy Spirit constitutes the enthronement of the Beloved Disciple. He is "beloved," that is, the "one whom Jesus loved (*egapa*)," because he is successor to Jesus, whom the Holy Spirit addressed at his baptism as, "My Son the Beloved" (*ho agapetos*; *Mark* 1:11) Thus the Beloved Disciple is metaphysically inseparable from the Woman, the Holy Spirit, the celestial Mother. The Paraclete is the Spirit of Truth, and 'Spirit'

---

2. Robert H. Stein, "Is the Transfiguration (Mark 9:2-8) a Misplaced Resurrection-Account?" *Journal of Biblical Literature*, vol. 95, no. 1 (March 1976), 88-89.

3. Ibid., 88.

4. See chapter 8 in Samuel Zinner, *Christianity and Islam*.

in Hebrew (*ruah*) and Aramaic (*ruha*) is feminine. Indeed in the Old Syriac (pre-Peshitta) version of *John* 14:26, we read: "The Spirit, the Paraclete, *She* shall teach you all things." Mary is the feminine dimension of the Paraclete, whereas the Beloved Disciple is perhaps the masculine mode. But the fact is that the Synoptics clearly state that all the male disciples fled from the cross. The Virgin Mary is unnamed in the *Gospel of John* because in this text she functions as a symbol or archetype, and as a symbol she cannot be reduced to her historical manifestation as Mary alone. The same must be said of the Beloved Disciple; yet the anonymity of the latter must also arise out of more esoteric considerations. We suggest that just as Mary in the Qur'an is spoken of in masculine terminology (she belongs to the masculine *saddiqin*, as well as functioning as a priest), so the masculine Beloved Disciple is none other than Mary Magdalene. This is no more odd than the Christian (Julian of Norwich) and Islamic (Ibn al-'Arabi) traditions which call Jesus "Mother." An equivalent metaphysical centrality of Mary in the Qur'an is achieved through the opposite technique: Mary is the only woman named in the Islamic holy text; all others remain anonymous, not to depreciate them, but to bring attention to Mary's unique role in Islam.

In a little-known essay from 1965, John Bligh offers intriguing evidence that the gospels in their crucifixion accounts portray Jesus as a fulfillment of the types Daniel, Elijah, and Melchizedek. But Bligh neglects to comment on the fact that all three of these figures either survive the assault on their lives, or are deathless immortals. The scriptural Daniel survives "safe and sound";[5] Elijah ascends deathless into heaven in a fiery chariot led by horses. We should here point out some of these connections made by Bligh. The cry from the cross, "My God, my God, why have you left me," a quotation from *Psalm* 22:1, *Eli, Eli, lamah 'azabatani*, followed by Jesus'

---

5. John Bligh, "Typology in the Passion Narratives: Daniel, Elijah, Melchizedek," *The Heythrop Journal*, vol. 6, no. 3 (July 1965), 305.

act of giving up the Spirit, or in *John*'s language, "handing on the Spirit," all of this functions as an allusion to the story of Elijah's ascent to heaven, before which his disciple Elisha asked "for a double share of your Spirit," and during which he cried, "My father, my father, the chariots of Israel and its horses!" Bligh notes that if Jesus, in crying out *Eli, Eli*, articulated the terminal *yodh* consonantally as *Eliy<sup>e</sup>, Eliy<sup>e</sup>*, then this could explain why the bystanders thought he was calling on Elijah.[6]

Bligh in fact suggests that Jesus intended his hearers to think of Elijah, which would imply that Jesus ascended to heaven from the cross at the moment he made the cry. Bligh, however, doesn't draw the parallel between the cross and the fiery chariot of Elijah, which is a significant point to make, for in that case the cross might be portrayed by the gospel writers as the *merkabah* chariot throne of God. This recalls Justin's quotation from a lost targumic reading of the *Psalms* which he applies to the cross: "The Lord shall reign from the tree," which is also paralleled in folio 9b of the *Book of the Resurrection of the Savior by Bartholomew the Apostle*: "I will set your enemies beneath your feet, and you shall reign from the wood of the cross." God thus rescues Jesus from death. Based on the evidence Bligh supplies, the Daniel example is generally convincing (with a few reservations regarding a few details); the Elijah example is less convincing, but still strong. The Melchizedek example is unconvincing viewed from a textual perspective; nevertheless, the comparison is theologically productive.

As Bligh points out, the cry from the cross is the only prayer recorded of Jesus that does not open with an address to the "Father," but we should qualify this since the explanation is that he was quoting *Psalm* 22, and not praying extemporaneously. Then *John* 19:26 has Jesus relinquish his mother to the mysterious "Beloved Disciple." In this way, Jesus becomes

---

6. Ibid., 307.

like Melchizedek, "without father, without mother" (*Hebrews* 7:3).[7]

The *Gospel of Philip* folio 72 gives us the following interpretation of Jesus' utterance on the cross: "'My God, my God, why have you forsaken me?' The Lord uttered these things on the cross, because there he was separated." This enigmatic interpretation is illuminated by the previous saying in folio 71 which states that when Eve was separated from Adam, death came into being. Therefore, what the saying in folio 72 may imply is that the female aspect of Jesus left him at the cross; and this female aspect will be the celestial Mother the Holy Spirit. It was the teaching of the Jewish-Christian Cerinthus that Jesus' words "My God, my God, why have you forsaken me?" referred to the celestial Christ, or Holy Spirit, which after descending upon Jesus at his baptism, departed from him on or shortly before the cross. The Jewish Christians very likely saw this departure of the Holy Spirit in the gospels' statement that Jesus "gave up" or "handed over the Spirit."

In this connection we should refer to *Odes of Solomon* 24, which opens with verses 1-2:

1. The dove fluttered over the Messiah, because he was her head;
2. And she sang over him and her voice was heard.

These lines are generally understood as referring to Jesus' baptism. Yet in the following verses all of creation begins to perish as chaos is unleashed. Instead of referring to Jesus' baptism, might this *Ode* instead be a description of the cross? In that case, verses 3-14 (the remainder of the *Ode*) would describe the upheavals of nature associated with Golgotha in the canonical gospels, as well as Jesus' *descensus ad inferos*, a theme treated extensively elsewhere in the *Odes*. If this surmise is correct, then how would one interpret verses 1-2? We suggest the possibility that the dove which "fluttered over the

---

7. Ibid., 308-09.

Messiah" is the Spirit who departed from Jesus on the cross; as verse 4 states: "The bird began to fly." Verse 7's "submersion of the Lord" would describe the *descensus ad inferos*. After the harrowing of hell, the *Ode* ends appropriately on a note of redemption in verses 13-14:

13. For the Lord disclosed his way, and spread abroad his grace;
14. And those who understood it, knew his holiness.

We have already had occasion to mention that Stroumsa has made an important study of origins of early Christian docetic understandings of the crucifixion as being rooted in part on the application to Jesus of the typology of the binding (*aqedah*) of Isaac, who was saved from sacrificial death at the last moment.[8] The Hebrew name 'Isaac' was understood to mean 'he will laugh', and this is the origin of the docetic traditions which portray Jesus as laughing at the suffering of the cross.[9] Origen dealt with this seeming incongruity by asserting that while Jesus "suffered in his flesh," the Logos "remained in incorruptibility."[10] According to Clement of Alexandria in his *Paedagogus*, Isaac laughed when he was delivered from death.[11] Yet both Origen and Clement hold that Jesus died and was raised from death; they therefore do not consistently apply the Isaac typology to Jesus.

Stroumsa notes the curious fact that Philo's treatise *De Isaaco* (*On Isaac*) has not survived; that this might be the result of an intentional censuring by Christians is suggested by the facts that Philo's writings were transmitted by Christians and that the section on Isaac's *aqedah* has been deleted from the surviving manuscripts of Philo's *Questions in Genesis*.[12] Philo

---

8. Guy G. Stroumsa, "Christ's Laughter: Docetic Origins Reconsidered," *Journal of Early Christian Studies*, vol. 12, no. 3 (2004), 267-88.
9. Ibid., 267.
10. See ibid., 277.
11. Ibid., 278.
12. Ibid., 284.

teaches that God was the father of Isaac (*Quod Det.* 124; *Mut. Nom.* 131); in *De Cherubim.* 42-5 and *Post.* 134, Philo explains that God made Sarah to be a virgin again in order to bear the Son of God, who is Isaac.[13] This portrayal of Isaac as the Son of God born of a virgin may have offended certain Christians, threatened by its perceived undermining of Jesus' uniqueness.[14] Yet Jesus' status as virgin-born Son of God would not have been the reason for censuring Philo, for after all, we still have his passages on this particular theme. We would suggest that what would have offended Christians to the point of destroying a manuscript, or portions of such, would have been what Philo might have said about the *aqedah*, which would probably suggest a docetic escape from death.

Stroumsa briefly mentions Islamic traditions regarding a laughing Jesus contrasted with a frowning John the Baptist, though without supplying references. We are not familiar with such a contrast, for the sources we know of present the reverse portrayal, as in the following two *ahadith*:

> In one of the books which have been translated [it is said] that John [Yuhanna] and Simon were among the disciples. John never sat in any company without laughing and making those around him laugh; and Simon never sat in any company without weeping and making those around him weep. [Once] Simon said to John, "How often you laugh, as though you had ceased from your work!" John replied to him, "How often you weep, as though you had despaired of your Lord!" Then God revealed to the Messiah, "The more attractive of the two natures to Me is John's nature."
>
> In a book also [it is said] that Jesus, son of Mary, met John [Yahya], son of Zechariah (Blessing and peace be upon them!) and John smiled to him. Then Jesus said to him, "Verily you smile the smile of a believer." John said to him, "Verily

---

13. Ibid., 285-86.
14. Ibid., 287.

you frown the frown of a despondent one." God then revealed to Jesus, "What John does is more attractive to me."[15]

However, since these two texts end with a revelation to Jesus that laughter is preferable to sorrow, they do in fact support Strouma's point.

---

15. James Robson, *Christ in Islam* (London: John Murray, 1929), 108-09.

# 7. Models of Early Christologies

**PART III**
The Angelic Christ and the Resurrection

There is yet another factor involved in the purely Jewish origins of docetism which Stroumsa does not cover, namely, angelic Christology, or the Ebionite view that Jesus (or Christ as the case may be) was an angel; this also accords with the Jewish esoteric conception of Isaac or Israel as an angel. Recall the story of the angel Raphael eating in the *Book of Tobit* with the stories of the resurrected Jesus eating in the canonical gospels; the difference being that the latter stress that Jesus is not a spirit (or angel) but really of flesh and blood, so that he is really eating. But this motif may represent more of a metaphysical than an historical dimension of the stories. Even Paul seems to have a docetic strain, which may be reflected in *Romans* 8:3's phrase "the *likeness* of sinful sarx" (which applies to Jesus' birth) and *Philippians* 2's term "the *likeness* of a servant" (which applies to Jesus' earthly end). An angel Christology is indirectly apparent in the *Letter to the Hebrews*, which allusively polemicizes against angel Christology in its first chapter, and also later directly states: "He did not take to himself the seed of angels, but the seed of Abraham." For the Ebionites, the "apparent" body would have been precisely just such an "angelic" body.

Alternatively there could have been a tradition that held the angel Christ had been truly human from birth, but that at the cross he became an angel, or assumed an angelic body. Early patristic literature commonly mentions the theme of saints being transformed into angels during their martyrdoms. And the resurrected, according to *Luke*, do not eat, drink, or marry, so that *Luke*'s own stories of the resurrected Jesus eating may have to be understood in the sense of an "apparent" eating in an angelic mode. Even Paul says that the kingdom of God does not consist of eating or drinking. This model suggests that docetism may have originated in the end of Jesus' earthly career, rather than at its beginning, a central point that Stroumsa insightfully makes in connection with the *aqedah*.

In Ebionite terms, Jesus is the human, Christ is the angel, incarnate in a series of prophets. The angelic Christ did not die, but ascended at the crucifixion. The unique characteristic of the Ebionite metaphysics was to mystically link Jesus and the Christ-angel. The *Gospel of the Hebrews*' phrase "rest in you forever"[1] implies that the maternal Spirit rested "in" Jesus even beyond the crucifixion, for although the Spirit departed from Jesus at the cross, implying a severance between Jesus and the angel Spirit-Christ resting in him, nevertheless the rest is forever, so that the departure would have to have been temporary.

If Jesus did not die, then he was made immortal, that is, what happened to him is what Paul says will happen to Christians who live until the *parousia*, who will not experience death, but an instantaneous transfiguration into the glorified, angelic state. One fact is clear, namely, the Ebionites believed in an immortal Jesus, "the living Jesus" (cf. the *Thomas incipit*). Perhaps Jesus called on Elijah on the cross, because it was commonly believed that Elijah would resurrect the dead, based on the story of Elijah raising the dead, and on the story of Elijah's own escape from death. According to the scriptures, Elijah and Enoch never died, and Enoch was transformed into the angel Metatron. The deathless ascensions of both Enoch and Elijah seem to have served as scriptural models for Jesus' own ascension, yet the Enoch-Elijah paradigms would not be applicable to Jesus' ascension if he

---

1. Compare "rest in," with *John* 1:14's "dwelt in," "tabernacled in."

had died previously. In *2 Enoch*, Enoch ascends by disappearing when darkness descends upon the earth. At the crucifixion there was an eclipse, and this darkening could imply the thought that Jesus ascended, like Enoch, during that darkness, after which an "apparent" body miraculously appeared on the cross at just that moment, precisely as Isaac had been, through a direct miraculous intervention, replaced by a lamb on Mount Moriah. Jesus would accord symbolically in this case with Isaac rather than with the lamb. In *2 Enoch*, Enoch is transformed (into Metatron), and then descends to teach on the earth for 30 days, but his angelic counterpart or higher self would still have been in heaven while he was on earth, a scenario reminiscent of what are apparently Jesus' words spoken on earth in *John* 3:13: "No one has ascended into heaven but the one who descended from heaven, even the Son of Man, who is in heaven." Later scribes, some puzzled by this verse's implication of a Son of Man simultaneously present in heaven and on earth, others puzzled by its implication that Jesus and the Son of Man were apparently somehow distinct entities, deleted the final clause "who is in heaven." In *Luke*'s Emmaus story and *John*'s Magdalene appearance story, Jesus is a polymorphic shape-shifter, like an angel.

The docetic understanding of Jesus' conception and birth is Jewish Christian in its deepest essence. *Odes of Solomon* 19 and the *Ascension of Isaiah* speak of a painless Virgin birth. The *Gospel of the Hebrews*' statement regarding "My mother, the Holy Spirit" and its portrayal of Mary as Michael incarnate, along with the *Gospel of Philip*'s Holy Spirit as feminine, all of these traditions are rooted in a Semitic mentatlity. A developed angeology entered Jewish thought after the exile to Babylon, but even before this there must have been ancient Near Eastern concepts in Israel, so that there is no need to see Greco-Oriental influences in docetism that already centuries before had not previously been integrated seamlessly into Judaism (e.g., *Tobit*), but this means, as Boyarin stresses, Judaism is itself in a sense a Hellenism or an Orientalism.

The *Gospel of the Hebrews* reflects the belief in an angelic Jesus and an angelic Mary. The belief in a further terrestrial angel is found in the Jewish-Christian text *Prayer of Joseph*, according to which the patriarch Jacob was an angel, or as the similar *Prayer of Jacob* phrases it, a "terrestrial angel." Goulder speculates that the *Letter to the Hebrews* may have been written to the church "in Rome or elsewhere."[2] The Ebionite Christology was not only tolerated in Rome in the late first-century and early second century, but prophets approved by the highest Roman church authorities promoted Jewish Christianity, as demonstrated by the example of the Roman prophet who wrote the *Shepherd of Hermas*, the composition of which extends probably from the 80s to about 100 CE. Yet given the similarities between the *Letter to the Hebrews* and the *Gospel of the Hebrews*, and given the Syro-Palestinian provenance of the latter, the former may have been directed either to a Syro-Palestinian church such as Jerusalem or Edessa, or perhaps even Antioch. But what event would have caused the author to write the *Letter to the Hebrews*? Something has transpired that has strengthened the position of the Ebionites in the congregation to such an extent that the author is driven to intervene by writing. The situation would be similar to what happened in Galatia; a church which had been Pauline was subsequently exposed to a successful Ebionite mission, prompting a forceful intervention by Paul. The *Letter to the Hebrews* seems to have been written from Italy (cf. 13:24), which could suggest the author is writing to the Roman church. If so, we may hazard to guess that the *Gospel of the Hebrews* was in circulation in Rome. The *Letter to the Hebrews* bears certain similarities to *1 Clement*, and the Roman Clement's intervention in the Corinthian schism is notable. Based on what we know of Corinth, the problem there in Clement's time would have been a revival of Pauline versus Jewish-Christian factions. It may be that the *Letter to the Hebrews* was written to the Jewish-Christian faction at Corinth. In any case, one is struck by the

---

2. Michael Goulder, "Hebrews and the Ebionites," *New Testament Studies*, vol. 49 (2003), 403.

peaceful co-existence of a Pauline Clement and a Jacobean Hermas in the leadership of the Roman church.

Above we remarked that the ascent of Jesus seems to have been associated with the darkness that descended on Good Friday. We find an illustration of this in the *Gospel of Bartholomew* chapter 1 where Jesus vanishes from the cross when the darkness falls upon the earth:

> 6) And Bartholomew said: "Lord, when you went to be hanged upon the cross, I followed you afar off and saw you hung upon the cross, and the angels coming down from heaven and worshipping you. And when there came darkness,
> 7) I beheld and I saw that you were vanished away from the cross.... Tell me, Lord, where did you go from the cross?"
> 8) And Jesus answered and said: "Blessed are you, Batholomew, my beloved, because you saw this mystery; and now will I tell you all things whatsoever you ask me.
> 9) For when I vanished away from the cross, then I went down into Hades, that I might bring up Adam and all that were with him, according to the supplication of Michael the archangel."[3]

In verse 20 we learn that Jesus brought the patriarchs from Hades "and came again unto the cross." Verse 21 reads: "Bartholomew says to him: 'I saw you again, hanging upon the cross, and all the dead arising and worshipping you,'" to which some manuscripts add a contradictory statement that has all the earmarks of an interpolation, "and going up again into their sepulchers." When the discourse is finished, we are told in verse 35: "And when he had said this he gave them the *shalom*, and vanished away from them." That the risen Christ could vanish is known from the canonical gospels; and that he could vanish already while on the cross suggests that on the cross he was already risen, indeed that the cross coincides with his ascent.

---

3. M. R. James, *The Apocryphal New Testament*, 167; modified.

The speeches of *Acts* do not contain the "third day" resurrection motif (which was itself based anagogically on the motif of Jesus' "three hours" on the cross). *Matthew* chapters 27-28 give us all the necessary clues to reconstruct what happened on the historical plane on Good Friday. To speak theologically, Jesus was raised to the divine Glory from the cross; others were seen resurrected, in a risen state, and this constitutes a *merkabah* ascent vision. But that a *vision* was involved does not imply that the events under discussion were not fully real; on the contrary, as Paul explains, what is seen passes away, but what is unseen is eternal. The resurrection appearances were visions of actual transcendent realities, but being manifested in the mode of divine visions, the general public could not see the ascent and descent of Jesus on Good Friday; only the women saw the vision; the guards were astounded not because they saw a vision of resurrected saints, but purely on account of the earthquake and other natural phenomena. Again, the word vision does not imply hallucination, but a divine gift of seeing into another dimension of reality which is more real than the corporeal terrestrial realm.

According to John Damascene, the Qur'an says that the Romans killed but a "shadow" of Christ, that is, "his likeness." Let us not forget that according to *Luke* the risen Jesus could walk through walls and appear in different forms so that people did not even recognize him. Dialectics are required here, for we are dealing with an atemporal death and an instantaneous ascension. The "shadow" could imply a *Doppelgänger* motif, and "shadow" also recalls the "shades" or "shadows" of Sheol. The ancient idea of "the double," which included concepts of a celestial counterpart that looked the same as one's earthly self, could be applied to the Ebionite idea of the two "natures" of Jesus Christ, because the glorified Enoch (Metatron) descends to earth for a temporary period to teach, after which he must then re-ascend to heaven. The celestial counterpart of Jesus was the celestial Christ, or the Holy Spirit, which descended upon him and entered into him at his baptism, and which separated from him at the cross. As Jesus was on the cross, his humanity was transfigured, and the Spirit ascended to God, leaving the transfigured humanity on the cross. This transfigured humanity was capable of shape-shifting and passing through solid matter, as we know from the canonical gospels. The transfigured Jesus could thus not sense pain on the cross. Such a body, according to ancient conceptions, is not wholly spirit, but rather consists of transfigured matter and spirit. It could be handled, but then be just as untouchable as before. Such a body could accordingly be handled and even buried, but yet it would not be truly lifeless.

With regard to the story in the *Gospel of the Hebrews* that Jesus gave his shroud to the servant of the High Priest, John Painter suggests that here "shroud" (*sindona*) may mean "body," based on a comparison of *Thomas* 21 and the Nag Hammadi *Treatise on the Resurrection* 45:15-40.[4] This is quite forced and unconvincing. More natural is Chilton's explanation that Jesus' gift of the linen *sindona* to the High Priest enables and authorizes the latter "to conduct acceptable sacrifice."[5]

The Qur'an exhorts believers: "Do not think of the martyrs as dead," for they live in another dimension, in a mode of life so real that earthly life is as death compared to it. The Jacobean conception of Jesus' crucifixion seems to assume a mirror image of Jesus' body; an image does not suffer; and a mirror image is a double, a metaphysical hologram, a temporary likeness composed perhaps not of ordinary matter or spirit, but of the substance from which both of these derive. According to the Qur'an some Jews brag, "we killed the Messiah," but the Qur'an insists that he is alive, for God raised him to the divine presence, which could mean that he didn't die truly, or permanently. The Qur'an here does not attack the Christian belief in Jesus' death; it only speaks against those

---

4. John Painter, *Just James: The Brother of Jesus in History and Tradition* (Columbia: University of South Carolina Press, 1997), 186.

5. Bruce Chilton and Jacob Neusner, eds., *The Brother of Jesus. James the Just and His Mission* (Louisville, Kentucky: Westminster John Knox Press, 2001), 155.

particular Jews who boasted of eliminating the Messiah by means of crucifixion. This sheds a whole new light on the passage. Similarly, all the Gnostic docetic accounts of the Passion serve the same purpose, that is, of denying the claims of certain enemies of Jesus of having exterminated the Messiah.

The Gnostic "separation" of Jesus and Christ may be compared with the dualism of body and spirit in Greek philosophical anthropology. It is clear in Nag Hammadi texts that the "likeness" of Jesus which was crucified means the body conceived as the "likeness," or inferior reflection, or shadow of the essential self. The Semitic mind sees a unit with physical and energetic aspects/modes, thus requiring the doctrine of the bodily resurrection, in contrast to the Greek conception of the immortality of the soul, which does not require a belief in a corporeal resurrection. On the other hand, even first century Palestinian Rabbinic thought had integrated Greek Platonism. And Paul held the resurrected body to be a spirit body (not implying a *"ghostly* body"), which in Platonic terms is nothing other than the pneuma. On the cross, Jesus' spirit separated from his body—this is one possible implication of Cerinthus' teaching regarding the departure of the Christ or Holy Spirit from Jesus at the cross. But because of the penetration of Platonic thought in first-century Palestine, we cannot say that Cerinthus' anthropology was "Hellenistic" in contrast to John's reputedly Semitic and "wholistic" (i.e., holistic) anthropology. To a large extent, this conflict was based more on John's and Cerinthus' diverse anthropologies than on their Christologies. In support of Cerinthus, the pre-existent Messiah-Logos is certainly to be distinguished from the human nature with which it united; in this respect Cerinthus and Thomas Aquinas coincide, in that the latter distinguishes between the Logos and the humanity of Jesus Christ. In support of John, the union of the Logos and the human nature justifies the "oneness of person" over against the "distinction of natures." The pre-existent Christ is the Logos and the Spirit.

# 8. Models of Early Christologies

**PART IV**
## Ebionite Christic and Marian Pneumatology

According to the synoptic gospels Jesus at his baptism sees the Holy Spirit descend as a dove, which as a symbol of peace suggests repose or rest. Hence the account in the *Gospel of the Hebrews* makes eminent sense when it introduces the theme of rest into its baptism narrative. And the Holy Spirit having rested, she shall reign over the All for ever; thus we recall that passage of the *Gospel of the Hebrews* mirrored in the *Gospel of Thomas* logion 2 and in Clement of Alexandria, in various forms: "Jesus said: 'He who seeks, let him not cease seeking until he finds; and when he finds he will be perplexed; and when he has been perplexed he will reign; and when he has reigned he will rest." In light of the fragments preserved from the *Gospel of the Hebrews* we suggest that this logion might on one level be applied to the Holy Spirit, who sought rest and found it in the true prophet. By indwelling Jesus at his baptism she finishes her work of creation. According to the Qur'an, when God finished the work of creation he rested upon his throne, which means transparently that having rested, he reigned, and that he reigned over the All is shown by the Throne Verse, which tells us that the divine throne is co-extensive with the heavens and the earth, that is, the entire cosmos, the All, the cosmic Pleroma.

We must here more deeply explore the implications of the concept of the Holy Spirit as Mother dwelling in her son the true prophet. The idea of a son dwelling in his mother is perfectly natural, but what of the perplexing converse imagery?

The key to a solution is that the Mother appears under her aspect of Spirit, which is the universal indweller or cosmic pervader (cf. *Wisdom* 12:1: "For thy immortal Spirit is in all things"). Just as, according to *John* 17 the Father dwells in the Son (and naturally the Son dwells in the Father), so the picture becomes complete when we remember that earlier in the same discourse the Son had spoken repeatedly of the Holy Spirit, the Paraclete, *she* who would indwell the apostles. The triadic interpenetration of persons, or hypostastic emanations, makes the maternal indwelling within the Son fully comprehensible. The standard scholarly form-critical judgment that the *Gospel of the Hebrews* represents merely a secondary elaboration of the reputedly primary canonical accounts of the events in question ignores the fact that even the canonical gospels narrate the events of Jesus' life from the point of view of theological elaboration. The critics also remain ignorant, generally speaking, to the fact that, theologically viewed, the Holy Spirit as the source of all truth may have inspired such "embellishment."

In the final analysis, theological insight is more important than a narration of historical events which fails to penetrate into the meaning and significance hidden behind or within outward events or phenomena. If one were to witness, for example, the ritual surrounding the Eucharist without the eyes of faith, one would be left with a bland and disappointing account about some meaningless phrases and actions performed by a priest passing his hands over ordinary bread and wine. However, were one to write a description of the same event from the eyes of faith, and to describe the descent of countless hosts of angels, the appearance of Christ and his mother, or the descent of the Spirit in the form of a dove, the unbelieving witness would charge the believer's account as being either a pious fraud or a delusion of religious fervor and fanaticism. Yet theologically speaking, the fact would remain that the account from the perspective of faith has sincerely and acceptably described the underlying spiritual significance of what has transpired on the occular plane.

After the Spirit's descent at Jesus' baptism and her declaration of Jesus' sonship, then each of the three synoptic gospels state that the Spirit then drove him into the desert to be tempted for 40 days. It is usually conjectured that the *Gospel of the Hebrews* refers to Jesus' temptation where we find the words, "My mother the Holy Spirit just now lifted me by the hairs of my head and brought me to Mount Tabor." But we would suggest that this might describe a *merkabah* ascent effected by the descent of the Holy Spirit at Jesus' baptism, and in fact, as we saw in the previous chapter, Origen interpreted Jesus baptism as involving a *merkabah* vision.[1] That Jesus is the Son of the Mother when the voice proclaims, "You are my son; this day have I begotten you," is supported by *Revelation* chapter 12 where the celestial Woman, who is doubtless the Holy Spirit, gives birth to the Son, although here the birth spoken of is that of the resurrection-ascension. But in light of the *Apocalypse of Peter*, which portrays Jesus' transfiguration as his ascension, we may conclude that, esoterically considered, Jesus' baptism, transfiguration, ascension, and even parousia might ultimately be but diverse refractions of a single luminous event which we may call the Messianic birth. The Holy Spirit as Mother gives birth to the Messiah. Jesus' resurrection-ascension as effected by means of the maternal Spirit is referred to by Paul when he writes: "If the Spirit of him who raised Jesus from the dead dwells in you, he [God] who raised Christ Jesus from the dead will give life to your mortal bodies also through his Spirit who dwells in you" (*Romans* 8:11). In a different yet related sense, we read in *1 Peter* 3:18 that Jesus was "put to death in the flesh but made alive in the Spirit."[2]

According to Philo, the First Adam (cf. *Genesis* 1:26ff.) is the intelligible Image of God, an androgynous archetype, simultaneously both masculine and feminine. The second or

---

1. David J. Halperin, "Origen, Ezekiel's Merkabah, and the Ascension of Moses," *Church History*, vol. 50, no. 3 (Sep., 1981), 261-75.

2. Peter's statements on Jesus' death must always be read against the background of the church's application to Jesus of the Isaac typology, according to which Isaac was rescued from death at the last moment.

final Adam (cf. *Genesis* 2) was the physical or natural Adam made of clay. For the Jewish Christians, the first and last Adam are both protological, whereas for Paul the last Adam is the eschatological Jesus the Messiah, or Jesus Christ. For Jewish Christianity the first Adam is the Holy Spirit, or an emanation from the Spirit of Holiness, and is precisely the divine "Spirit" or Breath which God breathed into the final or second Adam, in order to animate him. The pneumatic (= Spirit) Adam is the pre-existent "Christ," whereas the somatic (= bodily) Adam corresponds to the humanity of the prophet Jesus. The Jewish Christians thus believed, expressed of course in different language, in what later would be referred to as the human and "divine" natures of Jesus Christ. For Jewish Christianity, the "union" of "Jesus Christ" in Pauline theology "confused" through simplistic identification the two natures of Jesus Christ. Aquinas' doctrine of the distinction between Jesus' human nature and the divine pre-existent Logos is thus analogically subject to reconciliation with the Jewish-Christian Christologies. On the other hand, the "union" of the Spirit and Messiah is also taught in Jewish-Christian theology, for according to the latter, the Spirit entered into Jesus at his baptism. If Pauline theology's "union" of the two natures is understood as a true "distinctive" union rather than a "con-fusion," then the Great Church's and the Jerusalem Church's Christologies can be reconciled, at least in this regard.

In a previous chapter we discussed *1 Corinthians* 12:3 where Paul complains that certain Jewish Christians have proclaimed in the assembly: "Jesus is anathema!" We understand the word anathema in its non-pejorative sense: "Jesus is separated," that is, "Jesus is set aside" for God's sacred use. In *1 John*, in a section which possesses several parallels with the *1 Corinthians* 12 passage, the prophet is attacked who, according to a variant reading in certain manuscripts, "separates" Jesus Christ. Now the fuller exegesis of the *1 Corinthians* passage falls into relief: The Jewish-Christian Christology "separates" Jesus Christ into two natures, an earthly nature designated as Jesus, and a celestial nature designated as Christ or the Holy

Spirit. By contrast, Pauline Christology identifies or "con-fuses" both natures in the proclamation: "Jesus *is* Lord,"[3] or "Jesus *is* the Christ." Here, 'Christ' in the Pauline sense overlaps with *Kyrios*, and is therefore quite different in meaning and accentuation than the Jewish-Christian proclamation that "Jesus is Messiah." But we might offer a further precision, namely, that Jewish Christians understood the term "Messiah" to be the "heavenly pre-existent Holy Spirit," to use the terminology of *Hermas*, which is conceptually matched in the *Parables of Enoch*. That is, the Messiah is not an earthly human being, but a celestial power which "descends" in the last days. The Jewish Christians understood this pre-existent "Christ" as having descended upon Jesus at his baptism. Thus the Jerusalem church understood the phrase "Jesus Christ" to mean, "Jesus, the recipient of the Christ-Spirit," or "Jesus, the Anointed of the Spirit." Paul, by contrast, sees Jesus as the Christ, even as the pre-existent Christ. For Jewish Christianity, this verbal identification would have been acceptable if understood in an analogical sense implying "union," but not "con-fusion."

If Jesus is the Christ, then the human Jesus pre-existed, and Paul asserts this when he portrays "Jesus Christ" as pre-existing as the agent of creation (*Colossians* 1). Jewish Christianity, as well as standard Catholic theology, is more in line with the idea that the human nature of Jesus Christ did not pre-exist, but was created in time, in history, in the womb of the Virgin Mary. This created nature was then "united" with the "divine" nature, or the eternally pre-existent Logos, or Word of God. But Paul's doctrine can be reconciled with this standard paradigm if one understands his pre-existent "Je-

---

3. Incidentally, when the Aramaic speaking Christians of Jerusalem prayed "O Lord, come" (*Maranatha*), they were addressing God, not Jesus. These same Jewish Christians doubtless also prayed to Jesus, but not as to God. Yet their prayers to Jesus were not offered in the same mode as in Catholicism's invocation of saints or angels, because for the Ebionites Jesus had been united with the highest angel, who in fact was the supra-angelic Word of God.

sus Christ" doctrine as implying a non-con-fusing "union" of the two natures, so that analogically one may speak of "Jesus Christ" as pre-existent. But in the strict sense, what must be avoided is the literal assertion that Jesus' created nature is the eternal, uncreated Logos. To equate the created with the uncreated would be blasphemy, and it is this blasphemy of an overly simplistic identitative Christology which exhaustively equates Jesus with the uncreated Logos which Jewish Christianity and the Qur'an protests prophetically.

We must not equate Paul's Christology with some later Christians' simplistic identification of Jesus with the uncreated Logos, just as we must not identify every aspect of the later Jewish-Christian Christologies with the Jerusalem Christologies of the twelve apostles. However, in the final analysis, we must concede that there were serious areas of perceived conflict and tension between the Pauline and Jerusalem Christologies. This much is clear from the New Testament texts themselves. Not all theological tensions between these two Christological paradigms can be removed, given the limitations of human language and discourse; but an appreciable amount of the tension can be removed by the application of the Scholastic doctrine of analogical predication, and beyond this, of esoteric metaphysics; that is, both Christologies must to a certain extent be viewed in a non-literal or analogical (and in certain respects, metaphorical) light.

Generally speaking, Jewish Christianity identified Jesus' divine anointing with the "Christ" or Spirit as his baptism by John the Baptist. Again, Paul identifies Jesus and the Spirit by insisting that "the Lord (= Jesus) *is* the Spirit"—and *John* 7 goes so far as to say that there was no Spirit before Jesus' glorification. The Jewish-Christian understanding is reflected in the *Gospel of Mark*, which states that during his baptism "the Spirit *entered into* Jesus," so that a true union of natures, and not merely an outward or extrinsic "anointing" is envisaged by Jewish-Christian theology. According to *Matthew* and *Luke*, this moment of union is pushed back to Jesus' conception. Yet neither *Matthew* nor *Luke* identify Jesus with the Holy Spirit or with the pre-existent Logos. The question of when the union of Jesus and the Spirit occurred involves Jewish-Christian pneumatology and, by extension, Mariology.

Jewish-Christian theology understood the pre-existent Christ to be intimately associated with the Holy Spirit, which is reflected in the Targumic interchangeability of *Memra*, *Shekhinah*, and Holy Spirit. The same theological constellation of themes identifies the Christ with the angel Gabriel. One immediately thinks of Islamic tradition which identifies the Annunciation's Holy Spirit with the angel Gabriel. The Jewish-Christian *Epistle of the Apostles*, as well as the *Pistis Sophia*, identify the angel Gabriel with Christ. Note well, the angel Gabriel is identified with Christ, not with Jesus, though the two are "unified." For Jewish Christians, however, the Holy Spirit always possesses a feminine dimension, and this is in part associated with the Virgin Mary. It is no coincidence that certain "Gnostic" motifs are encountered in the Jewish-Christian literature. One recalls the previously discussed account in the *Gospel of the Hebrews* in Coptic Cyril, according to which the Virgin Mary (actually her celestial counterpart) pre-existed as a heavenly "power" (= angel), namely, the angel Michael. (When we recall that the *Shepherd of Hermas* identifies the angel Michael with the Holy Spirit, then we see that the *Gospel of the Hebrews* may be implying that Mary is a theophany of the Holy Spirit). Thus like Jesus Christ, the Virgin Mary possessed two natures, a human nature and an angelic nature, designated respectively by the terms "Mary" on the hand and by "Virgin" or "Mother" on the other. The Virgin Spirit descended upon or into Mary at the Annunciation, mirroring the descent of the Spirit into Jesus at his baptism. The descent of the Spirit upon or into Mary effects the humanity of Jesus; the descent of the Spirit into Jesus effects the angelic nature, the Christ. The constitution of Mary as the Virgin Mother, that is, Mary's unification with the Holy Spirit, takes place on the earthly plane at her immaculate conception, and proleptically in eternity. The same could be said of Jesus and the Word. For Jewish-Christian theology, the Holy Spirit, or the Christ, indwelt Adam (as did Eve), and this Spirit journeyed through the line of prophets through the ages, until at Jesus' baptism, the Spirit rested in the true prophet. But the same paradigm applies to the feminine dimension of the Spirit, who found plenary rest in the Virgin Mary. Such an elaborate system of Mariology is by no means only a "later" development in Christian theology, for its general paradigms are present implicitly from the beginning of Christian thought via the Jewish scriptures, namely, in *Proverbs* 8, *Sirach* 24, *Wisdom* 7, and *Baruch* 3-4.

If Jesus was anointed during his ministry with the Holy Spirit to work wonders and miracles, then his mother, unified with the same Spirit, could also work wonders, specifically the miracle spoken of in the *Gospel of the Hebrews*: "My mother the Holy Spirit took me by the hair of my head to the holy mount." This parallels the passage in *Ezekiel* 8:1-3:

> 1) ...the hand of the Lord fell there upon me. 2) And I saw, and behold, a likeness as the appearance of fire; from the appearance of his loins, and downward, fire; and from his loins, and upward as the appearance of brightness, as the appearance of amber. 3) And the likeness of a hand was put forth and took me by a lock of my head, and the Spirit lifted me up between the earth and heaven, and brought me in the vision of God into Jerusalem....

The prophet then sees "the idol of jealousy." Verse 2 alludes back to the *merkabah* vision of chapter 1:26ff, of the divine human form upon the throne of God, and the parallel in 8:2-3 with the *Gospel of the Hebrews* strengthens our previous *merkabah* interpretation of the *Gospel of the Hebrews*. Moreover, *Ezekiel* 8:3's reference to the evil "idol of jealousy" connects the *Gospel of the Hebrews* passage with the temptation of Jesus in the desert, where the evil Satan thrice appeared to him. In this context it is noteworthy that whereas the synoptic gospels record that Jesus "gave up" his spirit, according to the *Gospel of John* he "handed over" his Spirit just after he handed over Mary to the Beloved Disciple.

M. R. James argues that not only did Cyril not write the Coptic treatise, but that the passage in question did not form a part of the same *Gospel of the Hebrews* as quoted by Origen and Jerome. Dieter Lührmann (2004) makes the same argument.[4] However, Robert J. Miller, in an influential and widely used text, *The Complete Gospels*, assumes the authenticity of the Cyril fragment.[5] Miller writes that the *Gospel of the Hebrews* apparently taught the "pre-existence" of not only Jesus, but also of the Virgin Mary. Though the following connection is not generally made by scholars, we find the same doctrine of the angelic Mary in the medieval writings of the Gnostic Albigensians of Southern France; in their *Liber S. Ioannis*, the *Book of John* (*the Evangelist*), we read: "When my Father thought to send me into the world, he sent his angel before me, by name Mary, to receive me."[6] We see here the same Jewish-Christian teaching as found in the *Gospel of the Hebrews* according to the Cyril text: "It is written in the [Gospel] to the Hebrews that when Christ <u>wished to come upon the earth</u> to men [cf. *Liber S. Ioannis* 'thought to send me into the world'], <u>the Good Father</u> [cf. *Liber S. Ioannis* 'my Father'] called a mighty 'power' in the heavens which was called 'Michael', and committed Christ to the care thereof. And the 'power' came down into the world, and it was called Mary."

But in the *Liber S. Ioannis* we see a harsh polemic against John the Baptist, suggesting the possibility that this work was redacted at a time when there was fierce competition between a group of Jewish Christians and Mandaeans or some group with a similar anti-Jesus persuasion. (M. R. James misses this point by assuming that the references to the followers of John the Baptist in the *Liber S. Ioannis* function as a veiled code for Roman Catholics). This is intriguing since many elements of the *Liber S. Ioannis*, such as its Gnostic creation account and its non-acceptance of Moses, are in fact in agreement with classical Mandaean theology. This points

---

4. Dieter Lührmann, *Die apokryph gewordenen Evangelien*, 233, 237-38.
5. Robert J. Miller, ed. *The Complete Gospels. Annotated Scholars Version*, 428, 430.
6. M. R. James, *The Apocryphal New Testament*, 191.

to a quite early origin for these traditions enshrined in the *Liber S. Ioannis*, which was imported from Bulgaria by a bishop named *Nazarius*,[7] a name which conceivably may allude in some sense to the Nazoraean sect/s. James writes that the book "is a Bogomile production,"[8] but this only reinforces the likelihood that Gnostic groups such as the Bogomiles, Cathars, and Albigensians had preserved a number of quite archaic Jewish-Christian traditions.

As the Spirit came upon Mary at the annunciation, so the Spirit came upon Jesus at his baptism. Yet both were anointed by the Spirit from conception. More precisely, Jesus was united with the eternal "Son," the Logos, whereas Mary was united with the Holy Spirit, the uncreated Mother. And by virtue of the continuity between the anointer and anointed, Jesus and Mary "are" or "were" or "have been," via a retrospective protological projection, the eternal Son and uncreated Holy Spirit. Insofar as one can in this qualified and nuanced sense call or identify Jesus as the Christ or Son of God, so one can call Mary the Spirit of God. But if Mary, as human, cannot receive hyperdulia, neither can the human nature of Christ be "divinity"—Jesus' humanity cannot be worshipped or honored as strictly divine or as God as such. However, conversely, just as by virtue of the continuity established between the anointed and the anointed (or between the human and celestial natures), the humanity of Jesus united with the Son may receive human and angelic worship and honor—recall the Jewish and Qur'anic accounts of the worship of Adam (made in the divine image) by the angels, and this at the command of God—so the Virgin Mary by virtue of her anointing and unity with the Holy Spirit can receive the worship of heaven and earth; but always the celestial nature receives direct worship, while the human nature receives a relative, lesser worship or religious devotion. In Catholic parlance, this is illustrated by the devotion to the Sacred Heart of Je-

---

7. Ibid., 187.
8. Ibid.

sus, and to the Immaculate Heart of Mary, the latter two titles denoting the respective human natures of Son and Mother. By providential design, the Church places emphasis upon the unity between the two natures, while Islam accentuates the differentiation between the two natures. Both perspectives are valid, and both must be retained in order to preserve the legitimately diverse aspects of the truths underlying these metaphysical realities.

*1 Corinthians* 12:3's statement, "Jesus is anathema" as an allusion to the Ebionite separationist Christology may also help shed light on an engmatic passage from the Jewish-Christian *Gospel of Philip* which refers to Mary: "She is a great anathema to the Hebrews, who are the apostles and the apostolic men." If "anathema" here is understood in the positive sense of a sacred entity set aside for religious use in the Temple, then we may have here an allusion to the angelic Mariology attested in the *Gospel of the Hebrews*; Mary is a "great anathema," that is, a mighty power, in the estimation of the Jewish Christians. This same saying denies that Mary conceived by the Holy Spirit, because a woman does not conceive by a woman, which assumes the Jewish understanding of the Holy Spirit as the celestial Mother. This is by no means an unorthodox statement, for ante-Nicene theology held that Mary conceived by the Logos, not by the Spirit.[9] We present here the relevant *Philip* passage:

> Some said, "Mary conceived by the Holy Spirit." They are in error. They do not know what they are saying. When did a woman ever conceive by a woman? Mary is the virgin whom no power defiled. She is a great anathema to the Hebrews, who are the apostles and the apostolic men. No power defiled this virgin, [but rather?] the powers defiled themselves. And the Lord would not have said "My Father who is in Heaven" unless he had had another father, but he would have said simply "My father."

---

9. See J. N. D. Kelly, *Early Christian Doctrines*. Rev. Ed., 103, 144.

What Philip teaches here is that no power, in the sense of "spirit," impregnated Mary, not even the Holy Spirit impregnated her. The Ebionites held sex to be a "defilement" (cf. *Revelation* 14:4), so that not even the Holy Spirit could be said to have impregnated the Virgin. So no heavenly power "impregnated" Mary. The question remains, who was the father of Jesus? The *Philip* saying implies that Jesus had two fathers, the Father in heaven, who is the Unknown Father, and the creator demiurge. The creative demiurge is, however, nothing other than the eternal Logos, and this is the father of Jesus according to *Philip*, who thus agrees with ante-Nicene theology in general. The Father is Jesus' father, not the Holy Spirit, for the Holy Spirit is the *Mother* of Jesus. The saying is criticizing the Hellenistic masculine or neuter understanding of the Holy Spirit. Not the Holy Spirit, but God, metaphorically speaking, is the father of Jesus. But in this context "God" refers not to the Unknown Father, but to God the Word, God as demiurge-creator, or as Ibn al-'Arabi would phrase it, the God of beliefs.

# Part III

## The *Gospel of Thomas*

# 1. Jewish-Christian Features of the Gospel of Thomas

In a number of their works, Guillaumont and Quispel have stressed the Jewish-Christian complexion of the *Thomas* gospel. Quispel detected two layers in *Thomas*, one Jewish-Christian (from Jerusalem, ca. 50 CE), another Hellenistic and Hermetic (from Alexandria, ca. 100). In our commentary below on individual *Thomas* logia, we present philological and other evidence which call into question Quispel's Hermetic thesis. Quispel thought he had found a Hermetic source for logion 67, but this was in actuality a false lead, and as we mentioned in a previous chapter there is in fact a much closer parallel to logion 67 in Palestinian Rabbinic literature. Additionally, perhaps the most Hermetic and dualistic sounding logia in all of *Thomas* (87), turns out to be a curiously overlooked targumic-like rendering of a verse from the Biblical book of the prophet Jeremiah. The specifically Jewish-Christian character of the reputedly Hermetic *Thomas* logia has been missed chiefly because scholars have mistaken Jewish mysticism for Hellenistic Hermeticism. Authorities have *expected* to find Hermetic and Hellenistic thought in *Thomas*, and they have not failed to uncover a number of interesting quasi parallels. In the meantime, Rabbinic, Kabbalistic, and even Biblical parallels have gone unnoticed because unsearched, excluded a priori by flawed methodologies and their underlying assumptions. Since scholars even of the stature of Chilton have characterized certain components of *Thomas* as anti-Jewish we devote here an entire chapter to this question in order to examine the nature of Thomas' general theological *Tendenz*.

*Thomas* logion 53, which deals with the question of circumcision, presents the greatest challenge in all of *Thomas* with regard to the question of Jewish Christianity, for it seems, at least on a first reading, to advocate the Pauline metaphorical approach to circumcision.[1] Before we begin an analysis of the question, we must recognize that it would be unsound to view and interpret logion 53 in isolation, for as Callahan explains, logia 50-53 actually form a single dialogical exchange between Jesus and his disciples.[2] Once we join these logia together, we immediately receive interpretative benefits, for we at once recognize a connection between logion 50's "the *sign* of your father in you" and logion 53's theme of "circumcision," for circumcision is of course traditionally and Biblically designated the 'sign' ('*ot*, literally "letter") of the covenant between God and Israel, the 'chosen people'; it is therefore not without relevance that logion 50 also contains the claim, "we are the *chosen ones* of the living Father."

Since the *Thomas* gospel is an *esoteric* Jewish-Christian document, it would be useful to review the evidence regarding mystical beliefs concerning circumcision within Kabbalistic texts. Wolfson has published two helpful essays on the subject of circumcision beliefs among medieval Kabbalistic Pietists, and their beliefs were in many respects ultimately rooted in more ancient traditions, although modulations in details certainly must be acknowledged. However, the fact that, as we shall see, these medieval Pietist beliefs actually shed significant light on the *Thomas* gospel's basic esoteric trajectories, and that to a previously unhoped for degree, indicates that

---

1. Chilton and Neusner would insist that even Pauline Christianity is "a Judaism." See Bruce Chilton and Jacob Neusner, *Judaism in the New Testament. Practices and Beliefs* (London/NY: Routledge, 1996), 58-97. While we always welcome a broadening of understanding between various faith communities, especially one that promotes mutual tolerance and respect, we must also confront all the relevant evidence regarding a particular individual's self-identity with regard to religion. Paul clearly considers himself to have abandoned what at least he considered Judaism. The clearest statements on his position are found in *Galatians*, for example in 1:13 where he speaks of his "former life in Judaism." This position is precisely what generated conflict between Paul and the Jerusalem apostolic authorities.

2. Callahan, 420.

in this respect we are most likely on the correct exegetical trail. Already in the Rabbinic sources we learn that circumcision ensures entrance to the Garden of Eden at death,[3] and one recognizes that here we gain an immediate link with our block of *Thomas* circumcision logia, for logion 50 deals with the ascent of the soul after death, and logion 51 speaks of "the repose of the dead." Negatively stated, circumcision affords "protection from Gehenna," and is thus an apotropaic rite,[4] precisely as logion 50 with its apotropaic password-like formulae is clearly ritualistic in orientation. Rabbi Judah in the *'Arugat ha-Bosem* explains that as "the soul ascends," God "removes from it all the angels of destruction and the prosecutors, so that they will not come near it." This is because "the Tetragrammaton rests upon the soul," by virtue of the former being inscribed upon the circumcised phallus.[5] Notice that the Tetragrammaton *rests* upon the soul/phallus; compare this with the "sign" which is a "rest" in *Thomas* logion 50. According to Gikatilla's *Sha'arei 'Orah*, circumcision as "the covenant of the living God" is also called "the covenant of Sabbath." With this we may again compare logion 50's "the sign" as a "rest" (cf. a Sabbath).[6] According to *Hekhalot Zutarti* and *Hekhalot Rabbati*, as a person ascends, they reveal the relevant "seals" to the celestial gatekeepers, and thus gain entrance to the palace.[7] This, again, is the precise scenario we find in logion 50.

In the Rabbinic and Pietist texts, the main "seal" that is presented is the sign of circumcision; note again logion 50's

---

3. Cf. Elliot R. Wolfson, "Circumcision and the Divine Name: A Study in the Transmission of Esoteric Doctrine," *The Jewish Quarterly Review*, New Series, vol. 78, no. 1/2 (Jul. - Oct., 1987), 78.

4. Ibid., 80.

5. Ibid., 108.

6. Elliot R. Wolfson, "Circumcision, Vision of God, and Textual Interpretation: From Midrashic Trope to Mystical Symbol," *History of Religions*, vol. 27, no. 2 (Nov., 1987),

7. Elliot R. Wolfson, "Circumcision and the Divine Name: A Study in the Transmission of Esoteric Doctrine," 84.

"the sign of your Father in you." Among the medieval German Hasidim, it was held that circumcision enables one to anticipate to varying degrees the post mortem "cleaving" in this present life,[8] and we here refer the reader to logion 51's statement that the "repose of the dead" has already been realized. The anticipatory and post mortem cleaving to God are both founded upon the connection between circumcision and the Tetragrammaton.[9]

*Bereshit Rabbah* 49,2 explains that the "secret of the Lord" in *Psalm* 25:14 refers to circumcision; this implies the hiddenness of the phallus and the *sefirah* associated with it, *yesod*, 'Foundation', as the *Tsaddiq*, who may be portrayed as the "great hidden light" in *Sefer ha-Bahir*.[10] As Wolfson notes, *B. Hagigah* 12a alludes to the esoteric light that is "stored up for the righteous." Again, consider logion 50's prominent 'light' theme, and that this light is "established," which is semantically proximate to the concept of 'foundation', for 'to be established' may easily signifiy 'to be founded'. *Zohar* 3:11a designates *yesod* as "the Living God."[11] This coincides with logion 50's "the living Father," since in *Thomas* "Father" consistently reverentially stands in place of the term 'God'. In Rabbinic literature, circumcision implies "all the commandments," and for *Zohar* 1:197a "the covenant (of circumcision) is equivalent to the entire Torah";[12] compare the reference to the entire twenty-four prophets of Israel in our *Thomas* circumcision logia block (logion 52).

Wolfson next details how the *Zohar* presents circumcision as a prerequisite for the study of Torah, for the "covenant of the flesh" is necessary for the "covenant of the mouth," i.e., of the Torah.[13] Similarly, physical circumcision, which is accomplished by the seal of the Tetragrammaton upon the phallus,

---

8. Ibid., 95.
9. Ibid., 96.
10. Ibid., 100.
11. Ibid., 101.
12. Ibid., 103, 106.
13. Ibid., 104-05.

precedes the "circumcision of the heart" spoken of in *Deuteronomy* 30:6.¹⁴ *Tiqqune Zohar* 61 explains concerning the Tetragrammaton that its *yod* is the Lesser *Hokhmah* (= *Shekhinah*), the "'fruit of the tree' in the 'head of the Tsaddiq,'" which alludes to the phallic corona.¹⁵ According to *Tiqqune Zohar* 24: "In *the place* of circumcision and uncovering of the corona (the letters of the) Tetragrammaton *rest*."¹⁶ Again, compare *Thomas* logion 50's "*the place* (of) light" and the "sign" which is a "rest."

Whereas the Rabbinic sources associate the divine name *Shaddai* with circumcision, the Kabbalists teach that it is the Tetragrammaton which is inscribed. Menahem Siyyoni in *Sefer Siyyoni* writes concerning the "sign of circumcision" that *Shaddai* is the divine "seal," and explains that when a man's head and arms "are outstretched above," this resembles the letter *shin*; the extension of the left arm and the resting of the right arm resembles the letter *dalet*; and the phallus resembles the letter *yod*. Thus one obtains the name *Shaddai*.¹⁷ The *movement* and the *resting* of the arms here might conceivably be compared to *Thomas* logion 50's "sign" which is "a movement and a rest."

Note as well that the image of the *shin*, with its outstretched arms and head, is also reminiscent of the figure of a person suspended on a cross; this may be of significance for the interpretation of the Syriac Jewish-Christian *Odes of Solomon*, a work which contains frequent allusions to the rite of circumcision which are generally overlooked or "allegorised" away by Christian exegetes (cf. 4:8; 9:11; 11:1-3; ), despite the fact that the "Jewish-Christian" character of the *Odes* is widely touted. Especially significant in this regard is *Ode* 27:1-3: "I *extended* my hands and sanctified my Lord / for the *extension* of my hands is his *sign* / and my *extension* is the exalted tree." Charlesworth

---

14. Ibid., 107.
15. Ibid., 109.
16. Ibid., 110.
17. Ibid.

translates this as "the upright cross," but there is no cross, at least not a non-docetic one, in the *Odes*, for according to this text, Jesus did not die (cf. e.g., 28:17-18). *Odes* 35:7: "And I spread out my hands in the ascent of my soul," that is "in my ascent." The same noun found in *Ode* 27:3 occurs in *Ode* 39:10, where, however, Charlesworth renders it "a beam of wood." We shall presently return to *Ode* 39, which offers an important exegetical key for the present subject. *Ode* 42:1-2: "I *stretched out* my hands and approached[18] my Lord / for the *extension* of my hands is his *sign*. And my *extension* is the exalted tree / that was exalted on the path of the Righteous One." Charlesworth notes that the Syriac term here "also means 'wood', 'tree.'"[19] But he then explains he has translated the term as 'Cross' "because the Odes are Christian," and on account of "the special meaning" of the next line's Ethpeel form of "lifted up," which may refer to the concept of hanging on a cross. Thus Charlesworth entirely misses any of the possible allusions to circumcision, which include the outstretched hands (cf. *shin*), the *sign* of the *Lord* (cf. circumcision as "the sign" of the Tetragrammaton, i.e., the *Lord*), and the Righteous One, i.e., the *Tsaddiq* (n.b.). Moreover *Ode* 42:20 ends the hymnic compilation with: "And I placed my name upon their head," to which we may compare the theme of the inscription of the name LORD in circumcision. We are not necessarily arguing that *Ode* 42:20 directly refers to circumcision, but rather that it at a minimum reflects knowledge of the common Jewish themes associated with the rite, and that it therefore presupposes an acquaintance with and approval of the literal rite of circumcision. Now, to return to *Ode* 39; we read in verses 7-10:

> 7) For the sign in/on them is the Lord; and the sign is the path of those who cross in the name of the Lord.

---

18. According to Moses of Kiev, there is no "approach" to God except through circumcision; cf. ibid., 105.

19. James Hamilton Charlesworth, *The Odes of Solomon*, 146.

8) Therefore put on the name of the Most High and know him, and you shall cross without danger, for the rivers will be subject to you.

9) The Lord has bridged them by his word, and he walked and crossed them on foot.

10) And his footsteps stand firm on the water, and are not destroyed; they are as firm as a tree exalted upon truth.

According to the *Odes*, the *sign* is a *safe path* of *ascent* in the midst of *dangers*; this accords well with the Jewish idea of circumcision as a protection against the toll keepers encountered in the anticipatory or post mortem ascent, a situation reflected in *Thomas* logion 50 as well. In the *Odes*, the *sign* is the path of the *Tsaddiq*, which again conforms to the Rabbinic and Kabbalistic joining of the themes of circumcision and the *Tsaddiq*. The *Odes*' repeated image of the tree in this context may be related to the Kabbalistic circumcision traditions which identify the *Tsaddiq* as a tree (the tree of life), whose fruit is *Shekhinah*.

In a second important essay on circumcision, Wolfson has shown how medieval Kabbalists stressed that circumcision was a prerequisite for having visionary experiences.[20] This essay accentuates the link between circumcision and esoteric scriptural exegesis. Wolfon explains that exegesis renders the "concealed, hidden" as "disclosed," and textual "disclosure" corresponds to the unveiling of the phallus in circumcision.[21] Wolfson reminds us that Philo in his *Quaestiones et Solutiones in Genesin* 3,49 calls circumcision "the sign of election,"[22] and with this we may compare *Thomas* logion 50's "we are the cho-

---

20. Elliot R. Wolfson, "Circumcision, Vision of God, and Textual Interpretation: From Midrashic Trope to Mystical Symbol," *History of Religions*, vol. 27, no. 2 (Nov., 1987), 189-215.
21. Ibid., 191-92.
22. Ibid., 192.

sen (elect) ones," which immediately preceds the reference to the "sign of your father in you."

*Numbers Rabbah* interprets *Leviticus* 9:6's "This is the thing (*ha-davar*) which the Lord has commanded" as circumcision.[23] In the Syrian *Epistle of the Apostles* 18 we read in the Coptic version that Jesus declares: "I am the Word. I am become a thing unto him, that is to say, I am the perfect thought in the type (or, the thought fulfilled in the likeness). I came into being on the eighth day." Here Jesus says he has become "a thing" on the eighth day, but the eighth day is the day of circumcision, so that the imagery of the rite of circumcision would seem to hover in the background and is used here to describe Jesus' new state of existence. *Dabar*, like its Aramaic and Syriac cognates, may be translated both as 'word' or 'thing', and we see this reflected in this passage, which contains both terms: "I am the *Word*; I am become a *thing*."[24] At the minimum this suggests not only a possibly overlooked Semitism in this text, but it also suggests the antiquity of the *Numbers Rabbah* tradition. Additionally, the fuller Coptic passage refers to "the Voice" immediately before "I am the word." Intriguingly, we read in the *Zohar* 1, 98a that after circumcision, the Voice (= *Tif'eret*, 'Beauty') is unveiled and "united" with Speech (*dibbur* = *Shekhinah*).[25]

Wolfson deals extensively with the Kabbalistic androgynous aspects of circumcision, and in view of the *Thomas* gospel's interest in the state of androgyny, the Jewish mystical traditions linking circumcision and androgyny deserve our closest attention. We should note that the two logia immediately preceding logion 50 both allude to the androgyny theme; we suspect that this is not mere coincidence. Wolfson explains that in the *Zohar* circumcision involves the union of the masculine *sefirah Yesod* (= *Tsaddiq*) and the feminine

---

23. Ibid., 196.
24. We are reminded of the enigmatic *debir, debirim* in the Qumran *Songs of the Sabbath Sacrifice*.
25. Ibid., 203.

*sefirah Shekhinah* (= *Malkhut*, 'Kingdom').[26] The "vision" associated with the *raza di-berit*, the "secret of the covenant," denotes *Shekhinah*, and through circumcision the masculine *Yesod* is "united" with the feminine *Shekhinah-Malkhut*.[27] Recall *Thomas*' imagery of the 'wedding chamber', and that the androgynous attain the kingdom (= *Malkhut*) in logia 22 and 49. Wolfson notes that Jewish mystical traditions explain circumcision's "androgynous nature" by referring to the Rabbinic rules pertaining to the performance of the rite (cf. *BT Shabbat* 173b), namely the cutting of the foreskin, *milah*, and the exposure of the corona, *peri'ah*, and these two actions coincide esoterically with *Yesod* and *Shekhinah*.[28]

*Zohar* II, 36a teaches that Abraham was "closed and concealed" (*'atim ve-satim*) before circumcision; after circumcision he "opened" completely, "for the letter *yod* was revealed."[29] Because circumcision is a sign, literally 'letter' (*'ot*; cf. Arabic *ayat*), circumcision grants understanding of the esoteric secrets of the letters which constitute the Torah's text. As Wolfson insists, "that which is hidden must be brought to light," and the means of accomplishing this is circumcision.[30] Therefore, both textual exegesis and circumcision exhibit characteristics of the hidden and the revealed; and in fact, the one who seeks the hidden meanings of the sacred text "must be circumcised," for textual "penetration" constitutes a sexual penetration at the sefirotic level. Therefore study = unification.[31] Whether in a direct or indirect mode, clearly all of these themes are to various degrees relevant for the understanding of the *Thomas* gospel's general world of ideas.

Circumcision is the prerequisite of both the attainment of the visionary state and of textual interpretation. Indeed, as Wolfson phrases it, for the *Zohar*, the Torah is God's "corpo-

---

26. Ibid., 199.
27. Ibid., 201-02.
28. Ibid., 202.
29. Ibid., 205.
30. Ibid., 207.
31. Ibid., 210-11.

real form," so that penetrating a text "is a mode of visionary experience."[32] And with this we may compare the *Thomas* gospel's emphases on seeking the meaning of the esoteric text and of attaining the visionary state.

The *Zohar* I, 234b asks: "Why does the root *ngd* ('to tell', 'to speak') allude to the secret of wisdom?" The answer is that the *gimmel* and *dalet* are not separated, but united (sexually) in the root *ngd*. Adam separated these two letters and it brought forth death.[33] Wolfson explains further that in *ngd*, *gimmel* = *Yesod* and *dalet* = *Shekhinah*, for she is the 'poor one' (*dal*).[34] In any case, Wolfson notes that because a supernal sexual union is implied in the term *ngd*, which denotes speech, this implies a unitive sexual aspect to "speaking" and "discourse"; "speech (*ngd*)" therefore mirrors the "the play of divine sexuality" and circumcision's androgynous aspects. In circumcision, *Yesod* is unveiled, overflowing to *Shekhinah-Malkhut*; the *yod* of the phallic corona is the mediating "bridge" which "unites" *gimmel* and *dalet*. In the words of Wolfson, "discourse (*aggadah*)" flows forth from the union of *Yesod* and *Shekhinah*.[35] This again suggests that circumcision shares in the imagery of the reunification in the bridal chamber so prominent in Thomasine thought.

For the Kabbalists only the circumcised may enjoy the vision of God, read the Torah, and thus unify the supernal masculine and feminine energies; moreover, the "opening" involved in circumcision is a simultaneous "opening" in the sefirotic pleroma.[36] The penetration of textual secrets constitutes a "re-enactment" of the covenant of circumcision, each of which involves a "movement from closure to openness." When we "open" the Torah, this mirrors the unveiling that

---

32. Ibid., 212.
33. Ibid., 213. This is, incidentally, precisely the teaching of the *Gospel of Philip*, a text which shows extensive knowledge of the *Thomas* gospel.
34. Ibid. Does the spiritual poverty of *Shekhinah* have any connection with Jewish Christianity's self-designation as the Ebionites?
35. Ibid.
36. Ibid., 214.

takes place both on the physical plane in circumcision and in the supernal plane.[37]

In the light of all these Rabbinic and Kabbalistic traditions pertaining to circumcision which Wolfson has brought into such clear relief, we can at last begin to appreciate the extent to which the *Gospel of Thomas*, even when it does not directly treat of circumcision as such, reflects the terminology as well as the theological and esoteric conceptions underlying the rite. In the presence of such extensive verbal and conceptual conformities shared between *Thomas* and the various Jewish texts in question here, are we simply to dismiss all of this evidence with the non-chalant attitude that the latter are all inapplicable on account of their posterior temporal provenance? Or are we to recognize the possibility of commonalities arising independently on the basis of a shared inner world of ideas held together by the common link of Jewish mystical orality and textuality? The latter approach would seem to be the more judicious, not least of all on account of the fact that the earlier and later traditions under consideration in this context actually shed mutual light upon each other, which seems to indicate a shared conceptual genetic or organic linkage.

It seems rather clear that *Thomas* logion 50 refers to the sign of the covenant of circumcision operating as a seal which ensures the ascending soul safe passage to the place of light. When we then approach logion 53, it seems at a first reading to polemicize against physical circumcision. The stark contrast with logion 50 is glaring. But the similarity in logion 53's phraseology to the famous passage concerning the encounter between the pagan Rufus and Rabbi Akiva in *Tanhuma B*,7 (18a) may ironically hold one of the keys to the solution of the puzzle. In this passage, Rufus asks scornfully, "… why doesn't the child come out of the womb circumcised?" Rabbi Akiva explains that a child is not born circumcised because "God gave the command-

---

37. Ibid.

ments so that through them *Israel* would be led to obedience." Note well that Akiva assumes that the absolute need for physical circumcision applies only to *Israel*. One must remember that Rabbinic Judaism does not require, and never has required, that non-Jews be circumcised in order to attain salvation. Gentiles obtain salvation by following the ethical laws of Noah (cf. *Sanhedrin* 56a).

In light of the shared phraseology between *Tanhuma* B 7 (18a) and *Thomas* logion 53, it seems apparent that Jesus is here anticipating the only slightly later position of Rabbi Akiva. In other words, the disciples' question in logion 53, "Is circumcision of value or not?" would apply strictly to the Gentiles, and not to Jews. Yet logion 53 also, as we explain in the next chapter, implies that even for Jews physical circumcision has no value when unaccompanied by spiritual circumcision.

When we again remind ourselves that *Thomas* logia 50-53 actually represent a single pericope, we see that logion 50 constitutes a preparatory transition leading up to the discussion on circumcision in the dialogical block's final part, namely, logion 53. With regard to logion 50, *in nuce* and *in concreto*, it is implied that on one plane physical circumcision is useful for Jews, whereas according to logion 53 *spiritual* circumcision is useful for all human beings. We see no reason why the historical Rabbi Jesus could not have uttered the basic message of logion 53; indeed, if he did it would help explain why the Pauline mission was so successful in spite of its powerful opposition. Paul in *Romans* 2:28-29-3:1 may indeed be alluding to some version of the tradition contained in logion 53. Paul admittedly imposes a particular point of view upon this saying, but the fact that Jesus, in agreement with typical Rabbinical opinion, in his public teaching had not required the circumcision of non-Jews was something that Paul could use in his favor. A linguistic reconstruction of logion 53 (presented in our separate *Thomas* commentary) strongly suggests a Semitic *Vorlage*, and this increases the likelihood that it was crafted in a Jewish and Semitic-language environment, which would argue against it having been intended in any sense as inimical to physical circumcision for Jews.

The real issue behind the question of circumcision in the early church was the Torah requirement that only circumcised males partake of the Passover meal. The issue would inevitably flare up annually at the time of the "Easter" Eucharistic Passover feast in Jerusalem, as well as in the Diaspora. Jesus would not have required circumcision of Gentiles, but as a faithful Jew he most certainly would have insisted that only circumcised males could take part in Passover, and thus the rite of circumcision was destined to become a central theological matter of contention in the nascent churches. It would seem that the issue was resolved by a replacement of the annual Passover meal with the daily/weekly Eucharist among non-Jewish Christians.

In an essay which compares the *John* and *Thomas* gospels, Popkes stresses the parallels between Qumran and *John* (similar terminology of dualism of light-darkness, predestination of the sons of light and sons of darkness, etc., with, however, differences in actual meaning, which is all reminiscent of the inconsistency we saw earlier in Daniélou's argumentation). In contrast to *John*'s Christology, Popkes interprets *Thomas* logion 29 as docetic, and he sees proto-Gnostic light metaphors in this gospel. Popkes further argues that logion's 12 emphasis on James is not Jewish Christian but "Gnostic," and that in any event logion 13 cancels out James' importance and replaces him with Thomas. He portrays logia 6 and 14 with their counsel against praying, fasting, and alms as anti-Jewish. This, incidentally, can be answered from Lührmann, who points out that according to *Mark* 2:18-22 and parallels, Jesus did not fast, and in Paul's writings fasting is never once mentioned; the only apparent exception is *1 Corinthians* 7:5's "prayer and fasting," which, however, is an assimilative reading imported from the synoptic gospels.[38] Furthermore, in *Thomas*, prayer, alms, and fasting serve as symbols of mourn-

---

38. Dieter Lührmann, *Die apokryph gewordenen Evangelien*, 161.

ing, and according to the canonical gospels, mourning is inappropriate while the bridegroom is present. Popkes sees logion 52 as superlatively anti-Jewish, as the opposite of the *John* gospel which does not hesitate to cite the Old Testament prophecies concerning the coming Messiah.[39] Zöckler, however, has shown that logion 52's intention is not a carte blanche rejection of the Old Testament, but rather is to be understood against the background of its larger context, which implies that the disciples should not be overly focused on either the future (cf. logion 51) or on the past (cf. logion 52), but rather they should direct their attention to the present moment when God is intervening on their behalf in history.[40] According to Popkes, in contrast to *John*, "*Thomas* hardly contains any passages resembling the Qumran texts in either language or content."[41] But neither do the synoptic gospels contain much that can be compared to Qumran, yet this cannot be used to argue that they do not therefore contain any truly Jewish features. However, as we document throughout our textual-philological *Thomas* commentary, the *Thomas* gospel does in fact parallel a variety of Qumran texts in both thought and diction (this is especially the case with regard to 1QH).

Popkes' concluding remark that *Thomas*' lack of concern with a biographical narrative of Jesus' life[42] is also off the mark, for similarly Paul exhibits hardly any interest at all in

---

39. Enno E. Popkes, "About the Differing Approach to a Theological Heritage: Comments on the Relationship between the *Gospel of John*, the *Gospel of Thomas*, and Qumran," in James H. Charlesworth (ed.), *The Bible and the Dead Sea Scrolls. Volume Three. The Scrolls and Christian Origins* (Waco, Texas: Baylor University Press, 2006), 281-317.

40. Thomas Zöckler, *Jesu Lehren im Thomasevangelium* (Leiden/Boston/Köln: Brill, 1999), 244-52. One might in any case ask what sounds more anti-Jewish: *Thomas* logion 52 or *John*'s labeling the Judaeans as sons of the devil?

41. Enno E. Popkes, "About the Differing Approach to a Theological Heritage: Comments on the Relationship between the *Gospel of John*, the *Gospel of Thomas*, and Qumran," 312.

42. Ibid., 316-17.

this topic, and Popkes in any case ignores the stated genre of *Thomas*, which proclaims itself to be a collection of esoteric *sayings*, not *biography*, of Jesus. It is therefore a false methodology which Popkes applies throughout his essay when he compares *John* with *Thomas*, for they are of two essentially different literary genres, one being a short list of maxims, the other belonging to the genre of extensive biography.

Lührmann also complains of what he perceives as *Thomas*' non-Jewish texture: "No 'amen', and not even any Aramaic words," as opposed to *Mark* 5:41 (*talitha cumi*, "little girl, I say to you, arise"); 7:11 (*qorban*), 34 (*eph-phatha*, "be opened"); 15:34 (*Eloi, Eloi, lama sabach-thani*); *Matthew* 1:21 ("you shall call his name Jesus, because he shall save his people from their sins"); John 1:38 (*Rabbi*), 41 (*Messiah*), 42 (*Cephas*); 9:7 (*Siloam*), 20:16 (*Rabboni*), etc.[43] This creates a misleading impression, however, for the only reason the canonical gospels contain such phrases is that they are directed to non-Jewish audiences. The fact that they are missing from *Thomas* (except for the preamble where the Greek form of *Thomas* is given as *Didymos*) might on the contrary indicate that the traditions presented in *Thomas* were written by and for a Jewish-Chrstian audience that would not have needed any explanatory linguistic comments. Additionally, the Old Testament is by no means absent from *Thomas*; one thinks of logion 3 which is a *midrash* on *Deuteronomy* 30, and as we show in our commentary, logion 87 is a targumic paraphrase from *Jeremiah*. Furthermore, competent scholars have documented Semitic layers underlying the Greek and Coptic versions of *Thomas*.[44] Lastly, it is ironic that when

---

43. Dieter Lührmann, *Die apokryph gewordenen Evangelien*, 178.

44. For possible, and we stress *possible*, Syriac elements, see Nicholas Perrin, "NHC II,2 and the Oxyrhynchus Fragments (P. Oxy 1, 654, 655): Overlooked Evidence for a Syriac *Gospel of Thomas*," *Vigiliae Christianae*, vol 58 (2004), 138-51; for Aramaic elements, see April DeConick, *The Original Gospel of Thomas in Translation*, 11-12. However, Perrin's work has received frequent poor reviews by Syriac experts. Aramaic therefore, rather than Syriac, remains a strong possibility for a *Thomas* Semitic *Vorlage*. In our

so-called Gnostic texts contain several Aramaic or Hebrew words used in their correct senses, this is then inconsistently dismissed as possible evidence for an early dating, or as being indicative of a Jewish provenance.

---

textual-philological *Thomas* commentary in preparation we argue that textual evidence rather than grammatical arguments alone offers more assistance for determining *Thomas*' temporal and geographic origins.

## 2. The *Gospel of Thomas*
## A Contextual Commentary

In this chapter we offer a contextualized commentary on the entirety of the *Thomas* gospel. By contextual we mean that our exegesis of *Thomas* is developed first with reference to the document itself, that is, the various logia shed light upon each other, and this dynamic is the principle guide in our interpretation. Second, contextual refers to the historical setting of the Jewish, Christian, and Islamic esoteric trajectories we have established through reconstruction in Parts I and II of the present monograph. We include reference to the Islamic paradigms as well because although they originate several centuries after *Thomas*' composition, nevertheless Islamic sources have preserved many earlier Jewish, Christian, and Jewish-Christian traditions that seem genetically related, archetypally or historically as the case may be, to the general world of ideas enshrined in *Thomas* and similar texts.

The central key to unraveling the perplexities of the *Thomas* gospel is contained basically in the first three logia. According to logion 1, which is actually a statement by the apostle Thomas, not by Jesus, the one who finds the interpretation or meaning of Jesus' secret sayings will not taste of death. Logion 2 reinforces and fills out logion 1's theme of finding by presenting the steps by which the interpretation of the secret meanings will be achieved, the first step of which is seeking. Logion 2 tells us that the one who seeks will find. In light of logion 1, what is sought in logion 2 is transparently the interpretation of Jesus' secret sayings. This finding in turn results in perplexity, astonishment, and finally in a ruling, and by implication resting, which will be equivalent to logion 1's state of not tasting death. Finally logion 3 next informs us concerning precisely what kind of knowledge is implied by the secret sayings of Jesus. That is, the basic meaning of the sayings which constitute the *Thomas* gospel as a whole is that what one is seeking is self-knowledge. As logion 3 states, if one does not know oneself, one is in poverty, which implies that if one does know oneself, one has attained true wealth.

These themes of seeking and finding ultimately rest on the traditional Jewish sapiential books' themes of seeking and finding Wisdom, which is ultimately the hypostatic Lady Wisdom known from such foundational texts as *Proverbs* 8, *Sirach* 24, and *Wisdom* 7. According to these texts the seeking and finding of Wisdom results in reigning, resting, immortality, and true wealth, demonstrating that the world of ideas in which *Thomas* moves is that of Judaism, not Hellenism or Hermeticism, although to be sure the latter had been integrated within first-century Palestinian Judaism. But the main point to be observed is that the ideas in *Thomas* would emanate principally from Palestine, and if Alexandrian traditions are present, they will have been assimilated directly from within a Palestinian context, and would not stem directly from Alexandria, *pace* Quispel and DeConick. The implied presence of Lady Wisdom in *Thomas* is a vital key to understanding the gospel as a whole, for as in later Kabbalism, in *Thomas* Lady Wisdom would seem to coincide with the Kingdom, *Malkhut*, a central *Thomas* theme as well as a centrally important feminine *sefirah* in Kabbalism

Logion 4 then proceeds to clarify just what type of self is involved in logion 3's self-knowledge. According to logion 4's ending, the self involved is 'a single one'. This alludes to several layers of meaning which include celibacy as a return to the state of primordial unitive androgyny which was possessed by the Primal or Perfect Human, which is a more accurate rendering than Perfect Man, since what is indicated by the term, which is known in Islam as well, is not the masculine gender, but the simultaneously male and female androgynous state which prevailed while Eve still dwell within Adam. Yet one must be aware that the Hebrew word 'Adam' denotes the generality of humanity, male and female, and thus the

Androgyne as such, and only secondarily does 'Adam' refer to the first human male. It is vital in this context to correct Quispel's and DeConick's over-emphasis on 'a single one' as celibacy, for although celibacy is certainly involved, logion 4's unitive state is not to be restricted reductively to it. That is, the unitive state may result in celibacy, but is not to be reduced or confined to such. Thus the close parallels in Jewish and Islamic sources which speak of adepts of esoteric mysteries as 'the unitary ones' or 'the united ones' are not to be discounted when interpretating *Thomas*.

The unitary state involves a return to the Primal Human in Eden, who according to various sources (such as Irenaeus in his *Proof of the Apostolic Preaching*) was understood to have been a child or childlike and innocent, which accords with Adam and Eve's lack of shame concerning their nudity. This explains logion 4's reference to "a child of seven days." Logion 4's phrase "the place of life" is a central Mandaean term also attested in the Nag Hammadi *Dialogue of the Savior*. This should come as no surprise, since as we show in our separate textual-philological commentary on *Thomas*, logia 1 and 2 are alluded to in Mandaean texts.

Logion 5's "Know what is in front of you" refers to the disciple, in other words, Jesus is exhorting the listener: "Know yourself." Then "what is hidden will be revealed to you." The hidden meaning of Jesus' sayings will be revealed, which by implication means that if you know yourself, then your true self will be revealed to you. And one's true self is the primordial Edenic androgynous self, which in turn emanates from one's preexistent self which subsists in the supernal light, as indicated by logia 83 and 84.

Logion 6 begins *Thomas*' repeated theme of eating, which is continued in logia 7, 8, and 9, which involve a progression from meat (logion 7), to fish (logion 8), to vegetarian fare (logion 9). The original answers to the three questions presented in logion 6 have been displaced to logion 14. Logion 7 is not to be understood with reference to Hellenistic sources such as Plato, but with reference to what Idel calls "the widespread Kabbalitsic concept" which involves a higher entity, such as a human, eating a lower life form, a mystical rite which results in the "elevation" of the lower life form to a higher state of spiritual existence.[1] This interpretation of logion 7 is confirmed by logion 11's reference to eating dead things and thereby making them live. Logia 6-9's theme of eating, which builds up to vegetarian fare in logion 9, may also serve as a preparation for logion 12's introduction of James the Just (*Tsaddiq*), who according to tradition was a vegetarian. Logion 8's *single* large fish which is chosen over the many small fish implies the knowledge of the unitive or unitary self alluded to in earlier logia.

Logion 10's "fire" would form a wordplay with Coptic logion 11's "light" in either Aramaic or Syriac, a wordplay repeated in logia 82 and 83.[2] Logion 11 continues the theme of eating found in logia 6-9. It is significant that logion 10 contains the light theme, since the next logion introduces the figure of James the *Tsaddiq*. According to Kabbalistic sources, the *Tsaddiq* as foundation of heaven and earth, is constituted of the primordial light of creation referred to in the opening verses of *Genesis*.[3] In short, the *Tsaddiq* is the primordial light. The possibility that logion 11's light alludes to James is strengthened by the reference to eating "what is alive" in contrast to "what is dead," which would seem to refer to live plants in contrast to dead animals. This would give us an allusion to James' well-known vegetarianism. This vegetarianism represents a symbolic return to primordiality, since according to *Genesis* humans were vegetarians from the time of Eden to the Deluge of Noah. Thus the theme of vegetarianism as allusion to the primordial Edenic state explains logion 11's ending with a reference to the one becoming two, that is the single

---

1. See Moshe Idel, *Kabbalah: New Perspectives*, 72.
2. Cf. Nicholas Perrin, *Thomas and Tatian: The Relationship between the Gospel of Thomas and the Diatesseron* (Leiden: Brill, 2002), 156.
3. On the Tsaddiq in Kabbalah, see Gershom Scholem, *On the Mystical Shape of the Godhead. Basic Concepts in the Kabbalah*. Tr. from the German by Joachim Neugroschel (NY: Schocken Books, 1991), 88-139.

Primordial Androgyne was separated into the two sexual genders of male and female, Adam and Eve.

Logion 12 proclaims that heaven and earth came into existence for the sake of James the *Tsaddiq*, which is a confirmation of the antiquity of the medieval Kabbalistic doctrine of the luminous *Tsaddiq* as pillar and foundation of heaven and earth, which also accords with the Islamic Sufi doctrine of the *Qutb*.

Contrary to appearance, logion 13's main emphasis does not lie upon the question of Jesus' true identity, but upon Thomas attaining an equal status with Jesus, which cancels the former master-student relationship, so that Jesus proclaims that he is no longer Thomas' master (Rabbi, teacher). As we seek to establish in our separate textual-philological commentary, the three secret words which Jesus speaks to Thomas are not, *pace* DeConick, *Ehyeh asher Ehyeh*, "I am who I am," but rather the sequence of the three divine names *Yahweh, Elohenu, Yahweh* as they occur in the *Shema*, whose emphasis upon the divine Unity is surely related to *Thomas'* theme of the unitary or unitive self of those who find the meaning of Jesus' secret sayings. *Yahweh*, not *Ehyeh asher Ehyeh*, is the *Shem ha-meforash*, the *nomen proprium* of Judaism. The implication of logion 13 is that the unitive self of the initiate reflects and participates in the divine Unity. In other words, the doctrine of the *unio mystica* is being alluded to.

Since logion 14 was at first joined to logion 6, there was originally no separation between logia 13 and 15. Logion 15's theme of visionary beholding is to be explained by logion 13's allusion to the divine Essence, which formed a part of the *merkabah* traditions, which culminate in the *visio Dei*.[4] This also explains the theme of destruction by fire in logion 13, for this scenario is repeatedly joined to the *merkabah* narrations in Rabbinic literature. Since according to Rabbinic proscrip-

---

4. But since logion 15's phrase "one not born of women" likely refers to the celestial Adam, the *visio Dei* here will be indirect via the celestial Adam as *imago Dei*. This is quite reminiscent of Mandaean thought.

tions the *merkabah* could not be taught except to a single individual alone, Jesus therefore takes Thomas apart in private to give him an esoteric interpretation of the supernal triadic implications of the *Shema*.

Logion 16, like logion 4, ends on the theme of unity. This is the unity of the primordial and pre-existent celestial self as emanation of the divine Self alluded to in logion 13. Logion 17, widely paralleled in Islam in the form of a *hadith qudsi*, promises the revelation of what is unseen. In context, this will refer to the hidden self (which is called the hidden luminous image in logion 83), which must be discovered and known via a knowing and finding of the interpretation of Jesus' esoteric doctrine. The knowledge which is implied in logion 17 is further clarified in logion 18, for self-knowledge is a return to "the beginning," to the Edenic androgynous state when death did not exist. Therefore, if one knows one's primordial self, which will be through self-knowledge, then, as logion 1 promises, one will, in contrast to Adam, not taste death. Logion 19 clarifies logia 17 and 18 even further. What is blessed is the pre-existent self or image which exists before an individual assumes an earthly egohood or transient self. If one listens to and understands Jesus' esoteric words, the stones of Paradise (see *Ezekiel* 28) will introduce them to the five trees of Paradise. The five trees represent the five books of the Torah. Jesus' words are esoteric teachings of the Torah. Logion 19 is based on *Psalm* 1's promise of immortality to those who meditate day and night in the Torah. Jesus has fulfilled this constant abiding in and search of the Torah, he has sought and found the esoteric interpretation of the Torah and thus will not taste of death. This is the meaning of the *incipit*'s reference to Jesus as "the living one." The disciple who in turn listens to and finds the Torah's esoteric secrets as explicated by Jesus will avoid death as well. The central secret is self-knowledge, but this is not the earthly ego but the Edenic androgynous self which is identical to one's celestial self which pre-exists in the supernal light, which in view of logia 11 and 12 would seem to allude to the light of the *Tsaddiq*, which is manifest on the earthly plane as James the Just. This indicates that the person of James possesses a previously overlooked metaphysical centrality throughout the *Thomas* gospel. This gospel is all about the disciple's attainment of self-knowledge, not about the attainment of the knowledge concerning Jesus' true identity. The four exoteric canonical gospels are about Jesus; the esoteric *Thomas* gospel is about the disciple's Self-realization. This Self-realization is effected by finding the meaning of Jesus' secret Torah-based teachings. But logion 12 indicates that Jesus has departed from the terrestrial sphere, and has entrusted James with the esoteric secrets, so that it is through the mediation of James the *Tsaddiq* that one will attain self-knowledge and avoid the taste of death. This would accord with the general Kabbalistic paradigm according to which all souls, even the soul of the Messiah, descends and originates from the cosmic *Tsaddiq*. In this sense the *Tsaddiq* predominates over Jesus as his successor, whereas in logion 13 Thomas is Jesus' equal, not his successor. Therefore logion 13's praise of Thomas by no means implies a displacement of the earlier logion 12's positioning of James as supreme leader of souls.

Logion 20's smallest of seeds will refer to self-knowledge. Logion 21's childlike nudity theme will refer to the Edenic androgynous self. In our separate textual-philological commentary we present reasons against restoring the sentence "Let there be among you a person of understanding" to logion 24. The reference to the crop ripening seems to have been displaced, most likely from logion 9.

Logion 22 refers to a return to the primordial unitive state which transcends the duality of inside-outside, male-female, now-then, I-Thou, etc. This unitive state reflects the well-known transcendence of dualism in the *unio mystica*.[5] Logion 23's ending repeats this theme of unity. Logia 22-23's unitive state is by implication the 'place' where Jesus dwells according to logion 24. The place, *topos*, is therefore an ontological

---

5. See Thomas Zöckler, *Jesu Lehren im Thomasevangelium*, 211-42.

*tupos*, 'type'.[6] Jesus refuses to answer the disciples' question about his own identity and status and instead directs them to their own interior identity as a person of light, which again refers to the pre-existent light and images of logia 83-84, which in view of logion 12's background will refer to the hidden light of the *Tsaddiq* James.

Logion 25's theme of the "eye" connects the saying back to logion 24's theme of a person of light illuminating the world's darkness, which makes logion 25's sight via the eye possible. The illumination, however, is of an esoteric and moral order, as is shown by logion 25's theme of love and logion 26's condemnation of judging one's neighbor, which is an illustration of the darkness of logion 24. Logion 26's exhortation to be aware of one's own faults, which implies the need for self-introspection, prepares the reader for logion 27. Logion 27's idiom, usually rendered "Sabbath as a Sabbath" actually reflects the Hebrew idiom "Sabbath of Sabbaths," which traditionally refers to Yom Kippur, which is known for its required total fast, and this will be the meaning of logion 27's "fast from the world," that is, "fast from everything." Logion 27 is thus another of *Thomas*' Jewish-Christian markers, for in effect it says: "If you do not keep the complete fast [of Yom Kippur], you will not find the kingdom. If you do not keep Yom Kippur, you will not see the Father." Important to observe here is the connection between the Sabbath and the Kingdom, or *Malkhut*. This is quite a striking combination, since it accords perfectly with the traditional Kabbalistic joining of the Sabbath and *Malkhut* as the Sabbath Queen, another indication that the kingdom in *Thomas* alludes on one plane[7] to Lady Wisdom.

---

6. See Callahan, 414. But Callahan's explicit textual emendation of *topos* to *tupos* is unnecessary, although 'place' is admittedly used in logion 24 in the sense of 'type' or 'state'.

7. But not of course on every plane, so that DeConick is justified when she disagrees with Davies' global identification of Kingdom and Wisdom to a point which excludes any apocalyptic dimension; see April. D. DeConick, *The Original Gospel of Thomas in Translation*, 296. However, DeConick fails to

Logion 28 continues logion 27's Yom Kippur theme, for logion 28's image of standing in the midst of the sinful people as intercessor is a central Yom Kippur component, as is the reference to repentance with which the logion ends. Logion 29's flesh and spirit do not reflect Hellenistic body-soul dualism, but the Biblical Semitic contrast between flesh and spirit as representative of the divine and natural categories of existence or being (as in *Genesis* 6, where God says his 'spirit' will not abide in humans forever, for they are 'flesh'). The great wealth is self-knowledge, while poverty is lack of self-knowledge, as is clear from logion 3. Logia 28 and 29 would be connected via a Hebrew wordplay between 'wine' (*hayayin*) and 'wealth' (*hon*), a wordplay reflected in the Qumran *Habakkuk pesher* as well.

Logion 30 carries forward logia 27-28's Yom Kippur theme. According to Rabbinic literature, when God gave the Torah to Israel, they were granted an immortal status as 'gods' (*elohim*). But they immediately proved themselves unworthy and lost their immortality. Jewish tradition applies *Psalm* 82's following statement to this incident: "I have said that you are gods."[8] Therefore DeConick is incorrect when she sees a mistranslation of *elohim* in logion 30, which she thinks should be rendered in the singular as 'God'. All exegetes agree that logion 30 is related to the Rabbinic teaching (applied to the Qur'an in an Islamic *hadith qudisi*) that wherever 1 to 10 people are gathered to study the Torah, the *Shekhinah* descends in their midst. It is often forgotten, however, that the Torah was given on what was later known as Yom Kippur; in this way logion 30 alludes to this most important sacred day. The emphasis upon the initiates' status as 'gods' is found frequently

---

recognize that the earliest Jerusalem church held to a realized eschatology, as shown by Michael D. Goulder, *Paul and the Competing Mission in Corinth*, 177-96. Thus on one plane Davies is justified in his de-emphasis on the apocalyptic dimension of the *Thomas*' kingdom concept.

8. See James S. Ackerman, "The Rabbinic Interpretation of Psalm 82 and the Gospel of John: John 10:34," *The Harvard Theological Review*, vol. 59, no. 2 (April, 1966), 186-191.

throughout the Dead Sea Scrolls, and *Thomas* logion 30's plural reading 'gods' reflects this ancient Palestinian esoteric usage. Logion 31 may carry forward the Yom Kippur theme even further if its rejected prophet alludes to the disobedience of Israel to Moses at the Mount during the giving of the Torah.

Logion 32's city that cannot fall is Jerusalem,[9] another indication of *Thomas*' Jewish-Christian matrix. Logion 31-32's theme of the revelation of what is hidden is continued in logion 33, which requires the making known of the esoteric doctrines. However, logion 34 by implication cautions that a spiritually blind person cannot teach the *arcanum* to those who are themselves spiritually blind. One must be sufficiently prepared, as pointed out in logion 35, before assimilating the secret doctrines of self-knowledge.

Logion 36 implies that one should be childlike in not worrying about who will supply clothing. This prepares the reader for logion 37's theme of sacred nudity, which alludes to the Primordial Human's subsistence in a childlike state of innocence and nudity.[10] But in *Thomas*, this Edenic androgynous unitive state is attained through Jesus' secret doctrine, and this is why logion 38 contains this particular theme. Logion 39 laments that some of the religious authorities have hidden the keys of gnosis. Yet the saying ends on a cautionary note: "As for you, be wise like serpents and innocent as doves." Therefore one is to exercise wisdom and innocence when revealing the secrets of self-gnosis. The "knowledge" referred to here is precisely the self-knowledge spoken of in logion 3.

---

9. See Gilles Quispel, *Gnostica, Judaica, Catholica*, 200.

10. Incidentally, metaphysically viewed the Androgyne existed on the subtle plane rather than on the physical plane; but since the higher subtle plane is more real and lasting than the lower physical plane, it would be misleading to say that the Androgyne existed "only" (in the pejorative sense of "merely") on the subtle plane. In any event, both Jewish and Islamic traditions hold that subtle entities such as demons and jinn reproduce and multiply just as do physical beings.

Logia 40-45 concern inappropriate responses to Jesus' secret teachings. Logion 46 forms a sort of transition to a more positive tone in its praise of John the Baptist and in its teaching on the child theme, which again alludes to the Edenic androgynous state of the Primal Adam or Perfect Human, which is regained by the disciple who finds the interpretation of Jesus' esoterc doctrine. This doctrine involves an overcoming of inner duality, such as is illustrated by logion 47's insistence that one cannot mount two horses or bend two bows simultaneously. Inward unity is necessary. This unity is explicitly referred to in logion 48. In our separate textual-philological commentary we present extensive documentation to show that logion 48's "house" is the Jerusalem Temple, and the "mountain" that will "move" alludes to the mountain of obstacles that stood in the way of the destroyed First Temple's rebuilding, as in *Zechariah* 4:7. *Ephesians* 2 strongly suggests that Paul knew the Jesus saying contained in logion 48. Interestingly, if one compares logion 48 with its doublet logion 106, and joins 48's beginning with 106's middle section, one arrives at: "If two *make peace*, you will become *sons of humanity*," which is nothing other than a variant of the beatitude found in *Matthew* 5:9 "Blessed are the *peacemakers*, for they shall be called *sons of God*." Now 'sons of God' is a standard Jewish term for 'angels', just as the term 'son of humanity' in Jewish texts such as *Daniel* and *Enoch* functions as a title for angels. Logia 48 and 106 therefore imply that those who achieve inward unity with the divine Self through the knowledge of the mediating primordial and celestial luminous self which pre-exists in *Shekhinah-Malkhut*, will attain an angelic-like status. In the words of Abulafia in *Ozar 'Eden Ganuz* 27a, the goal of humanity is to attain to the state "of the angels called *ishim*," that is, 'men' or 'humans'. But the two who become one in logion 48 alludes not only to the disciple and the inward temple, but also to God who unites with the feminine *Shekhinah-Malkhut* in the Jerusalem Temple, which itself in turn reflects the supernal structure of the *sefirotic pleroma* of the divine Nature. Indeed, according to standard Kabbalism, the inward androgynous unification of the initiate mirrors the unification of God and the *Shekhinah*.

In the light of the above comments it is of profound significance that the next logion, 49, speaks of the unified initiate's origin in the kingdom, *Malkhut*, which will allude to the ontic dwelling-place constituted by *Shekhinah* where the pre-existent self-images dwell. The pre-existent self-images, or the initiates' celestial counterparts originated in *Malkhut*, and they will return to *Malkhut*. This return is detailed in logion 50. We recognize in this logion the Mandaean term 'place of light', largely synonymous with logion 4's 'place of life'. Logion 50's self-established light will be the light of the *Tsaddiq*, who appears "in their image." This is a reverential evasive circumlocution meaning "in God's image." Logion 50's phrase "chosen ones of the living father" should be read with the qualification that in *Thomas* 'father' is a reverential substitution for 'God', for Jesus in the *Thomas* text reverentially avoids (with the sole exception of logion 100) the explicit mention of the name 'God', a praxis which accords well with known ancient Rabbinic tradition. Therefore logion 50's "the living father" should be understood as implying "the living God," which is a Kabbalistic designation of the luminous *Tsaddiq*. This indicates that logion 50 is to be understood from the background of Jewish esoteric traditions, rather than Hellenistic or Hermetic philosophy. This applies to logion 50's concluding phrase "It is turbulence and rest" as well. The translation "movement and rest" is based on a bias which sees in Thomas' more esoteric logia the influence of Hellenistic thought. The term must be rendered negatively as 'turbulence', 'tossing', or 'shaking',[11] which is clear from the usage of the verbal form of logion 50's substantive term elsewhere in *Thomas*, as in logion 78's reed which is "shaken" by the wind. Therefore logion 50 does not reflect the well-known Middle- and Neoplatonic

---

11. See Perrin, *Thomas and Tatian*, 102, who points out that the Coptic noun form for 'movement' in logion 50 is used in the Coptc New Testament in generally negative senses, as in the 'tossing' of a boat in a storm.

speculation on movement and rest or the unmoved mover. Rather, what is presupposed here is the Kabbalistic notion of *ni'anu'a*, the "shaking" which occurred within the divine Essence, *ein-sof*, a "movement" which was "from itself to itself"[12] (compare logion 50's *self-established* light), which gave rise to the world of archetypes, that is, to what *Thomas* calls the *Malkhut* (logion 49) where the hidden light and images dwell (logia 83-84). This movement is therefore the turbulences of the *tsimtsum*,[13] the intra-divine contraction that brought forth the various worlds of plermoatic and cosmic manifestation. At the end of the process of creation brought about by the *ni'anu'a*, God *rested* from the work of creation. This gives us a much more intelligible and coherent understanding of logion 50 than does the Hellenistic preoccupation with movement and rest, especially since logion 50's theme of light would likely be that of the *Tsaddiq*, for whom, according to logion 12, the *cosmos* came into being.

Logion 50's turbulence and rest are said to be attributes of "the sign" that dwells within God's chosen people. The linking of the terms 'sign' and 'chosen ones' constitutes as clear a reference as one could wish for to the Jewish rite of circumcision. But in what sense are the notions of turbulence and rest applicable to circumcision? Apart from the obvious movement and rest presupposed in the active physical motions required for the removal of the phallic foreskin and the subsequent repose of the passively exposed phallic corona, logion 50 will be alluding principally to the esoteric or metaphysical dimensions implied by and accompanying these active motions and the passive state of exposure which follows. Among such esoteric implications would be the Kabbalistic traditions concerning the rite of circumcision as involving an intra-divine unification between the active masculine and passive feminine halves of the Tetragrammaton *Yahweh*. This theme accords well with one of *Thomas*' central esoteric teach-

---

12. See Gershom Scholem, *Kabbalah*, 132.
13. Ibid., 133.

ings, namely the initiate's interior androgynous unity, which in turn reflects the intra-divine unity between God and *Malkhut* or *Shekhinah*, and on another level the union between the masculine *Tsaddiq* and the feminine *Malkhut*.

Logion 51 carries forward the previous saying's theme of rest. Jesus explains that the world to come has already come, and that the dead are already raised (a theme known from Sufism as well). This is paralleled in the Kabbalistic doctrine that identifies the *sefirah Binah*, Understanding, who is the supernal Mother, with the world to come which is, however, already in existence on a higher transcendent plane of reality. Logion 52 is linked to logion 51 by means of the theme of the dead. "The living one who is in your presence" may operate on several semantic levels which include God, the *Shekhinah*, and even the initiate's own transcendent self. Jesus is, however, not alluding to himself as "the living one." In *Thomas*, Jesus avoids bringing attention to himself, and instead focuses all attention on God, the *Shekhinah*, and on the initiate's need to find his or her own true self as united with (or as indistinguishable from) the supernal Self. The "dead" the disciples have spoken of is not a reference to the prophets, for the latter in *Thomas* are by no means dead, for they live together with the angles (logion 88), and in any event, according to logion 51 the dead have been raised already, *sub specie aeternitatis*. The "dead" would therefore refer to Israel as dead in their hearts, a common theme known from the Jewish scriptures, such as *Jeremiah* 9:26: "And all the house of Israel is uncircumcised in heart." This gives us the explanation of why the very next logion deals with the theme of the necessity of spiritual circumcision. Logia 52 and 53 are to be understood, not with reference to Paul's doctrine of metaphorical circumcision which abrogates the physical rite, but with reference to John the Baptist's preaching as recorded in the *Gospel of Luke*, where John attacks Israel as being dead and as standing in need of repentance, without which their status as circumcised children of Abraham will be of no avail to them. The disciples' question in logion 53 therefore implies not so much the usefulness of circumcision in itself, but whether or not circumcision is of any use when accompanied by an uncircumcised heart. Circumcision is alluded to positively in logion 50, where we read of the "sign" of the "chosen ones" of God, that is the chosen people Israel who possess the "sign of circumcision." Given logion 50's positive reference to circumcision, only a very forced reading of logion 53 would see in it a condemnation of circumcision as such or *en toto*, especially given the well-known preaching of Jeremiah, John the Baptist, and other Biblical prophets on the insufficiency of physical circumcision when unaccompanied by spiritual circumcision.

Logion 53's theme of the usefulness, or more literally, the worth or profit of circumcision, stands in contrast to logion 54's theme of the poor (i.e., the Ebionites), to whom belong the *Malkhut*. One is reminded of the Kabbalistic association of *Shekhinah* with the theme of poverty, since *Shekhinah* possesses no light of her own, but rather reflects the supernal light of the other *sefirot*, including the light of the *Tsaddiq*.[14] If logion 54's *Malkhut* is conceived of as the supernal Mother, this logion's kingdom theme would make for a smooth transition to logion 55's inclusion of the word 'mother', which creates a link back to logion 53's 'mother'. Those who do not despise their earthly families in the face of bearing their cross, which here functions as an image of mortal difficulties in general rather than to Jesus' crucifixion specifically, will not be worthy of Jesus.

Logion 56 continues the theme of unworthiness. Logion 56 and its doublet logion 80, use the words 'carcass' and 'body' respectively in the sense of 'self', a fact which is clearly demonstrated by these two sayings' triplet found in logion 111b: "Jesus says: 'Whoever has found oneself, of that one the world is not worthy.'" As we explain in great detail in our

---

14. This is the same situation we find in the Qur'anic Light Verse (*sura* 24:35), where we read that the celestial oil "would almost give light without being touched by fire," which implies that the oil actually does not shine by itself. This oil therefore coincides with the Qur'anic *Sakina* (= *Shekhinah*).

textual-philological commentary, logion 56's 'carcass' and logion 80's 'body' are most likely the result of the Coptic scribe interpretatively varying his translation of an underlying Greek *soma*, concerning which *Thomas* commentators in general fail to note can mean both 'body' and 'corpse'. Behind the Greek *soma* would in all likelihood have been the Aramaic *geshem*, which means 'body' as well as 'self', which would explain the variation between the 'corpse' and 'body' of logia 56 and 80 on the one hand, and logion 111b's 'self' on the other. The reason why the Coptic scribe has rendered *soma* in logion 56 as 'corpse' is explained by logion 55's reference to 'the cross', which implies a corpse hanging on it. The thought in logion 56 may be that one who has come to know the world, that is, everything, has discovered their true self by means of undergoing the death of their lower self, the transient ego. The theme of death is absent from the logia immediately leading up to and following the doublet in logion 80, so that the scribe translated the Greek *Vorlage*'s *soma* more neutrally there as 'body'. Therefore, there is no textual corruption involved in logia 56 and 80, but rather an intentional scribal interpretative targumic-like praxis. In light of logion 111b, it is evident that at least the previous Greek scribe who translated the underlying Semitic version had been aware of the underlying sense of 'self' involved in all three of these logia.

In *Thomas*, one finds the authentic self by means of penetrating the hidden dimensions of the Torah as explicated by Jesus. The opposite of this teaching are the bad weeds sowed among the good seeds of logion 57. One avoids such bad doctrine by toiling in the Torah, diligently seeking out its secrets, or better, *her* secrets, since the Torah, according to *Sirach* 24, is an earthly manifestation of primordial hypostatic Lady Wisdom. This is one of the implications of logion 58 which proclaims blessed the one who has toiled, for they have found life. The sapiential literature frequently calls the Torah and Lady Wisdom 'life' as well as the 'tree of life'. This offers us an important clue to understanding the 'living one' mentioned several times throughout *Thomas*, including in the following logion 59. The living one is not only God, but also the feminine *Shekhinah*, who in Rabbinic literature coincides with the maternal Holy Spirit. Logion 59's contrast between life and death is mirrored in logion 60's exhortation to seek a place of refuge lest one become a corpse and be eaten, like a lamb slaughtered in sacrifice. This connects logion 61 back to the theme of eating in logia 6-9 and 11. Logion 62 continues the eating theme by referring to Salome's table where Jesus eats. As we argue in our textual-philological commentary, an Aramaic *Vorlage* of logion 62 likely had Salome reproach Jesus for eating from her table 'as if you were a relative' (אחא), to which Jesus responds via a wordplay that he is from God who is One (חד; cf. Hebrew אחד). The Coptic then reads: "If one is destroyed, one will be full of light." 'Destroyed' is usually emended to 'whole' or 'unified'. Although this was probably the sense of the Semitic *Vorlage*, it is possible that 'destroyed' was an authentic textual or interpretative variant at either the Semitic or Greek-Coptic stage/s, for logion 56 implies that one's lower self must become a corpse. Additionally, it might be that 'destroyed' is a confusion of one of the several Aramaic verbs that possess the simultaneous meanings of 'perfect' or 'complete' and 'destroyed'. Logion 61's theme of unification or perfection which fills one with light (which will again be the light of the *Tsaddiq*, James the Just, or alternatively another mode of supernal light mediated via James the *Tsaddiq*), constitute the contents of the mysteries vouchsafed to those who are worthy, as we read in logion 62.

Logion 61 warns that if one is interiorly divided, one will be filled with darkness, which implies death, as light implies life. This state of darkness is illustrated by the various examples given in logia 63-66. Such division and darkness are the result of ignorance of self-knowledge, as is indicated by logion 67: "The one who knows everything yet lacks [knowledge] of oneself lacks everything." Those who by contrast do possess authentic self-knowledge are praised in the following logia 68-69 in a triadic series of beatitudes. Logion 68 praises the persecuted. Logion 69 praises those who go without food in order to feed the hungry. Logion 69 also blesses "those who have been persecuted in their hearts, for these have truly come to know the father." It is possible here that in an Aramaic *Vorlage* the passive sense of 'persecute' may have been an active sense of 'striving', so that those are blessed who have striven in their hearts, which would allude back to logion 58's blessed ones who have toiled in the Torah and have found the life who is Lady Wisdom. Logion 70 explains that if one brings forth what lies within, one will be saved; if one fails to do this, what lies within will destroy one. This alludes to the saving power of self-knowledge and the destructive power of ignorance of self.

The theme of destruction is reflected in logion 71's destruction of the Temple, which only Jesus will build again.[15] That Jesus will build the Temple again is indicative of *Thomas*' Jewish-Christian provenance. Logion 72 continues with the theme of division. Logion 73 contrasts with the *few* workers the *large* harvest, which is reminiscent of the contrast between one large fish and many small fish in logion 8. Similarly logion 74 contrasts *many* standing around a well with *nothing* being in the well, which would seem to be an even more forceful comparison of the relationship existing between the One and the Many. Logion 75 states that *many* stand at the door, but only those who are *alone* (as one) will enter the bridal or wedding chamber. The bridal chamber is the sacred *locus* of the heart's interior where the state of primordial androgyny is re-attained, and it is simultaneously the earthly Temple as reflection of the realm of the divine pleroma where God and the *Shekhinah* are united. The initiate attains such union by means of self-knowledge, which enables one to unite in the bridal chamber with one's primordial and celestial counterpart. This self-knowledge is the single pearl of great price in logion 76. Jewish esoteric sources frequently speak of a celestial crown of David or Metatron which is set with pearls that cast a light throughout the entire cosmos, and this is the

---

15. Cf. Aland, Kurt, ed. *Synopsis Quattuor Evangeliorum*. 15th ed. (Stuttgart: Deutsche Bibelgesellschaft, 1996), 537.

precise theme that appears in logion 77, indicating yet again that *Thomas'* most esoteric sayings are to be understood with reference to Rabbinic and Kabbalistic conceptions, despite the fact that many of the latter survive in literary documents that are temporally posterior to *Thomas*.

Logion 77 is the most curious saying in the entire *Gospel of Thomas*. No where else does Jesus so directly reveal his hidden identity. Throughout *Thomas*, whenever anyone asks Jesus concerning his true identity, he sharply turns the questioner back to their own pre-existent self. Jesus does not desire that the disciples know their master; he wants only that they know themselves in the deepest and most authentic sense. It may be significant indeed that the second half of logion 77 is a known displacement which occurs in logion 30 in the Greek version. We do not know where the second half of logion 77, which refers to Jesus being present with wood and stone, was originally placed in *Thomas*. In our textual-philological commentary we tentatively suggest a displacement from logion 71, for the wood and stone are known to refer to the wood and stones used for building the altar of sacrifice and for lighting the sacrifice.[16] This would imply that Jesus will be prepared to rebuild the Temple after its coming destruction. In any event, the strangeness of logion 77 is somewhat ameliorated when we observe that the emphasis does not lie on the opening proclamation "I am the light," but upon its closing declaration that all the cosmos attains to the light. This will then reflect the general *Thomas* accentuation upon the necessity of attaining self-knowledge which is a knowledge of one's pre-existent light image. Although speculative, it is not impossible that logion 77 was originally a saying of James the *Tsaddiq*, who is the primordial light of logion 11 and the cosmic foundation of logion 12.

Logion 78 alludes to John the Baptist, and in view of logion 77's portrayal of Jesus as the primordial cosmic light,

---

16. Cf. April D. DeConick, *The Original Gospel of Thomas in Translation*, 139.

perhaps there might be a polemic implied in logion 78, as in the *Gospel of John* chapter 1 where we are told that Jesus, and not John the Baptist, is the cosmic light. However, logion 79 again reminds us of how incongruent logion 77 seems to be compared to the rest of the text as a whole. In logion 79 Jesus refuses a woman's praise of him when she implies that he is the Messiah (a title never once assigned to Jesus in *Thomas*) by praising him with a traditional Jewish messianic blessing.[17] Jesus rejects the woman's praise and instead pronounces blessings on his disciples who do the will of the father. That Jesus here rejects interest in his own person is indicated by logion 80, which states that the world is not worthy of the one who has self-knowledge (see our comments above on logion 56). Logion 81 insists on the necessity of renunciation of wealth and power, a censure which reflects typical Ebionite values. It is possible a negative particle has dropped out of the text, so that it first read: "Let the one who has grown wealthy *not* rule." Such a negative particle may have been easily deleted intentionally in order to allude to the positive theme of ruling in logion 2.

Logion 82's 'fire' would constitute a wordplay in either Aramaic or Syriac with logion 83's 'light'. Rabbinic literature teaches that the body of the Sages is constituted of fire; similarly it is said that the Torah is built of fire. Thus logion 82's fire may refer to Jesus as an interpreter of the Torah's esoteric depths, the understanding of which leads to *Malkhut*, as indicated at the logion's end. Logion 83's theme of the primordial hidden light is best understood with reference to the Kabbalistic doctrine of the *Tsaddiq* as the primordial cosmic light. The likelihood of this is strengthened when we observe that coupled with logion 83's hidden light, an actual Kabbalis-

---

17. Brad Young and David Flusser in "Messianic Blessings in Jewish and Christian Texts," in David Flusser, *Judaism and the Origins of Christianity* (Jerusalem: Magnes Press, Hebrew University, 1988), 280-99 remark that the woman's beatitude seems to suggest that she is proclaiming Jesus to be the Messiah. In any case, Jesus firmly deflects any such popular implications.

tic title for the *Tsaddiq*, is logion 82's *Malkhut*, a Kabbalistic title for *Shekhinah* who unites in supernal union with the masculine *Tsaddiq* in order to bring forth celestial souls, which would be none other than the light images spoken of in logia 83 and 84. The image and likeness of logion 84 alludes to the image and likeness of God in which the Primordial Human was created according to *Genesis* 1:26ff. This interpretation is confirmed by the fact that logion 85 then goes on to mention the creation of Adam, who according to Callahan's emendation "was not worthy to rest,"[18] which would create a catchword association between logia 85 and 86.

Logion 87, "Woe to the body that depends on a body, and woe to the soul that depends on these two," is not a Stoic or otherwise Hellenistic dictum. It is instead a targumic-like paraphrase of *Jeremiah* 17:5. (For the extended philological and targumic evidence, see our textual-philological commentary). 'Body' therefore refers Semitically to a human person as such; the "soul" alludes to the *Jeremiah* text's 'heart' that trusts in humans rather than in God. It is interesting to note that logion 87's paraphrase of the text from the *prophet* Jeremiah is followed in logion 88 with a reference to "the angels and *prophets*." Logion 88 seems to allude to the Rabbinically attested idea that angels and prophets allow entry to Paradise to the those who show them the evidence of circumcision, as in logion 50, where the 'sign' of circumcision gains the children of light entrance to the Place of Light. Logion 88 seems to allude to the initiate's circumcision in the phrase 'what is yours' (cf. logion 50: "What is the sign of your father *in you*?"). According to Rabbinic and Jewish-Christian literature, the prophets as well as the angels are circumcised. This might be reflected in logion 88's 'what is theirs'.

Logion 89 exhorts one to both inward and outward purity based on this polarity's common origin in the one God, since the aspect of diversity inherent in the inward-outward dichotomy reflects the emergence of the Many from the One,

---

18. Callahan, 422.

which might in turn imply a unitive transcendence of the inside-outside dualism, as in logion 22. This unitive mode of purity constitutes in part the yoke of Jesus mentioned in logion 90. In Rabbinic and Kabbalistic terms, the phrase "to take upon oneself the yoke of the kingdom of heaven" refers to the recitation of the Shema (see our commentary above on logion 13). Jesus' yoke is his esoteric interpretation of the Shema, which implies by extension his interpretation of the esoteric depths of the Torah as Lady Wisdom. The yoke implies the Kingdom, that is *Malkhut* and *Shekhinah* as well, for as the *Zohar* teaches, when one takes the yoke of the kingdom upon oneslf by means of the Shema, then *Shekhinah* rests upon them and the two dimensions of the masculine and feminine supernal potencies are united as one. This gives us the exegetical key to understanding logion 90's 'yoke' as well as 'rest'. The secret dimension of the Shema is precisely self-knowledge, that is, knowledge that one's pre-existent luminous self reflects and participates in the divine Unity. Via the discovery of this self one is united with it in the celestial bridal chamber, which reflects both the union of the *Tsaddiq* with *Malkhut*, and of God with *Shekhinah*. In logion 91 "they," perhaps the disciples, ask of Jesus, "Tell us who you are so we may believe in you." Jesus deflects this curiosity and upbraids them, in precisely the same words found in logion 52, for their ignorance of "the one who is in your presence." As we explained in our commentary on logion 52, this phrase refers to the disciples, not to Jesus. It also implies ignorance of God and the *Shekhinah*. Jesus wants his listeners to seek and find their own transcendent self, and this is alluded to in logion 92. Logion 92's "what you asked me about" are the esoteric doctrines referred to in logion 93, truths which must be guarded from profanation by the unworthy. But lest one become discouraged in the quest for self-knowledge, which is the goal of all of Jesus' esoteric teachings, logion 94 reassures the reader that whoever seeks will indeed find. Again, what one is to seek and find is the same self-knowledge spoken of in logia 2 and 3. Logion 95 may imply that when one finds the self, one should not cling to it as one's own, for there is ultimately no self but the divine Self.

Logia 96-98 present three parables of the kingdom, of *Malkhut*. Logia 96 and 97 compare *Malkhut* to a woman, which is congruent with *Thomas'* hypostatic feminine conception of Lady Wisdom and Torah. Logion 98 reflects a negative attitude toward powerful rulers, which is reflective of Ebionite ethics. According to logion 49, the initiates have originated from and will return to *Malkhut*. The function of logia 96-98 are best understood against this background.

Logia 99-106 employ various terms from family life and relations in varying natural and esoteric senses. Logion 101 is unfortunately fragmentary at a crucial point: "For my mother [...], but my true mother gave me life." As in previous logia (e.g., logion 58) 'life' in *Thomas* denotes the Torah, which coincides with Lady Wisdom and *Shekhinah*, the latter being a Rabbinic equivalent of the maternal Holy Spirit. Logion 101 is therefore representing the Holy Spirit as the mother of Jesus, as does the *Gospel of the Hebrews*. The 'life' which his true mother the Holy Spirit has given him is constituted precisely of the secrets of the Torah regarding self-knowledge which deflects death and ensures immortality, as promised in logion 1. DeConick suggests filling logion 101's lacunae with "gave me death," but in our textual-philological commentary we suggest the Semitic *Vorlage* may have contained here one of the Aramaic terms for 'love' (either רחמא or אהבתא), implying a maternal tenderness and gentleness, which, based on the imagery of various ancient Jewish texts which portray God as midwife and infant nurse (e.g. 1QH and *Odes of Solomon* 19), would in turn suggest the act of breastfeeding. Among the advantages of our suggested restoration is 1) it is based on the vocabulary of logion 101 itself (which refers to loving one's mother and father, 2) the main Coptic terms for 'love' would fit within the damaged manuscript's missing spaces, and 3) if there was an implication of feeding in the lacunae, then this would form a link to logion 102's theme of eating.

Logion 105 has in all likelihood been misinterpreted by the Greek scribe who translated the Semitic *Vorlage*. The obejects of knowledge and the general theme of 'knowing' in *Thomas* are virtually exclusively positive. It is therefore stange to read in logion 105 a negative association, namely 'harlot', with *knowledge* of the father and the mother, who in the context of logion 104's reference to the wedding chamber, most likely would refer to God and the *Shekhinah* as maternal Holy Spirit. The solution is quite simple if we propose that the Greek scribe has misinterpreted a feminine form of the Biblical *qodesh*, 'holy one', in the sense of an angel, which in the feminine form would coincide with one of the Biblical terms for 'harlot', namely, *qedeshah*. This term for 'prostitute' literally means 'sacred one' on the basis of temple prostitutes having been consecrated to what was perceived by non-Jews as a sacred or religious service. The Greek scribe therefore failed to understand the Semitic reference to the maternal Holy Spirit as the feminine angelic Holy One and misinterpreted it as 'harlot', 'prostitute'. Therefore, the one who has known the supernal father and mother, God and the feminine Holy Spirit, will be called the child of a feminine angel, that is, the maternal Holy One. Or alternatively, the thought might be that the one who has known their earthly natural parents will come to be called a child of the angelic Holy Spirit. This would allude to the semi-angelic status of those who possess self-knowledge. This status as angelic child would be paralleled in logion 106's phrase "children of humanity," for since humans are already human, a promise that they will become human requires us to understand the term human in this context in an esoteric sense. In the *Book of Enoch*'s *Animal Apocalypse*, animals symbolize humans, while humans symbolize angels. The *Book of Daniel* and the *Parables of Enoch* describe the celestial Son of Man (or Son of Humanity) as an angelic being. Logion 106's term 'sons (or, children) of humanity' is the plural form of *Daniel* and *Enoch*'s term for the angelic 'Son of Man'.

Logion 107 speaks of a single and large sheep, which corresponds to the single large fish of logion 8, which forms a sort of literary *inclusio* linking the opening and closing sections of *Thomas*. The shepherd is said to love the single sheep that was lost more than the other 99 sheep. As Quispel observes, this represents the 'lost sheep of the house of Israel' which God loves above all peoples,[19] and for whom, according to the canonical gospels, Jesus came to find.[20] However, the one sheep better than all the others will also represent the all-important metaphysical reality of self-knowledge, which is simultaneously an overcoming of multiplicity (99 sheep) by unity (one sheep), whereby the two become one. This act of the two becoming one is spoken of in logion 108, according to which the one who drinks Jesus' esoteric wosdom teachings concerning self-knowledge will become equal to Jesus, but not mystically united with him so that the disciple actually becomes Jesus, as is incorrectly implied by most translations. What is meant is that the student will become as his master, that is, he will master his lessons and become equal to the teacher, precisely as in logion 13. This self-knowledge which is the content of Jesus' secret doctrines is described as a treasure in logion 109. Logion 110, a doublet of logion 81, requires that one who has found wealth is to renounce it. This is a worldly wealth in contrast to logion 109's true wealth of self-knowledge. Everything, even the world itself, must be renounced save self-knowledge, the most authentic wealth. The world deserves to be renounced, for after all, as logion 111 proclaims, heaven and earth will pass away, but the one who has gained self-knowledge will not pass away or taste death. As Quispel has established, logion 111 should be rendered as follows:[21]

> Jesus said: The heavens and the earth will roll up in your presence, and whoever lives from the living one will not taste death or fear.
>
> Jesus said: Whoever has found oneself, of that one the world is not worthy.

---

19. Qur'an *sura* 2:47 similarly insists that God chose and preferred Israel over all the peoples of the world.
20. See Gilles Quispel, *Gnostica, Judaica, Catholica*, 190-91.
21. Ibid, 220.

Therefore logion 111 actually consists of two separate logia, so that the common comparison of *Thomas*' 114 logia with the 114 *sura*s of the Qur'an is invalid. Additionally, Quispel's rendering reveals that logion 111a is a doublet of logion 37's conclusion: "and you will see the son of the living one and you will not fear." When we compare logion 37's phrase 'son of the living one' with logion 111's phrase 'the one who lives from the living one' we come to recognize that logion 37's 'son' is meant in the Semitic idiomatic sense found in such terms as 'sons of the resurrection' (i.e., the ones who are resurrected), 'sons of the bridegroom' (i.e., those who are associated with the bridegroom, that is, his friends or guests), and the Arabic Sufi term 'son of the moment' (*ibn al-waqt*). Therefore in logion 37 Jesus is not referring to himself as 'the son of the living one', but he is in fact referring to the disciples who will see themselves, or their true selves, when they gain self-knowledge. In light of logion 111's two sayings we can deduce that that 111a's 'one who lives from the living one' (which is the meaning of logion 37's Semitic idiom '*son* of the living one') is none other than the one who has found oneself (111b).

However, logion 112 immediately claries that the self which must be found is not the lower ego or self, for "cursed is the flesh that depends on the soul" and vice versa, which is a doublet and variant of logion 87, which is, as we discussed, a paraphrastic targumic reformulation of *Jeremiah* 17:5. The true self is not the natural person ('flesh') nor even the human heart ('soul'), but the supernal self which lives from the living one, who is, as we saw in our commentary on logion 50, the living God, which is a specific Kabbalistic title for the cosmic *Tsaddiq*. Therefore, as the *Thomas* gospel nears its end James the Just, Jacob the *Tsaddiq*, is once again alluded to, just as he is shortly after the same gospel's opening (in logion 11 implicitly and in logion 12 explicitly). And since the male *Tsaddiq* is the spouse of the feminine *Malkhut*, the very next logion, 113, deals explicitly with the kingdom. People do not, indeed, they *cannot* see the kingdom, for it is an interior reality, as logion 3 makes clear enough: "The kingdom is inside you." In this sense *Malkhut* includes the reality of inward or self-knowledge. Logion 3 then states that the kingdom is simultaneously "outside you," or more literally, visible to the outer eye, or eyesight. The meaning is that the kingdom is both unseen and seen, that is, hidden and revealed, a contrast repeated in logia 5 and 6, and then in later logia, including logion 108. Therefore, when logion 113 states that the "kingdom is spread out over the earth, and people do not see it," this means "the kingdom is *revealed* in the form of self-knowledge which is *hidden*, or concealed within people." Therefore there is no moral censure or failure on the part of people implied in logion 113's statement "and people do not see it," or more correctly, "do not see her," since 'kingdom' in Aramaic as well as Coptic is grammatically feminine. Additionally, logion 113's "spread out over the earth," which is conceptually equivalent to logion 3's "outside you," does not mean that the kingdom is physically visible in the outward creation. The "eye" to which *Malkhut* is visible is the eye of the heart, which means the same as: The kingdom is knowledge of the celestial self. The *Kingdom* is *Wisdom*, an identification which is a staple association in Kabbalah, namely, *Malkhut* is *Hokhmah*, but the latter specifically as hypostatic Lady Wisdom.

However, in light of logion 22's teaching on the transcendence and cancelation of the inward-outward dichotomy, we should qualify the formulation "inner knowledge." As we remarked, logion 3 literally reads "the kingdom, she is of your interior, and she is of your outward eye. When you will come to know yourself...." The outward eye does not mean the physical eye, but the spiritual eye of *perception*. The contrast therefore pertains less to the inward and outer domains as to the categories of concealment and revelation, which themselves also become unified and then pass away in the state of self-knowledge. The kingdom is therefore not "inside you and outside you," but it is "hidden as you and revealed to your perception." This does not contradict logion 113's teaching that the kingdom does not arrive "in an outward act of looking (i.e., observation)," for what is implied here is clarified in the following statement: "They will not say, 'Look, she is there', or 'Look, she is that one.'" This implies that the kingdom cannot be localized (here or there) or "individualized" or reified as an "object" of thought. That is, the kingdom overcomes the subject-object dichotomy of cognitive thought and transcends all the spatial and temporal and other polarities of logion 22. As the supernal Feminine, the kingdom is the pure and undifferentiated divine matrix. The kingdom is revealed to the earth, that is, to earth's inhabitants, but not in a physically visible mode. Near *Thomas*' opening, logia 5 and 6 promise that what is hidden will be revealed. By contrast, near *Thomas*' close, the reverse sequence is found in the declaration that the kingdom is revealed to the earth and yet is hidden. By this reversal, perhaps even the polarity of hiddenness and revelation is transcended, note well, by means of *Malkhut*, who is simultaneously revealed and hidden, and therefore neither of these separatively. This simultaneity parallels the presenced simultaneity of the masculine and feminine genders of the androgynous Primordial Human. According to logion 22, the male and the female lose their respective self-definitions, so that the male is no longer male and the female no longer female. Logion 3 and 113 indicate that the same paradigm applies to the categories of concealment and revelation, which are united and transcended by means of *Malkhut-Shekhinah*. But *Malkhut* is the origin and goal of the initiate who has attained self-knowledge, so that the gnostic also experiences the transcendence of the concealment-revelation dichotomy, but not "within" or "without," a polarity which has now been left behind. As children of *Malkhut* and *Tsaddiq*, those who possess self-knowledge have become the very reality of non-dichtomous transcendence as such. Naturally the word 'transcendence' is not used in this context in the sense of the opposite of 'immanence', for that would constitute yet another polarity in need of cancelation. But at this point we must admit that language itself proves inadequate to fully express or circumscribe the metaphysical and esoteric realities which it strives to describe.

We have now reached the final and perhaps most misunderstood and misrepresented logion of the *Gospel of Thomas*, logion 114. Nearly all the objections against this logion made by femininsts can be answered once we translate the saying correctly, which to our knowledge has been achieved only by Schüngel.[22] Based on his Coptic philological observations, we can now present a correct rendering as follows:

> Simon Peter said to them: "Let Mary depart from among us, for women are not worthy of Life." Jesus said: "Look, am I to force her to become male? In order that she also may become a living spirit, her spirit is equal to that of you males. For every woman who will make herself capable will enter the kingdom of heaven."

This is a substantial improvement over the standard but flawed interpretation which generally reads something like the following:

> Simon Peter said to them: "Let Mary depart from among us, for women are not worthy of Life." Jesus said: "Behold, I will guide her so that she shall become male, so that she also may become a living spirit resembling you males. For every woman who will make herself male will enter the kingdom of heaven."

In light of the embarrassment which this latter rendering understandably causes, it comes as no surprise when some commentators deal with the problem by simply wishing away logion 114 as a supposed later interpolation.

Mary's spirit is equal to that of the male disciples. Yet the message of logion 22 insists that the male and female contraeity be canceled. This transpires in the attainment of the androgynous state of the Primordial Human. Both Mary and the male disciples have become "living spirits," an allusion

---

22. In our textual-philological *Thomas* commentary, we present several pages of Coptic and Aramaic philological arguments which justify Schüngel's position.

to *Genesis* 2:7, according to which God breathed the breath of life into Adam (i.e., androgynous Humanity, not the first male named Adam) and Adam (i.e., humanity) became a "living creature," rendered by the Septuagint as "living spirit." Therefore it is clear that logion 114 presupposes the doctrine of the androgynous Primordial Human. "For every female who acts capably will enter the kingdom of heaven." The kingdom herself involves the theme of androgyny, for she and the *Tsaddiq* become androgynously one in the celestial wedding chamber, just as God and *Shekhinah* "become" androgynous in the supernal wedding chamber. Logion 114's acting capably is equivalent to logion 58's active and diligent seeking of the Torah's secrets concerning self-knowledge, which results in eternal life. To know oneself (logia 1-3) is to enter the kingdom (logion 114), the feminine *Malkhut-Shekhinah*[23] whose very metaphysical gender passes away in androgynous unitive transcendence with God in the supernal Temple of their wedding chamber.

---

23. To which we might compare the divine Layla in Sufi poetry.

# 3. *The Gospel of Thomas*

## A New Translation
## Based on the Coptic and Greek Texts

Here are the secret teachings of the living Jesus; and he wrote them, even Judah the Twin, and he[1] said:

1. "Whoever finds the interpretation of these teachings will not taste of death."

2. Jesus said: "One who seeks, let them not cease seeking until they find; and when they find, they will be troubled; and when they have been troubled, they will be amazed; and when they have been amazed, they will reign; and when they have reigned, they will rest."

3. Jesus said: "If those who push you around[2] say to you, 'Behold, the kingdom is in the sky,' the birds of the sky would enter her before you. And if they say to you that she is under the earth in the watery abyss, then the fish of the sea would enter her before you. But the kingdom of God is both inside you and manifest to the outer eye. One who knows oneself will find the kingdom, and when you know yourselves, then you will be known, and you will see that you are children of the living father. But if you do not know who you are, you will dwell in poverty and you will be that poverty."

4. Jesus said: "The man old in days will not hesitate to ask an infant seven days old concerning the place of life, and he

---

1. Thomas, not Jesus.
2. Coptic *sok*, *contra* Guillaumont not from Aramaic נגד, but from Biblical *sug* (סוג); compare the Arabic سق (*saqa*).

will live. For the many who are first will become last; and the many will become one."

5. Jesus said: "Know what is in front of you, and what is hidden from you will be revealed to you. There is nothing which is hidden which will not be made manifest."

6. His disciples asked him and said to him: "How should we fast? And how should we pray? And how should we give alms? And how should we observe dietary laws?" Jesus said: "Do not lie, and do not do anything against your conscience, for Heaven sees all things. For there is nothing that has been hidden that will not be made manifest."

7. Jesus said: "The lion that a man will eat is blessed, for the lion will become a man. But the man that the lion will eat is cursed, for the lion will become a man."

8. He said: "The man is like a wise fisherman who cast his net into the sea; he drew it up full of little fish from the sea. Among them the wise fisherman found a good large fish. He cast the little ones back to the sea; he chose the large fish without trouble. Whoever has ears to hear, let them hear."

9. Jesus said: "Behold, the sower went out, he filled his hands and cast forth. Some, indeed, fell upon the road; the birds came, they gathered them. Others fell upon the rock, and did not send roots down into the earth, and did not send forth ears reaching to the sky. And others fell upon thorns; they choked the seed, and worms ate them. And others fell upon good earth, and it produced good fruit (reaching) up to the sky. It brought sixty per measure, and one hundred twenty per measure.

10. Jesus said: "I have cast a fire upon the world, and behold, I watch over it until it burns."

11. Jesus said: "This heaven will pass away, and the one above it will also pass away. And those who have died are not alive, and those who are alive will not die. In the days when you ate what was dead, you made it live. When you come to be in the light, what will you do? On the day you were one, you became two, but when you become two, what will you do?"

12. The disciples said to Jesus: "We know that you will depart from us. Who will be our leader?" Jesus said to them: "Wherever you will find yourselves, you will go up to James the Just, the one for whom heaven and earth came into being."

13. Jesus said to his disciples: "Make a comparison and tell me what I am like." Simon Peter said to him: "You are like a righteous angel." Matthew said to him: "You are like a wise sage." Thomas said to him: "Master, my mouth will not allow me at all to say what you are like." Jesus said: "I am not your master; because you drank you were intoxicated from the bubbling spring I have measured out." And he took him aside and spoke to him three words. But when Thomas approached his companions, they asked him: "What did Jesus say to you?" Thomas said to them: "If I were to tell you even one of the things he told me, you would gather stones and cast them at me, and fire would come from the stones and burn you."

14. Jesus said: "If you fast, you will give birth to sin, and if you pray, you will be condemned, and if you give alms, you will harm your own spirits. And in any land you enter, walking in the districts, if they receive you, eat whatever is placed before you; heal the sick among them. For what enters the mouth will not defile it, but what comes out of your mouth, that is what will defile you."

15. Jesus said: "When you look upon him who was not born of woman, bow your face to the ground and worship him, for he is your father."

16. Jesus said: "Perhaps people think that I have come to cast peace upon the world, and they do not know that I have come to cast divisions upon the world: fire, sword, war. For five will be in a house; three will be against two, and two against three; the father against the son, and the son against the father, and they will stand on their feet as single ones."

17. Jesus said: "I will give you what eye has not seen, what has not been heard, and what hand has not touched, and what has not entered the human mind."

18. The disciples said to Jesus: "Tell us how our end will be." Jesus said: "Have you discovered the beginning so that you may inquire about the end? For where the beginning is, from there will the end come forth. Blessed is the one who will stand in the beginning, for they will know the end, and they will not taste of death."

19. Jesus said: "Blessed is the one who existed from the beginning, before they existed. If you come to exist as my disciples and if you will hear my words, these stones will serve you, for to you belong five trees in paradise which stay green in summer and winter, and their leaves do not fall. One who will know them will not taste of death."

20. The disciples said to Jesus: "Tell us what the kingdom of heaven is like." He said to them: "She is like a mustard seed, the smallest of all seeds. When, however, it falls onto the earth prepared for it, it sends forth a large branch which becomes a shelter for the birds of the sky."

21. Mary said to Jesus: "Who are your disciples like?" He said: "They are like small children living in a field that is not theirs. When the masters of the field come, they will say: 'Return our field to us.' They strip naked in front of them and return their field to them. Therefore I say, if the master of the house knows that the thief is coming, he will keep watch before he comes, and not let him tunnel into the house of his domain in order to take his property. You, however, keep watch beforehand. Gird up your loins in a great power,[3] so that the thieves do not discover a path to get at you, because they will find the defense you are counting on." Let there be among you one who understands. When the grain opened, he arrived with haste, his sickle in hand; he reaped it. Whoever has ears to hear, let them hear.

22. Jesus looked at some infants breastfeeding. He said to his disciples: "These infants breastfeeding are like those who enter the kingdom." They said this to him: "And so if we are infants we will enter the kingdom?" Jesus said to them:

---

3. Cf. "a great power" in logion 85.

"When you make the two one, when you make the inside like the outside, and the outside like the inside, and above like below, and when you make the male and the female to be only one, so that neither is the male male nor the female female, when you replace an eye with an eye, and a hand with a hand, and a foot with a foot, and an image with an image, then you will enter the kingdom."

23. Jesus said: "I will choose you, one from among a thousand, and two from among ten thousand, and they, being only one, will stand up."

24. His disciples said: "Show us the place where you are, because we need to seek after it." He said to them: "One who has ears, let them hear. Light dwells within a person of light, and they light up all the world. If they do not become light, they are darkness."

25. Jesus said: "Love your brother as your own soul. Guard him as the apple of your own eye."

26. Jesus said: "You see the splinter in the eye of your brother; the log, however, in your own eye, you do not see. When you dislodge the log from your own eye, then you will be able to see clearly enough to remove the splinter from the eye of your brother."

27. "If you do not fast from the world, you will not find the kingdom; if you do not keep the sabbath of sabbaths, you will not see the father."

28. Jesus said: "I stood in the midst of the world, and I went forth and appeared to them in flesh. I found them drunk, every one of them; I did not find a single one thirsting. And my soul grieved for the children of humanity, because their minds are blinded, and they do not recognize, for they entered the world empty, and they seek to leave the world empty. They are drunk now; but when they become sober, they will repent."

29. Jesus said: "It is a wonder if the flesh came into existence for the spirit; but it is the greatest of wonders if the spirit came into existence for the body. But I am amazed at how this great wealth dwells in this poverty."

30. Jesus said: "Where there are three gods, they are gods. Where there are two or one, I am with that one. Pick up the stone, and you will find me there; split the wood, and I am there."

31. Jesus said: "No prophet is accepted in his own village; no physician heals those who know him."

32. Jesus said: "A city built upon an elevated mountain, being fortified, can in no wise fall, nor can she[4] be hidden."

33. Jesus said: "What you hear in your ears,[5] proclaim it from your housetops. For no one lights a lamp and puts it under a basket, and neither does anyone put it in a hidden place. Rather, one places it upon the lamp-stand so that anyone who enters or exits may see its light."

34. Jesus said: "If a blind person pushes around a blind person, the two of them will fall into a ditch."

35. Jesus said: "It is impossible to enter the house of someone who is strong and take it by force without tying their hands; then you will be able to remove the goods from their house."

36. Jesus said: ["Do not worry] from early to late, nor from evening to morning about the food you are to eat, nor about the robe that you are to wear. You are much greater than the lilies which neither card nor spin. When you have no clothing, then what will you wear? Who can add to your lifespan? He will give you your clothing."[6]

37. His disciples said: "On what day will you show yourself to us? And on what day will we behold you?" Jesus said: "When you disrobe and are naked without shame, and when you place your garments upon the ground beneath your feet, like those infants, and you trample upon the garments, then

---

4. "City" in Coptic is grammatically feminine; there may be an allusion to the Jewish scriptural theme of Lady Zion.

5. The Coptic idiom, "in your ear, in the other ear," must not be rendered literally.

6. This is the Greek version. Logion 36 has been shortened in the Coptic to: "Jesus said: 'Do not worry from morning to evening, and from evening to morning about what you will receive to clothe yourselves with.'"

will you behold the son of the living one, and you will not fear."

38. Jesus said: "So many times you wanted to hear these words which I speak to you, and there is no other from whom to hear them. Days will come when you will seek for me and you will not find me."

39. Jesus said: "The Pharisees and the scribes took the keys of knowledge; they hid them. They entered not, and those who desired to enter they did not allow. You, however, be as wise as serpents and as innocent as doves."

40. Jesus said: "A grapevine has been planted outside of the father, and not being fortified, she will be pulled up from her root and will be destroyed."

41. Jesus said: "Whoever has something in their hand will receive [more], and whoever has nothing, the little they have will be taken from their hand."

42. Jesus said: "Go away!"[7]

43. His disciples said to him: "Who are you to say such things to us?" "In what I say to you, you do not recognize who I am. Rather, you have become like those Judaeans, for they love the tree, they hate its fruit, and they love the fruit, they hate the tree."

44. Jesus said: "Whoever speaks against the father will be forgiven, and whoever speaks against the son will be forgiven; whoever, however, speaks against the Holy Spirit will not be forgiven, neither on the earth nor in heaven."

45. Jesus said: "Grapes are not harvested from thorns, nor are figs gathered from thistles, for these do not give fruit. A good person brings out of their treasury house what is good; an evil person brings evil things out of their corrupt treasury house which is in their heart, and they speak evil things. For out of the surplus of the heart they bring out evil things."

---

7. Cf. Callahan, 418-19 for the justification of this reading. As Callahan points out, logia 42 and 43 actually constitute a single pericope, and Jesus' harsh words in logion 42 explains the anger of the disciples' words at the beginning of logion 43.

46. Jesus said: "From Adam to John the Baptist, among those born of women, no one is higher than John the Baptist, so that he should lower his eyes to anyone. But I have said this, that one who will be an infant among you will know the kingdom and will be exalted above John."

47. Jesus said: "It is impossible for one person to climb two horses, and stretch two bows, and it is impossible for a servant to serve two lords, they will honor the one and despise the other. No one drinks old wine and immediately desires to drink new wine. And new wine is not poured into old wineskins in order to split them. And old wine is not poured into new wineskins in order to destroy them. Old patches are not sewn onto new garments, because there would be a split."

48. Jesus said: "If two make peace in this one house, they will say to this mountain: 'Move away!' and it will move."

49. Jesus said: "Blessed are the unitary and chosen ones, for you will find[8] the kingdom, for you are from the kingdom and will return to her."

50. Jesus said: "If they should say to you: 'From where did you come into being?' Say to them: 'We originated from the light, where the light issued forth from itself; it arose and appeared in their image.' If they say to you: 'Are you the light?,' say: 'We are children of the light, and we are the chosen ones of the living father.' If they ask you: 'What is the sign of the father in you?,' say to them: 'It is a shaking and a rest.'"

51. His disciples said to him: "When will the day come when the dead rest? And on what day will the new world come?" He said to them: "What you are looking for has already come, but you do not see it."

52. His disciples said to him: "The twenty-four prophets of Israel, they all spoke concerning you." He said to them: "You have ignored the one who lives in your presence, and you have spoken of the dead."

---

8. Or 'inherit'.

53. His disciples said to him: "Circumcision, is it of value or not?" He said to them: "If it were of value their father would beget them from their mother circumcised. Rather, true circumcision in spirit is found to be entirely profitable."[9]

54. Jesus said: "Blessed are the poor, for yours is the kingdom of heaven."

55. Jesus said: "Whoever does not hate their father and their mother, they cannot be my disciple, and whoever does not hate their brothers and sisters and does not take up their cross in my way, they will not be worthy of me."

56. Jesus said: "Whoever has known the world[10] has found oneself; but whoever has found oneself, of that one the world is not worthy."

57. Jesus said: "The kingdom of the father, she is like a person who had a good seed; their enemy came in the night, he sowed a weed over the good seed. The person did not allow to pull up the weed. He said to them: 'So that when you pull up the weeds, you do not pull up the grain with it. For on the day of the harvest the weeds will be apparent; they will be pulled up and burned.'"

58. Jesus said: "Blessed is the one who has toiled; he has found life."

59. Jesus said: "Look upon the living one while you are alive, lest you die and then seek to see the living one, but be unable to see."

60. He saw a Samaritan carrying a lamb while walking to Judea. He said to his disciples: "That one over there is binding a lamb." They said this to him: "He binds it so that he may kill it and eat it." He said to them: "While the lamb is alive he will not eat it, not until he kills the lamb so that it first becomes a corpse." They said: "It can be eaten in no other

---

9. Mother and Spirit may be connected thematically here, since according to Jewish texts the Holy Spirit is the celestial Mother.

10. Coptic/Greek *kosmos*, but since the local-spatial concept of 'world' was unknown in Aramaic or Hebrew in the time of Jesus, the sense here will be "all things," or "everything."

way." He said to them: "You too should seek a place of rest for yourselves lest you become a corpse and be eaten."

61. Jesus said: "Two will rest on a bed; one will die, one will live." Salome said: "Who are you, man, to make your way like a relative[11] onto my couch and then to eat from my table?" Jesus said to her: "I am he who comes from the Unified; I have received of my father." "I am your disciple." "And therefore I say: If my disciple is destroyed,[12] they will be full of light, but if they be divided, they will be full of darkness."

62. Jesus said: "I tell my mysteries to those worthy of my mysteries. Let not your left hand know what your right hand will do."

63. Jesus said: "There was a wealthy person who possessed many riches. He said: 'I will use my money in order to sow and reap and plant and fill my treasury house with fruit so that I lack nothing.' This was what he was thinking about in his heart, and when the night came, he died. Whoever has ears to hear, let them hear."

64. Jesus said: "A man was receiving various guests, and when he had prepared the dinner he dispatched his servant to invite the guests. He went to the first; he said to him: 'My master invites you'. He said: 'I have some money to give to some traders who are arriving in the evening. I will go to them to place orders. Please excuse me from the dinner'. He went to another; he said to him: 'My master has invited you'. He said to him: 'I have purchased a house and I will not be available for a day; I will have no time for leisure'. He went to another; he said to him: 'My master invites you'. He said to him: 'My friend is to be married, and I am in charge of the dinner; I cannot come'. Please excuse me from the dinner'. He went to another; he said to him: 'My master calls you'.

---

11. Our textual-philological *Thomas* commentary contains the philological evidence for this emendation.

12. Usually emended to 'made whole' or 'unified'. It is conceivable, however, that the thought may be that when one's lower self is destroyed, or as in the words of logion 56 (compared with logion 111b), when one discovers their (lower) self as a carcass, then one will be filled with light.

'I have leased out a farm; I am going to collect the taxes. I cannot come; please excuse me'. The servant, he came and said to his master: 'Those you have invited to the dinner have begged to be excused'. The master said to his servant: 'Go outside into the streets; bring those you will find so that they may dine'. Buyers and traders will not enter into the places of my father."

65. He said: "A just man owned a vineyard; he leased it out to some tenants so that they would operate it and he might collect the produce from their hand. He sent his servant to the tenants to collect the produce of the vineyard. They seized his servant, they beat him almost to the point of death. The servant left; he spoke with his master. His master said: 'Perhaps he did not recognize them'.[13] He sent another servant; the tenants beat this one as well. Then the master sent his son; he said: 'Perhaps they will show some respect to my son'. The tenants there recognized him as the heir to the vineyard; they seized him, they killed him. Whoever has ears, let them hear."

66. Jesus said: "Show me the stone the builders have rejected; he is the cornerstone."

67. Jesus said: "Whoever knows everything, but lacks self [knowledge], lacks everything."

68. Jesus said: "Blessed are you when you are hated and persecuted, and a place will be found where they will not persecute you."

69. Jesus said: "Blessed are those who have been persecuted in their heart; these are the ones who have truly known the father. Blessed are those who are hungry in order to fill the stomach of the one who is in need."

70. Jesus said: "What you beget within you, that which is within you will save you; if it is not begotten within you, that which you do not have within you will slay you."

71. Jesus said: "I will destroy this house, and no one will build it again [except me]."

---

13. A quite apparent textual corruption for: "Perhaps they did not recognize him."

72. A man said to him: "Tell my brothers to divide my father's belongings with me." He said to him: "O man, who has made me a divider?" He turned to his disciples; he said to them: "Am I really a divider?"

73. Jesus said: "The harvest is indeed plentiful; the laborers, however, are few. Pray, however, to the master that he may send laborers to the harvest."

74. He said: "Master, many there are standing around the well, but there is no one in the well."

75. Jesus said: "Many stand at the door, but the unitary ones will enter the marriage chamber."

76. Jesus said: "The kingdom of the father is like a merchant who had a consignment of merchandise. He found a pearl. The merchant was wise; he got rid of the consignment and purchased the single pearl. You also, seek for yourselves his imperishable treasure that endures, there where no moth comes to devour and no worms to destroy."

77. Jesus said: "I am the light, the one shining upon all. I am the all. The all came forth from me, and the all attained to me."

78. Jesus said: "Why did you go out to the countryside? To look at a reed shaken by the wind? And to look at a man wearing soft garments like your kings and your powerful ones? These are they who wear soft garments, and they are not able to know the truth."

79. A woman in the crowd said to him: "Blessed is the womb which bore you and the breasts which nourished you." He said to her: "Blessed are they who have heard the word of the father, who have truly kept it; for the days will come when you will say: 'Blessed is the womb which has not conceived, and the breasts which have not given milk.'"

80. Jesus said: "Whoever has known the world has found oneself; but whoever has found oneself, of that one the world is not worthy."

81. Jesus said: "Whoever becomes wealthy will become a king; but whoever gains power, let him forsake it."

82. Jesus said: "Whoever is next to me is next to the fire; but whoever is far away from me is far away from the kingdom."

83. Jesus said: "The images are revealed to the person, yet the light in the images is hidden in the image of the father's light. He will be revealed, yet his image will be concealed by his light."

84. Jesus said: "You rejoice on those days when you behold your likeness; but when you look upon your images which existed before you did, which do not die, and which are not revealed, how much will you be able to bear?"

85. Jesus said: "Adam came into existence from a great power and a great wealth, but he was not worthy of you,[14] for otherwise he would not have tasted of death."

86. Jesus said: "Foxes have dens, birds have nests, but the child of Adam has no place to lay his head and rest."

87. He said: "Woe to the body that depends on a body, and woe to the soul that depends on these two."[15]

88. Jesus said: "The angels will come to you with the prophets, and they will give you what is yours; and you will give them what is yours, and you will say to yourselves: 'On what day will they come and take what is theirs?'"

89. Jesus said: "Why do you wash the outside of the cup? Don't you understand that whoever made the inside is also the one who made the outside?"

90. Jesus said: "Come to me, for my yoke is easy, and my lordship, she is a gentle man,[16] and you will find rest for yourselves."

---

14. "Of you"; Callahan, 422 rightly emends to "to rest."

15. That is, "Woe to the human being who trusts in another human being, and woe to the person's heart who trusts in those who trust in each other," rather than trusting in the Lord; cf. *Jeremiah* 17:5. On this logion, see our contextualized commentary above.

16. We have translated over-literally, but we feel justified in doing so in this case in light of the androgynous metaphysics of *Thomas*. The relevant phrase above is usually rendered adequately enough less literally as : "my mastery is gentle."

91. They said to him: "Tell us who you are so that we may believe in you." He said to them: "You read the face of the sky and the earth, and the one who is in your presence, you do not know him, and you do not know how to interpret this moment."

92. Jesus said: "Seek and you will find; but what you asked me about in those days, I did not tell you about it in those days. I would like to tell them to you, but now you do not even ask."

93. "Do not give what is holy to dogs, lest they cast them upon the dung pile. Do not throw pearls to swine, lest they [. . .]."[17]

94. Jesus said: "The one who seeks will find, and the one who is invited in, it will be opened to them."

95. Jesus said: "If you have money, do not lend it at interest. Rather, give it to one from whose hand you will not get it back."

96. Jesus said: "The kingdom of the father, she is like a woman; she took a little yeast; she hid it in dough; she made it into large loaves of bread. Whoever has ears to hear, let them hear."

97. Jesus said: "The kingdom of the father, she is like a woman carrying a jar full of meal, walking on a distant road. The jar handle broke; the meal emptied out onto the road behind her. She didn't notice the problem. When she entered into her house, she put the jar down; she found it empty."

98. Jesus said: "The kingdom of the father, she is like a man who wanted to kill a man in power. He drew his sword in his house; he thrust it into the wall, to see if his hand would be strong enough to thrust it in. Then he slew the man who had power."

---

17. As in *Matthew* 15:26 (and *2 Peter* 2:22), so here 'dogs' and 'swine' are ancient Jewish pejorative designations for Gentiles. Perhaps Paul was guided by this saying in his policy of forcefully forbidding his Gentile converts from the study and cultivation of Jewish esoteric traditions.

99. The disciples said to him: "Your brothers and your mother are standing outside." He said to them: "Those here who do the will of my father, they are my brothers and my mother. They are the ones who will enter into the kingdom of my father."

100. They showed Jesus a coin, and they said to him: "Those who belong to Caesar demand taxes from us." He said to them: "That which is Caesar's, give to Caesar. That which is God's, give to God, and that which is mine, give to me."

101. "Whoever does not hate their father and their mother in my way, they cannot become my disciple; and whoever does not love their father and their mother in my way, they cannot become my disciple. For my mother [. . .]; my true mother, however, she gave to me the Life."

102. Jesus said: "Woe to them, the Pharisees, for they are like a dog sleeping in the cattle manger, for neither does it eat, not does it let the cattle eat."

103. Jesus said: "Blessed is the one who knows where the thieves will enter, so that they may arise and unite their domain and arm themselves before the thieves enter."

104. They said to Jesus: "Come, let us pray today and fast." Jesus said: "What sin have I committed, or in what have I been overpowered? Rather, when the bridegroom will have departed from the bridal chamber, then let them fast and pray."

105. Jesus said: "One who knows the father and the mother will be called the child of a harlot."[18]

106. Jesus said: "When you make the two one, you will become children of Adam, and if you say to this mountain, 'Depart from here,' it will depart."

107. Jesus said: "The kingdom of the father, she is like a man who was a shepherd, who had a hundred sheep. One of them, the largest, got lost. He left the ninety-nine; he sought

---

18. "Harlot"; in all likelihood a scribal misinterpretation of Biblical *qedeshah*, the feminine form of 'a holy one' (i.e., an angel) for 'harlot'. The Coptic scribe simply translated the Greek *Vorlage*'s *porne* literally.

after the one until he found him. After thus troubling himself, he said to the sheep: 'I love you more than the ninety-nine.'"

108. Jesus said: "Whoever drinks from my mouth, they will become equal to me, and I will become equal to them; and what is hidden will be made manifest to them."

109. Jesus said: "The kingdom of the father, she is like a man who was unaware that he had a treasure hidden in his field. And when he died, he left it to his son. The son was unaware of it. He took possession of the field and sold it. And the buyer started ploughing; he found the treasure. He began lending money at interest to whomever he wished."

110. Jesus said: "Whoever has found[19] the world[20] and grown wealthy, let them forsake the world."[21]

111. Jesus said this: "The heavens will be rolled up, and also the earth, in your sight; and the one who lives from the living one will not behold death or fear."[22]

Jesus said: "Whoever has found oneself, of that one the world is not worthy."

112. Jesus said: "Cursed is the flesh that depends on the soul; cursed is the soul that depends on the flesh."[23]

113. His disciples said to him: "On what day will the kingdom come?" "She will not come with outward observation. It will not be said, 'Behold, over there!', or, 'Behold, that one.' Instead, the kingdom of the father is spread out over the face of the earth, and she is not to be seen."[24]

---

19. But the Biblical 'find' (*matsa'*) also can mean 'attain', 'acquire'.

20. The Coptic/Greek *kosmos*, but since the local-spatial concept of 'world' was unknown in Aramaic or Hebrew in the time of Jesus, the meaning here would be "everything."

21. See the previous footnote.

22. For this rendering, see the contextualized commentary above.

23. That is, cursed is the person who depends on the corrupt human heart, and cursed is the corrupt human heart that trusts in humanity rather than in the Lord (cf. *Jeremiah* 17:5). See the contextualized commentary above, and at greater length, our textual-philological *Thomas* commentary in preparation.

24. We understand the Coptic here as semantically passive.

114. Simon Peter said to them: "Let Mary depart from among us, for women are not worthy of Life." Jesus said: "Look, am I to force her to become male? In order that she also may become a living spirit, her spirit is equal to that of you males. For every woman who will make herself capable will enter the kingdom of heaven."[25]

---

25. See the contextualized commentary above, and at far greater length, our textual-philological *Thomas* commentary in preparation.

# BIBLIOGRAPHY

Abdel Haleem, M. A. S. *The Qur'an*. A New Translation. Oxford: Oxford University Press, 2005.

Abrams, Daniel. "The Boundaries of Divine Ontology: The Inclusion and Exclusion of Metatron in the Godhead," *Harvard Theological Review*, vol. 87 no. 3 (1994), 291-321.

———, "From Divine Shape to Angelic Being: The Career of Akatriel in Jewish Literature," *The Journal of Religion*, vol. 76, no. 1 (Jan., 1996), 43-63.

Ackerman, James S. "The Rabbinic Interpretation of Psalm 82 and the Gospel of John: John 10:34," *The Harvard Theological Review*, vol. 59, no. 2 (April, 1966), 186-191.

Aland, Kurt, ed. *Synopsis Quattuor Evangeliorum*. 15th ed. Stuttgart: Deutsche Bibelgesellschaft, 1996.

al-'Alawi, Shaykh. *Knowledge of God. A sufic commentary on al Murshid al-Mu'in of ibn al-'Ashir*. Edited by 'Abd as-Sabur al-Ustadh; translated by 'Abd al-Kabir al Munawarra and 'Abd as-Sabur al-Ustadh. Norfolk, UK: Diwan Press, 1981.

Aldridge, Robert E. "Peter and the 'Two Ways'," *Vigiliae Christianae*, vol. 53, no. 3 (August, 1999), 233-264.

Alexander, P. S. "The Historical Setting of the Hebrew Book of Enoch," *Journal of Jewish Studies*, vol. 28 no. 2 (1977), 156-180.

Arberry, Arthur John. Abu Bakr al-Kalabadhi, *Kitab al-Ta'arruf li-madhhab ahl al-tasawwuf. The Doctrine of the Sufis*. London: Cambridge University Press, 1935.

Bacher, W. *Die exegetische Terminologie der jüdischen Traditionsliteratur*. Vol 1. Leipzig, 1899.

Bammel, Ernst. "Rest and Rule," *Vigiliae Christianae*, vol. 23, no. 2 (June, 1969), 88-90.

Barker, Margaret. *Enoch the Lost Prophet*. London: SPCK, 1988.

———, "Enthronement and Apotheosis: The Vision in Revelation 4-5," in P. J. Harland and C. T. R. Hayward (eds.). *New Heaven and New Earth: Prophecy and the Millennium. Essays in Honour of Anthony Gelston.* Leiden: Brill, 1999), 217-227.

Bauckham, Richard. *Jesus and the Eyewitnesses. The Gospels as Eyewitness Testimony.* Grand Rapids, Michigan/ Cambridge, U.K., 2006.

Betz, Hans Dieter. *The Greek Magic Papyri in Translation. Including the Demotic Spells.* 2$^{nd}$ ed. Volume 1: *Texts.* Chicago, Illinois: University of Chicago Press, 1996.

Black, Matthew. "The Maranatha Invocation and Jude 14,15 (1 Enoch 1.9)," in B. Lindars ed., *Christ and the Spirit in the New Testament.* Cambridge University Press, 1973, 189-196.

Bligh, John. "Typology in the Passion Narratives: Daniel, Elijah, Melchizedek," *The Heythrop Journal*, vol. 6, no. 3 (July 1965), 302-309.

de Blois, François. "Naṣrānī (Ναζωραιος) and ḥanīf (εθνικος): Studies on the Religious Vocabulary of Christianity and of Islam," *Bulletin of the School of Oriental and African Studies, University of London*, vol. 65, no. 1 (2002), 1-30.

Boccaccini, Gabriele. *Beyond the Essene Hypothesis: The Parting of the Ways between Qumran and Enochich Judaism.* Grand Rapids, Michigan: Wm. B. Eerdmans, 1998.

———, *Enoch and Qumran Origins: New Light on a Forgotten Connection.* Grand Rapids, Michigan: Wm. B. Eerdmans, 2005.

Bromiley, Geoffrey. *International Bible Encyclopedia: K-P.*

Boyarin, Daniel. "The Gospel of the *Memra*: Jewish Binitarianism and the Prologue of John," *Harvard Theological Review* 94 no. 3 (2001), 243-284.

———, "Hellenism in Jewish Babylonia," in Charlotte Elisheva Fonrobert and Martin S. Jaffee eds., *The Cambridge Companion to the Talmud and Rabbinic Literature* (Cambridge: Cambridge University Press, 2007), 336-363.

van den Broek, Roelof, "Der Brief des Jakobus an Quadratus und das Problem der judenchristlichen Bischöfe von Jerusalem (Esebius, HE IV, 5, 1-3), in T. Baarda, A. Hilhorst, G. P. Luttikhuizen, A. S. van der Woude, eds., *Text and Testimony. Essays on New*

*Testament and Apocryphal Literature in Honour of A. F. J. Klijn*. Kampen: Uitgeversmaatschappij J. H. Kok, 1988, 56-65.
van den Broek, Roelof and van Heertum, Cis (eds.). *From Poimandres to Jacob Böhme: Gnosis, Hermetism and the Christian Tradition*. Amsterdam: Bibliotheca Philosophica Hermetica, 2000.
Brox, Norbert, "Nikolaos und Nikolaiten," *Vigiliae Christianae*, vol. 19, Nno. 1 (March, 1965), 23-30.
Buckley, Jorunn Jacobsen. "The Evidence for Women Priests in Mandaeism," *Journal of Near Eastern Studies*, vol. 59, no. 2 (April, 2000), 93-106.
\_\_\_\_, *The Great Stem of Souls*. Piscataway, NJ: Gorgias Press, 2005.
\_\_\_\_, "*The Knowledge of Life: The Origins and Early History of the Mandaeans and Their Relationship to the Sabians of the Qur'an and to the Harranians* by Sinasi Gündüz. Review" *Journal of the American Oriental Society*, vol. 116, no. 2 (Apr. - Jun., 1996), 301-302.
\_\_\_\_, "The Mandaean Appropriation of Jesus' Mother, Miriai," *Novum Testamentum*, vol. 35, fasc. 2 (April, 1993), 181-196.
\_\_\_\_, "A Rehabilitation of Spirit *Ruha* in Mandaean Religion," *History of Religions*, vol. 22, no. 1 (Aug., 1982), 60-84.
Budge, E. Wallis. *Coptic Apocrypha in the Dialect of Upper Egypt*. London: Oxford University Press, 1913.
\_\_\_\_, *Miscellaneous Coptic Texts in the Dialect of Upper Egypt*, vol. V. London: Oxford University Press, 1915.
Burkitt, F. Crawford. *Early Eastern Christianity*. London: John Murray, 1904.
Callahan, Allen, "No Rhyme or Reason": The Hidden Logia of the 'Gospel of Thomas," *The Harvard Theological Review*, vol. 90, no. 4. Jesus' Sayings in the Life of the Early Church: Papers Presented in Honor of Helmut Koester's Seventieth Birthday (October, 1997), 411-426.
Charles, R. H. (ed.). *Apocrypha and Pseudepigrapha of the Old Testament*, 2 vols. London: Oxford University Press, 1913.
Charlesworth, James Hamilton. *The Odes of Solomon*. London: Oxford University Press, 1973.
Chilton, Bruce and Jacob Neusner, eds., *The Brother of Jesus. James the Just and His Mission*. Louisville, Kentucky: Westminster John Knox Press, 2001.

\_\_\_\_, *Judaism in the New Testament. Practices and Beliefs*. London / NY: Routledge, 1996.

Church, F. Forrester, and Gedaliahu G. Stroumsa. "Mani's Disciple Thomas and the Psalms of Thomas," *Vigiliae Christianae*, vol. 34, no. 1 (Mar., 1980), 47-55.

Cohen, Jonathan. *The Origins and Evolution of the Moses Nativity Stor.* Leiden/NY/Köln: E. J. Brill, 1993.

Collins, John Joseph. *Between Athens and Jerusalem: Jewish Identity in the Hellenistic Diaspora*.

Corbin, Henry. "Divine Epiphany and Spiritual Birth in Ismailian Gnosis," in *Man and Transformation*. Papers from the Eranos Yearbooks. Bollingen Series XXX, vol. 5. New York: Pantheon Books, 1964, 69-160.

Daniélou, Jean. *The Theology of Jewish Christianity*. Chicago, Illinois: Henry Regnery Company, 1964.

Davids, Peter H. "Palestinian Traditions in the Epistle of James," in Bruce Chilton, Craig A. Evans, eds., *James the Just and Christian Origins*. Leiden: Brill, 1999, 33-58.

Davies, Stevan. *The Gospel of Thomas*. Boston/London: Shambhala, 2004.

Day, John. *Wisdom in Ancient Israel*. Cambridge: Cambridge University Press, 1995.

DeConick, April. D. "The Original Gospel of Thomas," *Vigiliae Christianae*, vol. 56 (2002), 167-199.

\_\_\_\_, *The Original Gospel of Thomas. With a Commentary and New English Translation of the Complete Gospel*. London/New York: T&T Clark, 2007.

\_\_\_\_, *Seek to See Him. Ascent and Vision Mysticism in the Gospel of Thomas*. Leiden: E. J. Brill, 1996.

Donfried, Karl Paul. *The Setting of Second Clement in Early Christianity*. Leiden: E. J. Brill, 1974.

Draper, J. A. "Ritual Process and Ritual Symbol in 'Didache' 7-10," *Vigiliae Christianae*, vol. 54, no. 2 (2000), 121-158.

\_\_\_\_, "Torah and Troublesome Apostles in the Didache Community," *Novum Testamentum*, vol. 33, fasc. 4 (Oct., 1991), 347-372.

Drijvers, H. J. W. and G. J. Reinink. "Taufe und Licht: Tatian, Ebionäerevangelium und Thomasakten," in T. Baarda (ed.), *Text and Testimony. Essays on New Testament and Apocryphal Literature in*

*Honour of A. F. J. Klijn* (Kampen: Uitgeversmaatschappij J. H. Kok, 1988), 91-110.

Dunn, James D. G. "When Did the Understanding of Jesus' Death as an Atoning Sacrifice First Emerge?" in David B. Capes, April D. DeConick, et al. (eds.), *Israel's God and Rebecca's Children Christology and Community in Early Judaism and Christianity. Essays in Honor of Larry W. Hurtado and Alan F. Segal*. Waco, Texas: Baylor University Press, 2007, 169-182.

Epp, Eldon Jay. "The Multivalence of the Term 'Original Text' in New Testament Textual Criticism," *The Harvard Theological Review*, vol. 92, no. 3 (Jul., 1999), 245-281.

Erlemann, Kurt, "Die Datierung des ersten Klemensbriefes—Anfragen an eine Communis Opinio," *New Testament Studies*, vol. 44 no. 4 (1998), 591-607.

Feldmann, Franz. *Syrische Wechsellieder von Narses. Ein Beitrag zur altchristlichen syrischen Hymnologie*. Leipzig: Otto Harrassowitz, 1896.

Flusser, David. *Judaism and the Origins of Christianity*. Jerusalem: Magnes Press, 1988.

Fossum, Jarl. "Jewish-Christian Christology and Jewish Mysticism," *Vigiliae Christianiae*, vol. 37 (1983), 260-287.

\_\_\_\_, *The Name of God and the Angel of the Lord: Samaritan and Jewish Concepts of Intermediation and the Origin of Gnosticism*. Tübingen: Mohr, 1985.

Friedländer, M. *Der vorchristliche jüdische Gnosticismus*. Göttingen: Vandenhoeck und Ruprecht, 1898.

Gieschen, Charles A. *Angelomorphic Christology. Antecedents and Early Evidence*. Leiden/Boston/Köln: Brill, 1998.

Goulder, Michael. "The Pastor's Wolves: Jewish Christian Visionaries behind the Pastoral Epistles," *Novum Testamentum*, vol. 38, fasc. 3 (July, 1996), 242-256.

\_\_\_\_, *Paul and the Competing Mission in Corinth*. Peabody, Massachusetts: Hendrickson Publishers, Inc., 2001.

\_\_\_\_, "A Poor Man's Christolgy," *New Testament Studies*, vol. 45 (1999), 332-348.

\_\_\_\_, "Hebrews and the Ebionites," *New Testament Studies*, vol. 49 (2003), 393-406.

____, "The Samaritan Hypothesis," in M. Goulder (ed), *Incarnation and Myth: The Debate Continued*. London: SCM, 1979, 247-250.

____, "The Visionaries of Laodicea," *Journal for the Study of the New Testament*, vol. 43 (1991), 15-39.

Grant, Robert, and David Noel Friedman, *The Secret Sayings of Jesus*. NY: Barnes & Noble, 1993.

Green, Arthur. *A Guide to the Zohar*. Stanford, California: Stanford University Press, 2004.

Gregory, Andrew. "The Third Gospel? The Relationship of John and Luke Reconsidered," in John Lierman (ed.), *Challenging Perspectives on the Gospel of John*. Tübingen: Mohr Siebeck, 2006, 109-122.

Gündüz, Sinasi. *The Knowledge of Life: The Origins and Early History of the Mandaeans and Their Relationship to the Sabians of the Qur'an and to the Harranians*. London: Oxford University Press, 1994.

Guthrie, Kenneth Sylvan. *Numenius of Apamea, the Father of Neo-Platonism: Works, Biography, Message, Sources, and Influence*. London: George Bell and Sons, 1917.

Halperin, David J. "The Ibn Sayyad Traditions and the Legend of al-Dajjal" *Journal of the American Oriental Society*, vol. 96, no. 2 (April-June, 1976), 213-225.

____, "Origen, Ezekiel's Merkabah, and the Ascension of Moses," *Church History*, vol. 50, no. 3 (Sep., 1981), 261-275.

Hannah, Darrell D. "The Ascension of Isaiah and Docetic Christology," *Vigiliae Christianiae*, vol. 53 (1999), 165-196.

Harris, Rendel, Alphonse Mingana, *The Odes and Psalms of Solomon*. Vol. II. Manchester: University Press, 1916.

Hartman, Louis F. and Alexander A. Di Lella. *The Book of Daniel*. The Anchor Bible. Garden City, NY: Doubleday, 1978.

Hawting, G. R. *The Idea of Idolatry and the Emergence of Islam. From Polemic to History*. Cambridge: Cambridge University Press, 1999.

Henrichs, Albert. "Mani and the Babylonian Baptists: A Historical Confrontation," *Harvard Studies in Classical Philology*, vol. 77 (1973), 23-59.

Hirschfeld, Hartwig. "Mohammedan Criticism of the Bible," *The Jewish Quarterly Review*, vol. 13, no. 2 (Jan., 1901), 222-240.

Horsley, Richard A. "Spiritual Marriage with Sophia," *Vigiliae Christianae*, vol. 33, no. 1 (March, 1979), 30-54.

Hornschuh, M. "Erwägungen zum 'Evangelium der Ägyter', ins besondere zur Bedeutung seines Titels," *Vigiliae Christianae*, vol. 18, no. 1 (March, 1964), 6-13.

Howard, George. *Hebrew Gospel of Matthew*. Macon Georgia: Mercer University Press, 2002.

Ibn 'Arabi, *Journey to the Lord of Power. A Sufi Manual on Retreat.* Tr. By Rabia Terri Harris. Rochester Vermont: Inner Traditions International, 1989.

Idel, Moshe. *Ascensions on High in Jewish Mysticism: Pillars, Lines, Ladders.* Budapest/NY: Central European University Press, 2005.

\_\_\_\_, *Kabbalah: New Perspectives*. New Haven and London: Yale University Press, 1988.

\_\_\_\_, *The Mystical Experience in Abraham Abulafia*. Jerusalem: Magnes/ Albany: State University of New York Press, 1988.

\_\_\_\_, and Bernard McGinn, *Mystical Union in Judaism, Christianity, and Islam*. NY: Continuum, 1999.

Ivanow, W. *Ummu'l-Kitab, Der Islam*, vol. 23 (1963), 1-132.

James, M. R. *The Apocryphal New Testament*. London: Oxford University Press, 1924.

Jeremias, Joachim. *The Parables of Jesus*. Tr. S. H. Hooke. NY: Charles Scribner's Sons, 1955.

\_\_\_\_, *Rediscovering the Parables*. NY: Charles Scribner's Sons, 1966.

Kato, Bunno; Yoshiro Tamura, and Kojiro Miyasaka. *The Threefold Lotus Sutra*. Tokyo: Kosei Publishing Co., 2003.

Kelly, J. N. D. *Early Christian Doctrines*. San Francisco, California: Harper & Row, 1978.

Knohl, Israel. *The Messiah before Jesus. The Suffering Servant of the Dead Sea Scrolls.* Tr. by David Maisel. Berkeley / Los Angeles / London: University of California Press, 2000.

Koester, Helmut. *Ancient Christian Gospels. Their History and Development.* Harrisburg, Pennsylvania: Trinity Press International, 1990.

Küng, Hans. *Islam: Past, Present, & Future.* Tr. by John Bowden. Oxford: Oneworld, 2007.

Lidzbarski, M. *Ginza: Der Schatz oder das grosse Buch der Mandäer*. Göttingen: Vandenhoeck & Ruprecht; Leipzig: Hinrichs, 1925.

Liebes, Yehudah. "The Shofar Blast Angels and Yeshu'a Sar ha-Panim," in *ha-Mistiqah ha-Yehudit ha-Qedumah* [=*Mehqerey Yerushalayim be-Mahshevet Yisra'el* vi: 1-2] (1987), 171-195.

———, *Studies in the Zohar*. Translated from the Hebrew by Arnold Schwartz, Stephanie Nakache, Penina Peli. Albany, NY: State University of New York Press, 1993.

———, "Who Makes the Horn of Jesus to Flourish," *Immanuel*, no. 21 (Summer 1987), 55-67.

Lightfoot, J. B. *The Apostolic Fathers*. Grand Rapids, Michigan: Baker Book House, 1974.

Lowe, Malcom. "'Ιουδαιο of the Apocrypha: A Fresh Approach to the Gospels of James, Pseudo-Thomas, Peter and Nicodemus." *Novum Testamentum*, vol. 23, fasc. 1 (Jan., 1981), 56-90.

Lowy, Simeon. *The Principles of Samaritan Bible Exegesis*. Studia Post-Biblica 28, ed. J. C. H. Lebram. Leiden: E. J. Brill, 1977.

Lührmann, Dieter. *Die apokryph gewordenen Evangelien. Studien zu neuen Texten und zu neuen Fragen*. Leiden/Boston: Brill, 2004.

Luomanen, Petri. "Eusebius' View of the 'Gospel of the Hebrews'," in Jostein Ådna (ed.), *The Formation of the Early Church*. Tübingen: Mohr Siebeck, 2005, 265-284.

———, "'Let Him Who Seeks, Continue Seeking': The Relationship between the Jewish-Christian Gospels and the *Gospel of Thomas*," in J. Ma. Asgeirsson, A DeConick and R. Uro (eds.), *Thomasine Traditions in Antiquity: The Social and Cultural World of the Gospel of Thomas*. Nag Hammadi and Manichean Studies 59. Leiden: E. J. Brill, 2006, 123-127.

Maccoby, Hyam. *The Myth-Maker: Paul and the Invention of Christianity*. NY: Harper Collins, 1987.

Macdonald, John. *The Theology of the Samaritans*. New Testament Library. London: SCM Press, 1964.

Marsh, S. F. *The Book which is called the Book of the Holy Hierotheos*. London: Williams and Norgate, 1927.

Marx, Alexander. "An Aramaic Fragment of the Wisdom of Solomon," *Journal of Biblical Literature*, vol. 40 (1920), 57-69.

Mason, Steve. "Josephus and Luke-Acts," *Josephus and the New Testa-*

*ment*. Peabody, Massachusetts: Hendrickson Publishers, 1992, 185-229.

Massingberd Ford, J. "A Possible Liturgical Background to the Shepherd of Hermas," *Revue de Qumran*, numéro 24, tome 6, fascicule 4 (Mars 1969), 531-551.

Meyer, Arnold. *Jesu Muttersprache. Das galiläische Aramäisch in seiner Bedeutung für die Erklärung der Reden Jesu und der Evangelien überhaupt*. Freiburg i. B./Leipzig: Akademische Verlagsbuchhandlung von J. C. B. Mohr (Paul Siebeck), 1896.

Meyer, Marvin. "'Be Passersby': *Gospel of Thomas* 12, Jesus Traditions, and Islamic Literature," in J. Ma. Asgeirsson, A DeConick and R. Uro (eds.), *Thomasine Traditions in Antiquity: The Social and Cultural World of the Gospel of Thomas*. Nag Hammadi and Manichean Studies 59. Leiden: E. J. Brill, 2006, 256-271.

\_\_\_\_, Ed. *The Nag Hammadi Scriptures. The International Edition*. NY: HarperOne, 2007.

\_\_\_\_, and Richard Smith, *Ancient Christian Magic: Coptic Texts of Ritual Power*. Princeton, NJ: Princeton University Press, 1999.

Miller, Robert J. Editor. *The Complete Gospels. Annotated Scholars Version*. Revised and Expanded Edition. Foreword by Robert W. Funk. Santa Rosa, California: Polebridge Press, 1994.

Miller, Selig J. *The Samaritan Molad Mosheh*. Samaritan and Arabic texts edited and translated with an introduction and notes. New York: Philosophical Library, 1949.

Miller, Troy A. "Liturgy and Communal Identity: *Hellenistic Synagogal Prayer 5* and the Character of Early Syrian Christianity," in in David B. Capes, April D. DeConick, et al. (eds.), *Israel's God and Rebecca's Children Christology and Community in Early Judaism and Christianity. Essays in Honor of Larry W. Hurtado and Alan F. Segal*. Waco, Texas: Baylor University Press, 2007, 345-358.

Montgomery, James Alan. *The Samaritans. The Earliest Jewish Sect. Their History, Theology and Literature*. Philadelphia: John C. Winston Co., 1907.

Morray-Jones, C. R. A. *A Transparent Illusion: The Dangerous Vision of Water in Hekhalot Mysticism: A Source-Critical and Tradition-Historical Inquiry*. Leiden: Brill, 2002.

Nasr, Seyyed Hossein. *The Garden of Truth. The Vision and Promise of Sufism, Islam's Mystical Tradition*. NY: HarperOne, 2007.

———, *Islamic Life and Thought*. Albany, NY: State University of New York Press, 1981.

Nevo, Yehuda D. "Towards a Prehistory of Islam," *Jerusalem Studies in Arabic and Islam*, vol. 17 (1994), 108-141.

Odeberg, Hugo. *The Fourth Gospel Interpreted in its Relation to Contemporaneous Religious Currents in Palestine and the Hellenistic-Oriental World*. Uppsala/Stockholm: Almqvist & Wiksells Boktryckeri-A.-B., 1929.

———, *3 Enoch or the Hebrew Book of Enoch*. London: Cambridge University Press, 1928.

Olson, Daniel C. "'Those Who Have Not Defiled Themselves with Woman': Revelation 14:4 and the Book of Enoch," *Catholic Biblical Quarterly*, vol. 59, no. 3 (July 1997), 492-510.

Orlov, Andrei A. *The Enoch-Metatron Tradition*. Mohr Siebeck, 2004.

Pagels, Elaine. *The Gospel of Thomas*. Audio CD. Boulder, Colorado: Sounds True, 2006.

Painter, John. *Just James: The Brother of Jesus in History and Tradition*. Columbia: University of South Carolina Press, 1997.

Palmer, Martin, in association with Eva Wong, Tjalling Halbertsma, Zhao Xiao Min, Li Rong Rong, and James Palmer. *The Jesus Sutras. Rediscovering the Lost Scrolls of Taoist Christianity*. NY: Ballantine Wellspring, 2001.

Pedersen, Johs. "The Sabians," in T. W. Arnold, Reynold A. Nicholson, eds., *A Volume of Oriental Studies. Presented to Professor Edward G. Browne*. London: Cambridge University Press, 383-391.

Perrin, Nicholas. "NHC II,2 and the Oxyrhynchus Fragments (P. Oxy 1, 654, 655): Overlooked Evidence for a Syriac *Gospel of Thomas*," *Vigiliae Christianae*, vol 58 (2004), 138-151.

———, *Thomas and Tatian: The Relationship between the Gospel of Thomas and the Diatesseron*. Leiden: Brill, 2002.

Perry Ken, ed. *The Blackwell Companion to Eastern Christianity*. Malden, MA/Oxford: Blackwell Publishing, 2007.

Pines, Shlomo. *The Jewish Christians of the Early Centuries of Christianity according to a New Source*. The Israel Academy of Sciences and Humanities Proceedings, vol. II. No. 13 (Jerusalem, 1966).

\_\_\_\_, "Notes on Islam and on Arab Christianity and Judeo-Christianity," *Jerusalem Studies in Arabic and Islam*, vol. 4 (1984), 135-152.

\_\_\_\_, *Points of Similarity between the Exposition of the Doctrine of the Sefirot in the Sefer Yezira and Text of the Pseudo-Clementine Homilies. The Implications of This Resemblance*. Proceedings of the Israel Academy of Sciences and Humanities, VII 3. 1989.

Popkes, Enno E., "About the Differing Approach to a Theological Heritage: Comments on the Relationship between the *Gospel of John*, the *Gospel of Thomas*, and Qumran," in James H. Charlesworth (ed.), *The Bible and the Dead Sea Scrolls. Volume Three. The Scrolls and Christian Origins*. Waco, Texas: Baylor University Press, 2006, 281-317.

Pourjavady, Nasrollah. "Stories of Ahmad al Ghazali 'Playing the Witness' in Tabriz (Shams-i Tabrizi's Interest in Shahid-bazi)," in Todd Lawson (ed.), *Reason and Inspiration in Islam* (London: I. B. Tauris, 2005), 200-220.

Quarles, Charles L. *Midrash Criticism. Introduction and Appraisal.* Lanham/NY/Oxford: University Press of America, 1998.

Quispel, G. "Another Seed: Studies in Gnostic Mythology by Gedaliahu A. G. Stroumsa. Review," *Vigiliae Christianae*, vol. 40, no. 1 (March, 1986), 96-101.

\_\_\_\_, "Die islamische Gnosis: Die extreme Schia und die 'Alawiten by Heinz Halm. Review," *Vigiliae Christianae*, vol. 37, no. 4 (Dec., 1983), 408-409.

\_\_\_\_, "Ezekiel 1:26 in Jewish Mysticism and Gnosis," *Vigiliae Christianae*, vol. 34, no. 1 (March, 1980), 1-13.

\_\_\_\_, *Gnostica, Judaica, Catholica. The Collected Essays of Gilles Quispel*. Leiden: Brill, 2008.

\_\_\_\_, "Gnosticism and the New Testament" *Vigiliae Christianae*, vol. 19, no. 2 (Jun., 1965), pp. 65-85.

\_\_\_\_, "The Gospel of Thomas and the Trial of Jesus," in T. Baarda (ed.), *Text and Testimony. Essays on New Testament and Apocryphal Literature in Honour of A. F. J. Klijn*. Kampen: Uitgeversmaatschappij J. H. Kok, 1988, 193-199.

\_\_\_\_, "The Gospel of Thomas and Christian Wisdom by Stevan L. Davies. Review," *Vigiliae Christianae*, vol. 38, no. 1 (March, 1984), 91-93.

\_\_\_, "Kosmologie und Heilslehre der frühen Isma'iliya: Eine Studie zur Islamischen Gnosis by Heinz Halm. Review," *International Journal of Middle East Studies*, vol. 12, no. 1 (August, 1980), 111-112.

\_\_\_, "Paul and Gnosis: a Personal View," in Roelef van den Broek and Cis van Heertum (eds.). *From Poimandres to Jacob Böhme: Gnosis, Hermetism and the Christian Tradition*. Amsterdam: Bibliotheca Philosophica Hermetica, 2000, 270-302.

Reiling, J. "Wisdom and the Spirit. An Exegesis of 1 Corinthians 2,6-16," in T. Baarda (ed.), *Text and Testimony. Essays on New Testament and Apocryphal Literature in Honour of A. F. J. Klijn*. Kampen: Uitgeversmaatschappij J. H. Kok, 1988, 200-211.

Resch, Alfred. *Ausserkanonische Schriftfragmente*. Leipzig: J. C. Hinrichs'sche Buchhandlung, 1906.

Riley, Gregory J. "Influence of Thomas Christianity on Luke 12:14 and 5:39," *The Harvard Theological Review*, vol. 88, no. 2 (April, 1995), 229-235.

Ritter, Hellmut. *The Ocean of the Soul: Men, the World, and God in the Stories of Farid al-Din 'Attar*. Tr. by John O'Kane with editorial assistance of Bernd Radtke. Leiden: Brill, 2003.

Robson, James. *Christ in Islam*. London: John Murray, 1929.

Rubin, Nissan, and Admiel Kosman. "The Clothing of the Primordial Adam as a Symbol of Apocalyptic Time in the Midrashic Sources," *The Harvard Theological Review*, vol. 90, no. 2 (April, 1997), 155-174.

Rudolph, Kurt; Dennis C. Duling, John Modschiedler, "Problems of a History of the Development of the Mandaean Religion," *History of Religions*, vol. 8, no. 3 (Feb., 1969), 210-235.

Sagerman, Robert. *Ambivalence toward Christianity in the Kabbalah of Abraham Abulafia*. Ph.D. dissertation, Department of Hebrew and Judaic Studies New York University, May 2008

Salaman, Clement, Dorine van Oyen, William D. Wharton, Jean Pierre Mahé, *The Way of Hermes. New Translations of the Corpus Hermeticum and the Definitions of Hermes Trismegistus to Asclepius*. Rochester, Vermont: Inner Traditions, 2004.

Schedl, Claus. "Die 114 Suren des Koran und die 114 Logien Jesu im Thomas-Evangelium," *Der Islam. Zeitschrift für Geschichte und Kultur des islamischen Orients*, Band 64, Heft 2 (1987), 261-264.

Schneemelcher, Wilhelm (ed.). *New Testament Apocrypha*. Vol. 1: *Gospels and Related Writings*. Revised Edition. Louisville/London: Jerome Clarke & Co., Westminster John Knox Press, 2003.

Schoedel, William R. "A Gnostic Interpretation of the Fall of Jerusalem: The First Apocalypse of James," *Novum Testamentum*, Vol. 33, Fasc. 2 (Apr., 1991), 153-178.

\_\_\_\_, "Scripture and the Seventy-Two Heavens of the First Apocalypse of James," *Novum Testamentum*, Vol. 12, Fasc. 2 (Apr., 1970), 118-129.

Scholem, Gershom. *Kabbalah*. NY: Meridian, 1974.

\_\_\_\_, *On the Mystical Shape of the Godhead. Basic Concepts in the Kabbalah*. Tr. from the German by Joachim Neugroschel. NY: Schocken Books, 1991.

\_\_\_\_, *Origins of the Kabbalah*. Philadelphia, 1987. Schüngel, Paul. "Ein Vorschlag, EvTho 114 neu zu übersetzen," *Novum Testamentum*, vol. 36, fasc. 4 (Oct., 1994), 394-401.

Schuon, Frithjof. *Christianity/Islam: Essays on Esoteric Ecumenism*, tr. byGustavo Polit. Bloomington, Indiana: World Wisdom Books, 1985.

\_\_\_\_, *Dimensions of Islam*. tr. by P. N. Townsend. London: George Allen and Unwin, 1970.

\_\_\_\_, *Gnosis: Divine Wisdom*. Translated from the French by G. E. H. Palmer. Pates Manor, Bedfont, Middlesex: Perennial Books, 1990.

\_\_\_\_, *Islam and the Perennial Philosophy*, tr. by J. Peter Hobson. World of Islam Festival Publishing Co., 1976.

\_\_\_\_, *Light on the Ancient Worlds*. Translated by Lord Northbourne; second edition. Bloomington, Indiana: World Wisdom Books, 1984.

\_\_\_\_, *Spiritual Perspectives and Human Facts*, tr. by P. N. Townsend. Pates Manor, Bedfont, Middlesex: Perennial Books, 1987.

\_\_\_\_, *The Transcendent Unity of Religions*. tr. by Peter Townsend. New York: Harper & Row, 1975.

\_\_\_\_, *Treasures of Buddhism*. Bloomington, Indiana: World Wisdom Books, 1993.

Segal, Alan F. *Two Powers in Heaven: Early Rabbinic Reports about Christianity and Gnosticism*. Leiden: Brill, 1977.

Shah-Kazemi, Reza. *Paths to Transcendence according to Shankara, Ibn Arabi, and Meister Eckhart*. Bloomington, Indiana: World Wisdom Books, 2006.

Stein, Robert H. "Is the Transfiguration (Mark 9:2-8) a Misplaced Resurrection-Account?" *Journal of Biblical Literature*, vol. 95, no. 1 (March 1976), 79-96.

Stroumsa, Gedaliahu G. "Aher: A Gnostic," in Bentley Layton (ed.), *The Rediscovery of Gnosticism*. Vol. 2: *Sethian Gnosticism*. Leiden: E. J. Brill, 1981, 808-18.

\_\_\_\_, "Christ's Laughter: Docetic Origins Reconsidered," *Journal of Early Christian Studies*, vol. 12, no. 3 (2004), 267-288.

\_\_\_\_, "From Esotericism to Mysticism in Early Christianity" in Hans G. Kippenberg and Guy G. Stroumsa (eds.), *Secrecy and Concealment: Studies in the History of Mediterranean and Near Eastern Religions*. Leiden: E. J. Brill, 1995, 289-309.

\_\_\_\_, "Form(s) of God: Some Notes on Metatron and Christ," *Harvard Theological Review*, vol. 76, no. 3 (1983), 269–288.

\_\_\_\_, *Hidden Wisdom: Esoteric Traditions and the Roots of Christian Mysticism*. Leiden: E. J. Brill, 1996.

\_\_\_\_, "Le couple de l'ange et de l'esprit: traditions juives et chrétiennes," *Revue Biblique* tome 88 (1981), 42-61.

\_\_\_\_, "Polymorphie divine et transformations d'un mythologème: l' 'Apocryphon de Jean' et ses sources," *Vigiliae Christianae* vol. 35 (1981), 412-434.

\_\_\_\_, "'Seal of the Prophets': The Nature of a Manichaean Metaphor," *Jerusalem Studies in Arabic and Islam*, vol. 7 (1986), 61-74.

Stuckenbruck, Loren T. "'One Like a Son of Man as the Ancient of Days' in the Old Greek Recension of Daniel 7,13: Scribal Error or Theological Translation?" *Zeitschrift für die neutestamentliche Wissenschaft und die Kunde der älteren Kirche*, Band 86 (1995), 268-276.

Tidwell, Neville L. A. "Didache XIV:1 (KATA KYPIAKHN ΔE KYPIOY) Revisited," *Vigiliae Christianae*, vol. 53, no. 2 (May, 1999), 197-207.

Tucker, W. F. "Rebels and Gnostics: Al-Muġīra Ibn Sa'īd and the Muġīriyya," *Arabica*, tome xxii, fascicule I (1975), 33-47.

Tugwell, Simon. *The Apostolic Fathers*. Harrisburg, Pennsylvania: Morehouse Publishing, 1989.

Ullendorf, E. "Hebraic-Jewish Elements in Abyssinian (Monophysite) Christianity," *Journal of Semitic Studies*, vol. I, no. 3 (July 1956), 216-256.
Vermes, Geza. *The Authentic Gospel of Jesus*. London: Penguin Books, 2004.
\_\_\_\_, *Jesus in His Jewish Context*. Minneapolis: Fortress Press, 2003.
Verseput, Donald J. "James 1:17 and the Jewish Morning Prayers," *Novum Testamentum*, vol. 39, fasc. 2 (April, 1997), 177-191.
Vööbus, A. *Celibacy: A Requirement for Admission to Baptism in the Early Syrian Church*. Papers of Estonian Theological Society in Exile, 1. Stockholm, 1951.
Wansbrough, John. *Quranic Studies. Sources and Methods of Scriptural Interpretation*. Amherst, NY: Prometheus Books, 2004.
Weiss, Johannes. *Paul and Jesus*. Tr. by H. J. Chaytor. London/NY: Harper & Brothers, 1909.
Wenham, David. "2 Corinthians 1:17,18: Echo of a Dominical Logion," *Novum Testamentum*, vol. 28, fasc. 3 (July, 1986), 271-279.
\_\_\_\_, and A. D. A. Moses, "'There Are Some Standing Here. ...' Did They Become the 'Reputed Pillars' of the Jerusalem Church? Some Reflections on Mark 9:1, Galatians 2:9 and the Transfiguration," *Novum Testamentum* vol. 36, no. 2 (1994), 146-163.
Wild, Robert A. "The Encounter between Pharisaic and Christian Judaism: Some Early Gospel Evidence," *Novum Testamentum*, vol. 27, fasc. 2 (April, 1985), 105-124.
Wolfson, Elliot R. "Circumcision, Vision of God, and Textual Interpretation: From Midrashic Trope to Mystical Symbol," *History of Religions*, vol. 27, no. 2 (Nov., 1987), 189-215.
\_\_\_\_, "Circumcision and the Divine Name: A Study in the Transmission of Esoteric Doctrine," *The Jewish Quarterly Review*, New Series, vol. 78, no. 1/2 (Jul. - Oct., 1987), 77- 112.
Young, Brad and David Flusser in "Messianic Blessings in Jewish and Christian Texts," in David Flusser, *Judaism and the Origins of Christianity*. Jerusalem: Magnes Press, Hebrew University, 1988, 280-99.
Zalcmam, Lawrence. "Christians, Noserim, and Nebuchadnezzar's Daughter," *The Jewish Quarterly Review, New Series*, vol. 81, no. 3/4 (Jan. - Apr., 1991), 411 -426.

Zinner, Samuel. *The Abrahamic Archetype: Essays on the Transcendent and Formal Relationships between Judaism, Christianity, and Islam.* Cambridge, England: Archetype, 2011.

\_\_\_\_, *Christianity and Islam: Essays on Ontology and Archetype.* London: Matheson Trust, 2010.

\_\_\_\_, *The Mother of the Book*: *Images of the Supernal Feminine. Volume I:Essays on Mandaean and Christian Gnostic Traditions.* Casablanca, Morocco: Unpublished Monograph, 2009.

Zöckler, Thomas. *Jesu Lehren im Thomasevangelium.* Leiden/Boston/Köln: Brill, 1999.

Zunz, L. *Die Gottesdienstlichen Vorträge der Juden.* Frankfurt, 1892.

# INDEX

Abraham (patriarch), 28
Abu Hanifa, 129
Abu Mohammed Ali (Cordova), 105
Abulafia, Abraham, 59, 70, 77, 94, 109, 110, 145, 271
Achamoth, 74, 78, 80
*Acts of Gregory of Armenia*, 210
*Acts of John*, 175
*Acts of Thomas*, 158
*Adam kasia*, 73
*Adam Qadmon*, 25, 62, 73
Addai, 74
*Adoil*, 22
aeons, 22, 79, 80, 81, 82, 90, 119, 143, 144, 145, 146
Aflaki, 113
*agape* (meal), 59, 151, 154
*agrammatoi* 116
Ahmad, 105
'A'isha, 106
Akiva, Rabbi, 37, 38, 39, 40, 42, 163, 255, 256
Albigensians, 239
*Aletheia*, 80, 81
Alexandria, 26, 27, 29, 38, 48, 57, 72, 88, 91, 206, 245, 262
'Ali al-Rida, 108
*alma* (plural, *almin*), 119
Amdi, 107
*amrad*, 106
*'amuda' de-'alma'*, 67
Amuli, Seyyid Haydar, 16

*'an'amta*, 118
anathema, 131, 132, 133, 142, 163, 233, 240
Ancient of Days, 107, 108, 110-11, 112
androgyny, 28, 29, 61, 114, 176, 232, 252, 253, 254, 262-63, 265, 266, 267, 270, 271-72, 274, 278, 288, 289-90, 303
Antioch, 5, 101-02, 134, 135, 150-51, 154, 158, 159, 173, 193, 195, 206, 225
*apekuesen*, 188
*Apocalypse of Animals, Enoch*, 284
*Apocalypse of James, 1* and *2*, 71, 72, 73, 76, 77, 78, 79, 80, 188
*Apocalypse of Peter*, 214, 232
*Apocryphon of James*, 6, 7, 59, 72, 85, 86, 187, 190
*Apocryphon of John*, 189, 207
Apollos, 130-31
apophasis, 17
*aqedah*, 92, 137, 170, 219, 220, 223
Al-'Arabi, Ibn, 16, 112, 216, 241
Arabia, 99-104
Aramaic, xii, 5, 26, 29, 34, 55, 56, 57, 59, 77, 80, 81, 85, 93, 119, 128, 133, 164, 179, 188, 206, 216, 234, 252, 259, 264, 276-78, 280, 283, 287, 289, 291, 299, 306
Archontics, 38

*Ascension of Isaiah*, 102, 207, 224
*Ascents of James*, 82, 83, 141
*Asrar al-Shari'ah*, 16
Augustine, 87, 154-55
*axis mundi*, 69, 113
*Baba Bathra*, 135
Baidawi, 100
baptism, 59, 137-39, 147, 157-58, 167-71, 174, 176-81, 184, 209-11, 213-15, 218, 227, 230, 232-37, 239
*baraq*, 117
Barnabas, 151
*Barnabas, Epistle of*, 164, 172
*Bartholomew, Book of the Resurrection of the Savior*, 54, 189, 191, 193, 217, 226
Basilides, 91, 92
*Bath Qol*, 42
Bauckham, Richard, 4, 5, 6, 56
*Bel and the Dragon*, 93
*Berakhoth*, 42
*Bereshit Rabbah*, 26, 136, 137, 248
*Binah*, 80, 90, 190, 274
Bogomiles, 239
*Book of Acts*, 12, 63, 65, 101, 116, 127, 135, 139, 143, 148, 149, 150, 153, 154, 156, 158, 159, 163, 173, 182, 185, 227
*Book of Enoch, Ethiopic*, 18, 101, 102, 107, 108, 109, 110, 133, 157, 175, 208, 234, 271, 284
*Book of Enoch, Hebrew*, 105,
*Book of Enoch, Slavonic*, 22, 207, 224
*Book of Thomas the Contender*, 59, 83, 259
*Book of Religions and Denominations* (Abu Mohammed Ali), 105
*Book of Wisdom*, 93
Boyarin, Daniel, 17, 20, 21, 23, 40, 60, 130, 224
bridal chamber, 131, 178, 180, 193, 254, 278, 282, 305
Brox, Norbert, 158-59
Buddhism, 16, 27, 47, 106
Bukhari, 100
*buraq*, 117
Cathars, 92, 239
celibacy, 129-30, 131, 144, 156, 157, 158-59, 169, 182, 262-63
Cerinthus, 185.86, 218, 229
Charlesworth, James H., 166, 168, 169, 170, 249-50
Circumcision, 143, 146, 147, 167-68, 169, 178, 181, 245, 246-57, 273-75, 281, 299
*Clement, 1* and *2*, 3, 49, 149-50, 175, 176, 225-26
Clement of Alexandria, 219, 230
Clement, epistles on virginity, 158
Clopas, 75
Codex Bezae, 159
*Commentary on the Account of Creation* (Ezra of Gerona), 69
*Commentary on Galatians* (Victorinus), 123-24
Coptic, xi, xii, 54, 68, 189, 190, 191, 193, 198, 200, 202, 206, 236, 237, 252, 259, 264, 272, 276.77, 283, 287, 289, 296, 299, 305, 306
Corinthians, *1* and *2*, 49, 51, 83-85, 125-43, 147, 156, 160, 161, 163, 200, 233, 240, 257
Cornelius (centurion), 153

*Corpus Hermeticum*, 26, 170
Cyril of Jerusalem, 191, 200-05, 207, 236, 237, 238
*dabar*, 264
*Daniel, Book of*, 39, 107, 108, 109, 110, 111, 112, 211, 216, 217, 271, 284
Daniélou, Jean, 54, 65, 91, 138, 257
Dead Sea Scrolls, x, 21, 47-48, 53, 54, 169, 258, 269-70
DeConick, April D., 11, 13, 23, 38, 48, 56, 57, 58, 136-37, 175, 184, 194, 259, 262-63, 265, 268, 269, 279, 283
Demetrius, bishop, 88
*Deutero-Clementines*, 49, 51, 82-83, 94-95, 145, 153, 171, 184-85
*Dialog of the Savior*, 59, 189, 263
*Diatessaron*, 10, 56
*Didache*, 56, 58-59, 132, 162-64
*dikhr*, 36
*din*, 118
docetism, 77, 104, 136, 137, 130, 173, 219, 220, 222-24, 229, 250, 257
*Duae viae*, 58
Ebion, 201, 202, 203, 206
Ebionite, ix-xi, 9, 32, 39, 51, 53, 57, 59, 68, 76, 79, 89, 92, 94, 99, 101, 103-05, 123-85, 194, 196, 210, 211, 215, 222-23, 225, 227, 230-41, 254, 275, 280, 283
Ecclesia (aeon), 89, 95, 175, 176
Edessa, 185, 194, 225
Egypt, 57, 72, 88, 185, 193
*Ehyeh asher Ehyeh*, 73, 265

*eikonion*, 26
*ein-sof*, 273
*'ekh-moth*, 117
Eleazar ben Azarya, Rabbi, 39
Elijah, prophet, 4, 138, 216-17, 223
*Elohim/elohim*, 35, 68, 90, 207, 269
Epiphanius, 82, 201, 205
*Epistle of the Apostles*, 6, 72, 149, 185-87, 189-90, 193-94, 207, 236, 252
*Epistle of Jacob the Contender*, 83
*Epistle of James to Quadratus*, 75
Epp, Eldon Jay, 10-13
Essenes, 53-54, 65, 101, 102, 105, 129-30
Ethiopia, 17-18, 99-104, 150
Eusebius, 75
*Ezekiel, Book of*, 27, 29, 35, 81, 109, 115, 117, 178, 211, 232, 237, 266
Ezra, 138
Ezra of Gerona, Rabbi, 69
Falasha Jews, 100-01
*al-Fatiha*, 118
*firash*, 106
Fitzmeyer, Joseph, 19
*Galatians, Letter to*, 5, 41, 68, 83, 84, 123, 124, 127, 132, 142-43, 149, 150, 152, 156, 185, 200, 246
Ge'ez, 101
*Genesis, Book of*, 25, 27, 28, 29, 32, 90, 114, 117, 129, 200, 219, 232-33, 264, 269, 281, 289-90
*geshem*, 276
*ghadab*, 118
*ghayral maghdubi*, 119

*ghayril maghdubi*, 119
Al-Ghazali, Ahmad, 113
Al-Ghazali, Imam, 113
Glaucias (interpreter for Peter, teacher of Basilides), 91-92
*gnosis*, 26, 35, 37, 38, 60, 71, 72, 76, 86, 93, 94, 95, 98, 104-05, 139, 144, 176, 177, 184, 187, 270
Gnosticism, ix, 33-35, 38-39, 41, 42, 47-52, 54-55, 57, 60, 66, 71, 72, 77, 79-80, 83, 87, 88-96, 98, 104-05, 111, 119, 143, 159, 184, 189-90, 198, 207-08, 229, 236, 238, 239, 257, 260, 288
*Gospel of the Ebionites*, 57, 178-79, 210, 211
*Gospel of the Egyptians*, 57-58, 186
*Gospel of the Hebrews*, 56-58, 73, 85, 128, 139-40, 174-75, 179, 180, 198-212, 213, 215, 223, 224-25, 228, 230-32, 236, 237-38, 240, 283
*Gospel of the Nazarenes*, 57
*Gospel of Truth*, 90-91
Goulder, Michael, 128, 132, 133-46, 173-75, 225, 269
Greek, xi, xii, 8, 9, 13, 14, 21, 26-27, 37, 39, 56-57, 59, 68, 75, 85, 90, 93, 101, 111, 116, 134-35, 138, 155, 181, 182, 188, 198, 200, 211, 229, 259, 276-77, 279, 283, 284, 296, 299, 305, 306
Gregory the Great, 17
*ha 'omedim*, 69
*Habakkuk pesher*, 269
*hadith*, 14, 15, 16, 36, 61-62, 97, 100, 103, 105-06, 107-10, 112, 114-16, 119, 129, 194, 195, 220-21, 266, 269
*Hagigah*, 25-26, 39, 61, 74-75, 76, 248
*Hagiographa*, 93
Haggadah, 100
*halakhah*, 36-37, 144, 152, 156, 158, 160
Hammad ibn Salama, 106
Harithah, 114-15
*hayayin*, 269
*al-hayyat*, 115
*Hayei ha-Olam ha-Ba* (A. Abulafia), 109
Hebrew, ix, x, xii, 8, 14, 15, 21, 26, 29, 34, 55, 56, 68, 74, 75, 77, 80, 81, 85, 89, 92, 109, 115, 117, 118, 119, 130, 131, 133, 138, 141, 146, 148, 164, 177, 179, 182, 188, 206, 207, 216, 219, 260, 262, 268, 269, 277, 299, 306
*hekhalot*, 22, 40, 116, 133, 141, 147, 168, 173, 191, 192, 247
*Hekhalot Rabbati*, 141, 247
*Hekhalot Zutarti*, 247
Hermeticism, x, 37, 38, 48, 104-05, 245, 262, 272
*Hesed*, 118, 190
*Hierotheos, Book of the Holy*, 54
*hikma*, 118
Hillel, Rabbi, 21, 42-43, 74-75
Hisham ibn Salim, 108
Hokhmah, 29, 34, 70, 74, 80, 90, 118, 130, 143, 190, 249, 287
*hon*, 269
Horsley, Richard A., 130-31
Ibn Abbas, 106
Ibn Jurayj, 106

Idel, Moshe, 37, 39, 42, 68-70, 73, 79, 93-94, 110, 263-64
Ignatius of Antioch, 7, 10, 149, 158, 173, 185, 193
India, 46, 196
*Iao*, 88
Irenaeus of Lyons, 49, 51, 174, 186, 263
*Isaiah, Book of*, 14, 76, 77, 92, 179, 208
'*ishq-i haqiqi*, 113
'*ishq-i majazi*, 113
Ismailis, 98, 104
*Iudicium Petri*, 58-59
Jacob, patriarch, 66-67, 69, 70, 72, 81, 82, 83, 224-25
Jabobites, 104
*James, Letter of*, 6, 66, 72, 80-81, 84, 85, 86, 126, 128, 146-47, 153, 188, 195-96
James the *Tsaddiq* ('brother of Jesus'), ix, 5, 6, 50, 54-55, 65-87, 98, 99, 105, 123-24, 126, 127, 128, 134, 140, 141, 142-43, 148, 149, 150-51, 152, 153, 154, 156, 159, 161, 173, 185, 187, 188, 194, 195, 199, 206, 257, 264, 265, 266-68, 277, 279, 286, 293
*Jeremiah, Book of*, 31, 245, 259, 274, 281, 286, 303, 306
Jeremiah, prophet, 4, 30, 275, 281
Jerome, 57, 73, 128, 139, 155, 174, 175, 177-78, 180, 238
Jesus (son of Mary), throughout, but especially pages 44-64, 198-307
Jesus the *Tsaddiq* (collaborator of Paul), 147-48
Jochanan ben Zakkai, Rabbi, 135
John, apostle (pillar of Jerusalem), 153
John the Baptist, 4, 6, 53-54, 180, 211, 220, 235, 238, 271, 274-75, 279-80, 298
*John, Gospel*, 7, 10, 56
John the Elder, 55, 56, 89, 185-86, 229
Josephus, 21
*Judith*, 93
Justin Martyr, 12
Kabbalah/Kabbalism, xii, 27, 35, 42, 47-48, 50-51, 54, 66, 67, 68, 71, 73, 77-78, 80, 89-90, 91, 93-95, 108, 110-11, 115, 117-20, 130, 133, 143-46, 164, 189, 207, 245-46, 249, 251-52, 254-55, 262-65, 267-68, 271-75, 279-82, 286-87
*kabod*, 81, 109, 214
*Al-Kafi* (by Kulayni), 108
*kalam*, 97
*Kaulakaua*, 93
*Keter*, 91, 110
Kneset Israel, 95, 130,
Koester, Helmut, 3, 4, 47, 62, 184
kosher, 144, 147, 152, 154, 158
Kulayni, 108
*Ladder of Jacob*, 81, 82
Lady Wisdom, 29, 31, 34, 118, 125, 130, 131, 143, 262, 268, 276, 278, 282, 283, 284, 287
Lady Zion, 95, 296
Levi, Jerusalem bishop, 74-75
*Liber S. Ioannis*, 238-39

Liebes, Yehudah, 20, 38-39, 94-95
*logikon*, 188
Logos, 29, 33, 34, 80, 89, 145, 146, 167, 188, 207, 219, 229, 233, 234, 135, 239-41
*Luke, Gospel*, 9, 10, 12, 45, 56, 127, 136, 149, 157, 158, 181, 201, 204, 209, 213, 223, 224, 227, 235, 274
Luomanen, Petri, 11, 56-57
Lurianic Kabbalah, 2, 50, 77, 93, 94
*ma'aseh bereshit*, 25, 26, 27, 28, 61, 116, 118, 120
*ma'aseh merkabah*, 25, 27, 28, 61
*malakut*, 119
*Malkhut*, xii, 69, 85, 119, 253, 254, 262, 168, 271-75, 280-83, 286-88, 290
*mamash*, 37
Mandaean/s, x, 53-55, 73, 88, 92, 104-05, 137, 170, 174, 177, 190, 210, 238, 263, 265, 272
Mandaic, xii
Mani codex, 93
Manichaeism, 54, 92-94
*Manual of Discipline*, 169
Marcion, 72, 158
*Mark, Gospel*, 3, 5, 6, 10, 12, 52, 56, 136, 147, 151, 155, 158, 174, 201, 204, 209, 213, 215, 235, 257, 259
Mary, of Magdala, 177, 216, 224, 289, 294, 307
Mary (mother of Jesus), 75, 95, 104, 125, 176, 181, 200-08, 216, 220, 224, 234, 236-41
*masahif al-amsar*, 15

*Matthew, Gospel*, 3-4, 5, 9, 10, 12, 21, 55, 56, 57, 66, 126-27, 136, 138, 141, 142, 145, 146, 151, 171, 174, 201, 204, 207, 209, 211, 213, 227, 235, 259, 271, 304
*Maya*, 74, 78
al-Maythami, 108
Meister Eckhart, 53, 78
*Memra*, 40, 188, 236
*merkabah*, 23, 25, 26-27, 28, 35, 61, 81, 83, 86-87, 98, 114-17, 133, 141, 145, 147, 168-69, 191-92, 211, 217, 227, 232, 237, 265-66
Metatron, 38-39, 79, 87, 105-06, 108-12, 145, 186, 223, 224, 227, 278
Meyer, Marvin, 72, 177, 178
Middle-Platonism, 272-73
*milah*, 253
*milta d-qushta*, 80, 188
Monophysite, 102
*Moralis in Iob*, 17
Moriah, mount, 137, 224
Mujiriyya, 104
*musterion*, 26
*na'ar*, 109-10
Nag Hammadi, 37, 48, 50, 59, 71, 72, 73, 76, 90, 189, 195, 196, 228, 229, 263
Nahmanides, 93
Narsai of Syria, 179-80
Nazaraeans/Nazarenes, 104, 174, 208, 239
*Nedarim*, 48
*nefesh*, 85
Negev, desert, 99
Neoplatonism, 27, 78, 90, 229,

*Index*

272-73
Nestorianism, 9, 96, 99, 102-04
*ni'anu'a*, 273
Nicolaitans, 158
Nicolaus, deacon, 158-59
*ni'mata*, 118
Nine Saints, 101
*Nirguna-Brahman*, 78
*Numbers Rabbah*, 252
Numenius of Apamea, 37-42
*Nur Muhammadi*, 194-95
Odeberg, Hugo, 39, 43, 55, 73, 111
*Odes of Solomon*, 7, 8, 54, 163-70, 218-19, 224, 249-51, 283
*ofanim*, 35
'*olam* (plural, '*olamim*), 119
Olson, Daniel C., 157-58
Origen, 41, 66, 105, 219, 232, 238
*Ozar 'Eden Ganuz* (A. Abulafia), 271
Pagels, Elaine, 22-23
Palestine, 6, 7, 26, 27, 28, 29, 34, 37-38, 40-43, 45-48, 52, 55, 57, 58, 61, 64, 72-74, 79, 86-87, 88, 104, 105, 130, 135, 181, 193, 225, 229, 245, 262, 270
Papias, 55-56
*Parables of Enoch*, 175, 234, 284
Passover, 59, 257
*Pater Noster*, 12
Paul, xi, 5-6. 10, 22, 36, 49-51, 68, 83-86, 89, 103, 123-52, 153-56, 158-61, 163, 170-71, 173-75, 181-85, 187, 189, 193, 196, 200, 210, 215, 222-23, 225-27, 229, 232-35, 246, 256-58, 269, 271, 274, 304

*peri'ah*, 253
*pericope adulterae*, 12
Peshitta, Syriac, 93, 216 (pre-Peshitta)
Peter, 4, 5, 6, 49-50, 58, 59, 68, 69, 91, 123, 127, 130, 131, 141, 142, 150, 151, 152, 153-55, 159, 188, 195, 214-15, 289, 293, 304, 307
Philip, apostle, 187
Philip, evangelist, 101
*Philip, Gospel*, 59-60, 131, 134, 145, 164, 165, 174, 176, 178, 180, 181-82, 186, 210, 218, 224, 240, 241, 254
Philo of Alexandria, 28-39, 55, 90-91, 145, 146, 170, 219-20, 232-33, 251
Pines, Shlomo, 196
*Pirqe Aboth*, 42
*Pistis Sophia*, 119, 207, 236
pleroma, 50, 85, 91, 167, 176, 178, 230, 254, 271, 278
Plotinus, 37
*pneumatikos*, 125
Polycarp, 185
Porphyrius, 37
Pourjavady, Nasrollah, 113-14
*Prayer of Jacob*, 67, 81, 225
*Prayer of Joseph*, 66-67, 70, 224-25
*Proof of the Apostolic Preaching*, 186, 263
*Protevangelium Jacobi*, 7
*Proverbs, Book of*, 29, 34, 93, 118, 237, 262
*Psalms, Book of*, 63, 84, 216-17, 248, 266, 269
*psuchikos*, 125
*qatat*, 107

331

*qedeshah*, 284, 305
*qodesh*, 131, 284
Quispel, Gilles, 7, 36, 48, 57, 60, 88, 97, 104, 105, 134, 150, 159, 184, 194, 245, 262, 263, 270, 285
Qumran, 53, 102, 257, 258, 269
Qur'an, x, 13, 15, 16, 54, 92, 104, 114-20, 129, 170, 173, 174, 175, 182, 198-200, 208, 216, 227, 228, 230, 235, 239, 269, 275, 285, 286
*qutb*, 113, 265
*rabbi-l-'alamin*, 119
*Rahamim*, 118-19
*rahma*, 119
*al-Rahman*, 118, 119
*al-Rahim*, 118
*Rahmanan*, 100
Ramakrishna, 78
Ritter, Hellmut, 106-07
*ruah*, 77, 216
*ruha*, 77, 85, 177, 210, 216
Rumi, 113, 194
Sabaeans (Sabians), x, 53-54
Sabians (Harranian), 104
Sabbath, 120, 147, 151, 169, 173, 247, 268, 295
Sahib al-Taq, 108
*sakina*, 117, 275
*Saguna-Brahman*, 78
*sajda-yi 'ashiqan*, 113
Samaritans, 41, 54, 55, 111, 206, 299
Sanhedrin, 14, 39, 256
Sarah (matriarch), 95, 220
Schlüngel, Paul, 289
Sde Boqer, 99
*Sefer ha-Bahir*, 248

*sefirot*, 69, 73, 77, 79, 80, 86-87, 89-90, 91, 95, 98, 118, 119, 130, 143, 144-46, 189, 248, 252-54, 262, 271, 274-75
Segal, Alan, 22, 184
Septuagint, 14, 290
Shaddai, 35, 168, 249
*shahid' bazi*, 113
Shams-i Tabrizi, 113
*shariah*, 36-37
*shaykh*, 109-10
Shekhinah, xii, 43, 50, 63, 64, 77, 80, 89, 90, 95, 117, 130, 188, 206, 236, 249, 251, 252-54, 269, 271-75, 277, 278, 281-84, 288, 290
*Shem ha-meforash*, 265
Shem-Tob Hebrew *Matthew*, 55, 138, 207
Shema, xii, 200, 265-66, 282
*Shepherd of Hermas*, 5-6, 18, 95, 102, 138, 150, 163-65, 175-76, 185, 225-26, 234, 236
*shi'ur qomah*, 25, 98, 110, 169, 190
shofar, 20, 39, 95
Simeon (bar Clopas), 75
Simon Magus, 41
*soma*, 276
Son of Man (Son/Child of Humanity), 4, 89, 107-12, 163, 165, 167, 224, 284
*Song of Songs*, 29
Sophia, 29, 30, 31, 33, 34, 50, 66, 72, 74, 77, 78, 80, 85, 87, 89-90, 125, 130-31, 143, 145, 156, 157, 159, 176, 177, 207
Stroumsa, Guy, 38, 69, 137, 207, 219, 220, 222, 223

*Sukka*, 42, 43
*Summa theologiae*, 36
Al-Suyuti, 106
Syria, 5, 6, 7-8, 9, 38, 41, 46, 54, 57, 58, 59, 67, 71, 72, 75, 88-91, 101, 104, 130, 149, 157, 158, 162, 178, 179, 181, 184-97, 225, 252, 259
Syriac, xii, 8-10, 56, 93, 131, 163, 179, 211, 216, 249, 250, 252, 259, 264, 280
Syro-Malabar, 196
Tabari, 100
*tafsir*, 14, 100
Talmud, 16, 17 19, 38, 100
*Tamid*, 135
*Tanhuma*, 255-56
Targum, 14, 19, 93, 188, 194, 217, 236, 245, 259, 276, 281, 286
*Targum Genesis*, 26
Tatian, 178
*tawhid*, 16
*teleios*, 125
Tetragrammaton, 165, 168, 186, 247-50, 273
Theboutis, 75-76
Theudas (student of St. Paul, teacher of Valentinus), 89-91
*Thobiyah*, 75
*thusia*, 169
*Tif'eret*, 69
*tiqqun*, 42, 43
*tiqra*, 14
Tobias, Jerusalem bishop, 75
Torah, ix, 14-16, 27, 34, 36, 37, 55, 59, 65, 66, 87, 118, 128-29, 136, 139, 142-44, 146, 151-52, 155, 156, 160, 164, 168, 169, 248, 253-54, 257, 266-67, 269-70, 276, 278, 280, 282, 283, 290
Trent, Council, 13
*Tsaddiq*, 68-71, 76, 148, 248-52, 264, 265, 266, 267, 268, 272, 273, 274, 275, 277, 280-81, 282, 286, 288, 290
*tsimtsum*, 273
Ullendorf, Edward, 100-02
'Umar, 115
*umm*, 116
*umm al-kitab*, 117-18, 175
*ummi*, 116
*unio mystica*, 37, 169, 186, 187, 188, 190, 200, 265, 267
*Upanishads*, 47
Valentinus, 72, 88-91, 105
Vegetarianism, 85, 263-64
Vermes, Geza, 19-23, 52, 97
Victorinus, 123-24
Vööbus, A., 130
Vulgate, Latin, 13
*wahdat al-wujud*, 113
Wolfson, Elliot R., 168, 169, 246, 247, 248, 251-55
Yehuda, Rabbi, 43
*Yesod*, 69, 248, 252-54
YHWH (Yahweh), 75, 76, 87 (Lesser YHWH), 205, 265, 273
Yom Kippur, 105, 163, 268-70
*Yoma*, 111
Yose, Rabbi, 39-40, 42
al-Zahiri, Ibn Hazm, 105
Zamakhshari, 100
*Zohar*, 22, 35, 43, 50, 69, 77, 90, 93-95, 98, 248, 249, 252-54, 282

TITLES IN THE MATHESON MONOGRAPHS

*Ascent to Heaven in Islamic and Jewish Mysticism*,
by Algis Uždavinys, 2011

*Christianity & Islam: Essays on Ontology and Archetype*,
by Samuel Zinner, 2010

*The Gospel of Thomas: In the Light of Early Jewish, Christian and Islamic Esoteric Trajectories*, by Samuel Zinner, 2011

*The Living Palm Tree: Parables, Stories, and Teachings from the Kabbalah*, by Mario Satz, translated by Juan Acevedo, 2010

*Louis Massignon: The Vow and the Oath*,
by Patrick Laude, translated by Edin Q. Lohja, 2011

*Orpheus and the Roots of Platonism*,
by Algis Uždavinys, 2011

*Sacred Royalty: From The Paraoh to The Most Christian King*,
by Jean Hani, tanslated by Gustavo Polit, 2011

www.ingramcontent.com/pod-product-compliance
Lightning Source LLC
Chambersburg PA
CBHW031613160426
43196CB00006B/120